OTHER MAGE TITLES BY WILLEM FLOOR

THE PERSIAN GULF

LINKS WITH THE HINTERLAND

*Bushehr, Borazjan, Kazerun,
Banu Ka'b, & Bandar Abbas*

Willem Floor

MAGE
PUBLISHERS

Library of Congress Cataloging-in-Publication Data

Floor, Willem M.
 The Persian Gulf : links with the hinterland : Bushehr, Borazjan, Kazerun, Banu ka'b, & Bandar
Abbas / Willem Floor.
     p. cm.
Includes bibliographical references and index.
ISBN 1-933823-46-1 (pbk. original : alk. paper)
1. Port cities--Persian Gulf Region. 2. Cities and towns--Persian Gulf Region--History. I. Title.
DS326.F636 2011
955'.7--dc23
                         2011034390

ISBN 13: 978-1-1933823-46-1
ISBN 10: 1-933823-46-1
Printed and Manufactured in the United States

Mage books are available at bookstores,
through the internet, or directly from the publisher:
Mage Publishers, Washington, DC
202-342-1642 • as@mage.com • 800-962-0922
visit Mage Publishers online at www.mage.com

CONTENTS

TABLES & FAMILY TREES

ILLUSTRATIONS

BENI KHÂN EL TSCHLLAB

Schat el Árab
Hafar Fl
Sable Fl
SRAQ
Zobejr
Dauasir
Goban
Hindiân
Delam
Ras Bang
Bang M.
Gnaze
Bender Rigk
Ka
Bubeân
r Abdill
Fer Isje
Cheueri
s. Kulle Gorgu
Rás Schat
Charedsj
s. Karek
Abufchâhhr
s. Busheer
Druffra
Rifchâhhr ruin
Halela
Chormuu
Nakau
Andsjero
Chôr Essire
Rás el Chân
Zezarine
Om en chäle
Rás Berdiftâ
Kenn
Konkûn
Schul
Tä
Rás Nabénd
s. Cap Nabon
N
Tarud
Schech
s.
Bahhrejn I
Iual
Ora
a piscatu con Charum
Samahe
Arâd s.
Ennebbi Salehh
Gattar
Adsjär
Huäle
margaritifarum
Iusofie
ce
Âl Muflim
R
A
B
I
Æ
Faräha
PARS
Beui I.

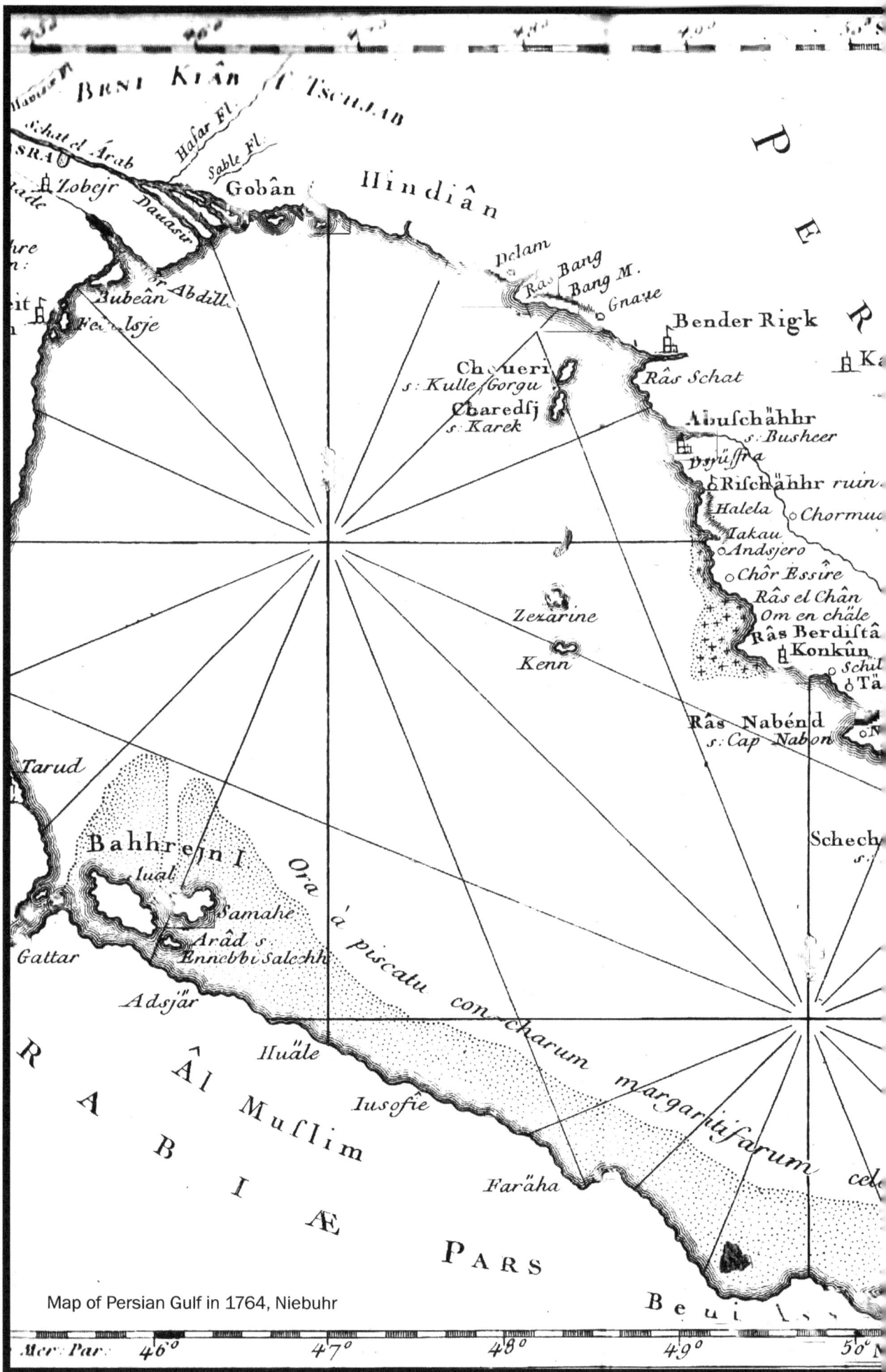

Map of Persian Gulf in 1764, Niebuhr

PER
Mer Par 46° 47° 48° 49° 50° N

SINUS PERSICUS

maximam partem
ad observationes proprias
A . MDCCLXV institutas
delineatus
a
C. Niebuhr

ruin:de
PERSEPOLIS

Schirâs

FARSISTÂN

Firûs abad

SIE

ERMESÎR

0   5   10   15   20   25   30
Milliaria Germanica 15 in uno Gradu

5   0   10   20   30   40
Leucæ Gallicæ 20 in uno Gradu .

PARS

LARISTÂN

Oriens

Beni Hule

Asban

Nachêlo

Tsjarâk

Siraf

Mogo

Ras el Dsjerd.
Ras el Hett

Lundtje

Kunk

Chamîr

Gambrên   Bender Abbâs

Minau

Hormus
s. Ormus

Lejt

Dsjisme

Djes : Drâs

Laresdsj s.
Larek

Hinderabi

Qäs
s. Kjen

Quesche

Beliôr
Polliôr

Tunb

Hindsjâm
Angar

Rafidu
Bassadore

Benatha

Salâme

Muffendom

Râs

Frûr s. Nobfleur

Schech Sure s. Surde

Tunb Namiu

Bumofe

Dsjülfâr

Râs
Fillam

Lima

Seer s. Dsjülfar

Seer Ditio

PARS

OMÂN

Dobba

Bâhr Omân

Scharedsje

Seer

Chôrfakân

Kälbe

TERRÆ   OMÂN

Höffefia

FOREWORD

I had no intention of writing this book. It came about by pure chance and the man to blame is Cyrus Mir, a friend, who in December 2009 asked me whether I could provide him with a list of references related to Kazerun. I did so and realized that I actually knew nothing about this town, despite visiting it in 1966 for the first and in 2000 for the last time. But since I do not know much about a great many things I just acquiesced in that natural state of mind until Cyrus Mir brought the reprint of Kazeruni 1383 to my attention in April 2010. This got my attention indeed, and after reading that interesting publication I immediately hit the books, even though I was finishing some other studies at that time. I submit herewith to you, dear reader, the result of this spontaneous urge to learn more about the vicissitudes of Kazerun. I hope that you will be as absorbed in reading it, as I was when I started digging for information and trying to make sense of it all.

Because Kazerun was an important station on the caravan road from Bushehr to Shiraz, from which it derived much of its revenues, I thought that it would be a good idea to publish my Kazerun study with two other earlier studies of mine. The first one is an earlier short study of the port of Bushehr, a kind of reconnaissance, as I am doing a more elaborate study of that town. The second one is a history of Borazjan, another important halting place for caravans going to or from Bushehr and Shiraz and likewise a center of disorder and rebellion after 1900. I have enlarged this study somewhat as more information was available to me since its conception as well as made a correction. The history of both Borazjan and Kazerun show the importance of the behavior of migrating tribes in keeping the caravan route safe and secure or not. Therefore, I thought it would be interesting to include another earlier study of mine, one that deals with the history of the Banu Ka'b in Khuzestan and, among other things, their role to promote trade or not and how that effected the role of Mohammareh. Finally, I have added a detailed description of the commercial route between Bandar Abbas and Isfahan during the Safavid period, which highlights the importance of the road infrastructure in linking a seaport with the markets in its hinterland.

It is because of this role played by these towns and tribal groups of being 'a link' in the commercial chain that I chose the title of this book. The ports in the Persian Gulf were but caravan termini. The ports themselves did not constitute a major market for imports. The real market for these goods was in the interior of Iran and therefore the road linking port and markets was a lifeline for both. What happened along that road, connecting the terminus and the market, determined to a great extent how much volume was shipped as well as at what cost, as this study makes clear.

I do not know whether I should thank Cyrus Mir as he made me work on a subject that I had no intention to get involved with, but I do it anyway, because it was fun doing so as well as rewarding and now I know at least something about Kazerun. I also wish to thank Mostafa Namdari Monfared, a PhD student in Shiraz, who was so kind to share with me his scans of Akhgar 1366 and of selected pages of the Shirazi newspaper *Fars*. Finally, Keith Openshaw was kind enough to check my English, once again – many thanks Keith.

CHAPTER ONE

The Rise and Fall of Bushehr (1560-1940)[1]

Introduction

Until 1734, Bushehr was an insignificant fishing village, but a small port of some local significance. After that date, it acquired an increasing and substantial economic and political importance. In the nineteenth century, it became Iran's most important seaport. Bushehr was a port city, but in contrast to many other Asian port cities of the colonial era, it was a port that was an integral part of a large independent state, Iran. Initially, the port had some measure of autonomy under a traditional sheikh. Unlike other Asian port cities, foreign merchant communities did not dominate Bushehr, a phenomenon typical of many other Indian Ocean ports, which has been the subject of much debate and study. What is of further interest to note is that Bushehr gradually changed from being a port-of-call to a port-of-transit and that this process coincided with the port's loss of its limited autonomy during the second half of the nineteenth century. As a result of this process we also note that there was less direct political interference with trade than under the autonomous port of Bushehr. The central government, through its local governor, provided a more equal opportunity to all merchants through a hands-off policy, where trade was concerned. This was partly due to the purely fiscal government interest in trade, and partly due to the strong political presence of Great Britain and other European consuls in the town after 1870. This reflects the larger policy context in which merchants had to operate in Qajar Iran, which was one where the state's role was mainly a fiscal one and which favored a *laisser-faire* attitude in the economic sphere, and the growing influence of European states on the political internal affairs of Iran.

---

1. Until now this study was only available in Persian, see Willem Floor, "Zohur va Soqut-e Bushehr," in Mostafa Zamani-niya ed. *Sayeh-ye sar-e mehrebani. Setayesh-e milad va karnameh-ye doktor Mansureh-ye Ettehadiyeh (Nezam-Mafi)* (Tehran, 1383/2004), pp. 377-435. Later this Persian version of the study was reprinted separately (Tolu`-e Danesh: Bushehr, 1387/2008).

In the case of Bushehr we observe that public spirited communal activities only came about under the influence of European ideas and lasted for a short period due to the failure of the political macro-context to provide the necessary incentives. It was only by 1925, with the advent of a new nation state imbued with a sense of mission to develop the country that public investments were made on a consistent and sustained basis, thus providing the basis for socio-economic and urban development, albeit at the cost of the loss of local decentralized democracy. Although Bushehr retained its role as the most important port in the Persian Gulf till the end of the Qajar period, the development of Khuzestan and the construction of the Trans-Iranian Railway reduced it to one of insignificance.[2]

Early History of Bushehr

Bushehr is situated at the northern end of a cigar-shaped peninsula of quaterny sandstone, about 12 miles long by 4 miles broad in the widest part, running parallel to the mainland and joined to it in the middle by a sandy plain about 20 miles wide, known as the *Mashilah*, which in winter more resembled a marsh. The town was a little above sea level, and until the early nineteenth century it was frequently an island, from rising tides.[3] In fact, in 1673 the town was described as being "surrounded on the west by a river, which is navigable for large boats, sand on the other side is embellished by woods and palm-groves. Most of the inhabitants are Arabs, the rest are Persians."[4] However, already by mid-nineteenth century this flooding of the marsh was a rare occurrence, while towards the end of the century Bushehr had in fact become a peninsula.[5]

Bushehr, though situated on a peninsula and where human settlement dates back at least 4,000 years, is a port-town of recent origin.[6] On the peninsula, Rishahr rather than Bushehr was the dominant ancient port, which was well-known and famous until the seventeenth century. It was only after Rishahr's sack in 1532 by the Portuguese and the razing of the fortress by the Safavids (1501-1732) in 1540 that other nearby ports could acquire prominence.[7] It is because of Rishar's sack that Bushehr began its development. For it is only in the 1580s that Bushehr is referred to in contemporary texts for the first time with certainty. The mentioning of Bushehr by

---

2. On this development see, e.g., Willem Floor, "Bushehr: Gateway to Southern Iran" (paper read at a Gulf/2000 conference at Sharjah in March 2009; forthcoming).

3. Waring 1973, p. 2; Kinneir 1973, p. 69.

4. Carré 1947, vol. 3, p. 835.

5. The origin of the name Bushehr is unclear. Popular etymology has it that the name means Abu Shahr or Father of the City, which is very doubtful. Equally doubtful is A. Houtum Schindler's suggestion that the name is a contraction of Bokht Ardashir (Ardashir has delivered). Curzon 1892, vol. 1, p. 231; E`temad al-Saltaneh 1294-96/1877-80, vol. 1, p. 300 mentions that Bushehr sometimes became an island. For the situation in 1913, see Report on the Trade 1913-14, p. 1.

6. The Bushehr peninsula was already inhabited in Elamite times. Inscriptions found date back to the 8th century BCE and are part of the remains of the ancient settlement of Liyan. van den Berghe 1959, pp. 165-74; Eqtedari 1348, pp. 138-201.

7. Qa'em-Maqami 1354, p.102; Rumlu 1357, p. 387.

Yaqut in the thirteenth century is a copyist's error; probably Rishahr was meant.[8] In May 1581, John Newbery reported, "wee were at Abousher, which is a Castle."[9] In 1586, the Venetian consul Balbi mentions the existence of the port of Abuscier.[10] According to Miles, Crowther and Steel examined various ports in the Gulf in 1614, amongst which was Bushehr, but they decided on Jask as the most convenient port to trade.[11] The Dutch captain Roobacker mentioned the flat promontory of Abier or Boecheer in 1645.[12]

The fact that Bushehr is hardly mentioned or found uninteresting as a port by the East India Company (EIC) staff indicates that, for the time being, Bushehr remained an unimportant fishing village where only some local trade was carried on. In fact, Tavernier in his discussion of Persian Gulf ports, did not even mention Bushehr, although he listed Rishar. The same holds for Mostowfi's *Mokhtasar-e Mofid*, a Safavid geography book, which mentions Rishar, but not Bushehr.[13] However, none of these persons had ever visited the location. Abbé Carré, who did in 1673, reported: "Rishahr was once inhabited, but is now deserted, but for some people."[14] By 1670, Bushehr had already acquired some regional importance. The sheikh of Bushehr was one of the leaders of the 'league' of Arabs of Khark, Rig, Dowraq and Bushehr, who together opposed the Hula Arabs of Lengeh, Charak, Chiru, Nakhilu, and Shilaw concerning who controlled the pearl fisheries of Bahrain. In 1673, the war between these two groups became so fierce that Shah Soleyman sent messengers, via the governor of Shiraz, to all sheikhs, ordering them to come to Bushehr, where the governor of Shiraz would attend the meeting to terminate the civil war. The royal interest was mainly due to the loss of revenue, because the war interfered with trade.[15] Bushehr had a Persian *shahbandar* and paid heavy dues to the shah of Persia.[16] By that time Bushehr also appeared on published European maps.[17]

It was only in 1734 that Bushehr was launched on the international scene by Nader Shah's (r. 1736-47) decision to make this port his base for naval operations and conquest in the Persian Gulf.[18] Undoubtedly, this decision had been partly influenced by the local availability of ships. Bandar 'Abbas, at that time still the major Persian Gulf port, was not selected, for unknown reasons. Both ports offered equal opportunity as far as port facilities were concerned, while Bandar

8. Schwarz 1993, vol. 3, p. 127.

9. Purchas 1905, vol. 8, p. 457.

10. Berchet 1976, p. 286.

11. Miles 1966, p. 206.

12. Hotz 1897, pp. 363, 387.

13. Thevenot 1971, vol. 2, p. 151; Mostowfi 1989.

14. Carré 1947, vol. 1, p. 94.

15. Carré 1947, vol. 1, pp. 94, 101, 103; vol. 3, pp. 824, 828-29.

16. Carré 1947, vol. 3, pp. 833-35.

17. See for example, Slot 1991, plates 7, 14-18, 23.

18. It was only after this date (ca. 1750) that Bushehr is depicted on published geographical maps, although Rishar continues to be depicted as well, either together with Bushehr or still instead of. It also often happened that neither place was depicted on the maps. Sahabi 2005, vol. 2, pp. 390 (d'Anville map), 394 (Bellin map), 400 (Tardieu map), 431 (Vaugondy map).

`Abbas also benefited from the presence of the Dutch East Indies Company (VOC) and the EIC. Moreover, the routes connecting both ports with the interior were better in the case of Bandar `Abbas, but, may be most importantly, food supplies were easier to obtain in Bushehr's than in Bandar `Abbas's hinterland. Also, according to the Dutch, Bushehr was "one of the best ports in this Gulf. At high tide, a ship drawing 12 to 13 feet of water can very easily be brought completely as far as the houses."[19]

In the 1730s, Sheikh Mazkur, not his son Naser who generally is known as the founder (*banna*) of modern Bushehr, was the main leader of the local population. He was the chief of the Al Mazkur clan who had migrated from Oman to Bushehr in the early eighteenth century.

> The Arabs inhabiting the district of Abu Shahr were not of the Huwala tribe. There were among them three eminent families; the first two of which had been from time immemorial settled in that place. The third, named Matarish, had come lately from `Uman, where they had been employed in fishing, and they soon entered into an alliance with the other two and found means to usurp the sovereign authority which they had been holding for several years before 1765.[20]

When the decision to start shipbuilding activities in Bushehr was made, this happened with Sheikh Mazkur's assistance. The Dutch described him as a kind of chief merchant, who was engaged in commerce on a daily basis and who had a good credit rating.[21] Despite Sheikh Mazkur's local importance, overall supervision of the construction of the fleet remained with Mohammad Latif Khan, the admiral of the fleet (*darya-begi*). The only European merchants in residence in Bushehr at that time were the Dutch, who at the invitation of Mohammad Latif Khan had established a branch office in 1738, while European so-called country traders also called on Bushehr.[22] Apart from the Dutch, Persian Armenian merchants had settled in Bushehr. Their number was limited, despite the fact that the Carmelites decided to establish a church in Bushehr in 1745, which shortly thereafter was abandoned. They returned in 1764 and from then onwards visited Bushehr, where there were 35 Catholics.[23]

Even before the death of Nader Shah in 1747 his grandiose plans to conquer Masqat and Oman had come to nothing. Part of his fleet had mutinied in 1741, and the leader of the expeditionary force, Mirza Taqi Khan, rebelled in 1745. After Nader Shah's death the former commanders of the fleet inherited the ships and Sheikh Naser I of Bushehr was one of them.[24] In

---

19. Floor 1979 b, p. 172.

20. Niebuhr 1774, p. 273; see also Floor 1979 b, p. 170 where the Arab group is referred to as Al Bu Mahair.

21. NA/VOC 2448 (18/2/1738), f. 2404-07. He also was referred to as being the *darugheh* of Bushehr. NA/VOC 2477 (12/1738), f. 567.

22. Floor 1987, pp. 31-53.

23. Anonymous 1938, vol. 1, pp. 614, 557-9, 695, 710.

24. Floor 2007, pp. 248-49.

1751, Sheikh Naser I, as well as other chiefs of the Gulf littoral, used his newly won freedom from central government control as well as his maritime assets to extend his sphere of influence to other parts of the Gulf, in particular to Bahrein.[25] The next decades were spent in extending his trading activities as well as defending his territorial interests. In both aspects Sheikh Naser I was reasonably successful.[26]

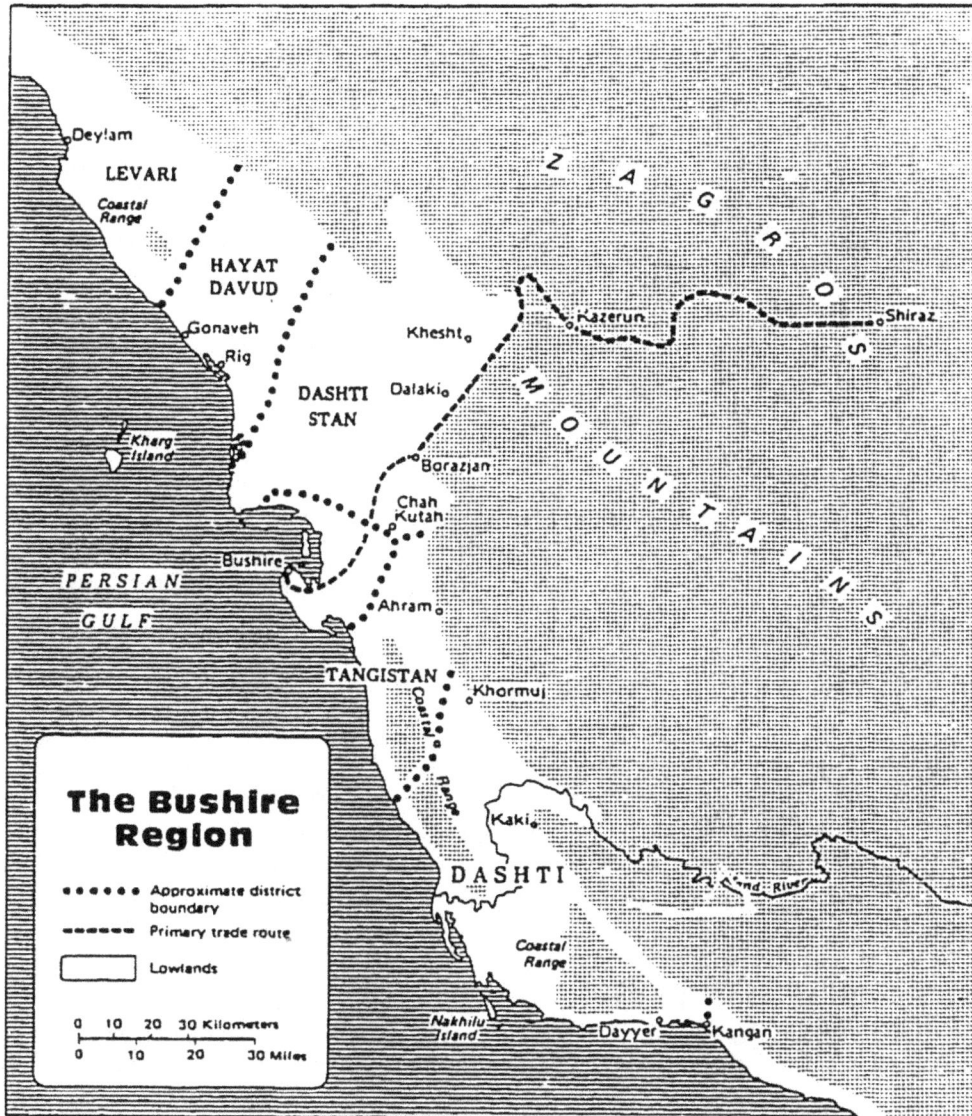

The Bushire Region

• • • • • Approximate district boundary
- - - - - Primary trade route
▭ Lowlands

0   10   20   30 Kilometers
0   10   20   30 Miles

Plan of Bushehr in the 1820s, Grummon 1985

25. Floor 1979 b.

26. Amin 1967, p. 128; Abu Hakima 1965, pp. 99-118.

Although the Dutch had established themselves in Bushehr in 1738 their stay was neither long nor very profitable. When in 1753, the VOC moved to Khark Island, close to Bushehr, it closed its factory in Bushehr much to the chagrin of Sheikh Naser. However, after initial enmity towards the Dutch, relations were patched up a few years later, when both found a common enemy in Mir Muhanna, chief of Bandar-e Rig.[27] In 1763, the Dutch were succeeded in Bushehr by their rivals, the English, who had abandoned Bandar 'Abbas in that year. The proximity of Shiraz, the new center of power in Persia, made Bushehr a better choice for trade than Bandar 'Abbas, because it was closer.[28] The EIC after abandoning its factory in Bandar 'Abbas moved its entire Persian operation to Bushehr when, in April 1763, the EIC reached an agreement with Sheikh Sa'dun of Bushehr by which, inter alia, no import and export "dues were to be levied, and only 3 per cent. charged on goods bought and sold to the English: woolen goods could be imported and sold to the English only, and no other European nation was permitted to settle at Bushehr as long as the English had a factory there.[29] In July 1763, a royal grant from Karim Khan was given at Shiraz and conferred various privileges of a similar nature. However, Bushehr was not attractive enough and the EIC moved for two years to Basra, but then moved back again in 1770 when Karim Khan, the ruler of the greater part of Persia, gave them special trading privileges. Although by 1780 Bushehr was no longer an important outlet for EIC trade, because a port for country traders it suffered from fierce competition with Masqat and Kuweit.[30]

Apart from political unrest and consequently insecurity on the roads in Bushehr's upcountry hinterland there was the continued pattern of interfering with trade by the sheikhs of Bushehr. Already, this pattern had manifested itself in the 1730-40s[31] and in 1754 contributed to the VOC's decision to withdraw from Bushehr, and it would also characterize the sheikhs' behavior during the first half of the nineteenth century. In the 1770s, trade suffered from interference by the governors of Bushehr and Basra.

> At Bushehr we are almost as much exposed to Oppression as we are at Bussora. The Sheikhs there interfere too much in the Trade of the Place; and the few Merchants with any Property who are there, are too much in a Combination to admit of our drawing any great Commercial Advantages from it wretched indeed as is the Situation in Bussora at Present it is much superior in Point of Trade than Bushehr.[32]

Apart from occasional necessity for funds or special goods, the reason why the sheikhs believed they could get away with this behavior was that, in the past, merchants had preferred Bushehr to the other ports, because of the presence of a number of Persian merchants in the town.[33]

---

27. Floor 1994, pp. 157-202.

28. Perry 1979.

29. Amin 1967, p. 125.

30. Amin 1967, pp. 138-39; Abu Hakima 1965, pp. 119-22, 165-6; Risso 1986, pp. 210f.

31. For example, Sheikh Mazkur was continuously interfering with trade and the Dutch had requested the central government to instruct him to stop this obnoxious behavior. See, e.g., NA /VOC 2546 (12/10/40), f. 1154.

32. Abu Hakima 1965, pp. 99-100.

33. Amin 1967, pp. 173-4.

However, by the 1780s Bushehr experienced a difficult period, due to the attraction of Basra, Masqat and Kuweit as alternative ports and a continued fierce competition between them.[34]

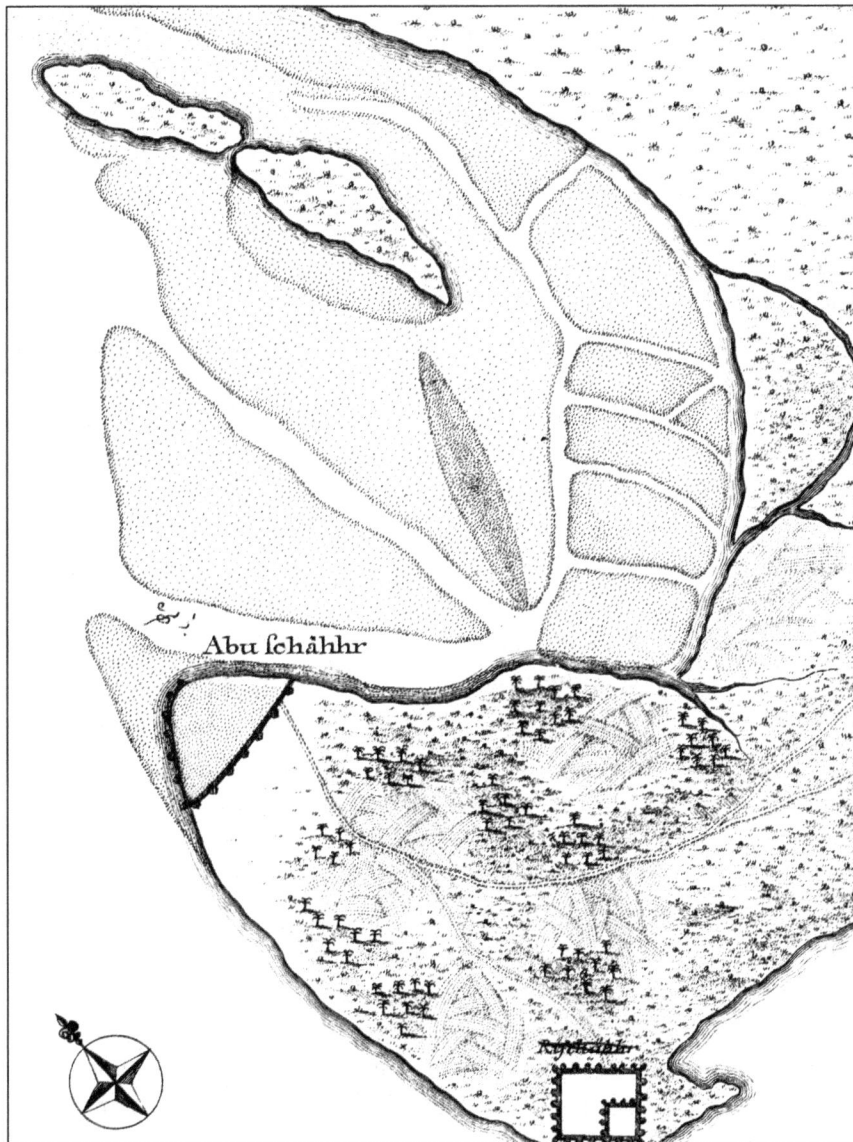

Plan of Bushehr in 1764, Niebuhr

Quasi-autonomy of Bushehr

Sheikh Naser I had been able to acquire considerable domains in the littoral, which he formally held for Karim Khan, with whom Sheikh Naser's children were placed as hostages for their

---

34. For a more detailed discussion of this early period of Bushehr's history, see Floor 2007, chapter 7.

father's behavior.[35] In exchange for his loyalty and payment of tribute, Sheikh Naser I was al-lowed to manage his own affairs. Sheikh Naser I died in 1789. He had built up wealth through trade with India and Masqat, which he left to his son, Sheikh Naser II. The last Zand Shah, Lotf ʿAli Khan (d. 1794), took much of this from him in 1792 in his bid to fight off the encroaching Qajars. Sheikh Naser therefore did not support Lotf ʿAl Khan and refused him entry to Bushehr. This put Sheikh Naser II in good standing with the new Qajar government.[36]

As of 1794, with the establishment of the Qajar regime in all of Persia, the sheikh of Bush-ehr remained nominally subject to the governor of Shiraz, and he paid tribute to the Shah, which he often withheld on the slightest pretexts, if he thought he could get away with it.[37] The next pe-riod can be characterized by efforts to keep the central government out of Bushehr's affairs as well as to fend off ambitious relatives. In May 1807, Sheikh Naser II died making the *hajj*, and a suc-cession struggle developed between ʿAbdol-Rasul, his son, and one of Sheikh Naser's brothers, Sheikh Khanom. However, despite the latter's presence in Shiraz, the Fars governor confirmed ʿAbdol-Rasul. Because of tax arrears and unwillingness to grant a loan to the prince-governor of Shiraz the latter granted the governorship of Bushehr to Mohammad Nabi Khan, a merchant who was the Persian ambassador at Calcutta. It was said that the latter had procured the governor-ship of Bushehr for 40,000 tomans. His brother Mohammad Jaʿfar Khan was proclaimed gover-nor *pro tem*.[38] However, this usurpation of the sheikhdom did not last long. In 1813, Mohammad Jaʿfar was replaced by Mehdiqoli Khan Qajar. He was inept and much of the littoral was insecure and the various sheikhs were fighting amongst each other and, therefore, in November 1814 he willingly agreed that ʿAbdol-Rasul take over as governor of Bushehr. With an absence of one year (in 1826, due to imprisonment by the Imam of Masqat) ʿAbdol-Rasul remained in power.[39]

In 1824, ʿAbdol-Rasul bought off Farmanfarma, the prince-governor of Shiraz, who want-ed to come to Bushehr as a staging point for the conquest of Bahrain. However, it would seem that these intentions were repeated regularly as a means to obtain money from ʿAbdol-Rasul. A similar event occurred at the end of 1831, but the sheikh was able again to buy off Farmanfarma. In March 1832, on his return from Shiraz, Sheikh ʿAbdol-Rasul was murdered by his enemies.[40] Although his son, Sheikh Nasr was after sometime confirmed as governor in his father's place, his position was soon challenged by Shiraz and he had to flee to Kuweit. However, due to Farman-farma's failed attempt to seize the throne in 1834, the field was free again for Sheikh Nasr. He returned to Bushehr in 1835, but still was ousted in 1838 even though he had paid his tax arrears, a common reason to dismiss a governor. The following years were quite confused with rotating governors appointed by Shiraz, who were regularly challenged by members of the al-Mazkur fam-ily and other local sheiks. In 1845, Sheikh Nasr was reinstated as governor of Bushehr in the hope that stability would return to the area. He ran into serious opposition from the sheikhs in Bushehr's hinterland as well as into financial problems. To meet his fiscal obligations, Sheikh Nasr

35. Grummon 1985, p. 98; Anonymous 1939, vol. 1, p. 668.

36. Fasaʾ i 1378, vol. 1, pp. 640, 648-69; Waring 1973, p. 7; Eʿtemad al-Saltaneh 1368, vol. 1, pp. 300-02.

37. Buckingham 1971, p. 351; Curzon 1892, vol. 1, p. 232.

38. Morier 1812, p. 25f; Lorimer 1915, pp. 1911-13; Fasaʾ i 1378, vol. 1, p. 702.

39. Grummon 1985, pp. 133-36.

40. Fasaʾ i 1378, vol. 1, pp. 749-50; Grummon 1985, pp. 125-26.

increased his grip on trade, which was resented by the merchants. The *malek al-tojjar* was in contact with the Qavams in Shiraz and intrigued against the Al Mazkurs. Sheikh Nasr had been able to resist a challenge to his rule in 1849 and received a robe of honor from Shiraz in January 1850. However, he did not pay his taxes, and Shiraz summoned Sheikh Nasr in late summer of 1850. On arrival he was sent to Tehran. The governorship of Bushehr, its dependencies and Dashtestan was given to Mirza ʿAli Khan, son of Qavam al-Molk, the powerful provincial magnate of Fars, with the title of *darya-begi*. When Hoseyn Khan, Sheikh Nasr's uncle heard this he gathered his levies and put Bushehr in state of defense. However, under the threat that "no quarter" would be given to the local population by the army sent by Tehran the Sheikh's relatives fled by ship taking the customs money with them never to play a role in local politics again.[41]

The sheikhs of Bushehr had made themselves unpopular due to their hostilities with the governor of Shiraz, the Imam of Masqat and the local chiefs of the Dastestan as well as by their sometimes oppressive behavior towards the local population of Bushehr itself. When the Bushehri sheikhs fell out with the neighboring tribes of Dashtestan and Tangestan, the shah used this dissension as an excuse to establish his own governor at Bushehr and to reduce the tribes of the Dastestan and Tangestan.[42] Local leaders such as Sheikh Hasan Al-e ʿOnsur, the major *faqih* and *Imam-e Jomʿeh* of Bushehr, assisted the central government in ousting the Mazkur sheikhs and appointing its own governor.[43]

One of the major reasons for local dissatisfaction with the Sheikhs was that e.g. ʿAbdol-Rasul was "a despotic tyrant, and guilty of every kind of excess and cruelty towards his subjects."[44] In addition there were the sheikhs' continued hostilities with the governor of Shiraz and other local chiefs; this had a negative impact on trade. Also, because the sheikhs interfered regularly with trade, this likewise had a negative influence on Bushehr as a port of call. In principle, clear rules existed aimed at attracting merchants, but these were not always respected and applied in such a way that it drove away rather than attracted ships.

> The customs duties are regulated by package and quality of the goods. The governor can take merchandise for his own use or sale, and instead of paying he runs up a balance in favor to the owners to be liquidated by remitting them the duties on further imports, till the amount is made up. This has a negative influence on trade. The governor was at war with some chiefs. He needed lead; there was a ship on the roads with that article, but refused to land afraid that the governor would seize it and pay much later. He went to Basra instead.[45]

---

41. Fasaʾi 1378, vol. 1, pp. 791-92, 794-95; Grummon 1985, pp. 146-69. Sheikh Nasr's descendants continued to live in Bushehr, but they were impoverished and did not regain their former status. In 1877, the Dutch consul bought a nice old door of the former sheikh's harem to be used as the main door of the new consular residence, *Hollandarabad*, that he was building on the peninsula. Because of local problems, the chief of the telegraph office sent a telegram to the governor of Shiraz claiming that it was the telegraph office's door. After some time this calumny was set aright. *NA*/Archief Ministerie van Buitenlandse Zaken (Ministry of Foreign Affairs) B 149, inv. 1. Keun to van der Does (2 August 1876) and appendices.

42. Pelly 1865 a, p. 41.

43. Sadid al-Saltaneh 1367, pp. 9, 11. For the Qajar policy to oust local ruling families see Floor 1999, pp. 254-59.

44. Kempthorne 1835, pp. 283-84.

45. Buckingham 1971, pp. 354-55.

Loss of Autonomy

Thus, as of 1850, the territory of Bushehr remained under a governor and local officers appointed by the central government in Tehran. Customs and revenues were either contracted by the governor or accounted for in detail to the royal treasury. The jurisdiction included Bushehr and some other neighboring Gulf ports.[46] The town was captured by Great Britain in 1856 as a result of the Anglo-Persian war.[47] As a result, the English political residents such as Colonel Ross, became if not the king of the Persian Gulf, certainly the real governor of Bushehr in the 1870s and thereafter.[48]

As of 1886, Bushehr became the seat of government of the Gulf Ports province. The town of Bandar ʿAbbas entirely, and the districts of Shamil and Minab were partly under the Gulf Ports governor, who also was in charge of the small ports between Minab and Bushehr, and for certain islands in the Gulf. In the various small ports the Gulf Ports the governor leased the customs for a stipulated sum as a rule to an enterprising merchant, usually an Indian; in larger places he put subordinate officials. The extent of the province was not more than a few miles inland, though about 32 miles behind the peninsula. Local chiefs, independent of the government officials, administered all the districts outside the peninsula.[49]

From Port-of-Call to Port-of-Transit

Until the mid-nineteenth century Bushehr remained a port-of-call that developed gradually into a port-of-transit. A port-of-call serves as a marketing and distribution center for long distance trade where two distinct sets of merchants met and exchanged goods. This exchange took place under market conditions, i.e. prices were determined by supply and demand. Merchants came looking for buyers or sellers, and would move on to another port if they could not find a ready sale or purchase. In 1750, Plaisted reports that "Here [in Bandar ʿAbbas] Capt. Robinson meeting with a good Market for his Cargo, was under no Necessity to go up as far as Bisheer, or Bowchier [Bushehr] to dispose of it here."[50] Connolly in the early 1830s, referring to the situation in Mashhad, reports "Thus, for want of a regular understanding many [merchants] bring goods at a complete venture, and if they do not suit the market, send them east or west, to any place at which there is a change of their selling."[51] This situation, which also existed in Safavid times, was determined by the fact that the Persian Gulf was one market where goods could be landed at many ports.[52] The availability of buyers and a positive reception (including low customs rates) by local governors

46. Pelly 1865 a, p. 33.

47. For details see English 1971, Chapters 5 and 6 in particular.

48. De Rivoyre 1883, p. 136; De Vilmorin 1895, pp. 349-50.

49. Report on the Trade 1910-11, p. 1; Curzon 1892, vol. 1, pp. 401-06.

50. Plaisted 1757, p. 7.

51. Connolly 1834, vol. 1, p. 347; see also Buckingham 1971, pp. 354-55.

52. Floor 2000.

determined the place where merchants would land their goods. This itinerant behavior came to an end when vertical integration was slowly established throughout the market chain and predictability of the behavior of customs authorities increased, thus reducing commercial uncertainty.

The market was dependent on the presence of merchants, who would come from upcountry to Bushehr to buy what merchants calling at the port were offering. This meant that market forces determined prices. Also, these merchants came to Bushehr only during the trading season, which was in the fall and winter. In summertime there was no trade to speak of. This also held for the big European companies such as the VOC and EIC which in their correspondence regularly refer to the seasonal aspect of trade in the Gulf ports, whether at Bandar ʿAbbas or Bushehr. Finally, the Sheikh of Bushehr, the largest merchant of the port, rarely took the goods he imported upcountry. He, like other importers, sold them to others who took the goods inland and distributed them.

This situation changed and gradually Bushehr became a port-of-transit, or a caravan terminus for the interior. This meant that henceforth Bushehr was a point of transfer between long-distance maritime trade and long-distance caravan trade. Goods bought in e.g. India were landed in Bushehr and forwarded immediately upcountry for distribution. The same owner managed all this. The shipper at Bushehr need not necessarily be the owner, but usually was an agent. Consequently, contemporary 19th century observers note that the merchant class of Bushehr consisted mainly of forwarding agents rather then merchants trading for their own account. This did not mean of course that if prices were more interesting in Basra than in Bushehr, contrary to earlier expectations, captains would continue their voyage to Basra instead. However, this became a much less frequent occurrence, and was the exception rather than the rule.[53]

This development was due to the fact that trade had increased with extraordinary rapidity during the early part of the reign of Fath Ali Shah (1797-1834) because of the greater security in land and greater attention paid by the Persian government to the Persian Gulf trade, the maritime security provided by the British fleet to small vessels as well as the continued economic growth in Persia itself. Bushehr continued to hold the predominant position as the major port for Persia in the Gulf, representing about 50% of total imports. The other smaller ports absorbed the remainder of imported goods.[54] However, during the 1830-40s the trade of Bushehr declined due to the increased use of the northern import route via Trabzon and Tabriz, in particular for British goods. Also, goods coming from India were diverted to Bandar ʿAbbas, to some extent, due to a lower customs tariff. However, despite this decline in the volume of trade, Bushehr remained the most important Persian Gulf port.[55] This decline coincided with the political problems of the Sheikhs of Bushehr and the consequent loss of local support.

Bushehr continued to keep its predominant position despite the fact that it had to compete with three other ports, which likewise functioned as a southern gateway to Persia. These ports were Bandar Abbas, Lengeh and Mohammareh (Basra also should be added to this list, but was located in Ottoman Turkey, though many of its imported goods were destined for western Persia). Some of these ports had even better anchorage than Bushehr, but through a combination of factors the latter port was, on balance, preferred by most merchants. First, its hinterland constituted

---

53. Floor 1988, pp. 59-77 and 179-182.

54. Issawi 1971, pp. 90-91; Lorimer 1915, p. 1955.

55. Amanat 1983, p. 86.

a very fertile plain of grain producing land for about 100 miles in Bushehr's hinterland. Consequently, Bushehr was a good center for the export of agricultural products. However, its chief advantage over the other ports was its active and prosperous commercial community and their close relationship with the merchants in Shiraz and Isfahan. For Bushehr's importance rose and fell in consonance with the level of economic activity in its hinterland, in particular Isfahan and Shiraz. Bushehr was not only a transit port, but it also served as a distribution center for southern Persia. This area consisted of the towns along the main caravan routes between Bushehr and Shiraz, and Shiraz and Isfahan, which meant outlets for goods and availability of pack animals, provided security prevailed and fodder was sufficient. Also, as of 1886, it was the seat of government for the Gulf Ports administration.[56] Thus, the prosperity of Bushehr depended largely on the up-country markets, security on the roads and a positive business climate. Further, the availability of factors such as labor and transport affected cost and the rapidity by which the market might be served.

Size and Composition of Bushehr's Population

The nature and the growth of the town's economic activities as well as its political situation were reflected in both the size and composition of the population, which changed over time. From an estimated population of some 8,500 at the beginning of the nineteenth century Bushehr grew into a port with about 20,000 inhabitants by 1920, and 40,000 in 1934.[57] The population's main occupation was trade, fishing, pilotage, and the navigation of their own vessels. It was a rather heterogeneous group of people, which was reflected in their dress, which was likewise a mixture. "The shirt, trowsers, and zuboon, or outer garment, are Persian; but the turban and the abba, or cloak, are Arabic, - the one is formed of the blue checked cloth of Muscat, or the brown cloth of Shooster [Shustar]; and the other of the manufacture of Lahsa, Kateef, and Coete [al-Hasa, al-Qatif, al-Quwait], on the opposite shore. The black sheepskin cap, the most peculiar feature of the Persian dress, is worn only by such as come down from the higher country, and is in no instance used by a native of Bushehr."[58]

Initially, the population consisted mainly of Arabs with the remainder Persians and some Indians, but by 1880 they were mostly Persian, and there were merchants from all over Persia. Most of the Indians had departed and were mostly in Lengeh, where they had a special bazaar.[59] As a result, the Bushehris spoke a corrupted form of Persian, which the Shirazis pronounced to be unintelligible. Although most understood Arabic, they also pronounced this with as little elegance as they did Persian, according to contemporaries.[60] The Persianization of Bushehr was due to the increased trade, which had led to an influx of Persian migrants from Behbahan, Kazerun, Dehdasht and Shiraz. Tribesmen from the Tangestan provided the labor class and fishermen,

---

56. Report on the Trade 1912-13, p. 7.

57. Ebtehaj n.d., p. 183.

58. Buckingham 1971, p. 349

59. Carré 1947, vol. 3, p. 835; E`temad al-Saltaneh 1368, vol. 1, p. 299. The Hindus lived unmolested in Bushehr, according to Waring 1971, p. 3.

60. Buckingham 1971, pp. 349-50.

not only in Bushehr, but elsewhere in the Gulf. As a result, towards the end of the 19th century the language mostly spoken was Persian. One-third of the population spoke Arabic, though few spoke it habitually. English was also spoken, which was the commercial means of communication with India. Sometimes even natives used it amongst themselves. In addition to the permanent population, there was a large floating population of traders, travelers, and temporary laborers. [61] Change was also taking place in the dress of the Bushehr. In the 1880s, the male inhabitants still dressed:

> very much like the Persian merchants in Masqat. Nearly all of them wearing the high Persian sugar-loaf shaped hat, of black dyed lamb's fleece, tight fitting coats, closed in front, and of black, green blue or brown color, with a white, or colored scarf round their loins, in which they generally carry a fine, silver-mounted, curved dagger, or a pair of long, single-barrelled pistols. Some of them wear also a short broad, double-edge sword, dangling from a leather belt. Nearly all of them had their finger nails painted crimson, and the palm of their hands dyed with henna.[62]

But by 1900, the ordinary dress "now consists of a long coat, a waist coat, pantaloons, woollen socks and imported shoes."[63]

Bushehr had no leisured class; most inhabitants were mercantile (merchants, brokers, shopkeepers), seafaring (mostly Arab) and coolie classes. Around 1828, the merchants of Bushehr were equally composed of Persian Moslems and Armenians. The latter had more connections with India, and were wealthier and thus more influential, also due to their contacts with the EIC resident.[64] With the growth of British trade the important Bushehri merchants held agencies for Manchester firms. By 1912, the European official and mercantile community numbered some 40 persons.[65] Like Bushehr's population at large, the mercantile community was not a homogenous group either, for there were ethnic, language, and religious differences. Nevertheless, it would seem that relations between these traders from different background were no major obstacle in social and commercial relations.[66] The well-known and influential Armenian Malkam (Malcolm) family was the repository of much of the wealth of the Moslem population of Bushehr, probably because of their reliability and their protected British status, which ensured that this wealth could not be directly interfered with by the Persian authorities.[67]

---

61. De Rivoyre 1883, p. 131. In addition there were 600 Persian Jews, 35 Armenians, 18 Iraqi Christians, some 40 Indians, and some 50 Europeans engaged in trade, official capacity and telegraph service around the turn of the 20th century. Lorimer 1915, pp. 343-44; Curzon 1892, vol. 1, p. 233.

62. Locher 1889, p. 51.

63. Lorimer 1915, p. 345.

64. Buckingham 1971, p. 350.

65. Report of the Trade 1913-14, p. 1.

66. Sadid al-Saltaneh 1362, pp. 2-12.

67. Sadid al-Saltaneh 1362, p. 6.

The Urban Environment

Bushehr's location, just being above sea level, was so low that the houses were revealed on coming from the sea, much sooner than the land on which the town was built.[68] Thus, when viewed from a distance, the town presented rather a handsome appearance.[69] The town was two miles in circumference, protected on the landside by a wall and various towers. The walls, which had protected the population as late as 1849, were already in ruins by the 1860s. The gates were still standing and maintained more or less, and guarded. But by 1900, while not actually demolished they were almost concealed amidst the recent extensions of the town in that direction, and only traces were visible here and there. At the gates "taxes are collected. Other role of government there is not; there is neither refuse collection department nor police."[70]

The houses were of stone and nearly all had an upper story: none had three stories and few had only a ground floor. There were about 1,400 houses by 1900, a number that had hardly grown since 1828 when the number was about 1,000. However, the population was dense and out of proportion to the number of dwellings. Therefore, besides these houses there were 1,000 to 1,200 huts, built of date-palm stocks and leaves and occupied by the lower classes and soldiers.[71] Because the town was densely built it had hardly any open spaces. The narrow six-feet winding lanes were not inconvenient in ordinary weather, but in the rain became a sewer of mud.[72] "After rain the narrow streets are in many places, sometimes from wall to wall, covered with green pools of stagnant filth, through which one may pass dry-shod on bricks or blocks, which long have been used as stepping-stones across these shallow pools. These filthy places might be filled in by a hundred men on one day's labor." [73]

Except for the EIC factory (and later the British political residency), the residence of the governor and a few good dwellings of merchants, in particular Armenians, there was hardly one comfortable house in Bushehr itself.[74] The wealthier town dwellers, whether olama, government officials, merchants or consuls of foreign nations, however, had gardens and comfortable country houses in the northern part of the peninsula (Sabzabad) and lived there, driving or riding every day to their business in town.[75] During the summer, most inhabitants left for Chah Kutah, 24 miles inland where they lived "in tents, or in large airy houses, cooled by 'tatteis', which consists of a light framework of date-wood filled in with camel-thorn, and kept constantly wet" and through evaporation "the tent or bungalow, enveloped by tatteis, is tendered cool and delightful."[76]

For its fresh water the inhabitants were dependent on wells, which were at about 3 miles distance. The town also had some mosques, both for the Sunnis and Shi'ahs, "who like other

68. Milburn 1813, vol. 1, p. 128.

69. Kinneir 1973, pp. 69-70.

70. De Rivoyre 1883, p. 135; Lorimer 1915, p. 341.

71. Curzon 1892, vol. 1, p. 234

72. Lorimer 1915, p. 341.

73. Arnold 1877, p. 429.

74. Buckingham 1971, p. 347; E'temad al-Saltaneh 1368, vol. 1, p. 299.

75. Lorimer 1915, p. 330; Sadid al-Saltaneh 1362, pp. 10-11; De Rivoyre 1883, p. 131.

76. Shepherd 1857, p. 154.

sectaries fight about shadows."[77] Bushehr further had an Armenian church, three baths and a miserable bazaar. There were one or two good caravanserais near the landing-place for boats, "occupied by and belonging to Armenian merchants; but those belonging to the Mohammadans hardly deserve the name."[78]

Neither Community nor Polity

In short, Bushehr was not a beautiful town. It possessed neither monuments nor relics of antiquity and to the outsider was a bewildering combination of narrow and tortuous passages winding in and out among overhanging mud houses, revealing only a thread of blue sky to the bewildered pedestrian.[79] The fact that the town looked dilapidated and that for its water supply it was dependent on sources outside town are indications that a responsible community organization had not yet developed. This situation was reinforced because most rich and influential people living in Bushehr were first or second generation immigrants from Fars, Azerbaijan, Khorasan and India (the latter often British subjects), who, apart from being Persian and merchants, had little in common, and with little if any special feeling for or commitment to Bushehr as a town or community. Also, they lived part of the year outside Bushehr which reduced their interest to develop a civic community, though it was not for an objective lack of projects that required the community's or polity's intervention to improve living and working conditions in Bushehr. Nevertheless, there was something of a literary community in Bushehr as is clear from the range of Sadid al-Saltaneh's friends and, for some of them, their common interest in Persian literature and politics.[80] Another area where some incipient communal project was realized concerned the construction of the only road in the peninsula fit for strongly built vehicles. The road was 6 miles long and ran from Bushehr to Sabzabad, with a branch to Rishahr, and led to the summer homes of the rich. Private subscribers under the supervision of the British residency maintained it.[81]

We therefore note that when national conditions were conducive to the development of local communal actions these opportunities were indeed grabbed. However, when these national conditions changed for the worse they had a negative impact on local communities, such as Bushehr. To illustrate these observations a discussion of some of pressing communal issues is offered here.

---

77. Shepherd 1857, p. 139 (with an example of these shadows); Buckingham 1971, p. 348.

78. Buckingham 1971, p. 348; Shepherd 1857, p. 143; De Rivoyre 1883, p. 166.

79. Report on the Trade 1913-14, p. 1.

80. Sadid al-Saltaneh 1362, pp. 6-20.

81. Lorimer 1915, p. 332.

Anchorage

Despite the fact that Bushehr was the major Persian port its anchorage

> was bad and had many physical disadvantages. Its roadstead is only partly protected against the prevailing winds from the NW. The anchorage is 4 miles from the landing place. Communication with shipping by boats is always slow either to and from the bandar, and is sometimes wholly cut off for days together during a strong North-wester. Boats cannot go off after sunset, nor move to land cargo until the Manifest has been seen by the governor. This is due to the fact that the landing and embarkation of goods at Bush are a monopoly of a hammal-bashi which he farms.[82]

As a consequence, at Bushehr shippers had to risk two transshipments, -one between the ship and the Bushehr Customs wharf and the other between Bushehr and Shif on the mainland. The Customs wharf was cramped and inconvenient and did not allow efficient storage. Also, damage, during handling and from exposure to sun and rain, was of frequent occurrence. At Shif, goods coming from up-country had to lie on the beach, exposed to the weather, waiting, often for weeks. When the boatmen finally picked up the goods, they caused much damage through overloading and inadequate covering, and often pilfered cargo confined to their care.[83]

To make access to the port easier a tender was made in the mid-1870s to dredge the channel, but nothing came of it, despite the fact that it had been estimated that the cost would not be prohibitive.[84] In 1935, the landing facilities were still inadequate. Steamers continued to be discharged in the open roadstead about 5 km from shore. So that goods still had to be brought in by lighters from ships anchored several miles from shore.[85]

Public Health

Sanitation was practically non-existent in all Persian towns. The practice of throwing the foulest garbage into the streets was universal. Drainage was non-existent and during the rains each street was a conduit unto itself. Fitful efforts at cleaning the streets were started towards the end of the nineteenth century in Tehran with little result.[86] As a result living and health conditions were bad. Diseases were endemic, sanitary conditions, in either the workplace or the city in general, were also bad.[87] Infectious diseases were rampant; there were no medical services or a no-

---

82. Pelly 1865 a, p. 49.

83. Gleadowe-Newcomen 1906, pp. 60, 64.

84. Stack 1882, vol. 1, p. 24.

85. Ebtehaj n.d., p. 183; Report on the Trade 1935-36, p. 3; Ibid. 1945, pp. 502-03, shows that by 1945 Bushehr had already been overtaken in importance by Khorramshahr.

86. Floor 1992 c, pp. 173-198; see also Floor 2004.

87. Ehlers & Floor 1995, pp. 251-75; Floor 2004.

tion of hygiene. Water sources generally were unclean and vectors for disease. VD, moreover, was widespread due to the promiscuous behavior of males. Clothing and footwear also were inadequate.[88] Bushehr was no exception to this rule, and like these other town regularly suffered from all kinds of endemic diseases of which malaria (due to the *ab-anbars*), rheumatic affections, eye diseases, diseases of the digestive organs, and venereal diseases were the most common.[89]

However, there was no organization whatsoever to deal with public health, which was left to look after itself. The town was crowded, badly built, and devoid of roads other than gaps between the houses. Inside the town there was no water supply other than the rainwater tanks in the houses, and arrangements for conservancy would be complimented when described by the adjective primitive. In the early 1850s, a large reservoir (*ab-anbar*) to collect rainwater was built on the sea front by a native merchant and was open for public use in April-May, but it was found that it was infested with Guinea worm.[90]

By the turn of the twentieth century not much had changed. The water of Bushehr still was bad, but by then almost every house had a well, with the exception of the many reed huts, of course. In addition, about 10% of the houses had reservoirs. However, the better classes still obtained their water from various places in the peninsula at considerable distance from the town. But even this water was slightly brackish; the Government of India chemist had declared all water on the peninsula unfit for human consumption. The British residency therefore obtained its water from Basra or Karachi by vessel.[91] This was not surprising given the fact that the public roads were used as refuse dumps.

> Refuse, excreta, human and animal, were deposited or thrown indiscriminately into the mud lanes that separated the houses from each other and are generously distributed over the town by the traffic that passes through these lanes. Many of the houses had their drains opening up to the lanes; in other pits in the houses were used for this purpose and the putrefying contents of these pits, often the accumulated filth of years, drained into such wells as exist and sent their stench to the air of the houses and the town.[92]

Nevertheless there was one area where some measure of community spirit developed, which focused on education and proved to be the basis for further future communal activities as part of the constitutional movement. This was only a normal consequence of the fact that education had been a prime target of reformers in Qajar Persia from the beginning.

---

88. Even among native contemporary chroniclers Bushehr was known as an unhealthy place; especially eye diseases prevailed. E`temad al-Saltaneh also notes that many people did not wear shoes, which exposed people to all kinds of parasitic diseases. E`temad al-Saltaneh 1368, vol. 1, p. 299

89. Report on the Trade 1915-16, p. 5; see in more detail, Floor 2012 (forthcoming).

90. Curzon 1892, vol. 1, p. 234

91. Lorimer 1915, pp. 346-47; Bradley-Birt 1909, p. 46.

92. Report on the trade 1921-22, pp. 1-2.

Education

During much of the nineteenth century there was no educational institution in Bushehr apart from the traditional *maktab* or Qoran school. E`temad al-Saltaneh stated that in Bushehr the population had neither a share in knowledge or art (*az 'elm va honar bahreh nadarad*),[93] although there was private tutoring for children of the wealthy.[94] In 1832, there was an Armenian church where, in its cemetery, a small school was kept up by the Armenians. It was founded by Joseph Wolff. British residents in Persia subscribed 700 pounds, but Wolff's interest in the institution ceased. Since his departure, after his brief stay, "none of the fair promises he made have yet been realized. The school possessed, while I was at Bushehr, no more than thirteen pupils, who were struggling through the rudiments of the Persian and Armenian languages, under the guidance of a sleepy old Armenian."[95] Soon thereafter, due to lack of funds, the school was discontinued.[96]

The first 'modern' public school was the Ahmadiyeh school founded by sheikh Ahmad in the 1880s, where the Koran, religion and Hafez was taught. After the founder's death, Sheikh Mohammad Baqer Behbahani, who modernized the curriculum, continued the school. When in 1892, Ahmad Khan Daryabegi was appointed governor of Bushehr he supported Behbahani in his drive for modernization materially and otherwise. He wrote to the Minister of Education for assistance in finding a principal. The latter sent Sheikh Mohammad Hoseyn Sa`adat, who arrived in Bushehr in 1899 and took charge of the school. Since then the school was known as the *Sa`adat-e Mozaffari*. Daryabegi and the well-to-do people of Bushehr raised part of the funds to build a school and people who had been reluctant to send their children to the school gradually did so. In 1900, there were more than 350 students. At the request of the trustees, Daryabegi put two hectares of land outside the town at the disposal of the school which belonged to Malek al-Tojjar and Mo`in al-Tojjar, two leading merchants and the wealthiest persons in town. The new school had six rooms, one salon, and other space for storage. Daryabegi asked Mozaffar al-Din Shah (1896-1907) for financial support, who assigned 1,000 tomans of the Bushehr customs for its construction. The school had not yet been finished when Daryabegi was recalled to Tehran. Matin al-Saltaneh and Mirza Yanis appealed to the merchant community to complete and support the school. At the suggestion of Mirza Yanes (an Armenian) one *shahi* per bale of imports and 0.5 *shahi* per bale of exports would be voluntarily levied to pay for the school. A school committee was formed that met once every Wednesday afternoon. The school moved to its new location at the end of 1901. In 1907, Daryabegi was re-appointed governor of Bushehr, and he stayed for two years. He exerted himself to complete the school and support its activities. The khans of the districts wanted to send their sons for education to Bushehr, but were afraid that they would be held hostage by the government in case of disputes. A request to Mohammad `Ali Shah (1907-10) resulted in a royal command banning the taking of the khan's sons as hostages for good behavior. An Armenian educated at Calcutta taught English, and the three upper classes spent one hour daily at the language. Other subjects taught were Persian, Arabic, arithmetic, geography, Islamic

---

93. E`temad al-Saltaneh 1368, vol. 1, p. 300. In general, see Afshar Sistani 1369, vol. 1, p. 446.

94. Sadid al-Saltaneh 1362, pp. 6-20 who mentions the involvement, including his own, of several people in the literary and grammar education of friends and their relatives.

95. Stocqueler 1832, vol.1, pp. 13-4

96. Curzon 1892, vol. 1, p. 233.

law and Persian history. There was also an Armenian school founded in 1909 and maintained by private subscription.[97]

The Establishment of a Municipality

As soon as the constitutional movement began in 1906 Bushehris participated fervently in the ensuing political debate. Interested parties created an *anjoman* or local council in which merchants such as the *malek al-tojjar* played an important role.[98] As soon as the law permitting the creation of a municipality was passed, Bushehris established such an organization. However, one of the problems that beset the new municipalities was that there were quite a few people who felt they were second to none, while most also lacked the education and experience on how to cooperate and manage the welfare of a community. Because of personalities battles the town was divided not along partly lines (because parties did not exist) but along individual interests. As a consequence, the results of the election were contested and accusations about irregularities were exchanged between various *primo dons*. It was only through arbitrage that the situation was finally resolved.[99]

Also, there were no funds to finance the activities that the municipality wanted to develop. All funds had to be requested from Tehran, which, if money was available, distributed such funds based on a proposed budget. These budgets, such as one from Bushehr, displayed much of the defects of the absolutist royal system that the revolution had claimed to displace.[100] "The net revenue from any other source is remitted to Tehran and not used for the province's needs at all. This has resulted in a growing dilapidated appearance of the town. The *vaqf*s also have fallen into a ruined state due to the poverty of the beneficiaries. Municipal leaders want to change this by introducing new taxes, but it is difficult to raise additional funds under current circumstances as well as to spend them judiciously and effectively."[101] This led to the decision of 12 February 1911 when taxes on alcohol consumption were decreed and collected, while the Municipality also laid down rules applying to drinking alcohol and gambling in public and by Moslems.[102]

In principle, a self-supporting municipal organization had established itself and started realizing an investment program of public works. As a result, the seawalls were rebuilt; new roads were laid down and steps were taken for the lighting of the town and the main road leading to the

---

97. Afshar-Sistani 1369, vol. 1, pp. 447-60. In 1905, a library was also founded by Bushehri well-wishers. Ibid., vol. 1, p. 478. For more details about the history of the school see Mashayekhi 1377; Report on the Trade 1913-14, p. 1.

98. RMM 4 (1908), p. 162.

99. RMM 10 (1910), pp. 585-86.

100. RMM 10 (1910), pp. 585-86.

101. Report on the Trade 1910-11, p. 1.

102. RMM 14 (1911), p. 158. Merchants were discussing the establishment of a Chamber of Commerce with a view to better organize trade in imitation of foreign models. There was also the occasional article in the press advocating the purchase of Moslem goods only and those made by non-Moslems only if there was no choice. However, the same paper (Mozaffari) shortly thereafter took exception to an anti-Jewish pogrom in Shiraz, of which many survivors fled to Bushehr, and wrote that this was a shame. RMM 15 (1911), pp. 162, 555

suburbs in 1913. Because of public health concerns there was continued removal of garbage by donkeys, though in insufficient numbers. The municipality had a prison and employed some 40 policemen recently provided with uniforms, blue for winter and khaki with red facings for summer. Most importantly, the central administration accepted the principle that municipal taxes should be spent in the location that raised them.[103]

Because the Persian government was unable to do something about the insecurity on the road to Shiraz, the killing of British officers by local tribesmen near Bushehr, the agitation of German agents and other political reasons the British occupied the port on 5 August 1915 and British martial law was instituted. This remained in force until 16 October 1915 when the town and peninsula were nominally restored to the Persian government and a Persian governor arrived to take over. However, British troops remained in charge of security as they did in other parts of Persia.[104]

After most British troops left Bushehr by 1919 the situation returned to normal again. By 1920, the municipality had a capable and energetic Persian at its head, who worked hard for the general welfare and made small improvements for the town and kept order. Still, Bushehr as a whole and especially its center remained a filthy place. An effort to repair the most important road leading to Bushehr was made, but permanent metalling was shelved due to lack of funds, and the doubt expressed by the British whether the soft stone and mud put down would last the winter was vindicated. Because the number of motorcars in Bushehr increased, the question of good roads likewise gained importance. However, the British consul expressed as his opinion that "It is doubtful whether something will be done by the government, despite the fact that a monthly tax of 5 tomans is levied on every car for the upkeep of the road."[105] In this opinion he also was correct and it would take another 15 years before Bushehr could boast of an all-weather road connecting it with the mainland, for construction on an all-weather road only began in 1935.[106]

Decline of Bushehr

Under the new Pahlavi regime (1925-79), established by Reza Khan (r. 1925-41), major changes were made in Persia, which also had their profound influence on towns such as Bushehr. However, these changes meant an end to the incipient local democracy. Even before Reza Khan had crowned himself shah of Persia he, as commander-in-chief, had already made it clear who was the real power in Persia and where he wanted changes. These changes were immediately felt in Bushehr. "The new army under Reza Khan made quite a difference in terms of safety on the roads. However, in Bushehr the military overrode civil authority. The governor was a mere figure

---

103. Trade Report 1913-14, p. 1.

104. Trade Report 1915-16, pp. 1-2. In general, see Moberley 1987; see further chapters two and three in this study.

105. Trade Report 1920-21, p. 1; Report on the trade of Bushehr 1921-22, p. 1; Trade Report 1923-24, p. 1.

106. Trade Report 1935-36, p. 3

head, the police subordinate to military commander, and various attempts were made to transfer municipal funds into the central treasury at Tehran."[107] Although after 1925 the municipalities remained in place they were but the executing instrument for the policies of the central government. However, this time the central government aimed to work also in the public interest. As a result of the changes in Persia, towns such as Bushehr lost their fragile and superficial municipal independence. In return, however, the government made major investments in health, education, roads, electric power, employment and other socio-economic sectors.[108]

This new policy led to the development of other ports in the Persian Gulf that were better situated and equipped than Bushehr and were better connected logistically with the Persian economy; this resulted in Bushehr losing its role as the major port of Persia. Whereas other ports in the Persian Gulf were being developed that of Bushehr was not. It was if development bypassed it. The failure to modernize the port, the growing importance of Khuzestan, and most importantly, the construction of the trans-Iranian railway totally marginalized Bushehr. In 1958, modern vessels still had to anchor at six miles (14 km) from the port and had to discharge cargo and passengers by lighter. A visitor characterized the lowly position of Bushehr in 1958 as follows: "Once a prosperous place of 60,000, now reduced to 14,000. Ten foreign consulates were once established there, in 1957 there was one foreign resident, a Russian maid servant."[109]

Conclusion

Bushehr was in some ways a town not representative of other cities in Qajar Persia. It was a port of which there were relatively few. Moreover, Bushehr was a town of recent origin in a country where towns often were at least hundreds of years old, if not much older. Bushehr only had acquired some importance since the mid-eighteenth century, and, because of the climatological conditions, it had a floating population, a feature that it had in common with other Persian Gulf ports. Otherwise the town operated in the same socio-political context as urban life elsewhere in Persia. I.e., as long as it paid its dues to the central government via its local representative, (in this case the sheikh), it was pretty much left to its own devices. Available local wealth and initiative was mostly spent on individual rather than communal needs. The rich had their large homes outside of town, obtained their water from faraway, and could have their children tutored according to their needs. This did not mean that the local business community did not defend its rights and interests as they saw fit. In fact they did, but within the confines of their parochial interests and not with a long-term communal view. This limited, short-term view was determined by the fact that the national political system did not provide the incentives to do so. When this situation changed as a result of the Constitutional Revolution of 1906 there was sufficient public interest to constitute a Municipality and start addressing the main communal problems such as: public health, education, and better transport. However, the failure of the political democratic movement to develop

---

107. Trade Report 1923-24, p. 1.

108. Ehlers & Floor 1995. In the same *Iranian Studies* 1995 volume there are additional articles dealing with other sectors during the Reza Shah period. See also Floor 2009.

109. Stevens 1979, p. 284.

itself into a mature, popular and sustainable system took away the political foundation for this incipient beginning of a local community to develop in a local polity.

In the twentieth century, therefore, the state started to play a major role in the country's development process. As of 1907, but increasingly so after 1925, it changed its traditional role of tax collector, conscriptor and intermittent keeper of the peace to that of the major investor in health, welfare and education, infrastructure, industrial and agricultural projects. Also, through the stimulation of private capital, the state co-financed the development of textile and engineering industries.[110] This developmental role of the state first had been embedded in the Municipality of Bushehr, which initiated a number of local, communal development projects. As of 1922, the Municipality became but the executive arm of the central government, which policy had consequences for Bushehr's future. This new reality led to the development of a national development policy to which the welfare of Bushehr was subordinated. It resulted, amongst other things, in the construction of competing ports, many of which became much more important than Bushehr, which by the 1950s had become a minor port of little importance.

---

110. Although, in 1931/1309, the Municipal Law was passed which defined the municipality's authority, the actual relevance was for Tehran only. For until 1949 the Ministry of the Interior was responsible for urban affairs. In that year the Law of Independence of Municipalities was passed, but till the 1970s the Ministry retained responsibility for some urban functions, amongst which was city-planning and land-use development. Habibi 1992, pp. 199-206; Mozayeni 1974, p. 266.

CHAPTER TWO

BORAZJAN

A RURAL MARKET TOWN IN BUSHEHR'S HINTERLAND[1]

Introduction

Studies that discuss communities of the Persian Gulf littoral are few, and they deal only with those situated on the coast, i.e. the ports. As far as I know, no analytical studies exist of communities in the immediate hinterland of the Gulf ports. The ports needed the communities in their hinterland for food supplies and services (e.g., pack animals) and, above all, for security against attacks from robbers on their economic lifeline, the caravan trade routes. It is therefore of no surprise that such hinterland communities sometimes tried to play, or even actually played, a more important political role than their size would permit in a different geographic location. The role of the market town of Borazjan is a case in point. It was the first major stop for caravans after they had crossed the watery way that separated Bushehr from the mainland. True, Ahmadi and Chah Kutah were in between, but they were so small, that apart from being an occasional halting place they played no other role. Borazjan was a much larger village, in fact, the political, economic and distributive center of the Dashtestan district and to a certain extent, may stand as a model of the role and behaviour of other similar district centres in the littoral, such as Daleki and Khormuj. A description of the Bushehr hinterland in 1912 nicely encapsulates its main characteristics.

---

1. This study was previously published as Willem Floor, "Borazjan in the 19th century," *IRAN* 2004, pp. 179-200 and translated into Persian by `Abdol-Rasul Kheyrandish, *Borazjan* (Tehran: Abad-e Dovvom, 1388/2009).

The land is dotted with villages at intervals of 5 miles with 100-500 dwellings, but most around 100. The houses are made of mud bricks, but a large part of mat huts. The village head usually resides in a mud fort. The villages have no markets and are supplied from the coast and a few towns such as Borazjun. However, pedlars monopolize the retail trade. The water supply is generally from wells, while most of the villages have date plantations, the produce of which is mostly consumed locally. Only date-growing centres such as Ahram, Khaviz (Tangistan) and Zirah export their output mostly. The population mostly depends on the cultivation of wheat and barley. Most able-bodied men cultivating one or two gaos [*gavs* or cows] of land: on the date crop, on vegetable produce with well irrigation, much of which is to supply Bushehr and other Gulf sea ports. Other crops include tobacco, cotton, millet, etc.[2]

Part of Borazjan's relative importance was derived from the fact that it was situated in the foothills of the mountain range that caravans had to cross on their way to and from Bushehr and Shiraz, the most important commercial supply route in Southern Iran. It was also for this reason that during the brief 1856 "war" between Iran and Great Britain, a British expeditionary force attacked Persian forces which were located between Chah Kutah and Borazjan. Depending on whom you believe, either the British or the Persians won, but in either case, both parties found much to celebrate in this sorry event.

Irrespective of the district's administrative status, whether it was under Bushehr or separately administrated from it, its traditional chief remained in power as administrator and tax collector (*zabet*). Borazjan henceforth developed as an important distributing center for its own hinterland by becoming a staple for imported consumer products for Dashtestan. Conversely, Borazjan also was the collection center for local products that were then transported to Bushehr for export to the world market.

With growing lawlessness around the turn of the twentieth century, the central government used the location of Borazjan to ensure the safety of part of the trade route to Shiraz. Finally, Borazjan became the terminus of the first railway built in Iran in the twentieth century, when the British occupation force built a small railway from Bushehr to Borazjan to facilitate supplying its forces in Southern Iran. In 1921, the railway was dismantled and returned to India. Borazjan continued with its role as a supplier of goods and services to Bushehr, but now as a more peaceful and quiet rural town.

---

2. Trade Report 1911-12, p. 1.

Drawing of Borazjan - Price 1832, p. 8.

Location

Borazjan, ordinarily pronounced Borazjun, is situated on the plain of Dashtestan, at an elevation of 750 m above sea level and dominated by the lofty crests of the Kisehkan Mountain less than 16 km eastward.[3] Borazjan is said to be a corrupted form of Gorazdan, or "Place of Boars," its alleged original name. The place used to be inhabited by wild boars before the re-establishment of settled government encouraged the extension of cultivation.[4] Whatever the truth, Borazjan was the principal place in the district of Dashtestan and the seat of the khan, who under the governor-general of Fars ruled the greater part of that district. Borazjan

---

3. Fasa'i 1378, vol. 2, p. 1636. Also written and pronounced as Gisekan.

4. Stack 1882, vol. 1, pp. 30-31, n. 1; Curzon 1892, vol. 2, p. 226.

should not be confused with the village of Rud-Bala-ye Seftiya, one of the four villages col-
lectively known as Arba'eh, near Firuzabad (Fars), which was also known as Borazjan.[5]

The district of Dashtestan from the village of Kolar (on the border of Ganaveh) to the village
of Manqal (Khormuj) measured 37 *farsakh*s, and from Rud Faryab village in the Kisehgan
Mountains to Shif measured 18 *farsakh*s.[6] The British consul Chick provided more detail. He
reported that the Dashtestan jurisdiction was bounded on the

> North: by the Rudhilla river from Hasht Jush, where it meets Angel territory
> to Durudgah, and thence by the Daliki or Shur river to some four miles past
> Buneh Mizan; the boundary with Daliki is about 3 miles past Qaraoul Khan at
> a sulphur stream crossing the caravan road, and this boundary line then mounts
> to the summit of the hills.
>
> East: boundary is along the summit of the Gisakun range past Kotal Bagh-i-Taj.
>
> South: boundary crosses the entrance to the Haft Mulla ravine, south of
> Nanizak and Jamileh: between Sarkurreh and Samal and Gulangun in
> Tangistan: then north of Bulferiz and Gandumriz in Tangistan: north of Ab-i-
> Tawil in Chahkutah and south of Isawand.
>
> West: boundary is north-east from Isawand, Nokal being in Angali and Jarafi
> in Borazjun, to Haft Jush.

There are four lists of the major villages that made up the district of Dashtestan. One
drawn up in the early 1860s and another made in 1875, both were written for the British by a
Persian official. The third list is by the nineteenth century Persian historian Fasa'i. The last list
is that of the new administrative structure of 1913, when Borazjan became part of the new
province of Dashtestan that was composed of eleven districts or *boluk*s (including Bushehr).
It is, but for one, identical to that of Fasa'i and thus reflects the political reality of the period.
The district of Borazjan had eighteen sub-divisions (*qaryeh*). There are differences between
the four lists, but many of the villages are the same. The differences undoubtedly reflect local
conditions at the time of writing, where one village was preferred to the other as being the
more important in any given location. Rahdar and Qara'ulkhaneh were not villages, but, as
their names suggest, guard-posts along the caravan route. In 1865 it was further noted that
Ziyarat was in the past a separate jurisdiction in the hands of *beg*s, but then one of the relatives of the khans of Borazjan resided there.[7] In addition there was the small district of Zireh,
which in 1913 was formally added to Borazjan, after an intermission of about eighteen years,
when the khan of Shabankareh held it.[8]

---

5. Anonymous 1865, p. 178.

6. Fasa'i 1378, vol. 2, p. 1319.

7. Anonymous 1865, p. 178.

8. Gouvernement Impérial de la Perse 1913, pp. 191-92; Ibid., RMM 1913, p. 77.

Table 2.1: List of the major villages of Dashtestan

1865	1875	1883	1913
·	·	Ahsham-e Jat	Ahsham-e Jayyet
Chah-e ʿArabi	Arabee	·	·
·	·	Anarestan	Anarestan
Bagh Hissar	·	·	·
Bagh-e Chenar*	·	·	·
Borazjan	Borazjoon	Borazjan	Borazjan
·	·	Bagh-e Taj	Bagh-e Ragh
Borgahi	Barkahee	Bargahi	Bargahi
Banar	Bunadee	Banar-e Soleymani	Banari-Soleyman
Bunneh	Baneh	·	·
Bunderuz	Bandaroos	Bandaruz	Bandeh-Orzon
·	·	Tell Behi	Talleh-Bahi
Jaim	Jemah	Jimeh	·
Jarrafi	Jarrafee	·	·
Jamileh*	·	·	·
Chah-e Khani	Chahkhanee	Chah Khani	Chah-Khanis
·	Huseinakee	·	·
Kharagah	·	·	·
Khurmi*	·	·	·
Khoshab	Khooshah	Khoshab	Khoshab
		Khest-e Jat	
Khoshmakun	Khashkoon	Khashugan	Khashukan
Dar-e Chatu	·	·	·
·	Dalakee	·	·
·	Dih Kaid	Deh Kayd	Deh-Qayed
Deh-e nao	Deh Nao	Deh Now	Deh-Now
·	Zulbehee	·	·
Rahdar	·	·	·
·	·	Rud-e Faryab	Rud-e Faryab
Ziyarat	Ziaret	Ziyarat	Ziyarat-Lar-Kasseh
Saifabad	Safeedabad	·	·
Sar Kurreh	Sarkurreh	Sar Korreh or Khorreh	·
·	Sarmal	·	·
Isawand*	Eeswandee	ʿIsavandi	Issa-vendy
Qaraʾul Khaneh	·	·	·
·	·	Gachi Deli	Katshi-Deli
·	·	Khosh Makan	Khosh-e Makan
Kakun*	·	·	·
Kullul	Kulul	·	·
Giz-e Bid	Gezbeed	·	·
·	Geeaakoon	·	·
Lardeh*	·	·	·

1865	1875	1883	1913
Ma`abad	-	-	-
Nakhi*	-	-	-
-	-	-	Zirah

Source: Anonymous, "A Brief Account," p. 178; Administration Report 1875-76, p. 18; Fasa'i 1378, vol. 2, p. 1325; Gouvernement Impérial de la Perse 1913, pp. 191-92; Ibid., "Les Réformes Administratives," p. 77. In 1808, according to Dupré 1819, vol. 2, p. 30, the district of Baradjoun [sic; Borazjan] included the following villages: Guissaroûn, Boundarouz, Bergoï, Issevandi, Deh-Kouner-Koûdjeki, Kochap, and Lerdè.
* = located in the Kisehkan mountains.

However, these measurements and list of villages do not give a feel for the physical milieu of the district. In 1821 Fraser wrote:

> Nothing can have a more uninteresting, and even depressing effect, than the appearance of that part of the province of Fars, called Dushtistan, or flat country. At this season it was peculiarly so, every vegetable production being burnt up, and nothing green meeting the eye, save an occasional grove of date trees, or a few tamarisk or caper-bushes, half smothered in dust. The road passes through a succession of low sand-hills, and patches of clayey soil; the latter being sufficiently fertile, and yielding good crops, when water for irrigation can be procured; although where that is not the case, it is as sterile and barren as the sand itself.[9]

It was in that harsh flat country that Borazjan is situated at 44 km [28 miles] northeast of Bushehr town. The ordinary route from Bushehr town to Shiraz passed by Borazjan, which by land is distant 76 km [48 miles] from Bushehr and 25 km [16 miles] from Daleki, the next stage beyond it; but the land-journey from Bushehr could be reduced to 44 km [28 miles] by taking a boat from Bushehr to Shif.[10] Borazjan was about 40 km [25 miles] from Shif.[11] It normally took two hours of travel from Ahmadi to the small village of "Seroond" and from there another two hours to Borazjan.[12] This village, Binning wrote, is at a considerable distance from the mountains, though owing to the purity of the atmosphere, they appear close at hand.[13] Borazjan was 3.5 to 5 km [two or three miles] from the bottom of the first range of hills.[14] However, that was the travel time under normal conditions traversing the hard white plain, whose monotony was only occasionally broken by a few palms and some clusters

9. Fraser 1984, p. 71.

10. Lorimer 1915, p. 328.

11. Weeks 1896, p. 127.

12. Buckingham 1971, p. 343.

13. Binning 1857, vol. 1, pp. 158-59.

14. Stirling 1991, p. 12.

of tamarisk trees.[15] Travelling over this plain was different after it rained, for it consisted of a type of soil known as *raml* or clayey sand.[16] This meant that, "In ordinary weather the ground is hard clay, mixed with sand; but the rain of the last few days had made the surface slippery and sticky, and had covered it with water. After seven hours of weary plodding ... we reached Burazjun."[17] In summer, Borazjan was very hot, and the discomfort was made worse by thousands of flies and mosquitoes.[18] A situation not unlike that of other locations in the Garmsirat reason why an unknown poet wrote:

دوزخ بورازجان وجهیم است دالکی
بوشهر هم یکی از قلاع جهنم است

Borazjan is Purgatory and Daleki is Inferno
And Bushehr is also a Hell's chateau.[19]

Origins and Housing

We do not know when Borazjan was established as a village. In the larger area there are traces that attest that the Dashtestan plain has been long inhabited, in fact since pre-Islamic times.[20] Borazjan is mentioned in the early Islamic period, but without any particulars and then there is total silence until the mid eighteenth century.[21] For it is only in 1786 that Borazjan is mentioned again in written sources. The British traveller Francklin, on his way to Shiraz, considered "Berazgoon, a considerable and populous village, surrounded by a brick wall, and flanked with turrets; under the dominion, and dependent of, Shirauz."[22] This implies that Borazjan must have existed for quite some time or else it could not possibly have been a

---

15. Weeks 1896, p. 127.

16. E`temad al-Saltaneh 1368, vol. 4, p. 2055; Moore 1915, p. 435 ("an interminable plain of bare yellowish grey earth").

17. Stack 1882, vol. 1, pp. 30-31.

18. Moore 1915, p. 437; Akhgar 1366, p. 112; Dupré 1819, vol. 2, p. 30. Captain Bruce, the British Resident in Bushehr had a summer-house in Borazjan in 1820, indicating that the heat in Bushehr was worse. Lumsden 2010, p. 30.

19. Akhgar 1366, p. 108.

20. Afshar Sistani 1369, vol. 1, pp. 265-78. In and near Borazjan there are still remnants of Achaemenid and Seleucid buildings.

21. Vothuqi 1375 b, p. 42; Jeyhani 1368, p. 110.

22. Francklin 1976, p. 41. It was only in 1831 that Borazjan is found on a geographical map for the first time, as far as I have been able to determine, see Sahab 2005, vol. 2, pp. 542, 544 (Long maps/1831), see also vol. 2, p. 520 (Wyld map/1842), p. 537 (Johnston map/1843).

populous village. Niebuhr took a different road to Shiraz than Francklin by passing east of Borazjan via Tangesir, Dashti, and Khormuj; he did not note Borazjan on his map either.[23]

In the first decade of the nineteenth century, foreign travelers did not change much in their characterisation of Borazjan as compared with Francklin. In 1800, Hollingberry, a member of Malcolm's embassy, considered "Berauzgoon, a tolerably large village, and well peopled."[24] Other travellers such as Waring and Kinneir considered Borazjan also a large village.[25] What struck these travellers furthermore was the physical aspect of the village. Kinneir described it as having a mud, not a brick, wall, flanked with towers, while Waring only mentioned the wall.[26] However, according to Morier, the village was a collection of huts, which were built around a fort, which "was a square, with turrets at each corner, which were cut into small chequers at the top."[27] Another aspect of the village, which was reached via a stony road half a mile before Borazjan,[28] was that thereafter the access to Borazjan was through plantations of date palms and tamarisk trees.[29] Although Ouseley stayed at Borazjan, none of the members of the embassy described the village, only referring to it. Price mentions that it was scene of some diplomatic grand-standing between Ouseley and the *mehmandar*, but he left us with a nice drawing of the village.[30] In the 1820s there was little change in the way Borazjan was seen by travellers. According to Fraser, it was a considerable town on the road,[31] while Buckingham dubbed it a large scattered village.[32] Stirling called Borazjan a large and populous village. He added, "There are two strongholds in this village, only one of which is occupied by the present authority for the purpose of defence and protection. The other is inhabited by, apparently, private families. The walls of the fort in which Salem Khan resides are high, perhaps not less than thirty feet, defended by several towers, and [it] is seated on rather a higher elevation than the rest of the town."[33]

In the mid-nineteenth century Borazjan was described as "a large straddling village. On one side of the village, is a fort."[34] According to Pelly, "All the villages, even Barazjan included, from Bushehr to the base of the hills, may be described as a series of simple forts of unburnt brick or rough stone, surrounded by straggling collections of temporary huts. Here and there a wealthier farmer may have built a mud-brick house, whose upper room peers drearily over the general huttage."[35] Thus it would seem that the wall to which the early travellers referred was that of the fort around which the villagers had built their simple dwellings.

---

23. Niebuhr 1992, p. 510 plus map.

24. Hollingberry 1976, p. 18.

25. Waring 1971, p. 17 (Birasgoon); Kinneir 1973, p. 363 (Borauzgoon).

26. Waring 1971, p. 17; Kinneir 1973, p. 363.

27. Morier 1812, p. 76 (Borazjoon); see also Dupré 1819, vol. 2, p. 30.

28. Kinneir 1973, p. 363.

29. Morier 1812, p. 76.

30. Ouseley 1819, vol. 1, p. 257; Price 1832, p. 8.

31. Fraser 1984, p. 71 (Boorauzgoon; Brauzejoon).

32. Buckingham 1971, p. 343 (Barazgoon).

33. Stirling 1991, p. 12 (Barrisgoon; Barrusjoon).

34. Binning 1857, vol. 1, p. 158 ("Brazgon, or more correctly Burazjan").

35. Pelly 1865 a, p. 143.

Borazjan had one fortress, although Stirling mentioned that there were two.[36] One of the forts was most likely a caravanserai, about which later. The ordinary houses were poor, built chiefly of unburnt bricks and mud, with flat roofs,[37] and, according to Pelly, as mentioned above, in general wretched.[38] The village "stands on a hard, gravelly soil; the stones forming the upper strate are large, ranging from the size of a pigeon's egg to that of a child's head. Running through the village there is the bed of a dry stream ... and there is no running water and is scarcely below the surface, it merely serves to convey off superfluous water when the rains are heavy.[39] The village has brackish wells, but below the surface there was drinkable water and the people were expert in digging temporary wells.[40] This explains why Lorimer and Sadid al-Saltaneh state that Borazjan's "water is from deep wells and is good and abundant."[41] However, it was difficult to have cool water due to the heat. The only way to do so was to use a leather vessel with three wooden legs, which was called *du lacheh*. By keeping the leather moist and putting it outside in the open air, especially at sunset, the water temperature decreased considerably.[42]

In 1856, Captain Hunt described Borazjan (Brásjoon) as having "A wall, with tower bastions at intervals, enclosed the whole, and detached square towers within overlooked all. A ditch fifteen feet deep ran round the outside, and beyond its gardens, with high thorns and cactus fences." He further commented that if the Persian force, whose entrenched camp the British army had just overrun, had taken up position in the village, then "in proper hands the capture of such a place must cost both time and many sacrifices."[43] Fortunately for the British, the Persian army had made it easy for them. From this and earlier descriptions it is clear that Hunt meant to describe the khan's fortress rather than the entire village itself, whose houses were spread out around the fort.

Population

All travellers consistently call Borazjan a large and populous village, but what did that mean? According to Morier, "I understand that the population of this district [Dashtestan] has been decreasing ever since the happy days of Sheikh Nasr."[44] This may have been due to the last fights between the Qajars and the Zands for the throne of Iran that took place in Bushehr's hinterland. Lotf ʿAli Khan Zand, the last Zand ruler, made a brief stop in Borazjan on his

---

36. Stirling 1991, p. 12.

37. Binning 1857, vol. 1, p. 158; Fasa'i 1378, vol. 2, p. 1325 (houses, which were all built with mud [*khesht va gel*]).

38. Pelly 1865 a, p. 143 (Barazjan); Lycklama 1873, vol. 3, p. 49 (large village).

39. Stirling 1991, p. 12.

40. Pelly 1865 a, p. 142; Waters 1876, p. 181.

41. Lorimer 1915, p. 328 Sadid al-Saltaneh 1362, p. 30; Fasa'i 1378, vol. 2, p. 1325.

42. Akhgar 1366, p. 112.

43. Hunt 1858, p. 206. For a Persian account of the events see Fasa'i 1378, vol. 1, pp. 810-17. Waters 1876, p. 180 reported that "Borasjoon contains at present no very substantial houses-consisting merely of an aggregration of huts."

44. Morier 1812, p. 77.

way to Bushehr, and from there to his final stand at Kerman.[45] It is only in 1808 that one of Borazjan's visitors (Dupré) made an estimate of the village's population, viz. 1,000 families or some 5,000 people.[46] The next estimate is from 1828, when according to Stirling, "The population of this village, from what I could understand from the enquiries I made, cannot be much less than three thousand souls."[47] In 1851, Binning estimated that the village contained about 1,500 houses.[48] This seems to have been a printer's error for 500, a temporary fluke, or a mistake in estimating the number of houses, for around 1860, according to Pelly, the village had 400 households.[49] In 1870, according to Rivadeneyra, it had 8,000 inhabitants. However, the 1871 famine reduced the population by one-third.[50] According to Fasa'i, Borazjan had 750 houses, or about 5,000 people, in 1885 or thereabouts.[51]

In 1890, the town reputedly boasted of 6,000 inhabitants.[52] According to Sadid al-Saltaneh, in 1896 Borazjan had 1,000 houses and about 5,000 people. However, a government survey carried out at his suggestion in Borazjan at that time showed that the number of houses was 885, or (assuming a family size of five) a population of about 4,500.[53] Lorimer's figure of about 500 houses with a population of 2,500 persons is too low for the beginning of the twentieth century, and since his study is based on a compilation of older data, this figure may refer to an earlier period.[54] If we discount Binning's estimate as an error, it would seem, that Borazjan's population increased during much of the entire nineteenth century, starting at 3,000 around 1825 and probably reaching some 5,000 persons towards the end of the nineteenth century. By 1911, Borazjan only had 800 houses and 4,000 inhabitants.[55] The decreased population may be due to the political unrest and the related violence in the area, about which later. The population size of Borazjan is in harmony with the estimated total population size of the districts at that time.

---

45. Shirazi 1888, p. 49.

46. Dupré 1819, vol. 2, p. 30.

47. Stirling 1991, p. 12.

48. Binning 1857, vol. 1, p. 158.

49. Pelly 1865 a, p. 172.

50. Rivadeneyra 1880, vol. 3, p. 9. In 1874, Waters 1876, p. 180 estimated its population at 1,500, "though at one time I was informed that it contained as many as twenty thousand."

51. Fasa'i 1378, vol. 2, p. 1325.

52. Curzon 1892, vol. 2, p. 226.

53. Sadid al-Saltaneh 1362, pp. 30-31, 612.

54. Lorimer 1915, p. 328.

55. Chick 1911, p. 3.

Table 2.2: In 1910 the estimated population of Bushehr and its main surrounding districts was:[56]

Bushehr peninsula	23,000
Dashti	20,000
Dashtestan	20,000
Hayat Da'ud and Liravi	20,000

Given the fact that Borazjan enjoyed economic growth during the second half of the nineteenth century, it is unsurprising that the population increased, but at the same time, possibly also lost population to other parts of the littoral. To make this point we need to have a closer look at the composition of Borazjan's population and its economic activities.

Borazjan was probably founded, or at least started its development, in the early eighteenth century and grew to its size of 500 households in the decades thereafter, due to the increasingly important commercial role of Bushehr. With the abandoning of Bandar 'Abbas in 1760 by the Dutch and English East India Companies (VOC and EIC), Bushehr became the most important port in the Persian Gulf. It became the emporium for the trade with Iran's political centre of the second half of the eighteenth century, Shiraz, and consequently the villages along that trade route benefited from the increase in trade that took place.[57] In the beginning of the nineteenth century, the Papari tribe reportedly ousted the original inhabitants of Borazjan, whom Lorimer reported to have been known as the Bag. However, the Paparis only constituted part of the population, because they were joined or preceded by a group called the Qayedan and the Ra'asa, whom Lorimer called recent immigrants, and by some sayyeds. "The remainder of the town's people are a medley of immigrants from other places, such as Busheris, Dashtis, Khishtis and Kazerunis."[58] By the beginning of the twentieth century, according to a local history, there were not less than forty important lineages or clans in Borazjan, in addition to many smaller ones.[59]

Table 2.3: List of the major lineages of Borazjan

Papari	Kamali	Khusravi	Qayedan	Ahangar	Farrashbandi
Shah Hoseyni	Ru'asa	Najjaran	Musavat	Sadat-e Mir Ja`fari	Zandavi
Shahneh	Baba`Ali	Ruzbeh	Abu'l-Fathi	Kalimi	Dehdashti
Vothuqi	Kamareji	Garmsiri	Banuvi	Aqa Majnuni	Laru'i
Shahrubandi	Bahreyni	Ujr	Mashayekh	Karbala'i Shamsi	Zahabi
Salmani	Barjal	Dadal-Mizani	Kuzehgaran	Akhundha	Haqiqat
Bahrani	Akhundha	Bahrani	Khvanin	Sadat-e Shoja`al-Dini	Dashti

---

56. Trade Report 1910-11, p. 2.

57. See Floor 2007, chapter 7.

58. Lorimer 1915, p. 328. For a discussion of the various lineages and their origins see Farrashbandi 1336, vol. 2, pp. 140-73. The Paparis probably were a sub-group of the Buyer Ahmadi tribe as there was a Papi group part of that tribe. Majidi Kera'i 1381, p. 417. Sections of the Mamasanis (another Buyer Ahmadi but large sub-group) also settled in Kazerun. Majidi Kera'i 1381, p. 353.

59. Farrashbandi 1336, vol. 2, p. 206.

The names of these lineages indicate partly professional origins (five groups), partly geographic ones (seven groups), but mostly personal ones (the remainder), and confirm Lorimer's characterisation of the population. Farrashbandi also states that the population came from different parts of Iran. In addition, they had all intermarried and thus formed one big family.[60] The name of a lineage could be misleading, for example, the Dashti group did not originate in the Dashti district, but came from Moz in Larestan. They were originally Naqshbandi Sufis (followers of Sheikh Habibollah), but converted to Bahaism after an internal conflict and moved to Dashti. One part of the group then moved on to Borazjan, the remainder staying in Khormuj and neighbouring villages.[61] In this respect Borazjan was a microcosm of Bushehr's population, which also was of motley composition, originating mostly from Bushehr's hinterland.[62] What therefore seems likely is that Borazjan's population indeed grew, but that Bushehr and other villages on the littoral siphoned off part of this growth. Also, there was a small Jewish community of ten families that resided in the village. Although their occupation is not mentioned, it is quite likely that they were engaged as peddlers (*pilehvar*), an occupation many rural Jews followed. "Their mullah, a venerable old man, gave us a touching, and artless description of their miseries and woes, and the affecting picture of indigence, poverty and degradation which we witnessed here [...] was sufficient to suffuse with tears eyes less accustomed to such sights than our own."[63] In addition, after 1865 there was one Armenian family living in Borazjan, whose male head was the operator of the telegraph office.

Economy

What drew these groups from the various parts of the Garmsirat of Fars to Borazjan and onwards? The explanation must be sought in the economy of Borazjan. Of what did it consist? Borazjan depended on dates and agriculture and upon the passage through it of the Shiraz and the up-country trade. Consequently, the people were mostly cultivators, traders or muleteers.

Initially, Borazjan must have been one of the many emblematic villages that Fraser so well described at that time.

> Villages are to be found wherever there is water; poor and wretched, but
> containing semi-barbarous inhabitants in considerable abundance; their food a
> few dates, and a bit of barley bread. Milk, indeed is abundant, and they possess
> flocks of sheep, reared chiefly for sale, and breed a number of horses, which
> though not so celebrated as those of Nejed, or Bahrein, are nevertheless highly

---

60. Farrashbandi 1336, vol. 2, p. 205.

61. Farrashbandi 1336, vol. 2, pp. 206-208, with a lot of stereotyped misinformation such as the sharing of women, etc.

62. Afshar Sistani 1369, vol. 1, pp. 423-31.

63. Stern 1854, pp. 109-10.

esteemed ... the villages are rarely in view, and are at best but collections of date-tree huts, so small and wretched as to be scarcely discernable from the inequalities of the ground.[64]

Borazjan had grown as the result of the increased long-distance trade that passed through its confines, and thus the village soon boasted of a caravanserai to attract caravans and their business. An earthquake destroyed its caravanserai in July 1824. At that time, according to Alexander, it was "a populous and thriving town: the walls can hardly be seen for the numerous stacks of grain which surround them. If a European happens to put up in the mehman-khana, or guest's-house, in the town, the chief of the place, Sheikh Suleem Khan, will provide him with every necessary, gratis. The origin of this custom was as follows: the life of an ancestor of the chief was saved by the interference of a European, and he strictly enjoined all his descendants to treat Europeans in general as above-mentioned."[65] Despite this alluring option Alexander slept outside on the ground.[66]

Initially, Borazjan was primarily a dry-farming agricultural settlement. Rich wrote, "On July 25 [1821], I arrived at Burauzgoon, passing through about two miles of plantations of dates and tobacco."[67] Borazjan had indeed many date groves.[68] Other travellers noted the *konar* trees when approaching Borazjan, and close to and surrounding the village the serried ranks of date-palm trees.[69] In addition to dates and tobacco, Borazjan had extensive fields of barley and wheat, amongst which grew wild oats, and the white and red poppy. "In some parts the crops had been cut and removed, in others they were ready for reaping, others again required a fortnight more to ripen them. The numerous fields into which these plains were subdivided had no hedges or banks to separate them from each other, or even from the woods; many parts were moist with salt water."[70] Binning noted that much wheat and barley was cultivated, and that there was an abundance of date trees. He further observed many lote or cornel trees (*konar*).[71] Stirling "saw no cultivation worthy of notice [March 19, 1828], and in fact none except those small vegetable gardens attached to some of the houses in the outskirts of the village."[72] These seemingly small gardens had a considerable output. Fasa'i states that Borazjan produced many vegetables (*boqulat-e gavchahi*), and the lettuce (*kahu*) of Borazjan was proverbially good. The watermelons of Sar Kurreh, one of the villages near Borajzan, were very big, sweet, and numerous and were exported to Bushehr in large quantities.[73] There

64. Fraser 1984, pp. 71-72.

65. Alexander 2000, p. 101.

66. Alexander 2000, p. 101.

67. Rich 1836, vol. 2, p. 195.

68. E`temad al-Saltaneh 1368, vol. 4, p. 2055, 2058 (Chah Kutah); Pirzadeh 1343, vol. 2, pp. 413-14 (*nakhilat*); Stern 1854, p. 109 ("the beautiful date-groves of Boraz-goon"); Akhgar 1366, p. 109.

69. Lycklama 1873, vol. 3, p. 49; Weeks 1896, p. 127.

70. Johnson 1818, pp. 28-29.

71. Binning 1857, vol. I, pp. 158-59; Fasa'i 1378, vol. 2, pp. 1325.

72. Stirling 1991, pp. 12-13.

73. Fasa'i 1378, vol. 2, pp. 1325-26.

also were regular plagues of locusts doing much damage to the crops; the only advantage was that the local people boiled and ate the locusts in the manner of shrimps.[74]

Apart for local consumption, Borazjan also produced for the market. Waring in 1804 observed that Borazjan carried on a considerable trade in cotton, wheat, barley and tobacco with Bushehr."[75] But trade was not only with Bushehr, but also with the passengers and handlers of the regular caravans that passed through Borazjan. "Corn and provisions, sufficient for the wants of the peasantry and of that of the passing muleteers, are found at all the forts. The surplus corn is exported; that which remains in store is buried in pits lined with straw. These are readily discoverable by probing; and the pit coverings are generally raised into mounds. The grain is sown in late autumn and reaped in late spring and early summer. Cotton thrives everywhere, but is carelessly sown, and the same bushes are left standing for an indefinite number of years."[76] This perception of negligence or lack of care was also described by Arnold. "Their agriculture is careless; their homes are miserable; their food, for the most, dates." ... "Cultivated patches, all unfenced, are few and far apart. In these, wheat was waving five inches high around bushes which the cultivators had not taken the trouble to remove."[77] Consequently, what mostly stood out in the mind of the foreign observers were its palm trees, for Borazjan was surrounded by date-groves which were most extensive on the west side, the reason why Curzon called Borazjan the palm-girdled village.[78]

There were no local manufactures in 1808, but the weaving of blue fabrics, which were "found all over the East."[79] Later in the nineteenth century, according to Lorimer, the women of Dashtestan district wove camel hair into material to make cloaks or 'abas. Their price in Bushehr was 50-250 qrans, according to colour and softness.[80] Also, the Dashti clan was almost exclusively engaged in cloth shoe making (shiveh kashi) and weaving (jula'i) and there was production of construction materials and pottery.[81] East of the village are the Kisehkan Mountains, which had mining potential. However, they were not easy accessible. Further there were many springs that were not used for agriculture. Also, there were many coal deposits that were not used either.[82] The increased importance of crafts may have been a later development, for the bazaar was qualified as "a wretched place," in 1808 as well as in 1851.[83]

---

74. Curzon 1892, vol. 2, p. 227.

75. Waring 1971, p. 17.

76. Pelly 1865 a, p. 142.

77. Arnold 1877, p. 401.

78. Lorimer 1915, p. 328; Curzon 1892, p. 226. According to Akhgar 1366, p. 109, the produce of one date palm could feed one family for one year. That was the reason why during local fights the hostile attacking force not only tried to kill people but also their palm trees by cutting their water supply and thus their livelihood.

79. Dupré 1819, vol. 2, p. 30.

80. DCR 3951 (Bushehr 1906-07), p. 19; E`temad al-Saltaneh 1368, vol. 4, p. 2055.

81. Farrashbandi 1336, vol. 1, p. 207, vol. 2, p. 150. On cloth shoe making see Wulff 1966, pp. 228-30.

82. Sadid al-Saltaneh 1362, p. 31.

83. Dupré 1819, vol. 2, p. 30 (with only a few shops); Binning 1857, vol. 1, p. 158.

However, in 1889 there were 50 shops of all trades,[84] and by 1900, the bazaar contained about 170 shops, according to Lorimer.[85] However, according to an 1896 government survey there were only 42 shops and nine farms (*mazra 'eh*s) belonging to Borazjan.[86]

Another economic activity was the supply of pack-animals, ensuring services for these animals (farriers) and the sale of food and fodder to caravans and travellers passing through, which was a monopoly belonging to the chief of Borazjan.[87] About 300-500 mules belonging to Borazjan were employed on the Shiraz route, depending on the fodder situation and the occurrence of plagues. Borazjan was the only trade centre in Dashtestan "and its trade is consequently an epitome of the trade of that district." Borazjan's 32 villages, which were situated within a radius of 12-15 km, supplied their goods to Borazjan for export, while Borazjan supplied them in turn with imported goods.[88] The exports all went to Bushehr and comprised wheat, barley, beans, melons, tobacco, gum, wool, firewood, charcoal and lime.[89] People at Bushehr preferred Indian charcoal to that of Borazjan district, if they could afford to buy it, because the latter contained a large quantity of powder.[90]

Table 2.4: Gum Arabica in Fars province was mainly produced by: [91]

District	quantity (in tons)
Maymand	100
Firuzabad	150
Borazjan	110
Shiraz (from various parts of Fars)	300
Kazerun	225
Kamarej	45
Khesht	75
Bandar-e Rig	130
Behbahan	350
Shustar, Ram Hormuz	175
Total	1,660

The imports in the opposite direction, for the consumption for the town and district, were chiefly cotton prints, rice, coffee, sugar, tea, opium and spices. The opium habit was very

---

84. Pirzadeh 1343, vol. 2, p. 414.

85. Lorimer 1915, p. 328.

86. Sadid al-Saltaneh 1362, pp. 30-31.

87. Sirjani 1361, p. 40.

88. Fasa'i 1378, vol. 2, pp. 1325-1326. Plagues indeed occurred such as in 1893, see Nezam al-Saltaneh 1361, vol. 1, p. 140.

89. Lorimer 1915, p. 328; Dupré 1819, vol. 2, p. 59.

90. DCR 4179 (Bushehr 1907-08), p. 17.

91. Trade Report 1911-12, p. 15.

prevalent by the end of the nineteenth century.[92] The currency of trade was Persian, chiefly silver *qeran*s; and the *man* of Borazjan was equal to 18 lbs. 11 oz. English, giving a *hashem man* (13 ordinary *man*s) of 139 lbs.[93]

Consequently, there were not only muleteers but also merchants in Borazjan who were in regular communication with Bushehr and the outlying villages of Borazjan. Binning, for example, mentioned the chief merchant of Borazjan whom he described as "a man well known to the Resident at Bushehr."[94]

Despite the economic activities in Borazjan and the growth in trade, and thus in income, the people of Borazjan did not did strike Stirling in 1826 "either as industrious or wealthy, nor can I say that I ever saw a well-dressed individual. The countenance and habits of all indicated much poverty and want, although there was no deficiency of pride in their emaciated and half-starved features and looks."[95] This may have been due to the rather harsh rule by the local khan and the fact that Borazjan was involved in several feuds at that time. For Stirling also noticed that, "there appeared to reign the spirit of desolation and desertion" among the population.[96] Fraser also implied this when he related that the sheikh of Borazjan wanted to sell him a beautiful Arabian, of the best blood. "But it had signs of firing on both legs. We declined, and later learned that the owner had purposefully blemished the animal to avoid having to cede it to the Sheikh."[97] He said it in even stronger terms, "everything we saw and heard strongly indicated that the government is even a more bitter enemy to the people's prosperity than their churlish soil."[98] In 1851, the people looked squalid and miserable, according to Binning. This was probably due to the fact that they just had been 'liberated' from the occupation by the Tangestanis.[99] Economically speaking things looked up during the second half of the nineteenth century, and Lorimer reported that "The standard of civilisation is higher at Burazjan than is usual in the coast districts about Bushehr, but the inhabitants avoid needless display of well-being and even allow their houses to remain unrepaired lest the Persian Government should be tempted to quarter a high official permanently among them; at the same time their attitude towards the Government is somewhat defiant.[100]

Despite its economic importance Borazjan did not have a caravanserai for much of the nineteenth century. Col. Johnson related that in 1817, "We arrived at Boorauzgoon, where there was no caravansarai. We were lodged under the thatched gateway of a Jew's house."[101] This lack of commercial infrastructure was soon thereafter corrected. In 1821, Rich reported, "We were lodged under the gateway of the caravansarai. Burauzgoon is in the style of Tchah-

92. Lorimer 1915, p. 329.

93. Lorimer 1915, p. 328.

94. Binning 1857, vol. 1, pp. 158-59.

95. Stirling 1991, p. 12.

96. Stirling 1991, p.13.

97. Fraser 1984, pp. 71-72.

98. Fraser 1984, p. 72.

99. Binning 1857, vol. 1, pp. 158-59.

100. Lorimer 1915, p. 328.

101. Johnson 1818, p. 28.

koota, but rather better and more extensive; with a caravansarai, which would not be amiss if it were finished"[102] It was probably this caravansarai which an earthquake destroyed in 1824. Stirling wrote in 1828, "There is no sarray here. I was obliged to get quarters in the fort by application to the men of the chief near the gateway."[103] Because of the destruction of the caravanserai, travellers had to find accommodation elsewhere. Binning "was conducted to the house of one Reihan, a Jew, and was accommodated in a small room adjoining the stable."[104] The chief merchant of Borazjan offered Binning lodgings in his house.[105] Fourteen years later there was still no caravanserai, for though the road through Borazjan was a major trade route one did not find a caravanserai till one reached Daleki.[106] However, there was the ruin of the old caravanserai, for in 1875 Ballantine wrote that there was a caravanserai, but it was totally tumbled down.[107] This means that either between 1865 and 1875 a caravanserai had been built, which in that short period had become ruined, which seems highly unlikely, or what is more likely, that it was the ruin of the caravanserai destroyed in 1824.

After 1865, the Indo-European Telegraph Department's line from Bushehr to Shiraz passed through Borazjan and was connected there with the Persian government telegraph, which went via Rig, Deylam, Behbahan, and Ahvaz to Mohammareh, Shustar and Dezful.[108] The Telegraph Department had built a station at Borazjan comprising a small building with two rooms, which foreign travellers often used and which had been built for that purpose. Locally the building was known as Kuti. In 1868 there were as yet no doors or chairs.[109]

However, the lack of a caravanserai was still sorely felt;[110] but this defect was soon to be remedied. In 1289/1872-73 the construction of a new caravanserai was started and in 1875 it was still under construction. It was not yet ready for use by travellers.[111] According to Ballantine, the new caravanserai was intended to be a substantial structure, "but the funds bequeathed for its erection, by a pious old Mussulman merchant, were constantly being drained by fraud and rascality, so that the work lagged." He and his party were lodged by an Armenian in the employ of the Telegraph Department in one of the two rooms of his office building.[112] Moshir al-Molk was the pious person who financed the construction of the new caravanserai, which was built under the supervision of the architect Hajj Mohammad Rahim. The cost figures given for the construction vary between 40,000 and 85,000 *tumans*.[113] By 1876, the caravanserai was ready, so that now Borazjan was described as consisting of "a

102. Rich 1836, vol. 2, pp. 195-96.

103. Stirling 1991, pp. 12-13.

104. Binning 1857, vol. 1, p. 158.

105. Binning 1857, pp. 158-59; see also Stern 1854, p. 109 (the gateway of a ruined caravanserai).

106. Pelly 1865 a, p. 142.

107. Ballantine 1879, p. 67.

108. Lorimer 1915, pp. 328-29.

109. Lycklama 1873, vol. 3, p, 49; Ballantine 1879, p. 67; Farrashbandi 1336, vol. 2, p. 224.

110. Curzon 1915, vol. 2, p. 226.

111. Sadid al-Saltaneh 1362, pp. 30-31; Ballantine 1879, p. 67; Waters 1876, p. 181.

112. Ballantine 1879, p. 67.

113. Farrashbandi 1336, vol. 2, p. 223; Sadid al-Saltaneh 1362, pp. 30-31 (85,000 *tumans*); Moshir al-Molk spent 40,000 *tumans*, according to Fasa'i 1378, vol. 2, p. 1325.

telegraph-station, a caravansarai, and a village."[114] Europeans mostly continued to lodge at the Telegraph station, if only because it was cleaner and had the additional benefit of the company of the Armenian operator.[115]

Caravânsérai de Borasgoun

Drawing of the *dezh*, De Vilmorin 1895, p. 344

The new caravanserai made quite an impression on European travellers. From afar it stood out as a landmark against the sky, looking like a two-tiered mediaeval castle with lofty and loopholed walls, ramparts, enormous towers and turrets. Everyone considered it to be the finest caravanserai in Iran, and although "it lost much of its impressiveness as one draws nearer," it was still a magnificent building. On the inside there was "a splendid suite of rooms for the governor or other travelling officials of high rank."[116] Although a caravanserai, the building was at the same time a stronghold "capable of being utilised as a fort, the reason why locally it was called *dezh* or fort. High Persian officials passing through Burazjan treat the Sarai as a residence."[117] Apparently, later some smaller additional caravanserais were constructed in Borazjan. According to a survey by 1896, the town had one large caravanserai and three small ones.[118]

---

114. Arnold 1877, p. 401.

115. Bradley-Birt 1909, pp. 61-62; Weeks 1896, p. 127; Stack 1882, vol. 1, p. 31.

116. Curzon 1892, vol. 2, p. 226 (with description); Weeks 1896, p. 127; De Vilmorin 1895, pp. 343-44. (with a detailed description and drawing); Bradley-Birt 1909, pp. 61-2; Williams 1907, p. 42; Sadid al-Saltaneh 1362, p. 30; Pirzadeh 1343, vol. 2, p. 413.

117. Lorimer 1915, p. 328; Farrashbandi 1336, vol. 2, p. 224. This caravanserai was used as the headquarters of the fourth battalion of the gendarmerie as of 1913. Akhgar 1366, p. 109.

118. Sadid al-Saltaneh 1362, pp. 30-31 (unless the small ones had already existed prior to 1876, but had been disregarded by Europeans, which seems unlikely).

Cultural and Social Life

As far as religious life is concerned, in 1828, there were no large mosques.[119] By 1896, according to a government survey, there were five mosques; whether they were large is unknown.[120] There were also several religious shrines of some importance.[121] Ouseley reported that: "Near our camp was the tomb of some modern Imamzadah or Mohammedan saint, whose name I did not take the trouble to record; a representation of it, however, is annexed, (Plate XII), not for any beauty in the view, but as it shews one form of those sepulchral edifices, which a traveller in Persia almost daily sees."[122] In 1896, there were at 12 km (2 *farsakhs*) south of the town two *imamzadeh*s; one was the alleged resting place of Ebrahim b. Musa Kazem and known as '*shir mard*.' It was famed for its many miracles.[123] There was a synagogue for the small Jewish community, "a dark miserable hut, consisting of four bare walls, and a broken uneven clay floor; there was not a book, except for a few parts of the Old Testament Scriptures, with which Dr. Wolff, many years ago, presented them."[124] To sustain religious life as well as other spiritual needs there were some local ulama, poets and calligraphers, who had achieved some renown. By the end of the nineteenth century, Borazjan even boasted of one *mojtahed*.[125] By 1890, there was a four-class "modern" school and a budget had been allocated for it, including for the teaching staff.[126]

For those who wanted more, there was also a set of good baths.[127] In 1832/1248, the then ruling governor or *zabet*, Salim Khan, built a new bath-house. By 1896 this one was still standing and was in good condition, while the other was in ruins.[128] For those who wanted physical exercise there was a very peculiar characteristic of Borazjan that, as far as I have been able to ascertain, was the only settlement in Iran where a kind of baseball (rounders) was played. In 1826, Stirling noted that, "The children however attracted my attention, from observing their play with the ball in much the same way boys play at home, but with less spirit and design. Their ball was bad, made chiefly of wound cotton cloth, and not even with worsted wound into a ball, which would have given elasticity. They were not a little pleased at my joining them and showing that I was not ignorant of the game."[129] That this game was no fluke, but had really captured the minds of the population is clear since the same game was

119. Stirling 1991, p. 13.

120. Sadid al-Saltaneh 1362, pp. 30-31.

121. Lorimer 1915, p. 328.

122. Ouseley 1819, vol. 1, p. 257.

123. Sadid al-Saltaneh 1362, pp. 30-31; Pirzadeh 1343, vol. 2, p. 413 mentions an *imamzadeh* of Nur al-Din, which may denote the other one that Sadid al-Saltaneh mentioned.

124. Stern 1854, p. 109.

125. Farrashbandi 1336, vol. 1, pp. 130-42, 146-202; Fasa'i 1378, vol. 2, p. 1325; Sadid al-Saltaneh 1362, p. 31.

126. Sadid al-Saltaneh 1362, p. 545.

127. Stirling 1991, p. 13.

128. Sadid al-Saltaneh 1362, pp. 30-31.

129. Stirling 1991, p. 13.

still played in Borazjan some 65 years, or two generations, later. Curzon reported that, "The village youths of Borazjun were busily engaged in rustic games, among which hockey and rounders (the precise equivalent to the English game) appeared to be the most popular."[130]

Borazjan had not more to offer in terms of amenities than had Bushehr, except for one thing. The living conditions were apparently slightly better, for in 1822, Lumsden mentioned that Capt. Bruce, the British resident at Bushehr, had a garden-house at Borazjan.[131] Also, here was the possibility to do some hunting, in which the local population took part. Rich reported in 1822 that "The Khan sent us a present of a very fine chamois or ibex, which tasted something like delicate beef."[132]

Taxation

In 1808, the people of Borazjan gave two-third's of their harvest to the chief of Borazjan, who each year paid the governor-general of Fars 4,000 *tumans*.[133] According to Stirling, who visited the town in 1828,

> The villages of Barrisgoon under Selim Khan yield annual revenue of 3,000 tomans. This sum includes everything in them, all abwalis [water dues from irrigated lands], customs and duties, with the exception of occasional presents, when in the presence of the Prince, which are supposed to be regulated by some known customs which have hitherto prevailed. Each of these district officers may be considered as the most considerable and wealthy of the local proprietors of the land; these estates from time immemorial have been in the possession of their families. Selim Khan, I was informed, at Barrusjoon only paid the sum of 1,057 toomans, while he collected annually 10,000 toomans, consequently only paying about one tenth of the assets of his estate. The rest of the chief men of districts pay in the same proportion. Out of one hundred maunds which are produced, he gives thirty maaunds to the Surkar [overseer of land rental].[134]

Around 1860, Borazjoon paid 4,000 *tuman*s in taxes including *pishkesh*.[135] According to Pelly, farmers paid taxes on the output per cow. "The crop borne by a cow of land 15 Krans or so per annum in money, and one maund of wheat and one of barley apparently for Kurneh, or expenses in collecting."[136] In 1879, Borazjan also had to pay 43,500 gold marks

---

130. Curzon 1892, vol. 2, p. 227.

131. Lumsden 1822, p. 77.

132. Rich 1836, vol. 2, pp. 195-6.

133. Dupré 1819, vol. 2, p. 30.

134. Stirling 1991, p. 23.

135. Pelly 1865 a, p. 172.

136. Pelly 1865 a, p. 42.

(GM) in taxes in addition to 3,200 GM as *pishkesh* and 640 GM as *khel 'at-baha*.[137] In 1898, the tax burden for the butchers was 800 *tumans*, according to Sadid al-Saltaneh. Eskandar Khan the *tofangdar-bashi* of the governor Hosam al-Saltaneh was the collector. He collected this tax in secret, because butchers and bakers' tax had been declared exempt by Mozaffar al-Din Shah.[138] The reduced fiscal burden for the khan of Borazjan probably had to do with the fact that Borazjan and its surroundings provided in 1879 as any as 1,000 *tofangchis*,[139] and this provision was in lieu of taxes. Borazjan troops therefore participated in the battle of Khosh-Ab on 10 February 1856, part of which was cavalry. "They had also in their charge the governor of Brásjoon, who-endeavouring to attract attention by placing a black Persian cap on a stick, and waving it as a signal to his countrymen-was immediately, and very properly, knocked off his horse, and forced to remain on his knees until the fortune of the day was decided."[140]

Also, two leading lineages, the Qayedun and the Ra'asa, were exempt from payment of taxes in 1879.[141] The population of the Dashtestan did not have a decreased tax burden, because they had to finance the cost of the military service that Borazjan had to provide. Some of the taxes they had to pay included *nakhilat*, a tax on date trees, which were taxed in Borazjan at 7.50 GM. This tax was collected in two payments, one at Nowruz and the other in the autumn.[142] The chiefs had to pay land tax to the governor of Bushehr or that of Fars and provide military levies when called upon, depending on whether the governor of Shiraz had farmed out the taxes of Dashtestan or whether he collected them directly. In the aftermath of the Constitutional Revolution, payment of taxes fell into arrears, as in so many other parts of Iran. Due to smuggling, the population of Dashtestan and neighbouring districts were well armed, which made them less amenable to pay taxes.[143] By 1911, the taxes (*maliyat*) of Borazjan were 5,300 *tumans*. The khan's revenue was 16,000 *tumans* in agricultural taxes and 20,000 *tumans* from *rahdari*, *'alafi*, taxation of caravans, sale of monopolies of gum, etc.[144] These taxes were not necessarily paid to the government. In 1913, the *kargozar* of Bushehr reported that Ghazanfar al-Saltaneh, the chief or *zabet* of Borazjan, nominally paid 6,000 *tumans* to the government, but collected a few times more than that from the peasants.[145]

137. Migeod 1990, p. 230, n. 1 (GM= *Gold Mark*, a value calculated by Migeod using the silver price at that time. Unfortunately, he does not give the conversion rate). On the terms *pishkesh* and *khel`at-baha* see Floor 1999, pp. 262-63, 430.

138. Sadid al-Saltaneh 1362, p. 31.

139. Migeod 1990, p., 233, n. 7.

140. Hunt 1858, p. 216.

141. Migeod 1990, p. 225, n. 5.

142. Migeod 1990, p. 228, n. 13, and 229, n. 6.

143. Administration Report 1905-1906, p. 16; Administration Report 1907-1908, p. 8; Trade Report 1911-12, p. 2.

144. Chick 1911, p. 3. The rate was adjusted occasionally. In June 1897, the governors of Dashti and Dashtestan did not accept the rate of 5 *shahi*s per animal in either direction. Sirjani 1361, p. 526. On the terms *rahdari* and `*alafi*, see Floor 1999, pp. 166-68, 379-99, 417.

145. Nava'i 1385, p. 126.

The Ruling Family

According to the British consul Chick, "The ruling family of the Borazjun khans are descended from a certain Muhammad, who came from the district of Kam Firuz. He was employed as a servant by the then ruling khan, married his daughter and became chief of Borazjun."[146] It is not known whether the original khan was a Bag (the original inhabitants) or a Papari (the "usurping" inhabitants). The new ruling family, the descendants of Mohammad, were not Paparis but belonged to a tribe called Meyman, according to Lorimer.[147] This probably was an error for Meymand, a sub-group of the Buyer Ahmadi tribe, were able to oust the Zanganeh tribal group from the area in 1762 led by Shah Mansur Gap (Big), Mohammad's grandson. To bolster his sway over the new land, Shah Mansur built a fort or *qal'eh*, which gave its name to the current 'fort quarter' (*mahalleh-ye qal'eh*) of the town. Karim Khan Zand gave Shah Mansur the title of khan; the latter's son Salim Khan took over from his father in 1803. He was succeeded by his son Mohammad Hasan Khan in 1832, who was captured by the British in 1856.[148] He was handed over to the governor of Shiraz, Ehtesham al-Dowleh.[149] In 1875, Mohammad Hasan Khan was still in charge of Dashtestan,[150] although he was arrested in that year together with his son Heydar Khan and dismissed as *zabet* of Borazjan. In 1877 it was reported that he was still kept prisoner at Shiraz and that one of his sons, presumably Heydar Khan, was executed at the orders of Mo'tamed al-Dowleh, the governor-general of Fars.[151]

Even before Mohammad Hasan Khan died in 1877, after having been ruling khan for 44 years, there was infighting among the ruling family, concerning the succession. This conflict raged in particular between 1870 and 1877; this led to a frequent change of khans.[152] This family struggle enhanced the already unruly reputation of the Dashtestanis due to its sometimes very violent nature. Brittlebank visited Borazjan in 1872 and met the village chief without mentioning his name. According the the chief of the local telegraph station, this chief's career was one of violence and crime, and "that he had obtained his position by the murder of his brother."[153] Only eight months prior to Rivadeneyra's visit (March 1875), Ah-

---

146. Chick 1911, p. 3.

147. Lorimer 1915, p. 328.

148. Atabegzadeh 1373, pp. 122-23; Chick 1911, p. 4. The Zanganeh group by that time may have been a sub-group of the Buyer Ahmadi, see Majidi Kera'i 1381, p. 416.

149. Atabegzadeh 1373, p. 123; Chick 1911, p. 4. In 1852 the governor was Mahomed Hossein Khan, according to Stern 1854, p. 110. Fasa'i 1378, vol. 1, p. 811. After the battle he had hidden himself and refused bread and fodder to the Persian soldiers released by the British. Another member of the family was Asad Khan Borazjani, who came to Bushehr with other chiefs in 1858. Some time later the British took Mohammad Hasan Khan prisoner and took him to Bushehr when they withdrew from Borazjan. Fasa'i 1378, vol. 1, p. 815; *Ruznama-ye ettefaqiyeh* 1373, p. 2583 (27 Shawwal 1274/June 10, 1858).

150. Administration Report 1875-76, p. 18; Pelly 1865 a, p. 172 (Its chief was Mahomed Hassan Khan); Sirjani 1361, p. 40 (In 1292/1875, Mohammad Hasan Khan was *zabet*); Migeod 1990, p. 68.

151. Administration Report 1877-78, p. 5; Sirjani 1371, p. 40.

152. Migeod 1990 p. 68, note 2. Not every one was a candidate. One who was not considered in this conflict was Gurgin Khan, a son of Mohammad Hasan Khan and a slave-girl. He lived in Deh-e Qa'id, but was not even a chief. Migeod 1990, p. 343, n. 5.

153. Brittlebank 1873, p. 123 (he and his men also drank alcohol).

mad Khan, governor of the time, asked his brother one day: "They tell me you have relations with my wife, I will kill you." And then he killed him on the spot by firing his revolver a few times.[154] It also put an end to the strife among the khans about who would hold sway over the village; it was the governor of Bushehr who won by taking over Borazjan's administration, according to Rivadeneyra. The result was that many poor Borazjanis left the town and reinforced the number of nomads and marauders. The reason for this departure was that many inhabitants felt a strong allegiance to the khan's lineage.[155]

The governor of Bushehr's takeover, if that was what it was, did not, however, last long. One of Mohammad Hasan Khan's sons, Mirza Hoseyn Khan, finally prevailed in the family fight. In the 1880s, Fasa'i wrote that the functions of *zabet* and *kalantar* of Borazjan had been for generations with Mirza Hoseyn Khan Borazjani, who is of the lineage of Salim Khan Borazjani.[156] Sadid al-Saltaneh reported that in 1896 Mirza Hoseyn Khan was *zabet* of Borazjan. A that time he was fifty-four years old, and had been already *zabet* for twenty-four years. He had two sons, Mohammad Khan and Mahmud Khan, who both had marriage ties with the khans of Shabankareh.[157] It would seem that the winner of the family feud had been forced to compromise, however. For Mirza Hoseyn Khan shared power with `Ali Khan, who ruled Borazjan alternately with him, until the latter's death. Although by 1911, Mirza Hoseyn Khan, then about seventy years old, was still living at Borazjan. His son, Mirza Mohammad Khan, Ghazanfar al-Saltaneh, had taken over from his father about one decade earlier. He was ousted from his position by Ejlal al-Dowleh in 1903 and was replaced by a duo of relatives, viz. Hajj Mohammad Khan and Hajj Khan, the son of `Ali Khan, for one year, when he took over again.[158] However, in 1906 Persian texts mention "the khans" of Borazjan, indicating that there was shared rule again.[159] Ghazanfar al-Saltaneh, with some interruptions, remained *zabet* of Borazjan till the end of the Qajar era.

---

154. Rivadeneyra 1880, vol. 3, p. 10. Maybe this is the same incident that Brittlebank referred to; an Ahmad Khan is not mentioned in the family tree (see below).

155. Rivadeneyra 1880, vol. 3, p. 9.

156. Fasa'i 1378, vol. 2, p. 1325.

157. Sadid al-Saltaneh 1362, p. 30; Sirjani 1361, p. 529 (In July 1897 the chief was Mirza Hoseyn Khan).

158. Chick 1911, p. 4.

159. Qa'immaqami 1359, p. 275.

Family Tree of the Khans of Borazjan

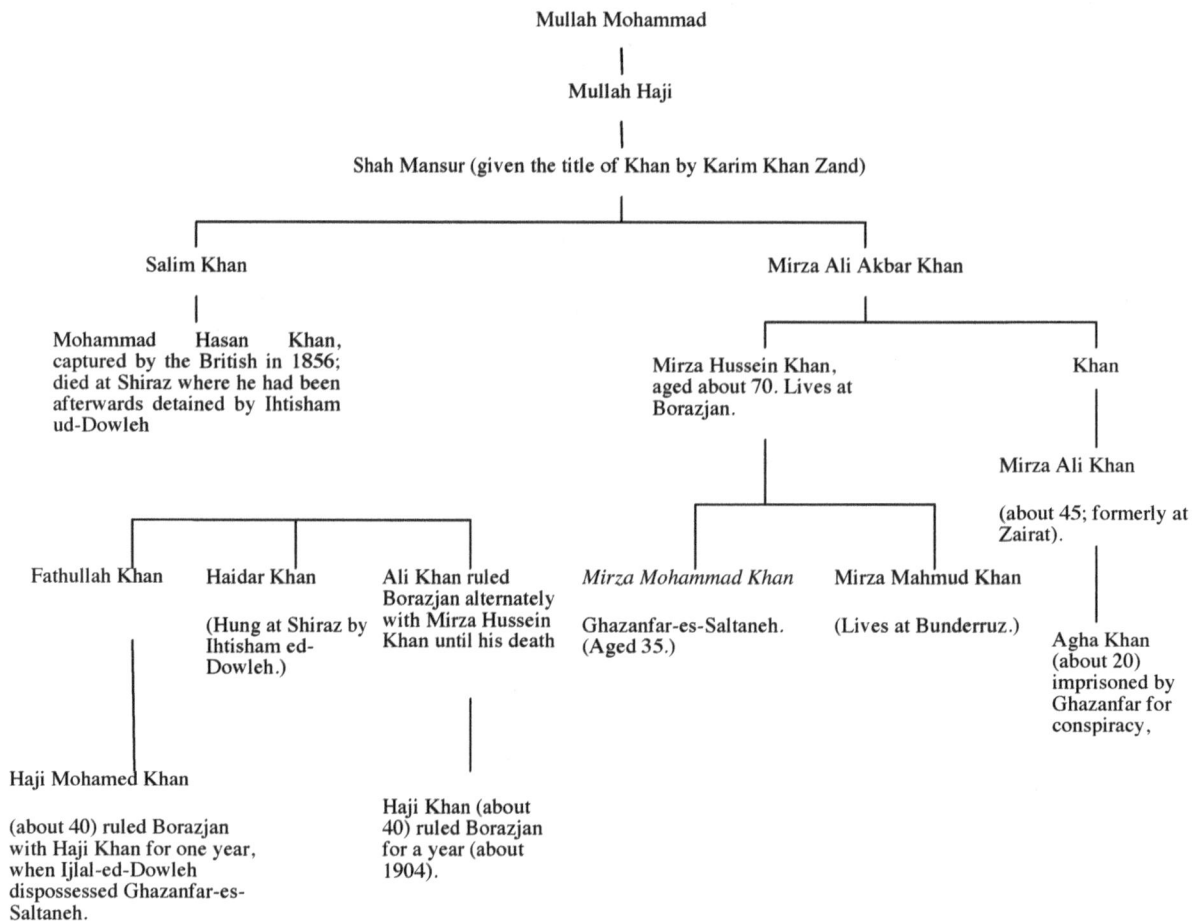

Mullah Mohammad

|

Mullah Haji

|

Shah Mansur (given the title of Khan by Karim Khan Zand)

Salim Khan — Mirza Ali Akbar Khan

Mohammad Hasan Khan, captured by the British in 1856; died at Shiraz where he had been afterwards detained by Ihtisham ud-Dowleh

Mirza Hussein Khan, aged about 70. Lives at Borazjan.

Khan

Mirza Ali Khan

(about 45; formerly at Zairat).

Fathullah Khan

Haidar Khan

(Hung at Shiraz by Ihtisham ed-Dowleh.)

Ali Khan ruled Borazjan alternately with Mirza Hussein Khan until his death

Mirza Mohammad Khan

Ghazanfar-es-Saltaneh. (Aged 35.)

Mirza Mahmud Khan

(Lives at Bunderruz.)

Agha Khan (about 20) imprisoned by Ghazanfar for conspiracy,

Haji Mohamed Khan

(about 40) ruled Borazjan with Haji Khan for one year, when Ijlal-ed-Dowleh dispossessed Ghazanfar-es-Saltaneh.

Haji Khan (about 40) ruled Borazjan for a year (about 1904).

Administrative Structure

In the Safavid period Dashtestan was an *olka*, or an administrative jurisdiction, under a governor (*hakem*) assisted by a deputy-governor (*na'eb*).[160] In 1737, Hasan ʿAli Beg (Hassan Alie Beek), was the *na'eb* of Dashtestan. The *na'eb* was often at Zireh (Ziera), five miles inland.[161] It is not known whether he was one of the original Bag owners of Borazjan or from some

---

160. Afshar Sistani 1369, vol. 2, pp. 604-18 (three royal decrees concerning the governor (*hakem*) of the *ulka-ye* Dashtestan).

161. VOC 2448, Instruction to Schoonderwoerd (03/07/1737), fol. 482-494; VOC 2448, Journal Bushehr, fol. 1548 (Hossain Chan Becq, the brother of the *na'eb* of Dashtestan). Ibid. (24/8/1737), fol. 1500-07.

other local group, or where he had his seat of government. However, the *na'eb* of Dashistan was the superior of the sheikh of Bushehr at that time, for Bushehr was part of the Dashtestan administrative region (*olka-ye Dashtestan*). After the fall of the Zands, Bushehr and Dashtestan remained a separate jurisdiction under one governor, answerable to the governor-general of Fars province.[162] Bushehr, under the sheikhs of the al-Mazkur family had asserted its independence and had been able to become a separate jurisdiction. This situation lasted until 1850 when the al-Mazkurs were expelled from Bushehr, which led to the administration by governors appointed by Shiraz and later Tehran. Initially, Bushehr, Dashtestan and Dashti constituted one governorship, although the traditional local chiefs remained in function as *zabet* and *kalantar*.[163] Pelly noted that, "these Arab villages are farmed and administered by their own Sheikhs, who arrange their own civil disputes, and pay a lump sum of revenue per annum. Murder would be compensated by blood money; but the Sheikh would not send the murderer to Bushehr for punishment. The Sheikh in turn would levy rent on the farmers by the cow."[164] This administrative construction lasted till 1888 the new governorship of the Gulf Ports (*mamlakat-e banader*) was established, who resided in Bushehr, although his jurisdiction included all Iranian ports between Bushehr and Jask, but usually without Dashtestan and Dashti.[165] As before, the traditional chiefs remained in place to ensure the tax collection, law and order. The relationship with the outside governor was not always flawless. Several times troops had to be sent to Dashtestan and Dashti to collect the taxes.[166] In 1885-86, for example, a conflict had broken out between Malek al-Tojjar, the governor of Dashtestan, and 'Ali Khan, the chief of Borazjan. The soldiers sent against him were defeated and the governor requested the governor of Shiraz to send some cannon to settle the matter, which the latter refused.[167] Tax collection was not always without its problems either. In January 1886, this gave rise to disturbances that required the sending of troops from Bushehr. Similar serious disturbances occurred in April 1886.[168] In 1889, these districts were much disturbed due to feuds between local chiefs, mainly those of Borazjan and Angali.[169] In 1889, Nowzar Mirza was governor of Dashti and Dashtestan; he was succeeded by Mohammad Hasan Khan Sartip

162. Fasa'i 1378, vol. 1, p. 702 (Mohammad Ja`far Khan governor of Bushehr and Dashtestan in 1225/1810-11)

163. Fasa'i 1378, vol. 1, pp. 794 (Bushehr, its dependencies and Dashtestan was given to Mirza `Ali Khan, son of Qavam al-Molk in 1266/1849-50), 820 (in 1275/1858-59, Dashti, Dashtestan and Bushehr were given to Hasan Khan Qarachadaghi Azarbayjani), 822 (in 1276/1859-60 to Soleyman Mirza), 823 (in 1277-1860/61 to Mehr `Ali Khan), 825 (in 1279/1862-63 to Ahmad Khan `Amid al-Molk Nava'i).

164. Pelly 1865 a, p. 42 (the cow, *gav* or *gao*, means here a land measure). The situation was different in the case of "the Persian villages (not like the Dashties sufficiently strong to defend itself,) the Hakem or Sheikh, or Moollah, would be removed from his Government at the pleasure of the Bushehr Governor. Criminels [sic] would be sent to Bushehr; and revenues, if not punctually paid, would be levied by a Mohussil, or failing this way, by force." Ibid.

165. ; Lorimer 1915, p. 1460, note ("The Gulf Ports form a mamlakat and are governed by a hokmran.")

166. Fasa'i 1378, vol. 2, pp. 854.

167. Sirjani 1361, pp. 260-61.

168. Administration Report 1885-86, p. 7; Ibid., 1886-87, p. 9.

169. Administration Report 1889-90, p. 8; see also Ibid., 1893-94, p. 11.

in that same year, who also held this function in 1890-92.[170] Towards the end of the nineteenth century, Dashtestan was returned to Fars. Therefore, the governor of the Gulf Ports, if he at the same time was also governornor of Dashtestan farmed Borazjan along with its dependencies from the governor-general of Fars. In 1906, not the governor of the Gulf Ports, but Sadeq al-Mamalek was governor of Dashtestan.[171] Therefore, Lorimer noted that it "belongs to the government of Fars and is the seat of the khan who administers the greater part of the Dashtestan district. A deputy-governor also resides here on behalf of the governor-general of Fars."[172] In 1913, pursuant to the new administrative reforms, Dashtestan became a separate jurisdiction administered by the khan of Borazjan.[173]

Political Role

The tribal levies of Bushehr's hinterland not only served to secure the caravan routes but also to keep the ambitions of the Bushehr sheikhs in check. The period between 1760-1850 was one where Borazjan played an important role as Shiraz's instrument in its disputes with Bushehr. Sheikh Naser of Bushehr, from the very beginning of his administration, had plans for his family and his town. He realised the importance of fostering ties with the Dashtestan tribes in order to resist demands from the overlord at Shiraz.[174] The ties with Shiraz were often of a shifting nature, and when Sheikh Naser refused to give in to certain demands, Karim Khan incited the chiefs of the Tangestan and Dashtestan to attack and lay siege to Bushehr. By December 1767 Sheikh Naser agreed to Karim Khan's demands and the tribal levies retreated in January 1768. His son was sent to Shiraz to stay at court. This event showed that without a secure hinterland (i.e. support of Dashtestan) Bushehr was not able to develop an independent stance.[175] Sheikh Naser did not forget this slight and blow to his ambitions, and when the last Zand ruler came to Bushehr for military assistance the sheikh closed its gates. He then pursued Lotf ʿAli Khan with the help of, amongst others, troops from Dashtestan and Borazjan was their staging place.[176] Although the new Qajar régime was grateful for Bushehr's help, at the same time, it was suspicious of the al-Mazkur sheikh's political ambitions. Borazjan's levies once again would play the role of the Qajar stick. In 1800, the chief of Borazjan with a party of horse and infantry came a distance of four miles to meet the EIC envoy John Malcolm, "for whose entertainment they practiced a series of evolutions and mock skirmishes, which they continued until we reached our encampment at the village."[177] These

---

170. Nezam al-Saltaneh 1361, vol. 2, p. 92; Administration Report 1889-90, p. 8; Ibid., 1890-91, p. 9; Ibid., 1891-92, p. 10.

171. Qa'emmaqami 1359, pp. 54, 75, 110.

172. Lorimer 1915, p. 328.

173. Gouvernement Imperial de la Perse 1913, pp. 191-92; RMM 23 (1913), p. 77.

174. Nami Esfahani 1363, p. 348; Grummon 1985, p. 74.

175. Grummon 1985, pp. 97-98.

176. Fasa'i 1378, vol. 1, p. 648.

177. Hollingbery 1976, p. 18; Morier 1812, p. 76 (for the ambassador Ouseley in 1810).

men were intended not only for the defense of Borazjan itself but also to provide protection along the road. In 1821, for example, the khan of Borazjan sent a man with Rich's party to the next guardhouse.[178]

Borazjan's involvement in politics was determined by its location, both geographically and administratively. The entire region was tribal in nature, and since the fall of the Safavid dynasty there had been little control there by the central government. Consequently, lawlessness thrived and caravans were attacked at times. Rivalry with other district centres was normal and incursions, temporary occupations, and killings frequently occurred. Because Dashtestan fell administratively directly under the prince-governor of Shiraz, the tensions which developed between Bushehr and Shiraz, also had their impact on Bushehr's hinterland, in particular on nearby Borazjan. This led to rivalry between the traditional chiefs of Bushehr and of Borazjan, and as well as between the latter and other chiefs of Dashti, Shabankareh, and Tangestan, the other neighbouring districts.

According to Pelly, "all the khans are at near perennial feud." Each district (*nahiyeh*) had its own *zabet* and *kalantar*, who did not recognise the control of any other, and the people only accepted the rule of their own chief.[179] This did not mean that the feuding chiefs did not collaborate at times. They did, such as in 1303/1885-86, when the chiefs of Dashtestan and Tangestan jointly opposed the appointment of Malek al-Tojjar as their governor. To induce the governor-general of Shiraz to accept their proposal, they offered to pay their taxes immediately and to give an additional *pishkesh* of 2,000 *tumans*.[180] As the chiefs, so were their followers. Fraser characterised the "typical" inhabitant of Dashtestan in 1822 as follows: "Every thing is directly the contrary of that which would be sought for the fit habitation of man; yet, in this desolate region, where the intensity of heat seems calculated to curdle and destroy his faculties, he is found brave and independent, like his great ancestor; his hand against every man, and every man's hand against him. Even the power of the most absolute Kings exercised but questionable and imperfect authority over the tribes of the Dushtistan."[181]

Although there are not many reported incidents of regular banditry and attacks on caravans, the hinterland was not a peaceful place. In 1826, the Dashtestan had become an unsettled state, caused mainly by the "grasping disposition of the Sheikh of Bushehr, who is endeavouring to get under his jurisdiction the whole of the low country." When he sent a body of troops to claim tribute from Borazjan, it resisted and fifteen of the Bushehr forces were killed.[182] At that time Stirling observed: "This chief was absent on an expedition against the people of Thungistan. The tribe denominated Thungistanians are a factious set, and are apparently always engaged in warfare against their neighbours or among themselves. They are powerful, and are the great disturbers of the peace near Bushehr. They are dreaded and feared by the chiefs in whose vicinity they reside. They have rebelled and refused to pay Salim Khan

178. Rich 1836, vol. 2, p. 195-6.

179. Pelly 1865 a, p. 143; also see Anonymous 1865, p. 180; Nezam al-Saltaneh 1361, vol. 1, p. 92; Qa'immaqami 1359, p. 288; Sirjani 1361, p. 529 (Borazjan chief attacked Daleki in July 1897); Government of Great Britain 1910. There also were raids by tribal groups from outside Dashtestan. Sirjani 1361, p. 54.

180. Sirjani 1361, pp. 252, 289 (they did not want Hajji Samsam al-Molk either in June 1887).

181. Fraser 1984, p. 71.

182. Alexander 2000, p. 100.

the dues to which he, as representative of His Majesty, is entitled to demand. Salim Khan is however, not tributary directly to the King of Persia, but to the Prince of Sheeraz, one of the King's sons. This chief is reported to levy about ten thousand toomans from the country in which he rules, and pays only annually one thousand and fifty seven toomans."[183]

In November 1828, Rezaqoli Mirza and Timur Mirza, sons of the prince-governor of Shiraz, led an army consisting of Dashtestanis, Tangestanis, Dashtis and soldiers from Shiraz against Bushehr, where Sheikh 'Abdol-Rasul of Bushehr wanted to extend his rule. They sacked the town and after two months of looting withdrew. The merchants complained to the shah, who ordered the governor to restore the plundered goods. When the people of Dashtestan refused to return the goods, the governor of Shiraz tried to come to an agreement with the chief of Bushehr to settle the matter. The latter wrote to hand over to him the chiefs concerned, in which case he would compensate the merchants. The governor of Shiraz then moved to Dashtestan in order to win over the khans and entered Bushehr. The prince then arrested all the khans and released them to 'Abdol-Rasul, who after having paraded them in the bazaar took them to Khark, where he drowned them all save one who fled.[184]

Although 'Abdol-Rasul had placated Farmanfarma, the prince-governor of Shiraz, this was only temporary. By the end of 1831 the prince was again in Bushehr in order to squeeze him or to replace him as governor. 'Abdol-Rasul promised to pay 20,000 *tumans* per year more in taxes and paid the prince a return visit in February 1832. On his return, prominent Tangestanis and Dashtestanis who lusted for his blood, because he had killed some of their relatives who had participated in the 1828 sack of Bushehr, killed him at Borazjan.[185] He was returning from Shiraz, "when he received a warning at Daliki, about the intentions of the Borazjanis. He ignored the warning and stayed the night in the fortress of Borazjan. The fort was surrounded by armed Borazjanis who offered *bakht* or free quarter to the sheik's followers, who accepted that. The sheikh withdrew to a small narrow tower of the fort where he could sell his life most dearly. After he had killed seven or eight of his assailants they set fire to the tower; he had to exit and was killed immediately. His corpse was burnt to ashes and scattered to the winds."[186]

Under 'Abdol-Rasul's successors there was continued conflict with Shiraz, and both parties tried to ally themselves with the coastal khans. Shiraz was sometimes even able to get the support of the khans of Rohilla and Shabankareh, usually allies of the al-Mazkurs of Bushehr. The Tangestanis and Dashtestanis usually supported Shiraz. Thus, neither Bushehr nor Shiraz could count on the reliability of their allies. At the same time, these allies continued their infighting even when pursuing common goals. For example, the Bushehris resented Rezaqoli Mirza's harsh fiscal policy, while the Tangestanis did not like his inroads into their affairs. As a result, Aqa Jamil Khan, an al-Mazkur ally, engineered a coup against the prince supported by Heydar Khan Dashti, with whom he also had strong economic ties. The alliance did not hold however; Heydar Khan killed his Tangestani counterpart on 1 August

183. Stirling 1991, p. 12.

184. Fasa'i 1378, vol. 2, pp. 745-47.

185. Fasa'i 1378, vol. 2, p. 753.

186. Binning 1857, vol. 1, pp. 158-159.

1833 because he was jealous of his power.[187] In January 1835, the Shabankareh and Rohilla khans attacked Borazjan and renounced their allegiance to Shiraz.[188]

The coastal khans also collaborated with the British. Mirza Asad, governor of Bushehr, had quarreled with the EIC and Baqer Khan of Tangestan. The latter moved against Bushehr in January 1839. At that time the British and Mohammad Shah (r. 1834-48) had differences over Herat, and this resulted in the EIC withdrawing from Bushehr to Khark. The British maintained a correspondence with Baqer Khan and other khans, which made the position of Mirza Asad untenable, and therefore, he was replaced in June 1839.[189] In 1845, Sheikh Nasr was reinstated as governor of Bushehr. He had his problems, mainly with Baqer Khan, whom he could not please and their differences erupted into a conflict in 1848. Baqer Khan took Borazjan in 1845; Shabankareh, Angali and Zirukh were also under his authority by that time.[190] When the Bushehris fell out with the neighbouring tribes of Dashti and Tangestan, the Shah used this dissension to establish his own governor at Bushehr and at the same time to reduce the power of the tribes of Dashtestan and Tangestan, together with some minor tribes such as the Rohillas.[191]

However, central government control over the coastal hinterland remained weak, despite the fact that there now was a subordinate governor at Bushehr. In fact, except when there was a strong governor, the situation was as if nothing had changed. Strong governors would take tough measures to subdue disobedient chiefs. In 1877, Ehtesham al-Dowleh arrested Mohammad Hasan Khan and his son Heydar Khan and put them in prison, where the former died. What happened to his son I have not been able to learn.[192] Although around 1900, as tax farmer, the governor of the Gulf Ports officially had control over the Dashtestan and other coastal districts; he kept 200 infantry and 50 gunners at Bushehr for his own protection and to enforce his orders. "In this area the khans of Borazjan, Shabankareh, Angali, Hayat Davud, and Liravi and the sheikh of Chah Kutah are constantly engaged in intrigues against one another and form combinations and counter-combinations among themselves for the promotion of their ends. Cattle raids and thefts occur which are followed by military altercations, every man having a modern rifle and a cartridge-loading machine."[193] The population of Borazjan, as did those of Tangestan and even more so, therefore enjoyed a poor reputation; hardly a year passed by when there were not murders under extraordinary circumstances, reported the Spanish traveller Rivadeneyra in 1875.[194] In 1876, Arnold noted that the men at Borazjan were shooting throughout the evening, which seemed their one amusement. "They are only interested to improve their markmanship. Their agriculture is careless; their homes are miserable; their food, for the most, dates; they are subject to the

---

187. Fasa'i 1378, vol. 2, p. 717; Lorimer 1915, pp. 1918-19.

188. Grummon 1985, p. 159.

189. Grummon 1985, pp. 165-66.

190. Fasa'i 1378, vol. 2, p. 791; Grummon 1985, pp. 167-69.

191. Pelly 1865 a, p. 41.

192. Fasa'i 1378, vol. 2, p. 851; Chick 1911, p. 4.

193. Lorimer 1915, p. 1465; see also Akhgar 1366, pp. 108-110.

194. Rivadeneyra 1880, vol. 3, p. 10; Fasa'i 1378, vol. 2, p. 1326.

most cruel tyranny." ... "their one delight is to be ready against their neighbors with their rifles." Their head-man or sub-governor shot a shepherd just to test his markmanship, he was told this as a true story by a local resident.[195] Curzon also "noticed at Borazjun that all men were armed with a big pistol, loosely stuck in the belt; and, upon inquiring the reason of this singularly un-Persian habit heard that it is peculiar to Borazjun and a few surrounding places, the inhabitants of which revel in the open profession of robbery, and in the luxury of blood-feuds."[196] This situation had not changed fifteen years later, when Williams noted the "ruffianly looking appearance of the inhabitants, who, apparently have many feuds, consider it essential to load themselves with rifles, pistols, and knives."[197] Despite its somewhat violent reputation, in 1896, Borazjan was also a refuge for political dissenters from Bushehr, who fled there when the situation became too hot for them there.[198] It should be noted that visitors and passers-by were well treated.

With the decreasing authority of the central government, the willingness of the coastal khans to pay taxes and to spurn illegal activities also declined. In 1324/1906, the Persian government used Borazjan as a staging post to suppress the rebellion of Esma'il Khan Shabankareh.[199] A Persian military detachment of 150 infantry with one mountain gun then occupied the *dezh* of Borazjan. Riflemen (*tofangchis*) from Borazjan itself were used against Mirza Esma'il.[200] Ironically, at that time Mirza 'Ali Khan, the local administrator and tax administrator ('*amel*) of Borazjan, refused to pay taxes and with his son Aqa Khan sought refuge with Esma'il Khan Shabankareh, his sister's husband. From the mountains they engaged in brigandry and killing people. Ghazanfar al-Saltaneh, who was still heeding government orders and had been the administrator and tax collector in the past, replaced him.[201] Ghazanfar al-Saltaneh was married to the daughter of Esma'il Khan of Shabankareh, but they had a bitter feud because of the district of Zireh, which in the past had been farmed by the khans of Borazjan, but had been leased by Nezam al-Saltaneh to the khan of Shabankareh for the last fifteen years. He had tried several times to usurp his father-in-law's position, and as a result, raids between Borazjan, Zireh and Shabankareh were common. Another conflict with Mirza Esma'il Khan arose because of the imprisonment in the autumn of 1911 by Ghazanfar al-Saltaneh of his cousin Mirza 'Ali Khan, headman of the village of Kulul, and his sons on a charge of conspiracy against him.[202] Because they were kept in chains, Esma'il Khan of Shabankareh, who was also related to them, in vain interceded on their behalf. Therefore, Ghazanfar al-Saltaneh's wife, daughter of Esma'il Khan, left him with her young son and returned to her father. Negotiations to reconcile both sides failed. Totally unexpected, in June 1914, Mokhber al-Saltaneh, the governor-general of Fars ordered the governor of the Gulf

---

195. Arnold 1877, p. 401.

196. Curzon 1892, vol. 2, pp. 226-27.

197. Williams 1907, p. 43.

198. Sadid al-Saltaneh 1362, pp. 31, 44.

199. Vahram 1351, p. 192f.

200. Lorimer 1915, p. 328; Qa'emmaqami 1359, pp. 275, 280, 376.

201. Vahram 1351, pp. 206-07, 209; Qa'emmaqami 1359, pp. 213, 275.

202. Chick 1911, p. 5; Qa'emmaqami 1359, p. 288.

Ports (who also was in charge of Dashti, Dashtestan, Shabankareh and Borazjan) to instruct Esma'il Khan, via the gendarmerie officers, to immediately return his daughter and grandson to Ghazanfar al-Saltaneh. A force of 100 gendarmes went to Sa'dabad, Esma'il Khan's chief village. Esma'il Khan was unable to oppose them and abandoned the village leaving his daughter and grandson behind. The British protested in Shiraz to the use of the gendarmerie, whose task it was to police the Telegraph road only, rather than injudiciously interfering in tribal quarrels. The commander of the Fars regiment, Col. Uggla, did not apologize, but "by stipulating for conditions involving a surrender of territory by Ismail Khan, made the only suitable reparation, the release of Esma'il Khan's relations imprisoned by the Ghazanfar impossible."[203]

To a certain extent, Borazjan became the base of operations against the British after they had occupied Bushehr in 1915. To start his anti-British operations the German Consul Wassmuss marched to Borazjan to seek the support of Ghazanfar al-Saltaneh, who was known for his anti-British stance. After his Persian partisans had arrested the staff of the English consulate in Shiraz in 1915, Wassmuss transported them all to Borazjan. Here the gendarmerie commander, Captain Ahmad Khan Akhgar handed them over to Za'er Khezr of Ahram.[204] The choice of that area was an excellent one, because the local chiefs had been for years defying the Persian government and anti-British feelings were high due to British efforts to curtail their smuggling and highway robbery activities. According to O'Connor, the imprisoned British consul, "For years they had abused their position and hampered trade by levying illegal taxes on all caravans of merchandise passing through their territory, and neither the orders of the Persian Government nor the protests of the British representative had been effective in restraining them."[205] According to the British, Ghazanfar al-Saltaneh was the most noted buyer of and dealer in smuggled arms and ammunition among the headmen of the Bushehr littoral and hinterland. He and his father had acquired great wealth from extortion on passing caravans, and especially from the monopoly of the sale of grain to animals.[206] The British considered Ghazanfar al-Saltaneh to be a difficult hostile man, as he had previously shown in 1909 and 1911 when he had been actively agitating against the arrival of British-Indian troops.[207]

Following the arrest of the German consul Dr. Listemann in early 1915 and the agitation by Wassmuss, Mirza Mohammad Khan Ghazanfar al-Saltaneh organized an anti-British confederacy of Khans consisting of himself, Sheikh Hoseyn of Chahkutah, Ra'is 'Ali of Delvar, and Za'er Khezr of Ahram and in letters threatened to attack Bushehr. In reaction Heydar Khan of Hayat Davud aligned himself with Esma'il Khan of Shabankareh as well as with the Khans of Liravi, Rudhilleh. The pro-German Mokhber al-Saltaneh made contact with Ghazanfar al-Saltaneh and the gendarmerie force of Borazjan, which became a center

203. Administration Report 1914, p. 11; the British did not protest when the gendarmerie undertook similar actions elsewhere in Iran, because those were favoured by them, see Cronin 1996, pp. 112-13. Borazjan was also the base of operations of the gendarmerie against Buyer Ahmadi rebels in 1913. Oberling 1974, pp. 121-22.

204. Oberling 1974, pp. 130, 134; O'Connor 1931, pp. 220, 239; Cronin 1996, p. 122.

205. O'Connor 1931, p. 222.

206. Chick 1911, p. 5.

207. Chick 1911, p. 5.

of pro-German intrigue. In May 1915, Ghazanfar al-Saltaneh took action against Esma'il Khan of Shabankareh by supporting the latter's nephew Agha Khan to rebel. Esma'il Khan asked and received help from the Khans of Rig and Rudhilleh and fighting continued over the entire hot season at great cost to Esma'il Khan. The British were pleased because this fight prevented Ghazanfar al-Saltaneh joining Sheikh Hoseyn and Za'er Khezr in attacking Bushehr; instead he sent them small presents of ammunition and arms from time to time. Daryabegi who had been on a dubious mission to Borazjan for Mokhber al-Saltaneh was appointed governor of the Gulf Ports. By the end of September 1915, the riff-raff of the Shiraz bazaar, who called themselves *mojadehin*, led by Sheikh Ja'far, "a venal mujtahid," left Shiraz to join the fighters near Bushehr. Most of them already deserted at Dasht-e Arjan, but those remaining reached Borazjan at the beginning of October 1915. One of the leading *mojahedin* was 'Ali Akbar Khordel, who had once tried to kill Qavam al-Molk. On arrival at Borazjan, Sheikh Ja'far, much to the disgust of Ghazanfar al-Saltaneh, tried to take charge of things in Borazjan and to line his pockets. The Shirazi *mojahedin* were starving despite collections made for them in Shiraz as most of the money was said to remain with the collectors and Sheikh Ja'far; as a result their numbers dwindled and finally the last group returned to Shiraz.[208]

The fight against the British during the years 1914-18 gave a nationalist and heroic hue to the business-as-usual predatory activities of the Dashtestanis. The chiefs could not only have their cake, but eat it as well, this time not as highwaymen but as defenders of Iran's neutrality against imperialist oppressors. It is difficult, almost a century years later, to distinguish between the normal anti-authoritarian attitude of the coastal population and genuine nationalism. One thing is certain, in my opinion at least, it definitely was not only nationalism that drove these men to activities that up till then had been their normal way of life. The British described Ghazanfar al-Saltaneh as "an educated man, one of the most rapacious of the roadside chiefs. His consistent anti-British attitude was due to his fear of losing his privileged position of practical independence."[209]

World War I ended disappointingly for the opponents of Great Britian who rewarded its friends. "Early in April a gathering of local Khans was called at Borasjun to attend the ceremony of investing Haidar Khan of Hayat Daud with the C.I.E. [Commander Indian Empire]. Twelve Khans, as well as the Imam Juma of Bushehr and several big Bushehr merchants were present. After the ceremony the assembly were entertained to lunch, sports and a display by the Air Force. Such a gathering is unique in the history of South Persia."[210] In early March 1919, Ghazanfar al-Saltaneh was captured by Agha Khan of Borazjan in Fariyab, but he was allowed to escape by his *tofangchi*s, indicating that he still enjoyed popular support. Ghazanfar al-Saltaneh first joined with Za'er Khezr and Sheikh Hoseyn, but one month later

---

208. Administration Report 1915, pp. 3-4, 7 Captain Ahmad Khan Akhgar commanded at Borazjan and was involved in attacks on Bushehr, but he did not report anything negative about the auxiliary force from Shiraz. Cronin 1996, p. 120; Akhgar 1366, pp. 206-09.

209. Moberley 1987, p. 374. From the description of the military operations, local resistance was offered by only a few score of men, which is also clear from O'Connor 1931, p. 241 who had been their prisoner. It goes without saying that in Persian hagiography, *Shahid* Ghazanfar al-Saltaneh has attained semi-divine status. A thorough and dispassionate analysis of this man and his fellow-travellers during this period seems to be called for.

210. Administration Report 1919, p. 3 (CIE means Commander Indian Empire).

he surrendered to Farmanfarma in Shiraz, "having no stomach for an outlaw's life in the hills." In early June 1919, Asaf al-Dowleh arrived, who on behalf of Daryabegi was deputy-governor in Dashti, Dashtestan and Tangestan and was headquartered at Borazjan.[211]

As a result of British military operations against the Khans along the Telegraph road, a light railway was laid between Bushehr and Borazjan, about 40 miles in length, and a considerable portion of the Bushehr-Shiraz road was made passable for motor traffic. By the end of 1918 this road was safe and trade boomed.[212] The Bushehr-Borazjan railway was opened to civil traffic in May 1919 and helped to boost trade to Shiraz, but it was too short to make a real difference; however, the new safety on the roads did. One advantage of the railway was that the muleteers could leave their donkeys at Borazjan, rather than go to Bushehr, which had no grazing, and they then went back to Borazjan where they could graze.[213] During 1919, the railway earned 1,51,338 *qrans* for passengers and 2,30,139 for goods, or a total of 3,81,523 *qrans*. It was not as much used as expected, because merchants, including foreign ones, were conservative. The British hoped that by erecting sheds the railway would attract more business in 1920.[214] This indeed happened, because the annual earnings in 1920 were: 191,276 *qrans* plus Rs 98 for passengers and 514,591 *qrans* for freight.[215] However, as Great Britian wanted to reduce its footprint in Iran it tried to find a buyer for the railway. When negotiations with APOC failed the government of India, in November 1920, ordered to dismantle the railway. Then Mo`in al-Tojjar tried to create a syndicate of Bushehri merchants to buy the railway, but he was not able to even raise one-fifth of the asking price and thus the dismantling continued. "As, however, the water for the railway comes from Borazjan, the main line had to be left till the last and public traffic continued, while spare stores were collected and subsidiary lines pulled up." On 21 March 1921 the railway ceased to carry passengers and public goods, the railway was further dismantled by June and shipped to India before the end of August 1921.[216]

In 1922, Ghazanfar al-Saltaneh was allowed to return to Borazjan, where he remained. However, according to the British, he had "lost nothing of his old aptitude for intrigues, though outwardly he has kept his promises of good behaviour he gave to the Residency when he was brought back to Borasjun in 1921." He was actively involved in the desultory fighting between *zabet* Sohrab Khan and his relative Agha Khan, who defended the rights of Jahangir Khan, the younger brother of Sohrab Khan. Some troops from Borazjan tried to divide the district between Sohrab Khan and Jahangir Khan and there was fighting. Finally, the governor-general of Fars decided that Sohrab Khan was the only *zabet* or district chief.[217] To show that things had changed in Iran, in the fall of 1923 the military forced Ghazanfar al-Saltaneh to henceforth pay 10,000 instead of 6,000 *tumans* in revenue. When he protested he was immediatly replaced by his nephew `Ata Khan, who, assisted by Sheikh Mohammad of Chah-

---

211. Administration Report 1919, p. 4.

212. Trade Report 1918-19, pp. 1-2; Moberley 1987, pp. 87, 374-76, 408-10.

213. Trade Report 1919-20, pp. 1-2.

214. Administration Report 1919, p. 6.

215. Administration Report 1920, p. 6.

216. Trade Report 1920-21, p. ii; Administration Report 1920, p. 7.

217. Administration Report 1922, p. 6.

kutah collected the additional money.[218] The government of Iran clearly remained suspicious of Ghazanfar al-Saltaneh, for in 1925, he was under house arrest in Shiraz for the greater part of the year, but on payment of a certain sum was finally allowed to return to Borazjan.[219]

He remained the administrator/tax collector (*zabet*) of Borazjan, but in the beginning of 1930, Ghazanfar al-Saltaneh rebelled in protest against the 'Disarming Campaign,' which had begun in November 1929. This was a campaign where the Persian army started disarming the Dashtestanis and Tangestanis, which lasted until the end of the first quarter of 1930. He robbed caravans and flocks of sheep and gave receipts for what he took. As a result, many people joined his ranks. A few Khans of Dashti joined the rebellion as well, emboldened by the setbacks that the Persian army suffered at Firuzabad and elsewhere in Fars against rebelling Qashqa'is. To avoid a broader-based rebellion of tribal elements, or even the rekindling of the Qashqa'i revolt, he was killed by a local competitor, in true Dashtestani tradition. Sardar-e Entesar, the governor of Bushehr induced Sheikh ʿAbdol-Rasul Khan, son of Sheikh Hoseyn of Chahkutah, to kill Ghazanfar al-Saltaneh, his fellow-nationalist hero, which happened on 27 February 1930. Some of his followers were also killed and the rest dispersed, while the Dashtis were defeated as well. Sheikh ʿAbdol-Rasul Chahkutaki and Hajj ʿAli of Chahpir received medals for their help in disarming the tribes. By the end of March 1930 order had been restored.[220] Henceforth, government troops were permanently stationed in the *dezh* of Borazjan, a sign that the old violent way of life was not longer tolerated and that a new era had begun.[221] This did not mean that there was not the occasionally robbery or some other marring event, but these were the exceptions rather than the rule.[222]

Discussion

Borazjan was the chief market town of the district of Dashtestan. Its economy, like that of its neighbouring districts depended on agriculture, but with one major difference; Dashtestan also benefited from the transit trade between Bushehr and Shiraz and beyond. Administratively, the district was part of Fars province and the khan of Dashtestan acted as the governor's local agent (administrator, tax collector). Part of Dashtestan's taxes was paid in kind, i.e. by the supply of riflemen to serve in the governor of Fars's army. Because of its location, the

---

218. Administration Report 1923, p. 7.

219. Administration Report 1925, p. 13; Afshar Sistani 1369, vol. 2, p. 578; Bamdad 1351, vol. 6, pp. 194-95.

220. Administration Report 1929, pp. 14-15; Administration Report 1930, pp. 2, 6; Bamdad 1351, vol. 6, pp. 194-95; Afshar Sistani 1369, vol. 2, p. 578.

221. There had already been Persian troops stationed in Borazjan as of 1924, but after 1930 their number was increased. Administration Report 1924, p. 6.

222. On 21 July 1931, Hasan Khan Matin al-Soltan Farzad, former head of the Finance Department of Bushehr, and his wife were robbed of everything they had, including the clothes they wore, near Borazjan. Two sets of clothes were sent to them from Bushehr. Earlier in May, the deputy governor of Borazjan, Mirza Nasrollah Khan Hekmat was arrested and taken to Tehran having been accused of taking bribes. Administration Report 1931, pp. 3-4.

people of Dashtestan and other neighbouring districts were used as enforcemers by whoever ruled in Shiraz. Normally, this meant keeping the caravan routes safe from highwaymen. In particular, in the first half of the nineteenth century, it meant combatting the ambitions of the sheikhs of Bushehr, which ran counter to those of the governor of Fars. If the Dashtestanis were not fighting the Bushehris or keeping the roads safe, they were fighting and raiding their neighbors.

The traditional chiefs maintained their power through a number of interlinked economic, social and political instruments. The economic instruments included the monopoly of the sale of fodder, the supply of pack animals and related services as well as the distribution of the fiscal burden over the peasants. The chiefs also bound the peasants to them by granting of "credit" in case of their inability to pay taxes on time and by supplying seed in case of failed crops. In short, peasants in the Dashtestan were pretty much bound by strong economic ties to the chief's lineage. The chiefs through their role in the community, the distribution or otherwise of largesse as well as of favors were also able to influence their peasants' behavior and allegiance. From a social point of view, each community felt, rightly or wrongly, that other similar neighboring communities were hostile to them, which created a feeling of the "in group" and thus the need of individuals to identify with the group's goals, which were defined by the chief. Politically, it was the chief who decided when, where, and who was going to be raided and robbed. Also, he decided who could participate, not only in the raid, but also in the spoils. Thus, by being the major employer, the major provider of services and other economic opportunities, as well as the only provider of protection, the traditional chiefs had very effectively bound their peasants to them and could and did receive their unquestioned allegiance. If need be, force was used to bring dissenters back into the fold. The apparent unity of the Dashtestanis was occasionally sundered by infighting among the members of its "ruling" family about who was in charge. After a bout of serious internal family conflict between 1870 and 1877 the leading candidate, Mohammad Hoseyn Khan, won, but he had to share his administration with another leading member of his family.

Despite the fact that a governor appointed by the central government administered Bushehr in 1850, government control over the Bushehr hinterland remained tenuous. In fact, the Dashtestanis and Tangestanis did pretty much of what they liked within certain bounds. Those bounds became enlarged during the first decade of the twentieth century. The authority of the central government was questioned in the country at large and finally lost much control over the country after the Constitutional Revolution of 1906. As a result, many people along the Bushehr-Shiraz caravan route started plundering caravans or imposed high, illegal "protection" fees on passing ones. Because the caravan road to Shiraz and beyond was the major channel for British exports into and imports from Iran, Great Britain took a particular interest in what happened in that part of Iran. Also, the smuggling of arms to and by the coastal population ran counter to Persian and British policy in the Persian Gulf. At the request of the Persian government, the British Indian Navy therefore vainly tried to put a stop to it, while the occasional passage over the caravan road by small groups of British Indian troops did not put a stop to the robberies and illegal exactions either. The khans of Dashtestan, Dashti and Tangestan resented these British actions against what they considered to be their legitimate interests. These same khans also opposed the armed intervention by the Persian government, whether by its army or later by the gendarmerie, in order to suppress their predatory activities. When British troops entered Iran to provide security in the south and east as well as to stiffen resistance against the Turks during World War I, Persian nationalists very much resented British intervention. The coastal khans now became national heroes, for they were no longer simply opposing forces that wanted to suppress their banditry, but were now fighting against alleged enemies of Iran. However, once the war was over and the British troops had left, the khans went back to their old ways, which were no longer tolerated by the new Pahlavi government. The killing of Ghazanfar al-Saltaneh in 1930, the ensuing imposition of government control and the building of the new paved road between Bushehr and Shiraz resulted in the end of an old and no longer acceptable way of life.

APPENDIX 2.1

SHABANCARA AND ZIRA

It is convenient to take these districts together, as for many years they have been under the control of one family.

The district of Shabancara is bounded on the —

North: by the Machur (low hills) of Shabancara, running more or less north-west south-east.

East: by the river Shahpur, or Shirin (from where the Mahur descend towards the river north of Saʿadabad in Zira) down to its junction with the Shur or Daliki river at Durudgah.

South: by the combined river from Durudgah between the villages of Mukaberi and Mainun in Rudhilleh.

North-west: by the river between the villages mentioned up to the Shur-i-Bidu at Anjiru.

West: from the Shur (or salt stream, later known as Shur-i-Bidu) flowing from the Mahur-i-Shabancara: then between Khalifeh and Chaharrustai in Hayat Daoud about 1 mile from the latter place, and past Anjiru.

Zira is bounded on the —

West: by the Shahpur river.

East: by the Daliki river.

North: boundary is south of Siah Mansur and of mazarai up to the foot of the mountains.

On the East the district also marches with that of Daliki from between Behnera and the Daliki date-groves, west of the river, down to the siuth-west of Sarkeverdun in Daliki country.

The Shabancara district contains some 33 villages: Zira about 12.

Shabancara	*Zira*
Deh Kuhne (the capital= about 250 houses, largest)	Sa`adabad
Khalifeh (about 100 houses, next largest)	Jutta
Saifabad	Tul-i-Sirku
Bunari	Tul-i-Qatil
Dashti	Durudgah
Cham-i-Tangu	Nazar Agha
Basri	Tul Alesfi
Mukaberi	Tul-i-Khargai
Anjiru	Sar-i-Qanat
Boiri	
Darvei	
Dehdarun	
Muhammad Jemali	
Band	
Tayyibi	
Sikanderabad	
Chehil Gazi	
Chahdul	
Chahmushki	
Seh Konari	
Bahramabad	
Zakaryai	

Shabancara, which is part of Dashtistan, is assessed for the maliyat at 5,200 tomans. Zira is the personal property of Nizam-us-Saltaneh and has been leased by him to Ismail Khan of Shabancara for the past 15 years for 11,000 tomans annually.

Shabancara is purely an agricultural district, but is noted for horse breeding. The wealth of Zira lies in its date gardens, which are very extensive.

The districts are divided up into spheres amongst the members of the ruling family, which has bene in Shabancara for some 18 generations, it is said. Ismail Khan himself resides in, and controls Zira. His elder son Muhammad Ali Khan acts as his father's deputy at Deh Kuhne and manages the western part. Rostam Khan, a brother of Ismail Khan, looks after the part from Boiri north and sosuth: Agha Khan, son of the deceased brother of Ismail Khan, resides at Darvei and rules over the southern part of Shabancara. The Shabancara and Zira districts are said to be able to muster 1,500 tufangchis.

The small but rich district of Behbera, consisting of two villages only, had also been assimilated to Zira in recent years by Ismail Khan.

In 1909 there was a quarrel between the Kashkulis and Ismail Khan over the rich district of Mazarai, lying in the coast plain north of Zira and across the Shahpur river, which in former times formed part of the sub-government of Khisht. After a raid by the Kashkulis right across Shabancara the question was settled by arbitration of Hayat Daoud, the revenue being paid to the Kashkuli Khans each year, while the control of the district is left to one of the Shabancara Khans, viz., Agha Khan, who sent his brother as his deputy.

Mazarai numbers in its [sic] villages –

Mazarai

Siah Mansur

Dasht-i-Gur

Palangi

Shuli

Kun-i-Surkh.

The chief political feature is enmity and blood-feud with Borazjun and Daliki on account of Zira: relations with Hayat Daoud are very cordial.

The ruling family is:

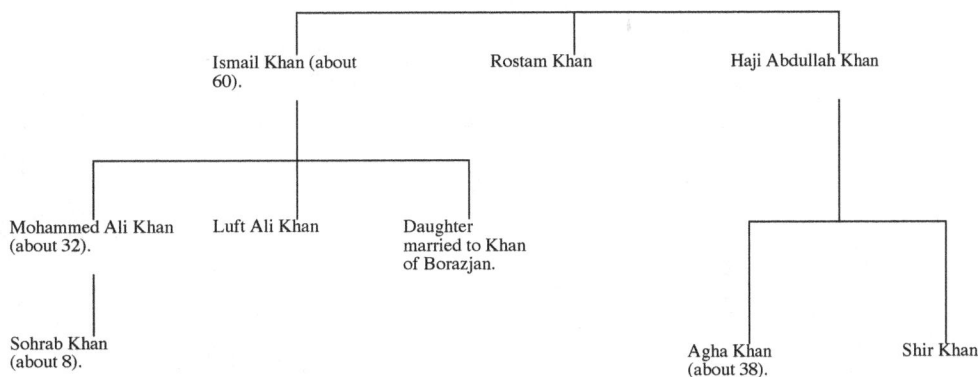

Source: Administration Report 1911, Appendix II, pp. 9-10 (Notes by Mr. H.G. Chick, commercial adviser to the political residency in the Persian Gulf, upon various districts of Fars and of the Gulf Ports).

View of Kazerun Johnson 1818, p. 47

CHAPTER THREE

KAZERUN – HALFWAY STATION TO SHIRAZ

THE TOWN OF KAZERUN

Origin

The district of Sabur Khurrah (the Glory of Shapur) was the smallest of five *khurrah*s or districts of Fars. Its chief town was Shapur or Bishapur - a city as large as Istakhr. The town was named after its builder Shapur (r. 241-272), son of Ardashir Babakan. However, by the tenth century, although still a rich town, it had become run-down and part of the population migrated to the neighboring rising town of Kazerun. As the fortunes of Kazerun rose those of Shapur fell, thus Kazerun became the most important town of Shapur district. Kazerun had already attained sufficient importance by the beginning of the seventh century that it boasted of a judge.[1] Kazerun itself was an amalgamation of three villages near Shapur that slowly merged into one town. These three villages were named Nowdar, Darist, and Rahban, which had been founded by the mythical king Tahmurath the Demonbinder. Later, Firuz (r. 459-484) the great-grandson of Bahram Gur made the three villages into one town called Kazerun, while Kavud (r. 488-531) enlarged it, making Kazerun a dependency of Bishabur. These three

---

1. Vahraman 1997, p. 37 (5, 5-8).

villages were built on watercourses of the same name, which in the tenth century were still found as the names of Kazerun's town quarters.[2]

According to Istakhri, Kazerun was the name of the district, while the town's name was al-Gannegan.[3] Other sources claim that Kazerun originally was named Kuh-e Zarran and it was pronounced as Gazerun. It was also called Gazerat because the mountains were auriferous.[4] These various names led to the invention of popular etymologies, such as the one reported by MacGregor. "Kaziroon, it is said, is properly Gaziroon, from Gazir, a washerman, the place being said to have been once famous for its washing, or the home of the people of this occupation."[5]

Geographical Situation

Kazerun is situated 850 m above sea level in a valley with a N.W. to S.E. direction, which has a long, narrow, fertile plain about 30 miles long and 4-8 miles wide, between two ranges of saddle-shaped hills composed of limestone, varying from white to yellow and pink, "which is the great geological characteristic of this part of Persia." According to Ballantine, Kazerun valley "was dotted over with vineyards and orchards, where we found the fruits of the tropics and the products of colder climes growing side by side. In fact, the trees, gardens, and fields are far more extensive, and the water more abundant, than in any place we had as yet visited." He was not the only one who was enthralled by the floral display, for in the tenth century the neighboring pastures called Maghzar Narkis or narcissus meadows were famous. In 1816, Johnson remarked on the many flowers etc. that bloomed in Kazerun valley. Binning saw several forts and towers in the plain. The remainder of the district was mostly hilly country intersected by numerous streams, plains and hills being covered with *konar* (lote, cornel or cherry tree), zizyphus, wild almond and oak.[6]

---

2. Le Strange 1905, pp. 262, 266 (Nurd, Darbast and Rahshan); Ibn al-Balkhi 1912, p. 55; Abru 1378, pp. 130-31; Mustawfi 1919, p. 125. Later, certainly in the nineteenth century, Shapur was but a dependency of Kazerun. Administration Report 1911, Appendix II, p. 15 ("Shahpur was in former times a separate district, but its maliyat (taxation) is now payable from Kazerun and it may be taken together with Kazerun").

3. Schwarz 1993, vol. 1, p. 33.

4. Kazeruni 1381, p. 40.

5. MacGregor 1879, vol. 1, p. 21.

6. Le Strange 1905, p. 267; Kinneir 1973, p. 65; Johnson 1817, p. 49; Buckingham 1971, p. 329; Dupré 1819, vol. 2, pp. 20-21; Stirling 1991, p. 24; Binning 1857, vol. 1, p. 177; Anderson 1880, p. 50; Weeks 1896, p. 122; Ballantine 1879, p. 88; Stack 1882, vol. 1, p. 37; Houtum-Schindler 1911; RMM 23/1913, p. 26 (Kazerun district is 14 *farsakh* or 84 km long and 10 *farsakh* or 60 km wide); Fasa'i 1378, vol. 2, p. 1430 (for a detailed description); Anonymous 1368, p. 58; Pirzadeh 1343, vol. 2, p. 420; Keyhan 1310, vol. 2, pp. 227-28.

The Kazerun plain was bounded on the:

South-West: the Kih-i-Mast mountain, separating the district from that of Kumarij.
North-east: the mountain range separating it from the Nedun valley.
North-West: the Chakkun defile, and the Mulla Na`l Shikan pas, separating it
from the (Shulistan) Mamasenni district, distant about 22 miles from Kazerun town.
South-east: Pul-i-Abgineh and the Mulla Arab pass, distant about 7½ miles from
Kazerun and separating it from the Famur district.[7]

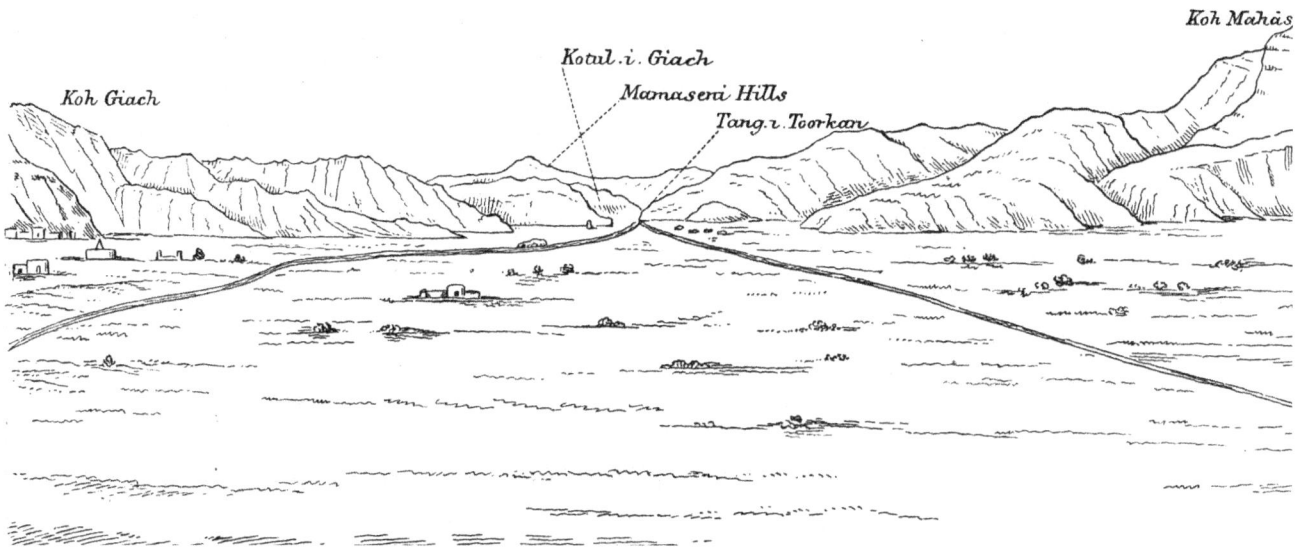

Kamarej plain, MacGregor 1879, vol. 1 p. 18

According to Col. Pelly, "Kauzeroon is the principal town and a sort of half-way point between Bushehr and Shirauz."[8] It was 113 km from Shiraz and 155 km from Bushehr. Coming from Bushehr a traveler went via Borazjan, Daleki, and the Kamarej plain to the entrance of the valley of Shapur, "which was protected by neglected defense works is called Tang-e Chitun."[9] The distance from Kamarej to Kazerun was about 30 km. "Passing a guardhouse at the end of Tengi Toorkan, we entered the plain of Kauzeroon; and a little after sunrise, reached the remains of the ancient town of Direz, where there is a small village constructed of the old ruins. The roadside was covered with masses of ruins; and on the right hand I observed a rudely-sculptured stone lion. Direez is six miles from the town of Kauzeroon."[10] After a while, the traveler arrived at the town of Kazerun, which was situated "almost at the foot of the eastern boundary, which is a range of lime-stone mountains."[11]

7. Administration Report 1911, Appendix II, p. 15. "Pul-i-Abgineh is in the independent control of Mohammad Ismail Khan, its Kedkhuda, who is a near relation of the Kedkhuda of Kaluni in the Dasht-i-Barm." Ibid., p. 16.

8. Pelly 1865 b, p. 146.

9. Johnson 1818, p. 47.

10. Binning 1857, vol. 1, p. 176; see also Dupré 1819, vol. 2, p. 24.

11. Buckingham 1971, p. 329. It was situated at the foot of Mt. Davan, Anonymous 1368, p. 58.

After leaving Kazerun the next stop on the road to Shiraz is Dasht-e Arjan, at a distance of 50 km with two passes. It was 12 km from the town to the first pass. The road was pretty good for the first six miles, "until it leads over a rough stone causeway, crossing a swampy ground." To the right at about 2.2 km there was a salt water lake running in an easterly direction.[12] "Along the roadside runs a rude attempt at fences (the first I have seen in Persia) made of thorn bushes."[13] Before leaving the valley the traveler passed a causeway called The Bridge of the Mirror (*Pol-e Abgineh*) where a bas-relief may be seen showing Timur Mirza, who was governor from 1826-1834.[14] Then the traveler had to cross two very difficult and dangerous passes. The road rose abruptly 500 meter to the Pass of the Daughter (*Kotal-e dokhtar*) and, after 8 km, it rose another 1,000 meter to the Pass of the Old Woman (*Kotal-e pir-e zan*), at 2,200 m. The surrounding mountains are more than 600 meter higher and some even reach 3,600 meter and are covered with snow for six months of the year.[15]

Caravan road from Kazerun plain up Kotal-e Dokhtar,
Government of Great Britain, 1945, p. 545

---

12. Johnson 1818, p. 49.

13. Moore 1915, p. 419

14. Mostafavi 1978, p. 72; Rivadeneyra 1880, vol. 3, p. 45.

15. St. John 1868, p. 412. In medieval times these passes were known as Malan (now, *pir-e zan*) and Hushanak (now, *dokhtar*). Mustawfi 1919, p. 177. In 1665, the villagers still referred to the pass as Ouschanac. Thevenot 1971, vol. 2, p. 149 and apparently still in 1808. Dupré 1819, vol. 2, p. 19 (Aouchanek). For a detailed description of the road between Bushehr and Shiraz, see Clerk 1861.

The district of Kazerun is bounded on the north by a salt lake, and watered by a number of streams of excellent water. A mid-tenth century 'Geography of the World' mentions that "Kazrun lies near the lake Yun." The same source describes Lake Yun as being "10 parsangs long and 8 parsangs broad. Round it lie inhabited lands and it has many useful products."[16] A century later Arab geographers called the lake near Kazerun Lake Muz, Buheyreh Muz or Murak, which was 12 *farsakh* long and came close to Muz. It was salty, and many fish were caught in it.[17] In modern times the lake is called Lake Famur or Parishan, "which encompasses 42 sq km at about 820 m [above sea level] near Kazerun, is fed by about 80 fresh and brackish springs with a discharge of about 800 litres/second and supports a fish fauna near the springs."[18]

Modern travelers, give conflicting information, although most call it a large lake. According to Francklin, Lake Parishan was about six km east, while Hollingberry situated it at about 12 km to the east of the town. Whereas early nineteenth century travelers stated that the lake was salty, Abbot in 1849 reported that "A small shallow Lake of fresh Water occurs near Kazerun."[19] The different opinions on the salty or sweet nature of the lake's water are perhaps due to the fact that: "During periods of low rainfall, Parishan becomes a shallow saline lake and presumably fish habitat is limited to the immediate vicinity of freshwater springs."[20] Fasa'i adds that in periods of drought the lake dried up and in its place many black berries grew. Near the village of Parishan there was a small cave connected to the lake that was half and sometimes fully filled with water. Fish liked to come there because of the warm water. There was a hole in the cave, of the size of a well mouth. The people of Parishan took turns to wait at that opening to catch fish by lowering a woven basket into the hole. When they hauled it up it was full with fish, which were sold at low cost to caravans that came to the village. In the lake there were red fish weighing from six to ten kg from which the people produced oil.[21]

The climate was agreeable, warm to very warm dry climate in summer, temperate to cold in the other seasons, the variations being largely due to altitude. North-eastern winds could be very vehement in March, so that Rivadeneyra one night feared that the house he was staying in would be blown away. These winds certainly broke the telegraph poles. After the period of stormy weather there was a period of rapid growth of mushrooms, he reported. In spring the winds coincided with the rains, which grew in intensity in November and December, the time of sowing. Fall was a mild season, but people were afraid of the locusts/insects. Earthquakes were frequent and the shocks were and still are invariably along the

---

16. Anonymous 1937, pp. 54, 127.

17. Schwarz 1935, vol. 1, p. 10; Le Strange 1905, p. 267.

18. [http://www.briancoad.com/introduction/gulfbasin.htm]

19. Francklin 1976, p. 256; Hollingberry 1976, p. 25; Monteith 1857, p. 117 (Salt Lake); Amanat 1983, p. 177; Rivadeneyra 1880, vol. 3, p. 44 (10 x 2 km).

20. [http://www.briancoad.com/introduction/gulfbasin.htm]

21. Fasa'i 1378, vol. 2, pp. 1600-01. According to Rivadeneyra 1880, vol. 3, p. 44 people caught fish with a little canoe made of reed and wood called *lumbun*; Anonymous 1368, p. 58 (much fish in Lake Famur); Pirzadeh 1343, vol. 2, p. 423 (good fish).

North-South direction of the faultline.[22] This is because valley of Kazerun and the adjacent areas are situated on a fault line and thus earthquakes are not exceptional. However, the one that hit Kazerun in March 1824 was a major and devastating one.[23] An Englishman who visited the town in May 1824, two months after the earthquake, wrote:

> A town in Persia, even in its best state, wears the looks of age and dilapidation, with its unfinished, and mud-built habitations, tottering chimnies, broken doors, and crevices, and apertures forced, as if by thrusting stones out, to make windows. But here was total ruin: the road was blocked up: and after scrambling over heaps of dust and dirt, we found the inhabitants all collected in wood-frame cottages without the town.[24]

He wrote the following about the after shocks:

> The shocks are totally different from those I experienced at Bushire. There they resembled the notion of a cradle rocking slowly and gently to and fro; here, you are first startled by a heavy thundering noise rapidly passing beneath you, and this is succeeded by a kind of a jerk, as if its progress had been suddenly and powerfully impelled. At Bushehr the sensation produced giddiness and slight inclination to sickness; here it is too swift and rapid; there seems to be no motion, or if sensible it is as quick as a flash of lightning.[25]

Urban Morphology

According to Ibn Howqal (943-69), Kazerun was well-built and the houses were of stone set in mortar. Istakhri (tenth century) commented that the houses in Kazerun were like those elsewhere in the province of Shapur, viz. they were built of adobe, but stones and gypsum also were used. Because of the size, development, and fertility of the district and the closed nature of the grouping of the houses they usually were very well built. Kazerun also had larger buildings, villas, more fertile soil and better air than Nubendegan. In those respects Kazerun was the healthiest town in Iran.[26] The entire urban area was filled with villas, orchards and palm groves that extend to the left and right. Kazerun was a walled town with a suburb, and it produced many fruits.[27]

---

22. Rivadeneyra, vol. 3, p. 22; Fasa'i 1378, vol. 2, p. 1431; Sirjani 1361, pp. 140, 250; Stirling 1991, p. 34; Pirzadeh 1343, vol. 2, p. 420.

23. Fasa'i 1378, vol. 1, p. 724.

24. M[oney] 1828, p. 23.

25. M[oney] 1828, pp. 24-25.

26. Schwarz 1993, vol. 1, p. 33.

27. Schwarz 1993, vol. 1, pp. 33-34.

Most of the houses as well as the mosque were built on a hill, and were accessible by steps. The bazaars and villas of the merchants were situated in the valley. The brokers had beautiful well-constructed villas in the neighborhood. Kazerun valley reminded Istakhri of Sistan, for there was nothing but fields, massive houses built next to one another with palm hedges. Moreover, there were no permanent rivers, but only watercourses and wells. Most importantly, at half a *farsakh* from Kazerun was a cupola, "which is the center of the world."[28] Unfortunately, this cupola has since disappeared and with it the center of the world.

View of Kazerun, MacGregor 1879, vol. 1, p. 20

As there are no other descriptions of Kazerun, but one, until the nineteenth century, one is struck by the fact that 900 years later the situation had not changed very much. In 1665, when de Thevenot passed through he noted that "*Karzerum* is a Town of many Houses, but all so miserable, that in our Country the greatest Compliment that could be put upon it, would be to call it a *Bourg* or Village, because it has a Market-place."[29] This does not tell us much about the town and could apply to any other similar market-town in Iran. True, Kazerun was in many ways like other towns in Iran, but not entirely in the non-descript manner as suggested by de Thevenot. Nevertheless, Fraser and others may have agreed with him, for he wrote that the city and plain of Kazerun were disappointing, the town "is little more than a heap of ruins without one object of curiosity of interest."[30] In fact, Price is the only traveler who is altogether positive, relatively speaking, for he wrote: The town "has gone much to decay, but the domes of its mosques and other public buildings, give it an air of grandeur."[31]

---

28. Schwarz 1935, vol. 1, p. 34; Abru 1378, p. 131 (the houses in the rural areas were fortress-like, because of the threat of the Shabankareh Kurds).

29. Thevenot 1971, vol. 2, p. 149.

30. Fraser 1984, p. 79; Rich 1839, p. 214 ("with the exception of the governor's house, [it] is a very dismal-looking place."); Abbott 1857, p. 184 ("there is nothing of interest"); Rivadeneyra 1880, vol. 3, p. 24.

31. Price 1832, p. 9.

When you approached the town at night, the barking of its dogs alerted you to the proximity of the town before you saw its houses.[32] Otherwise, what struck all those who approached the town was that it was situated at the foot of two hills and surrounded by fields of tobacco and maize. Moreover, it was quasi hidden by orchards with peach, apricot, pomegranate, and in particular orange trees as well as date palms.[33] According to de Panisse, the entire scene looked Arabian and reminded him of Egypt.[34]

Once visitors entered the town they all remarked on the fact that it must have been a large city, "and in size little inferior to Shirauz."[35] This was because the town extended over at least two km if not more. According to Buckingham, "The greatest length of the town, from north to south, is about a mile, and its breadth from east to west, somewhat less." ... "This space contains more ruined and deserted dwellings than inhabited ones."[36] Thus, many parts of the town were uninhabited, because they were in ruins and falling apart, while others were just dilapidated.[37] The people of Kazerun, according to Buckingham, believed the town "to have been once so large as to have extended for several fursucks in length; but of this they offer no satisfactory proofs. It may however have been once nearly double its present size, as vestiges of ruined buildings are seen on each side, beyond its present limits."[38] By 1850, not much had changed in the appearance of Kazerun, which was still considered to be a large town, but in ruins for the greater part.[39]

There were two reasons for the ruinous state of the town. The first one was the result of the destruction of the town in 1790 by Ja`far Khan Zand.[40] This was not the first time that this had happened, for Ibn Balkhi reported in the twelfth century that "the city of Kazirun lies in ruins," this time as the result of an attack by the Shabankareh Kurds.[41] The other one was the heavy earthquakes that hit Kazerun, the last major one in March 1824, which destroyed many buildings and unsettled many more.[42]

Before 1790, the town had walls and ramparts, but these were mostly destroyed by Ja`far Khan Zand. As a result, its walls and skirts were almost all in ruins and "in a decayed and falling state."[43] These walls were decaying quickly indeed, because by 1816, Buckingham

---

32. Buckingham 1971, p. 322.

33. De Windt 1891, p. 206; Alexander 1826, p. 119; Stack 1882, vol. 1, p. 37; Ballantine 1879, p. 92; de Vilmorin 1895, p. 329; Mustafa 1904, p. 194; Williams 1907, p. 102

34. De Panisse 1867, p. 222; Mustafa 1904, p. 194 wrote that it reminded him of Mesopotamia.

35. Francklin 1976, p. 256.

36. Buckingham 1971, p. 329.

37. Morier 1812, p. 92; Ouseley 1819, vol. 1, p. 272 (see plate XVI); Waring 1971, p. 22; Buckingham 1971, p. 323; Johnson 1818, p. 47 (drawing of Kazerun); Rich 1839, p. 214; Fraser 1984, p. 79; Alexander 1826, p. 119; de Bode 1845, vol. 1, p. 204.

38. Buckingham 1971, pp. 328-29; Alexander 1826, p. 119 ("a long and prosperous town, but half in ruins from earthquakes.")

39. Binning 1857, vol. 1, p. 177.

40. Rich 1839, p. 214.

41. Ibn al-Balkhi 1912, p. 55.

42. Fasa'i 1378, vol. 1, p. 724; Alexander 1826, p. 119; Stirling 1991, p. 24 (The town of Kazeroon was nearly destroyed by the earthquake which occurred three of four years ago); de Bode 1845, vol. 1, p. 204.

43. Morier 1812, p. 92. Waring 1973, p. 22. According to Dupré 1819, vol. 2, p. 21 Kazerun had

had difficulty identifying the functions of the remains of the walls. "There are some vestiges of a wall with round towers in some places, but it is not easy to determine whether they are portions of an enclosure to the whole, or parts only of some part within the town."[44] The same observation also holds for the houses. Already in 1816, many of the houses were dilapidated and "only a few were good, stood detached, and have all the enclosures near them."[45] In passing through the town of Kazerun in 1826, Alexander "did not find a single upper story standing, and the lower ones were so hidden by the ruins of the upper, that the houses appeared buried underground."[46] In 1889, Pirzadeh remarked that he had never before seen such destruction like in Kazerun, and he estimated that for each well-built house there were ten dilapidated ones.[47]

The houses were mostly built of unhewn limestone, roughly placed in white mortar, while the walls were whitewashed with plaster, which was abundantly available. The result not only gave a cheerful appearance, but also a clean one, "unlike the generality of Persian cities," de Bode commented. It was not only the white plaster, or the almost absence of the monotony of everlasting baked mud and clay that foreign visitors appreciated. They further remarked on the fact that most courtyards had palm trees and/or were surrounded by them, "a feature quite peculiar to Kazerun, which is the first place to the west of Shiraz where the palm prospers."[48] According to Abbott,

> Many of them are fortifications, possessing parapets and loopholes for musketeers. Barricades had been constructed on the roofs, and the marks of shot showed there had been fighting in some earnest.[49]

However, the stone white plastered houses were not the only type to be found in Kazerun. "Some of the older buildings were, however, of unburnt bricks; and there are among the ruins a number of sheds, simply matted over, and used as halts for passengers to smoke their nargeels, and refresh themselves on the way."[50] Later travelers create the impression that the mud houses dominated in Kazerun. Weeks described the town, which with its "low red walls and a fringe of date-palms rising from its gardens, resembles an Egyptian village," while

---

no walls.

44. Buckingham 1971, p. 329. According to Pelly 1865 b, p. 147, the town was "nearly wall-less," while Houtum-Schindler 1911wrote that the town was without walls. In 1840, Anonymous 1368, p. 58, wrote that the town had no walls, but that north-west of the town there was a fort with high walls and its own well that could accommodate a regiment.

45. Buckingham 1971, p. 323; Johnson 1818, p. 47.

46. Alexander 1826, p. 119

47. Pirzadeh 1343, vol. 2, p. 420; on p. 421, after having visited the town he wrote that of ten dilapidated and ruined houses two to three were well-built and inhabited. The houses had neither walls nor foundation.

48. Buckingham 1971, p. 329; de Bode 1845, vol. 1, p. 204; de Windt 1891, p. 206; Binning 1857, vol. 1, p. 177; Kazeruni 1381, p. 40; Pirzadeh 1343, vol. 2, p. 420; Ainsworth 1888, p. 135.

49. Abbott 1857, p. 184.

50. Buckingham 1971, p. 329.

de Vilmorin wrote that the houses were constructed of stone and mud.[51] A twentieth century traveler does not mention the white houses either, but only the "low mud houses interspersed with date trees."[52] By the turn of the twentieth century, Kazeruni wrote that his town had about 4,000 strongly built and durable houses made from stone and gypsum, thus correcting the impression that mud houses prevailed.[53]

Photo of a street in Kazerun, Hinz 1938, Tafel 54

Because timber was expensive, little or nothing at all of this material was used in the construction of houses. Stirling observed that:

> Most of the houses have the rooms arched as wood is not procurable, and upon these a great weight is usually placed. Some of the arches have a space of not less than twenty feet, they are ordinarily of peaked shapes but have always what may be called interval abutments placed at equal distances, and have the appearance of being composed of several separate arches which have been joined together in the interior of the building.[54]

According to Abbott, Kazerun consisted of an upper (*bala*) and lower (*pa'in*) town, an aspect about which nothing further is known, other than that they were antagonistic. He

---

51. Weeks 1896, p. 122; de Vilmorin 1895, p. 330. However, Pirzadeh 1343, vol. 2, p. 420 reported that fired bricks were hardly used. Waters 1876, p. 196 ("Kazeroon consists of a number of flat-roofed ancient-looking little houses.")

52. Moore 1915, p. 420.

53. Kazeruni 1381, p. 40

54. Stirling 1991, p. 24.

even submits that Kazerun "hardly deserves the name of a town, as it is, more properly speaking, a conjunction of two large villages,"[55] probably because the town is the amalgation of three villages. Another aspect of the urban configuration was that Kazerun had irregular narrow and winding streets, which radiated from the market-square in the center of the town.[56] By the early twentieth century, the government offices and the military barracks were at the edge of town.[57] There also were a number of unremarkable shrines, mosques and caravanserais (see below). The Indo-European Telegraph station, an imposing building of two stories, was located near the caravanserai and the Masjed-e Now on the Meydan-e Kheyrat.[58] The ground floor was dedicated to storage, while the upper rooms contained living rooms and an instrument room. Opposite this building was the office of the Persian government telegraph station.[59] As the telegrapher led a lonely life, travelers were always welcome to stay the night and/or have dinner there.[60]

55.   Abbott 1857, p. 184; Administration Report 1911, Appendix II, p. 15; Curzon 1892, vol. 2, p. 205.

56.   Pelly 1864, p. 147; Motahharizadeh 1383, p. 12; Norden 1928, p. 126.

57.   Norden 1928, p. 128.

58.   Sadid al-Saltaneh 1362, p. 36. For a picture with the Bagh-e Nazar in the foreground see Yate 1917, p. 339.

59.   Norden 1928, p. 128; Rubin 1999, pp. 315-16.

60.   Stack 1882, vol. 1, p. 39; Wills 1893, p. 349; Mac Gregor 1879, vol. 1, p. 19; Rivadeneyra 1880, vol. 3, p. 43; Mustafa 1904, p. 195; Williams 1907, p. 102. The telegraphers were Armenians, such as Abid Malcolm, C. Johannes Carapit (who was third signaler in Kazerun in 1873 and remained there until 1888) and Markar who was married. Mac Gregor 1879, vol. 1, p. 19; Ballantine 1879, p. 89; Rubin 1999, pp. 280, 306, 307. In 1896, the chief telegrapher was Markar, an Armenian, but there also was an Iranian Moslem telegrapher. There also was Mirza Hoseyn Yavar, the chief of the Persian telegraph office. Sadid al-Saltaneh 1362, pp. 36-37 and earlier Mirza `Ali Khan *telegrafchi*. Mafi et al. 1361, vol. 1, p. 144.

Overview picture of Kazerun in 1892, de Vilmorin, 1895, p. 329

All travelers agree on one thing, viz. that "The city, excepting a mosque, and the Governor's palace and gardens, has nothing remarkable in it."[61] And even that Buckingham considered a bit optimistic, for "Kazim Khan's residence is the best and only conspicuous building in town, and even that is not remarkable, were it not for two square towers, called bad-girs."[62] According to Chesney, Kazerun had two squares and and three mosques in the 1830s.[63] The saving grace of the town was, among other things, that the climate was better, which together with its water and fruit trees made it an agreeable location.[64] According to MacGregor, "Kaziroon is not a pretty place, but has much to recommend it in its coolness, its good water, and its fruit."[65] Within the town itself travelers noted the role of the date palms as shade trees, although Pelly wrote that there were a few date trees, and that "the date does not ripen well at Kauzeroon."[66]

Around the town there were many gardens.[67] Their number was higher than suggested by Pelly, who noted only three or four fine gardens of oranges, pomegranates, in the

---

61. Francklin 1976, p. 256; Hollingberry 1976, 25; Stirling 1991, p. 25.

62. Buckingham 1971, p. 329.

63. Chesmey 1868, p. 103.

64. Ballantine 1879, p. 88; Curzon 1892, vol. 2, 205; Mustafa 1904, p. 194.

65. Mac Gregor 1879, vol. 1, p. 20; Boehm 1904, p. 84.

66. Pelly 1865 b, p. 147; Arnold 1877, p. 393; Lycklama 1873, vol. 3, p. 16.

67. Kazeruni 1381, p. 41 (with a list of their names and some details); Pirzadeh 1343, vol. 2, p. 422.

suburbs of the town.[68] The most famous garden was the Bagh-e Nazar, lying 1,500 m south of the town. There was also a caravanserai at some distance. The twelfth century historian Ibn Balkhi already mentioned its existence, but it is moot whether that was the same garden and at the same location. What made it such a beloved location to both native and foreign visitors were its avenues of orange trees planted by ʿAli Qoli Khan, governor of Kazerun in about 1767.[69] Everybody sang its praises, noted its paradisiacal character and observed that its like was not to be seen anywhere else in Iran, and may be even beyond.[70] Orange groves were planted along four avenues and its side streets. Two of these avenues are nearly 200 yards long, and another avenue is more than 150 yards long."[71] According to Buckingham, in 1816 the garden "had long alleys of large orange trees, whose spreading branches completely over-caponied the walks; and the date and cypress" both flourishing.[72] Some sixty years later Weeks wrote of the 200-year old orangerie: "The trees are of such size and their foliage is so dense that only a few slender rays of sunlight filter through and sparkle like gold coins on the black soil."[73] Like the other gardens, other trees were planted such as cypress and pomegranate, while, according to Alexander, it also "abounded with apples, apricots, cherries, plums, grapes, &c."[74] According to Stack, the people of Kazerun were proud of their orange gardens, "but the oranges are either sour or bitter." Sweet oranges were imported from Baghdad.[75] By the end of nineteenth century its annual rent was 200 *tuman*s, of which one-fifth was the revenue of an endowment. The gardens received water once per week from the Kheyrat canal.[76] In 1874, however, Dr. Waters opined that "the Bagh-i-Nazar can no longer take precedence in beauty over Bagh-i-Now: to my mind the latter is much the nicest, though the former has the widest and greatest reputation."[77]

The Bagh-e Nazar belonged to government, because each traveler mentions that it was the governor's garden, and each time it was a different governor. Most travelers were able to spend the night there either in a tent or in the pleasure house, which was situated at the entrance of the garden, from which the principal avenue and garden were visible. It had been

---

68. Pelly 1865 b, pp. 146-47; Pirzadeh 1343, vol. 2, p. 422; Waters 1876, p. 198.

69. Fasa'i 1378, vol. 2, p. 1437; Houtum-Schindler 1911; Sykes 1902, p. 318; Kazeruni 1381, p. 40; Arnold 1877, p. 393; Weeks 1896, p. 122. According Dupré 1819, vol. 2, p. 23 the garden was west of the town.

70. Kazeruni 1381, p. 40; Sykes 1902, p. 318.

71. Fasa'i 1378, vol. 2, p. 1437; Kazeruni 1381, p. 41; Pirzadeh 1343, vol. 2, p. 419.

72. Buckingham 1971, pp. 325-26. Dupré 1819, vol. 2, p. 23 also mentions that cypresses had been planted. In 1836, possibly in this same garden, Ainsworth 1846, p. 478 and Ibid., 1888, p. 136 noticed that "the pathway was made of pebbles embedded in decent cement, and so raised as to afford a dry walk when the garden, as is usual in these countries, should be flooded in the evenings."

73. Weeks 1896, p. 122.

74. Alexander 1826, p. 119; Morier 1812, p. 92; Ballantine 1879, p. 89.

75. Stack 1882, vol. 1, p. 37; Arnold 1877, p. 395; Boehm 1904, p. 84; Pirzadeh 1343, vol. 2, pp. 418-19, who reports there were *bakra'i* trees, which in Kazerun were called *bakra'i-ye talkh* or bitter citrus fruit trees. These trees were common in the Kazerun valley; the fruits were sold for two *shahi*s or 500 *dinar*s per Kazerun *man* or five *charak*.

76. Sadid al-Saltaneh 1362, pp. 34-35; Mafi et al. 1361, vol. 1, p. 144.

77. Waters 1876, p. 198. The Bagh-e Now was owned by a firm of Armenian merchants in Bushehr.

built by governor Imamqoli Khan around 1800. The house was spacious and two-storied and travelers always stayed in one of the upper rooms. Apparently, at least according to Buckingham, the governor "only occupied, or visited occasionally, during the heats of summer." There were a few of his servants there, who were permitted to admit strangers for a few days during his absence.[78] The garden had some important visitors in the course of its history, the most well-known being Fath ʿAli Shah in 1830 and his son Farmanfarma, the governor-general of Fars, in 1832.[79]

In 1809, the upper rooms were "neatly matted and stuccoed, with painted glass windows."[80] In 1816, "The accommodation consisted of a small upper room facing the garden, and an open balcony looking towards the town, with galleries, and a terrace above." [81] Close to the house was "a tank filled with grayling, of which we caught many dozen with the rod, several of three pounds weight."[82] In 1820, according to Lumsden, there were two houses in the garden, one of which was larger than the other and in between was the grove of orange trees. The first house seems to have been the gate house, because Lumsden writes that "the room in which we breakfasted was over the gateway of the garden, and had painted glass windows to the north and south." At the other end of the garden was the larger house, "consisting of an open room in the centre, with passages on its right and left, and on each side of those, neat rooms, about 24 by 16 feet, with Gothic painted glass windows, recesses in the walls, and an arched roof."[83] By the 1870s, the house or kiosk was "sadly in need of repair, close to a broken fountain, and situated in a beautiful garden of oranges and pomegranates."[84] By the end of the nineteenth century the garden was flanked by two nice buildings, which were both occupied by government officials.[85]

---

78. Buckingham 1971, p. 325; Morier 1812, p. 92; Johnson 1818, pp. 47-48; MacGregor 1879, vol. 1, p. 22; Weeks 1896, 122; Curzon 1892, vol. 2, 205.

79. Fasa'i 1378, pp. 742, 746.

80. Morier 1812, p. 92; see also Lumsden 2010, p. 32.

81. Buckingham 1971, p. 325.

82. Alexander 1826, p. 119

83. Lumsden 2010, p. 32.

84. Ballantine 1879, p. 89. These two buildings had been built by Hosam al-Saltaneh, but by 1889 had become dilapidated. Therefore, Ehtesham al-Dowleh, governor-general of Fars had given orders to renovate them. People were also making a mess of the garden. Pirzadeh 1343, vol. 2, p. 419. Already in 1877, Hajj Sayyah remarked that the garden had been neglected and was dilapidated. Sayyah 1346, pp. 14-15. Mafi et al. 1361, vol. 1, p. 144. Nezam al-Saltaneh ordered a large water storage to be built for the Bagh-e Nazar and on top of it a number of rooms where the womenfolk of travelers could stay. In 1903 he asked what been done about it. Ibid., vol. 2, p. 320.

85. Sadid al-Saltaneh 1362, p. 35, who further commented that the government officials and their staff had not littered the garden too much, which, therefore, still could be called a garden.

Population

According to Lt. Hollingberry, who accompanied John Malcolm on his first embassy visit to Iran in 1800, Kazerun was "a tolerably large place, but thinly inhabited."[86] The reason for this reduced population was that Kazerun had become depopulated during the civil wars that had raged during the last years of the Zand dynasty. Its population, which allegedly had been 70,000 to 80,000 under Karim Khan Zand had dropped to 3,000 to 5,000 people by 1800, a process possibly reinforced by misrule of the governors of Kazerun.[87]

Table 3.1: The Population of Kazerun 1800-1912

Year	Population size	Source
1800	3,000 – 4,000	Kinneir 1973, p. 65
1808	3,000*	Dupré 1819, vol. 2, p. 21
1809	4,000 – 5,000	Ousely, vol. 1, p. 272
1816	3,200 *	Buckingham 1971, p. 330
1821	10,000	Rich 1839, p. 214
1828	5,000	Stirling 1991, p. 25
1840	7,500 *	Anonymous 1368, p. 58
1841	3,200 – 4,200	de Bode 1884, vol. 1, p. 204
1848	7,500 – 10,000 &	Amanat 1983, p. 185
1851	12,000 ("larger than that of Bushehr")	Binning 1857 vol. 1, p. 177
1857	4,000	Clerk 1861, p. 63
1863	3,000	Pelly 1864, p. 146
1867	3,000 – 4,000	Lycklama, vol. 3, p. 25
1875	5,000 - 6,000	Mac Gregor 1879, vol. 1, p. 20; Ballantine, p. 90; Rivadeneyra 1880, vol. 3, p. 21; Waters 1876, p. 196 (3,000)
1881	8,000	Stack 1882, vol. 1, p. 37
1889	10,000*	Pirzadeh 1343, vol. 2, p. 419
1889	6,000	de Windt, 1891, p. 206
1896	Twice that of Bushehr! >20,000	Sadid al-Saltaneh 1362, p. 36
1905	8,000	Houtum-Schindler 1911
1912	12,000	RMM 23/1913, p. 26
1914	20,000	Nyström 1925, p. 192

* The figures were given in number of families and I have assumed that there were five persons per family. & The figure was given in inhabited houses, which I have assumed each had a family of five persons.

86. Hollingberry 1976, p. 24.

87. Kinneir 1973, p. 65; Ouseley 1819, vol. 1, p. 272.

Photo of Kazerun in 1915, Mustafa 1904, p. 197

Apparently, the population number only slowly increased, for throughout the nineteenth century visitors of Kazerun hardly ever give a population that is higher than 5,000.[88] Rich, Abbott, Binning and Stack are the only ones that give a figure that is double the average, but there is no reason to assume that their figures are more or less reliable than those given by other travelers as these differences may be due to seasonal variations in population. Kazerun, like most population centers in Iran suffered from a high death toll in the years 1870-73 due to the Famine, during which time it allegedly lost 1,000 people.[89] According to Stack, although many died during the famine, "many more had to leave the place and seek work and food in Bushehr or Shiraz."[90] In 1874, Goldsmid reported that, "We were told that, of its 10,000 inhabitants, 4000 had died from want, 4000 had left the place, and that only one-fifth remained."[91] This also suggests that the population figure prior to 1870 was higher than 5,000. If the figure of 12,000 people given in 1912 by the government of Iran reflects the reality, then a higher figure than 5,000 seems the one that is a more likely indication of its population. Moreover, a Persian source states that Kazerun in the first decade of the twentieth century had a population that was twice that of Bushehr. If that is true, then Kazerun had a population of some 40,000 people, which seems highly unlikely.[92]

---

88. In the 1830s the town had 2,000 houses, according to Chesney 1868, p. 103.

89. Mac Gregor 1879, vol. 1, p. 20. Rivadeneyra 1880, vol. 3, p. 24 also noted the impact of the famine on the population.

90. Stack 1882, vol. 1, p. 37. On the famine in general, see Okazaki 1986.

91. Goldsmid 1874, p. 195.

92. Motahharizadeh 1383, p. 12, n. 45. For the population figure of Bushehr, see chapter one.

Because so many of the houses in Kazerun were destroyed, dilapidated or uninhabited the people lived in the center of town.[93] In the fourteenth century, the original three villages, which merged and grew into the town of Kazerun, formed three distinct quarters, "each with its magnificent and mighty palace and each is like a castle."[94] In the nineteenth century, the town's population was distributed over fourteen quarters separated by wide and large open spaces, which were situated in the upper (*bala*) and lower (*pa'in*) town. Their names were as follows: Imamzadeh, Chabi, Kuzehgaran, Torkman, Dugh-forushan, Bazaar, Ahangaran, Jonbad, Shiveh-Kashan, Mosalla, `Oliya, Moqanni, Tarreh-bari, Dashtak, of which the most important were: the Bazaar, `Oliya or Bala (Upper), Jonbad, and Mosalla quarters.[95] The names of the other ten quarters are often found to indicate the location of specific buildings (see below). Each quarter had a chief (*kadkhoda* or *bozorg-e mahalleh*), and above these quarter chiefs there was a *kalantar* for the entire town, who together were responsible for security and tax collection in the town. Each quarter was different and there was rivalry and fights between them.[96]

Although sayyeds and ulama dominated as the notables of the town, in some of the town's quarters other professionals also figured among the notables around 1900. In the Oliya or Upper quarter resided many professional religious families, who were in this occupation since Safavid period, while many of its other notables were gentleman-farmers, religious scholars, physicians, and merchants. In the Ahangar quarter the notables comprised of physicians, merchants, traders (*`attar, bazzaz*), artisans as well as *kalantar* Lotfallah. The notables of the Jonbad quarter were money changers (*sarraf*), merchants, a surgeon (*jarrah*) and some seven eye physicians (*kahhal*) as well as three former and one serving *kalantar*, to wit: Aqa Baba, Hasan `Ali; Ebrahim, and `Abdollah. The Mosalla quarter prided itself on its many sayyeds and ulama, merchants, of whom one was also a farmer as well as on a recently built caravanserai. The Bazaar quarter was a large and well-developed ward with among its notables: many sayyeds, ulama, mullahs, merchants, farmers, grey-beards (*rish-safidan*), and the head of the tailors (*khayyat-bashi*).[97]

Most of Kazerun's inhabitants were Shi`ite Moslems, and less than one percent were Jewish, despite Lt. Col. Johnson remark in 1816, that they were numerous in proportion to the population.[98] In that same year, for example, there were an estimated 600 Moslem Shi`ite families and 40 Jewish ones, according to Buckingham.[99] A similar situation still existed in the 1840s and in 1875.[100] The number of Jews must have been higher in the past. This is what

---

93. Motahharizadeh 1383, p. 12.

94. Mustawfi 1919, p. 125.

95. Kazeruni 1381, p. 40; Fasa'i 1378, vol. 2, p. 1437; Abbott 1857, p. 184; Administration Report 1911, Appendix II, p. 15; Sadid al-Saltaneh 1362, p. 36. According to RMM 23/1913, p. 26, the names of the four main quarters were: Bazaar, Bala, Gonbad, Sofla; Houtum-Schindler 1911.

96. Motahharizadeh 1383, p. 12.

97. Kazeruni 1381, pp. 46-61.

98. Johnson 1818, p. 47.

99. Buckingham 1971, p. 330. According to Dupré 1819, vol. 2, pp. 21-22 there were 600 families in total of which 25 were Jewish families.

100. De Bode 1845, vol. 1, p. 204-05 (the Moslem population is a few thousand plus 40 houses of

the rabbi reported in 1845, stating that "Their community, which was formerly very consid-erable, has been diminished by persecutions, sickness, earthquakes, and other calamities; so that their number at present does not exceed one hundred souls."[101] Around 1000, Kazerun had a considerable Jewish population (see below). A memento of that once larger presence probably was "The old Jewish fort [which in 1817] is uninhabited, and in ruins, overgrown with grass."[102] The Jews lived in a separate quarter, which was situated on the outskirts of the town.[103] "Their houses had an neat and comfortable appearance, and that assumed indigence and wretchedness, which their countrymen frequently display in order to avoid extortions and exactions, was not practiced here, the people being evidently aware that the Jews had not much to lose, and the other had not much to hazard."[104]

There were no Armenians in town, although after the establishment of the telegraph office in the 1860s, the telegrapher usually was an Armenian, who sometimes was married.[105] One source reports the presence of Indian merchants in Kazerun without indicating their number.[106]

The population of Kazerun was a mixture of people of Arab, Turkish and Lori ex-traction. Otherwise they had no default, according to Kazeruni's odd formulation.[107] This mixture made for interesting observations. Whereas the Panisse noticed that the turbans that people wore accentuated Kazerun's Arab, Bedouin types, Binning observed that "The people here are much fairer, and better looking, than the inhabitants of the low country. Some of the young boys I saw, were little, if at all, darker than English children."[108] This mixture of diverse ethnic groups also had a cultural impact, because "They speak a very curious dialect, which contains many words of old Persian."[109]

The inhabitants allegedly lived, for the most part, on dates.[110] However, it is quite likely given the abundance of other fruits as well as the cultivation of grains, that bread and fruit formed a major part of people's diet as in most parts of Iran. Meat was also eaten, but

---

Jews); Rivadeneyra 1880, vol. 3, p. 21 (50 Jewish families); Clerk 1861, p. 63 (30 families).

101. Stern 1854, p. 115. "Their dwellings are in general well constructed." Johnson 1818, p. 47; Rivadeneyra 1880, vol. 3, p. 21.

102. Johnson 1818, p. 47; Waring 1973, p. 22 ("it is now [1802] converted into a corn-field").

103. Johnson 1818, p. 47; Stern 1854, p. 114.

104. Stern 1854, p. 115. "Their dwellings are in general well constructed." Johnson 1818, p. 47.

105. However, in 1836 an Armenian merchant lived in Kazerun. Ainsworth 1846, p. 478 and Ibid., 1888, p. 135. Mac Gregor 1879, vol. 1, p. 19; Ballantine 1879, p. 89. The wife of the Armenian telegrapher Makar was robbed near Kazerun in June 1890. `Abbasi and Badi`i 1372, p. 39.

106. RMM 23/1913, p. 26.

107. Kazeruni 1381, p. 40. This comment may have been triggered by what Abru 1378, p. 131 reported, viz., that the people of Kazerun were gripers (`avan) and slanderers (ghammaz). According to Boehm 1904, p. 85, the people outside Kazerun had "a bad reputation all over Persia."

108. Binning 1857, vol. 1, p. 177; de Panisse 1867, p. 222.

109. Rich 1839, p. 214. For a poem in Kazeruni dialect plus a short word list, see Fasa'i 1378, vol. 2, pp. 1553-54; see also vol. 1, p. 82.

110. Arnold 1877, p. 393.

probably, like elsewhere in Iran, mostly by the wealthy. Kazerun not only had a butcher,[111] but people caught animals (see below) to enrich their diet. The valley teemed with all kinds of wild birds such as pheasants, partridges, and woodcocks, which were easily caught with simple means, while other animals were sold by the butcher at relatively low prices.[112]

According to Kazeruni, the people of his town were generally poor, but friendly, a sentiment with which the American traveler de Windt agreed in general, for he found that "the people seemed more civilized and prosperous-looking than those in the villages north of Shiraz."[113] Other travelers had a similar nuanced appreciation of people's poverty. Arnold, for example, commented on "The poverty of the people, the squalor of their huts (many of them made of mats hung on poles)." ... "But nobody shivered or looked pinched and hungry. Two pounds' weight of dates makes a good meal, and can be bought for about the value of a half–penny in English money."[114] The Jewish inhabitants of Kazerun were "still more poor and wretched than the rest"[115] The people were, of course, in even worse circumstances during and immediately after the 1870-71 famine. In 1873 Goldsmid reported that,

> Among the scraps of intelligence gathered at Kazaran [sic], the truth of which, if I could not certify from personal knowledge, neither could I dispute, on presumptive or other evidence whatever, was, that for one person buried, ten corpses were eaten by dogs, or left to rot exposed. In illustration of this statement may be mentioned the assertion of one of the children relieved-that its father had died some time before, and been buried, but that its mother had been exposed and devoured after death: a child was, moreover, actually seen by a member of the mission struggling with a dog for the entrails of a sheep. We distributed 220 lbs. of rice and 60 lbs. of bread to the sufferers during the two days of our stay; but the task was not an easy one, owing to the crowd of applicants.[116]

Kazerun was in many ways a frontier area. Coming from the coast, it was located where, for example, the climate became better (i.e., it was cooler and less humid), it was the last place where dates still grew, but also the location where people changed headgear. Rich and others noted that "We here lose the turban, and the black cap commences."[117]

Women are rarely mentioned in connection with Kazerun, but since it has been around for such a long time they must have formed a considerable part of the town's population, I

---

111. Norden 1928, p. 126 (photo of butcher).

112. Rivadeneyra 1880, vol. 3, p. 21 (in 1875, the price of chicken was 1 riyal, and prices of goat, buffalo, sheep were in a similar price range); Fasa'i 1378, vol. 2, p. 1430. In its neighborhood there also were many boars, buffaloes and bears, but these were not eaten. Sirjani 1361, p. 316. There also were lions in the area. Brittlebank was told "that the muleteers had heard that some lions had been seen prowling in the neighbourhood of the path which we should have to traverse the next day, and that they were unwilling to proceed farther on the journey." Brittlebank 1873, p. 134.

113. Kazeruni 1381, p. 40; de Windt 1891, p. 206.

114. Arnold 1877, p. 393. There were juicy according to Rivadeneyra 1880, vol. 3, p. 21.

115. Buckingham 1971, p. 330.

116. Goldsmid 1874, p. 195.

117. Rich 1839, p. 214; Ouseley 1819, vol. 1, p. 301 (lamb-skin caps); de Panisse 1867, p. 222.

would say about 50%. Some sources confirm their presence. In 1809, when making his entrance into the town, Ouseley noticed women among the people welcoming the ambassador, "many of whom were well-dressed and did not conceal their faces; some were comely."[118] In 1927, Norden noticed women, who this time were properly veiled, shopping in the bazaar.[119]

Employment

Although most people in Kazerun were poor, throughout the centuries it usually was described as "a large and prosperous town with much wealth," such as in the tenth century.[120] This wealth was due to its production of linen and fine gauzes, an imitation of Egyptian brocades known as *dabiq*, as well as fringed towels. Moreover, the weaving of *tazi* or *tavazi* fabrics made it a wealthy place. These fabrics took their name from the nearby rich and populated town of Tavaz, where people's weaving skills were superior and their fabrics consequently were also better than those woven at Kazerun.[121] Because it was an important textile center of the linen trade, with many respected brokers, and a much frequented bazaar. Muqadassi (946-1000) called Kazerun the 'Damietta of Iran.' In addition, Kazerun derived much wealth from its involvement in the overland trade.[122] To stimulate Kazerun's activities, the Buyid ruler ʿAzod al-Dowleh in 935 built a large caravanserai or market hall (*dar*) for the brokers dealing in the *tavazi* fabrics. This was an excellent investment as it yielded a revenue of 10,000 *dirham*s daily.[123]

> The cloth called *Tazi* [originally coming from Tawwaj] which they make here are woven from the fibre of the flax-plant. Of this, first they tie up the fibrous stalks in bundles and throw these into a tank full of water, leaving the fibre loose until it has rotted. It is next gathered up, the fibre being separated out, and the flax is then spun into lined thread. Next, this linen thread is washed in the water of the Rahban water-channel; and through the water here is but scanty, it has the property of making white the linen thread that is washed in it, and if it be washed in any other water it never becomes white. Now, this Rahban water-channel is the property of the royal Treasury, and the custom is now established that the profit thereof belongs to the house of the Amir, the Treasury having granted the usage thereof to the weavers who weave the cloths under the orders of the Treasury. There is an inspector who oversees on behalf of the Treasury, and there are the brokers who set a just price on the cloths, sealing the bales

---

118. Ouseley 1819, vol. 1, p. 271. In 1836, Ainsworth 1846, p. 478 and Ibid., 1888, p. 136 found when waking up in the princely residence in a garden of Kazerun that a young woman was fanning him, who immediately left when he woke up.

119. Norden 1928, p. 136.

120. Anonymous 1937, p. 127.

121. Schwarz 1993, vol. 2, p. 67; Le Strange 1905, p. 294; Anonymous 1937, p. 127; Muqadassi 433.

122. Schwarz 1993, vol. 3, p. 147.

123. Muqaddasi 433; Schwarz 1935, vol. 1, p. 34; Le Strange 1905, p. 266.

with a stamp before they are delivered over to the foreign merchants. In times past it was all after this wise. The brokers would make up the bales of the Kaziruni cloth, the foreign merchants would come and buy the bales and they stood thus made up, for the placed reliance on the brokers, and in any city to which they were carried the certificate of the Kaziruni broker was merely asked for and the bale would then be sold at a profit without being opened [for examination]. Thus it often happened that a load of Kaziruni bales would pass from hand to hand ten times over, unopened. But now, in these latter days, fraud has become rife, and the people becoming dishonest all confidence is gone, for the goods with the Treasury stamp are often found deficient, whereby foreign traders have come to avoid the merchandise of Kazirun. This fraud was especially common during the reign of Amir Abu Sa`d, whose bad government and tyranny were manifest to all. If, however, this evil state of things could be changed, much wealth would still accrue from this manufacture. Further, in addition to the revenues to be derived from the Kaziruni cloths, which belong to the house of the Amir, there are the land-tax and the customs, both of which would increase greatly under a just and stable government.[124]

In the fourteenth century, there are reports on the continued production of textiles in Kazerun, while the town still played an important economic role as it was a center of the fruit trade. According to Mustawfi, "Much cotton is produced here, and Kazeruni muslin is exported to all parts; some linen is also made. ... Most of these Kazirun stuffs, unless they be washed in the waters of the Rahban watercourse, do not retain their freshness."[125] Information on Kazerun becomes rare in later centuries, because it was off the beaten tracks, which led via Lar to Hormuz and after 1622 to Bandar Abbas.[126] When reference is made to Kazerun during the Safavid period one does not get the impression that it was a very important town. According to Tavernier, there were no caravanserais between Kazerun and the coast (although supplies were ample), while the town itself was but "a small badly built town."[127] However, this impression may be wrong as its natural endowment was excellent and thus its products must have been as much in demand before 1800 as after that date, when more data become available. This is, for example, indicated by the fact that in 1705 Kazerun's tobacco was an important product traded in the Persian Gulf.[128] Nevertheless, the nineteenth century was an era of growth, certainly compared with the disastrous end of the eighteenth century, which was marred by fights between Zand pretenders. Moreover, the Qajars brought stability, while the town benefited from the development of Bushehr, which assured an outlet for its exports. However, that development took time, because in 1808 Dupré described Kazerun as having a miserable bazaar, with no trade, and two dilapidated caravanserais; the only economic activity was the weaving of printed fabrics.[129] However, with the growth of trade of Bushehr the situation of Kazerun also improved.

124. Ibn al-Balkhi 1912, pp. 55-56; see also Abru 1378, p. 131.

125. Mustawfi 1919, p. 125; Abru 1378, p. 131.

126. For a description of that commercial road, see chapter five in this study.

127. This is also reflected in geographical maps, where Kazerun only occurs in 1679 for the first time, but only regularly in eighteenth century maps. Sahab 2005, vol. 2, pp. 310 (Rossi map), 335 (Danckerts map ca. 1680); see also Thevenot 1971 vol. 2, p. 149 and Tavernier 1683, vol. 2, p. 144.

128. NA, VOC 1747, f. 528 (14/12/1706).

129. Dupré 1819, vol. 2, p. 22.

Photo of a butcher in Kazerun, Norden 1928, p. 126

For example, the horse trade was very important, in which Kazerun played an important role. Kazerun was an important market for horses, which were bred in its hinterland and purchased by the India army. That is why by 1821 "most horses were gone." Nevertheless, it was this trade that "gave the dilapidated and ruined town some importance."[130] In fact, "The principal occupation of the more wealthy Moslems is the purchase and sale of horses for the Indian market, and raising a cross-breed between the Turcoman and Arab race, which are called Kauzerooni, and are celebrated for their excellence as journeying, or road horses, but are inferior to the Arab in beauty, and to the Turcoman in strength."[131]

Many Persian and Hindu merchants lived there, who were engaged in, among other things, the export of fruit to India and Arabia (figs, nuts, almonds, raisins, prunes) as well as the general import-export trade. They often resided part of the time in Shiraz, where the main market was, or in the Bushehr area.[132] From the statistics of the number of mules (plus some donkeys) that passed though Kazerun, either coming or going to Bushehr/Shiraz it is clear that the town had an important intermediary function. In fact, Kazerun, next to Shiraz, was the headquarters of the muleteers in the province of Fars, thus providing much direct and indirect employment to the people of the town and the district.[133]

---

130. Fraser 1984, p. 80; Stirling 1991, p. 25.

131. Buckingham 1971, p. 330.

132. RMM 23/1913, p. 26; Fasa'i 1378, vol. 2, pp. 1068, 1323, 1448 (the prominent Malek al-Tojjar Kazeruni family); Kazeruni 1381, p. 40.

133. Rich 1839, p. 215; Pelly 1864, p. 147; Mac Gregor 1879, vol. 1, pp. 20-21; Curzon 1892, vol. 2, p. 205. "Kazerun and Dawun are also noted for the numbers of mules used on transport work, and owned by the inhabitants." Administration Report 1911, Appendix II, p. 16.

Table 3.2: Number of pack animals transiting through Kazerun in March-August 1913

From Kazerun to Bushehr	From Bushehr to Kazerun	Date
1571 mules	404 mules	March 1913
1199 mules	2268 mules	April 1913
7350 mules	4908 mules	May 1913
1230 animals incl. donkeys	2380 animals incl. donkeys	August 1913

Source: Persia 1914, no. 1, pp. 67, 94, 117, 161.

To sustain these caravans and its merchandise, Kazerun boasted of a number of caravanserais. These were also needed to house travelers, because in the seventeenth century, many a pilgrim en route to the Persian Gulf or returning from there made a stopover in Kazerun, despite the difficult and arduous route.[134] In 1665, there "two to three good *Kervanserays* in it,"[135] while in 1816 Buckingham stayed in one of five that existed then, which he qualified as a poor caravanserai.[136] In 1828, Stirling noted only one caravanserai, "but in such a dilapidated state as not to be fit for occupation."[137] The lower number undoubtedly is due to the destruction wrought by the earthquake of 1824. Thereafter more caravanserais must have been built, for it is reported that Kazerun had many.[138] In 1926, one caravanserai also served as a coffee-shop, "which is, in itself, an inn of sort, since wayfarers often spread their sleeping-rugs between the stone columns supporting the roof."[139] It had to compete with a little tea-house, where in 1932 Merritt-Hawkes and her friends had lunch consisting of "huge slabs of Persian bread which were wrapped round chickens, salad and fried fish." ... "The men drank some very precious beer. I only looked on, for it was so difficult to procure that I felt it would be a sin to drink it when it was, to me, just beer and not nectar."[140]

Local trade does not seem to have been very important. In 1828, Stirling remarked that "It is place of no particular importance in regard to trade, and has no remarkable buildings and public edifices, and even the *bazar* is such as not to deserve the name, as scarcely a thing is procurable either in respect to provision, dress, or those superfluities and necessaries which the inhabitants require."[141] This situation had not changed much some twenty-five

---

134. Sistani 1344, pp. 479, 483.

135. Thevenot 1971, vol. 2, p. 149. However, Tavernier 1683, vol. 2, p. 144 reports that there was but one miserable caravanserai, where no traveler wished to stay. Other European travelers, coming from Rig, also had nothing in particular to report about Kazerun. In 1629, Philippi à SS. Trinitate 1649, p. 80 mentions "Casaron" as a town with palm groves near Lar, while in May 1661 de Béryte mentions that "Calzeron" was a small town that had been much bigger in the past. Furthermore, its climate was more pleasant than that of Rig. As he was there during the month of Ramazan de Béryte describes how Moslems perform their fast. de Bourges 1661, pp. 67-71.

136. Buckingham 1971, pp. 323, 329.

137. Stirling 1991, p. 25.

138. Motahharizadeh 1383, p. 12.

139. Norden 1928, pp. 126-27.

140. Merrit-Hawkes 1935, p. 41.

141. Stirling 1991, p. 25.

years later. Abbott reported that the town only had "about 100 miserable-looking shops."[142] In 1875, Ballantine reported that Kazerun had "a scanty bazaar, where English cloth and homespun prints were exposed for sale. There was also pottery and iron ware in little niches for shops, half a dozen in which would hardly fill one of our large show windows."[143] Some ten years later, the French traveler de Vilmorin wrote that Kazerun had two bazaars, both of which were established in the open air under mats held up by poles. For sale were mainly British products such as matches, and quincaillerie such as needles, yarn, etc.[144] Concerning the sale of the various imported products to the outlying villages and nomad camps the Jews of Kazerun, as in so many other parts of Iran, played an essential role. They made a living "as pedlars, and go in little parties on foot, carrying their loads of Indian spices on their backs, between Bushehr and Shiraz."[145] They hawked a limited selection of articles, which they bartered with the sedentary and transhumant rural population. In addition, their other "principal occupation consists in writing fictitious charms and talismans for the Mahomedans, [and] telling fortunes," while they also worked as physicians and as musicians.[146]

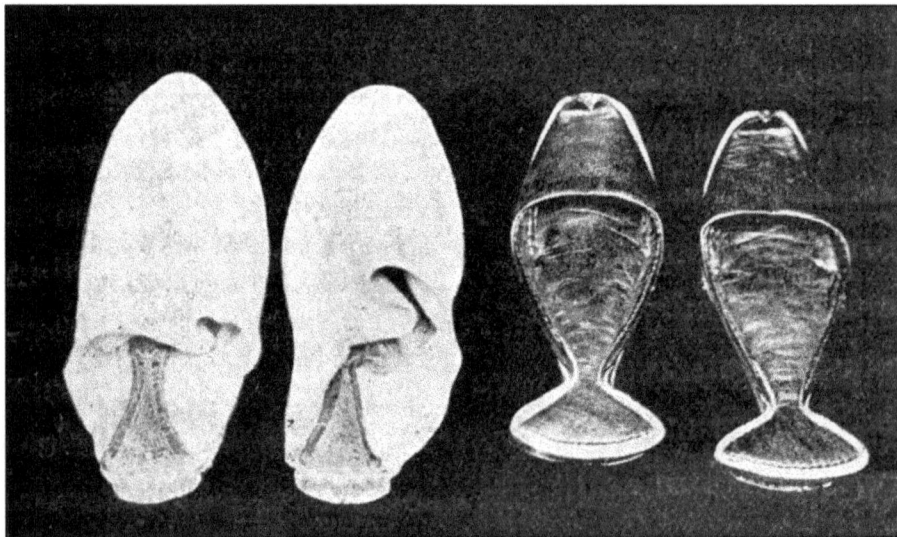

Maleki shoes, Collins 1896, p. 45

The old bazaar, after which the *Bazar-e Vakil* of Shiraz allegedly was modeled, had a long street. Apart from the hot season, the other seasons it was open to all.[147] The bazaar was the home to a variety of craftsmen who catered to the needs of the local population, both in the town and its surrounding district. From the square the bazaar-streets starts its twisting,

---

142. Abbott 1857, p. 184.

143. Ballantine 1879, p. 90.

144. De Vilmorin 1895, pp. 330-31. According to Pirzadeh 1343, vol. 2, p. 421, the bazaar was built with reeds and earthenware.

145. Buckingham 1971, p. 330.

146. Stern 1854, p. 114; Rivadeneyra 1880, vol. 3, p. 21.

147. Kazeruni 1381, p. 40.

and turning way, lined with open shops and the dwelling shacks of the merchants."[148] According to Buckingham, "The lower orders of the people live by their humble labours; but among them there is manufacture, except a particular kind of shoes made of plaited cotton. ... These are made also in other parts of Persia, but are nowhere so good as here."[149] These particular shoes were known as *maleki*, and Kazerun was famous for their manufacture.

> They are very strong, light and easy, and prove beyond doubt that leather is not the only, if it is even the best material, out of which shoes can be made. The uppers of these are made of white ribbed cotton cloth, and the soles of old rags pressed together, only the toe and heel being tipped with a few stripes of raw hide. They cost from one kran for a common pair, to five for the best, and are used by all the inhabitants of Fars, and the soldiers of Persia generally. The soles are very broad, and the uppers are most soft and comfortable, and though always used on the most trying roads for shoes I have ever seen, they last a long time.[150]

They were still being produced when Curzon and Collins passed through Kazerun around 1890.[151] In about 1926, there still "were many shoemakers in the bazaar. Kazarun shoes, like those of Abadeh, are famous throughout Persia."[152]

Although a far cry from the famed *tavazi* fabrics, in 1828 there were "about three hundred weavers of coarse cloth which are in some demand in the neighbourhood, and three or four printers."[153] Given the importance of the trade in horses and mules, as well as the size and frequency of passing caravans (see below) there were many farriers, saddlers, coppersmiths and black-smiths in the bazaar.[154] For example, in the Ahangar (Smith) quarter lived families who were engaged as black-smiths (*haddad*), farriers (*na'lband*), and copper-smiths (*nahhas*).[155] There were also saddlery and butcher shops in the bazaar.[156] The Spanish traveler Rivadeneyra, clearly mistakenly, wrote that the only industry in Kazerun was the tanning of skins and the making of cases for muskets made of wood from Mazandaran.[157] By 1896, there

---

148. Norden 1928, p. 127.

149. Buckingham 1971, p. 330.

150. Mac Gregor 1879, vol. 1, p. 22

151. Curzon 1892, vol. 2, p. 205; Collins 1896, p. 45 (photo).

152. Norden 1928, p. 135.

153. Stirling 1991, p. 25. The printers are those who made chintzes by printing with a block patterns on unbleached fabrics imported from India, see Floor 1999, and Ibid., 2009.

154. Norden 1928, p. 137.

155. Kazeruni 1381, p. 48

156. Norden 1928, p. 137.

157. Rivadeneyra 1880, vol. 3, p. 22 (*cajas de espingarda*).

was a photographer in town, named Mirza Hasan, who probably had learnt his art in Bombay.[158] Some of the religious scholars made a living working in the religious court.[159]

Istakhri (10th century) mentioned that Kazerun was much forested.[160] Although most of these forests have disappeared, in 1816, Buckingham remarked that firewood was abundant and cheap in Kazerun, which was exceptional for Iran, where firewood was scarce and expensive, in general.[161] This was still the case some ten years later, when Alexander "passed several cafilas of dromedaries laden with fire-wood."[162] That was because "there are several rich and well wooded valleys."[163] Almost 40 years later, Col. Pelly noted that "unless for the gardens above noticed, the plain of Kauzeroon is not well wooded. Firewood in any quantity would have to be collected at considerable trouble from the neighbouring hills."[164] By 1912 wood was still listed as one of the products of the Kazerun district.[165]

Girl carrying wood, Norden 1928, p. 126

Another appreciated commodity was that of snow, which was collected and sold in town. Pelly opined that "With care this snow can be taken to Bushehr on a relay of mules

---

158. Sadid al-Saltaneh 1362, pp. 36, 38.

159. Sadid al-Saltaneh 1362, p. 36.

160. Schwarz 1993, vol. 1, p. 33.

161. Buckingham 1971, p. 323.

162. Alexander 1826, p. 119.

163. Monteith 1857, p. 116.

164. Pelly 1865 b, p. 147.

165. RMM 23/1913, p. 26.

even during the hottest months, but it keeps only a few hours after arrival."[166] Some 20 years later, Ballantine also noted that snow was for sale. He wrote that it was fetched from the mountains "at the close of winter, and placed in pits, where it was trodden hard to prevent its melting." In summer the owners of the snow-pits brought every day some snow down to the bazaar, "which, being very cheap, was indulged in by all classes."[167]

Williams was not impressed with the quality of the workmanship found among the craftsmen, at least the one he had business with. His gun barrel had broken off at the stock, but after 'repairs' in the bazaar of Kazerun, the barrel fell on the ground when he wanted to shoot as the plate was not riveted but had only be glued on![168]

In short, Kazerun was a market town in an agricultural district, serving a distribution center for both the district's exports as well as its limited number of imported goods. Further, it derived income from the transit trade by providing pack animals and related services to merchants and travelers. However, there were very few wealthy people in Kazerun, and there was none who owned 5,000 *tuman*s. Those Kazerunis, who were very rich, were those living and trading in foreign parts.[169]

Religion

Whether during the days of the Persian Empire, or later when Islam had taken over from Zoroastrianism and Judaism, the people of Kazerun made religion their business. Even as late as the mid-tenth century, various Arab geographers noted that there were two venerated fire temples, named Gefteh and Gul Adhar at Kazerun.[170] It was only after the year 1,000 that the people of Kazerun started to abandon their old religions for that of Islam. Sheikh Abu Eshaq Ebrahim Kazeruni (342-426/963-1034) is credited of having converted the people of Kazerun to Islam, because they still were Zoroastrian or Jewish. Despite the opposition of the Zoroastrian governor of Kazerun, Khurshid, he allegedly converted some 24,000 people to Islam.[171] The Moslems in Kazerun all belonged to the Shafe`i school of Sunni Islam.[172]

---

166. Pelly 1865 b, p. 148. Waring 1973, p. 22 reported in 1802 "that ice and snow are sold all the year in the market at Kazeroon, and are even occasionally conveyed to Bushehr on mules."); Rich 1839, p. 211 ("snow coming from Kauzeroon").

167. Ballantine 1879, p. 90.

168. Williams 1907, pp. 96-97.

169. Pirzadeh 1343, vol. 2, p. 420; see also Kazeruni 1381, p. 40.

170. Schwarz 1993, vol. 1, p. 33; Anonymous 1937, p. 127. For a description of the four-arched fire temple near Kazerun and in adjacent districts, see Mostafavi 1978, p. 74-79, 329-30. To the southeast "of the city on a huge mound are ruins of buildings with underground chambers, popularly known as Kal`eh i Gabr, 'castle of the fire-worshippers.'" Houtum-Schindler 1911

171. Algar 1960.

172. Mustawfi 1919, p. 125.

By that time there was already a mosque, crowning a hillock.[173] Those who converted
were soon followed by others, as it was rewarding to become a Moslem in more than one
sense. For example, the descendants of Salman-e Farsi, who was from near Kazerun and a
companion of the prophet Mohammad, were exempt from the poll-tax until the Mongol
period. During the reign of the Abbassids his descendents received money from the state
treasury (*beyt al-mal*). The Salman-e Farsi cemetery still exists in Kazerun and is visited.[174] In
the twelfth century, Ibn Balkhi reported that:

> In various of the townships of Kazirun there are mosques for the Friday prayers.
> The people, however, are covetous and needy; further, they are a slanderous
> folk. In all these parts there are places where [a criminal] may take refuge, as it
> were in a *Harim* [or Sanctuary], and of such is [the shrine] of Shaykh Abu Ishaq
> Shirazi, whom Allah sanctify![175]

According to Amin al-Razi, Kazerun "was always a source of scholars and mine of
theologians," and in the Safavid and Qajar period the town also boasted many of the same.[176]
One of those leading lights was the above mentioned Sheikh Abu Eshaq Shirazi or Kazeruni
who was the founder of the influential Kazeruni order, who not only converted his fellow
Kazerunis, but sent his disciples as 'fighters for the faith' (*ghazis*) to enlarge the realm of
Islam. He, therefore, earned the title of Sheikh-ghazi. Both in Kazerun itself and in a large
number of other places in Fars, his adherents established convents to assist the poor and travelers, which was the spring board for the later spread of the Kazeruniyeh order. The order was
found as far west as Edirne and as far east as China (Canton) and many places in between.
The seaborne expansion was aided by the fact that soil from Kazeruni's grave was said to calm
stormy seas and have healing powers. Around 1507, the central convent of the order at Kazerun was destroyed by the Shi'ite Safavids.[177] Thereafter the Kazeruni order faded away, also in
Anatolia, in the seventeenth century.[178] Sheikh Eshaq's tomb was neglected thereafter and the
devotional focus of the now Shi'ite Kazerunis was henceforth aimed at the tombs of other
worthies.[179] Other Kazeruni Sufi leaders, who were adherents of Sheikh Abu Eshaq and who
were also partners in the later neglect, included Sheikh Owhad al-Din 'Abdollah Balyani
(d. 683/1184) whose tomb is near Balyan village. The same holds for that of Sheikh Amin

173. Le Strange 1905, p. 266.

174. Kazeruni 1381, pp. 40-42; Fasa'i 1378, vol. 2, pp. 1437-38.

175. Ibn al-Balkhi 1912, pp. 56-57.

176. al-Razi 1974, vol. 1, p. 208 ff; Zarkub 1350, p. 131ff; Hazin 1830, pp. 95-96; Fasa'i 1378,
vol. 2, p. 1445-48; Kazeruni 1381; Mustawfi 1919, p. 125.

177. Algar 1960; Fasa'i 1378, vol. 1, p. 337 (ruler of Fars came to pay his devotion); Filiz Çağman
and Zeren Tanıdı 2002, show that the Shiraz convent of the Kazeruni order was a center of
manuscript and miniature production.

178. Algar 1960.

179. Mostavafi 1978, p. 258.

al-Din Balyani (d. 1344) of which little is left.[180] Another leading Kazeruni Sunni scholar was Mohaqqeq-e Davani (d. 1502) whose dilapidated tomb may be found near Davan village.[181]

After the establishment of Safavid rule, the people of Kazerun once again converted, this time to Shi`ism. They were probably induced in doing so soon after Shah Esma`il I had killed four thousand Sunni preachers in Kazerun in 1504, as people took the hint.[182] Initially, the adhererence to Twelver Shi`ism must have been skin deep, for only 100 years later a Kazeruni still preserved a precious keepsake, viz., a book allegedly in the hand of the cursed Caliph Yazid, the murderer of the second Shi`ite Imam Hoseyn. The owner of this rarity presented it to Shah `Abbas I (r. 1578-1629), who happened to need a rare present for the Ottoman Sultan. The shah had the volume gilded and studded and sent it to Istanbul as a gift.[183] Although this sinner had at least realized the error of his ways, others, even after 200 years, still refused to see the light, because in villages such as Somghan people remained Sunnis. Hence they were only too happy to assist the Sunni Afghan general, Zabrdast Khan in 1724 with the siege of Shiraz.[184]

After Shi`ism had taken over from Sunnism as the dominant religion, other exemplars, therefore, took the place of the Sunni leaders, who could not be considered models to be followed, of course. As a result, the faithful Kazerunis henceforth shared their time and devotions among seven shrines:[185]

1. Sayyed Mohammad Kashi in the Gonbad quarter.
2. Sayyed Mohammad a.k.a. Zeyd, in the center of Gonbad quarter.
3. Sayyed Mohammad Rahdur, in the Ironsmiths' quarter (brother of no. 1).
4. Aba Fath, in the bazaar quarter.[186]
5. Shah Hamzeh, in the bazaar quarter.[187]
6. Imamzadeh, in the form of a tower, in the Imamzadeh quarter.[188]
7. Sayyed Mohammad Amin al-Din north of town near the mountain.[189]

---

180. Mostavafi 1978, pp. 258-59; Fasa'i 1378, vol. 2, p. 1438.

181. Mostafavi 1978, p. 259; Fasa'i 1378, vol. 2, p. 1439-40, who also has information concerning other famous ulama, physicians and scholars.

182. Aubin 1959, p. 58; Ibid,. 1988, p. 86.

183. Natanzi 1351, p. 472.

184. Khurmuji 1380, p. 420. On Sunni support for the Afghan invaders, see Floor 1983 and Ibid., 1988.

185. Mostafavi 1978, p. 256; Buckingham 1971, p. 329 (seven tombs of different holy men with a dome). According to Sadid al-Saltaneh 1362, p. 36, there were many of these shrines.

186. Allegedly a son of `Ali b. Abi Talib, the first Shi`ite Imam. Sadid al-Saltaneh 1362, p. 36.

187. Allegedly a son of Musa Kazem, the seventh Shi`ite Imam. Sadid al-Saltaneh 1362, p. 36. Shahzadeh Hamzeh, son of Imam Musa is buried here. Rich 1839, p. 215. "There is also a very old building of a circular form of Shah Humza, a peer or saint, to whom is ascribed the power of effecting miraculous cures on those who will testify their faith in his sanctity by prayers, accompanied with sufficient offerings in his shrine." Johnson 1818, p. 48.

188. Allegedly Mohammad, the son of Hasan `Askari, the eleventh Shi`ite Imam, is buried here. Sadid al-Saltaneh 1362, p. 36.

189. "A couple of miles north of the city behind a low range of hills are the imposing ruins of

In addition to these various shrines, the Moslems of Kazerun also frequented five mosques, "which are kept up and well attended."[190] These mosques had domes of mud, and minarets of sun-baked bricks.[191] Apart from the Salman-e Farsi cemetery,[192] or perhaps the same, there was a cemetery in Kazerun with among other things many massive, sometimes natural-sized, stone lions.[193]

By 1900, there was a host of local families who for scores of years or longer not only were the notables of their quarter and town, but also holders of inherited religious functions such as that of Sheikh al-Eslam, some as far back as the Safavid period. Various sayyeds families were in particular prominent among these hereditary religious entrepreneurs, who literally made religion their business.[194] It is, therefore, not surprising to learn that the leading notables of the town, according to Pirzadeh, were ulama and sayyeds, who were all knowledgeable and pious.[195] Between 1890 and 1910, the uncontested religious leader of the town was Sayyed Mahmud, who, because he had a namesake, was called Sayyed Mahmud-e Bozorg, because he was tall man.[196]

The Jews had a rabbi and, in their own quarter, a synagogue, "a humble unadorned room, with no other furniture except a few mats and several pieces of worn-out carpets. The blind mullah, who was led by a boy, acted as guide, he assured us that within his recollection, Kanzeroon [sic] contained two synagogues."[197] One may assume that the Jews had their own cemetery.

Water

Over the centuries it would seem that neither the climate nor the water supply system of Kazerun has significantly changed. In the tenth century, its inhabitants had to use well water just as they continued to until recent times.[198] According to the twelfth century historian Ibn Balkhi, Kazerun's climate was hot, "like that indeed of Bishabur, and all the water they drink has to be taken from wells, for there are no running streams, only the three under-

---

a marble building said to stand over the grave of Sheik Amin Nasr al-Din Mahommed b. Zia ed din Mas`ud, who died A.H. 740 (A.D. 1339)." Houtum-Schindler 1911; Fasa'i 1378, vol. 2, p. 1438.

190. Buckingham 1971, p. 329; Stirling 1991, p. 25; Dupré 1819, vol. 2, p. 22 (four miserable mosques). Motahharizadeh 1383, p. 12 (many mosques). The Masjed-e Now was built in 1017/1608. Ibid, p. 15, n. 14.

191. Arnold 1877, p. 393.

192. Kazeruni 1381, p. 42.

193. Rivadeneyra 1880, vol. 3, p. 24; Ballantine 1879, p. 91.

194. Fasa'i 1378, vol. 2, pp. 1442-44. Kazerun also had an *imam-e jom`eh*. Motahharizadeh 1383, p. 111. On religion as a source of income see Floor 2001.

195. Pirzadeh 1343, vol. 2, p. 420.

196. Sadid al-Saltaneh 1362, p. 35.

197. Stern 1854, pp. 114-15; Johnson 1818, p. 47; Dupré 1819, vol. 2, pp. 21-22.

198. Schwarz 1993, vol. 1, p. 33.

ground water-channels [of the villages above-mentioned]."[199] It was still that way in 1665, when Thevenot visited Kazerun. He observed that "the water they drink there, is brought above half a League from the Town, but both in it and the *Kervanserays* there is water good enough for Beasts and the Kitchin."[200] In 1816, the water supply system had not changed, i.e., there was no river supplying it.[201] The town still relied "three or four separate springs which supply the town." The quality of the water was pure and better than that of Shiraz, Buckingham reported.[202] Water came from the Wadi, Kheyrat, and Qaracheh *qanats* (underground channels); the latter had been built in 1132 and was financed by Atabeg Qaracheh, hence the name.[203] The Kheyrat *qanat* was built by a former governor Khvajeh Hosam al-Din Afshar.[204]

According to Stirling, the water supply by *qanat*s was good. Water was "brought nearly into every tenement, and has besides numerous wells and reservoirs which preserve rain water."[205] He is the only source mentioning water reservoirs, a water supply option that was typical for the southern coastal zone (*Garmsirat*). Therefore, the prevalence of water cisterns (*berkeh*) is typical of the entire Larestan area, and also of Kazerun.[206] Pirzadeh, who visited Kazerun in 1889, reported that the *qanat*s contained little water. The biggest canal had not more than one *sang* of water.[207] Kazerun suffered from the almost general drought that struck Iran in 1870 and consequently also suffered severely in the subsequent famine. The *qanat*s on which the water supply depended dried up. Many people died, and many more had to leave the place and seek work and food in Bushehr or Shiraz.[208] Hajj `Abdol-Hoseyn, a merchant, told MacGregor that over 1,000 people had died in Kazerun during the famine, or about 20% of its population.[209]

Although the climate of Kazerun was considered to be healthy,[210] already in the tenth century al-Muqaddasi noted the feeble eyesight of the people of Kazerun.[211] This was a problem that was universal in Iran and in particular in the coastal areas. It is of interest to note that although a few physicians are mentioned, many more ophthalmologists (*kahhal*) are listed among the town's notables. In the nineteenth century, in the Jonbad quarter, apart from one

---

199.   Ibn al-Balkhi 1912, p. 55; Mustawfi 1919, p. 125.

200.   Thevenot 1971, vol. 2, p. 149.

201.   There is little water in the town's creek. Kazeruni 1381, p. 40.

202.   Buckingham 1971, p. 330

203.   Fasa'i 1378, vol. 1, p. 243; Sadid al-Saltaneh 1362, p. 36; Khurmuji 1380, p. 147. Motahharizadeh 1383, pp. 12, 18, n. 43 states according to the endowment deed (*vaqfnameh*) Sheikh Amin al-Din Balyani was the benefactor. For information on the Wadi canal, see Ibid, n. 44.

204.   Fasa'i 1378, vol. 2, 1441.

205.   Stirling 1991, p. 25; Pelly 1864, p. 146 (Drinkable water is sufficiently abundant).

206.   Mahmoodian 2007, p. 47; Dupré 1819, vol. 2, p. 24; see also chapter 5 in this publication.

207.   Pirzadeh 1343, vol. 2, p. 419.

208.   Stack 1882, vol. 1, p. 37. In case of little or no rain the people pray for rain by engaging in an ancient ritual that includes sung invocations, see Hatami 1375.

209.   Mac Gregor 1879, vol. 1, p. 20.

210.   Johnson 1818, p. 48.

211.   Schwarz 1993, vol. 3, p. 140; Muqaddasi 1906, p. 439.

surgeon (*jarrah*) at least seven ophthalmologists are mentioned.[212] In December 1890 there was an outbreak of cholera in Kazerun and many people fled. People and caravans coming from Kazerun were not allowed to enter Shiraz. Then it was learnt that the disease was not cholera and the quarantaine was lifted.[213]

The presence of baths or *hammam* is only reported as of the beginning of the nineteenth century. However, given the ritual purity requirements of Islam made it necessary that such an institution also existed during almost the entire period that Islam became the majority religion of Kazerun. In 1816, according to Buckingham, there were two small baths in Kazerun.[214] When in 1804, Waring wanted to take bath in one of them he was prevented from having one, because people were afraid that he would make the place ritually impure.[215] Buckingham apparently did not have that problem in 1816, or at least he did not mention it. He went to visit one of the baths, which he described as follows: "It was small and dark, but of exactly the same plan as all those we had seen in Persia, and more highly heated than any. The attendants, too, were more skilful in their duty than even those of the best baths in Shiraz and Ispahan; and in their method of moulding the limbs and muscles, approached nearly to the Turks."[216] Somewhat more than one century later, Norden enjoyed the steam bath in Kazerun, which with two towels only cost one *qran*.[217] Like elsewhere in Iran, on particular days, the bath horn (*buq-e hammam*) sounded to announce that the bath was open to women.[218]

Education and Amusements

Kazerun had several elementary schools (*maktab-khaneh*) where the Koran and some poetry were taught. These were usually located in a religious building.[219] One of the first modern schools in Kazerun was established by Naser-e Divan and, therefore, the school was called Madraseh-ye Naseri. He invited all the notables of the town to the opening ceremony in October 1915.[220] In 1922, there also was a government school in Kazerun.[221]

Apart from schools of learning, Kazerun was "famed as having been the school, and perhaps the birth place of many of the most renowned Pylewauns, or wrestlers of former

---

212. Kazeruni 1381, p. 49. Also a few physicians are mentioned in the Ahangar quarter. Ibid., p. 48. For the prevailing diseases in Qajar Iran and the treatment by eye doctors, see Floor 2004.

213. Sirjani 1361, pp. 420, 438, 440.

214. Buckingham 1971, p. 329.

215. Waring 1973, p. 23

216. Buckingham 1971, p. 325.

217. Norden 1928, pp. 136-37.

218. Ouseley 1819, vol. 1, pp. 301-02.

219. Motahharizadeh 1383, p. 12, 18, n. 40 (there was already such a *maktab* in the eleventh century); Sadid al-Saltaneh 1362, p. 35.

220. Motahharizadeh 1383, p. 95.

221. Motahharizadeh 1383, p. 182 (doc. 120).

times; and it still has a zourkhauna or gymnasium, which retains a portion of its ancient notoriety."[222] In fact, allegedly most of the male inhabitants were said to be wrestlers.[223] When Brydges-Jones traveled as ambassador to the court of Fath Ali Shah in 1809, he was greeted at 3 km from the town by a welcoming party. "Most of the male inhabitants of that city, to the number, at least of five thousand, had assembled about us; and here we were met by wrestlers and pahlewans, who exercised their heavy clubs, called *meels*, and went through various feats of agility and strength, immediately before Sir Hardford's horse."[224] Given the relationship between wrestling and certain forms of clannish group formation it is unsurprising to learn that "the inhabitants are a *lootie* set, like those in Shiraz."[225]

Wrestling was not the only pastime in which the people of Kazerun were engaged. A Kazeruni speciality was the catching of sparrows, which were eaten and sold in the market.[226] In 1822, Fraser described the method used in Kazerun, which probably was used elsewhere in Iran.

> The mode of catching sparrows is ingenious; and, if taken merely from description, would appear to depend of a kind of fascination, which the persons practising it exercise, *commanding*, as it is said, the birds to enter their nets. The fact, however, is simply as follows: observation has shown, that the birds return in flocks from their feeding places to roost, at a certain hour, and in certain directions; and a net so contrived as to be raised on end by a person concealed, is placed in this line: a number of stakes are planted also along the line, in two rows, but they do not appear to be of any further use than to assist the deception. When the flight of sparrows approach, another person, also concealed, flings over them a clod or stone, uttering at the same moment a shrill cry like that of a hawk, on which the little animals immediately sink, and fly close to the ground through the opening where the net is placed; this is tilted up, and sometimes one, sometimes a number of sparrows are taken. But they do not always succeed well; and on the occasion when they exhibited for our amusement, they assuredly were not eminently successful.[227]

Perhaps the most important event in the year was the commemoration of the martyrdom of Imam Hoseyn, an event whose celebration grew in importance during the Qajar period. Arnold, who observed the theatrical presentation in 1875, noted that the courtyard of the principal mosque was full of men; the surroundings roofs were filled with women and children.

---

222. Johnson 1818, p. 48.

223. Rich 1839, p. 214; Fraser 1984, p. 80; Curzon 1892, vol. 2, 205.

224. Brydges-Jones 1976, p. 73 ("the distance from Derais to Kazerun is 7 miles, which took us 6 hours because of the performances and the crowd.")

225. Abbott 1857, p. 184; Sirjani 1361, p. 131 (Rabi` II 1298). For the link between wrestlers and *luti*s, see Floor 1971.

226. Fasa'i 1378, vol. 2, pp. 1430-31 (who gives a description of the method of catching sparrows with a small drawing).

227. Fraser 1984, p. 80.

In the centre, about fifty men had formed themselves into a ring, holding each other's hands. In this formation, they expanded and contracted the circle, advancing and retreating with the cry 'Ah, Houssein!' uttered in the tone of the profoundest grief. This was kept up with mechanical regularity for about an hour. Then, when every man's brain was reeling with the exercise and with watching it, at a word from their leader the men sat down, and each beat his bare breast with his open palm, and then clapped his hand on his thigh with the common cry. This, too, was done with the same precision. We left them at this work, and soon after it was understood that the two parties, one holding that day to be the proper anniversary and the other preferring the morrow, were disposed to fight over the difference. There was some tumult, and the governor ordered that there was not to be the usual procession in the streets, of which the leading feature is the slashing of their faces and persons with knives, and the consequent staining of their white garments with blood, by the most devoted mourner for Hossein.[228]

THE DISTRICT OF KAZERUN

Sedentary Population

Around the year 1000, the district of Shapur was the smallest one in the province of Fars; Kazerun was its capital.[229] Not much is otherwise known about Kazerun's situation, be it that Ibn Balkhi lists Mur and Shitashgan as Kazerun's most populous districts.[230] In the late 1730s, the district was reduced in size when Nader Shah separated Khesht from the district of Kazerun and made it a separate governorship.[231] It is only in the nineteenth century that more is reported about the extent of Kazerun's jurisdiction. The British consul Keith Abbott, who was on a fact-finding tour in southern Iran in 1849, reported that Kazerun district had 13 villages, while those of its dependent sub-districts comprised another 19 villages, viz., "Kuh Marreh Posht-e kuh (10), Kuh Marreh Shekhan (6), and Kuh Marreh Jerruk (3), or a total of 32 villages."[232] Two other sources, Fasa'i and Houtum-Schindler report that the district of Kazerun had 46 villages, with a population of about 15,000, which were distributed over four sub-districts:

---

228. Arnold 1877, p. 394; see also Rivadeneyra 1880, vol. 3, pp. 24-26. On this festival, see Floor 2005.

229. Aigle 2005, p. 72.

230. Ibn al-Balkhi 1912, p. 57.

231. Fasa'i 1378, vol. 1, p. 586.

232. Amanat 1983, p. 185. Chick mentions the names of 22 and other villages. Administration Report 1911, Appendix II, p. 15.

Shahpur, its center is `Amu'i;

Kuh-e Marreh-ye Posht-e Kuh a.k.a. Fashquyeh, its center is Nowdan;

Kuh-e Marreh-ye Jeruq, its center is Sartabeh; and

Kuh-e Marreh-ye Mashkan (Mashgan), its center is Buranjan.[233]

However, by the turn of the twentieth century, a local historian listed 63 villages.[234] Around 1910, according to the government of Iran, the district had 56 villages with a sedentary population of 35,000, excluding those of Kazerun town.[235] These last two lists appear to reflect the reality on the ground more than the other sources mentioned. This discrepancy in the number of villages probably is due to what the reporters considered to be a village and what was not.

The sedentary rural population was engaged in agriculture (producing wheat, barley, rice, beans, melons, dried fruits, citrus fruit, tobacco, opium, sesame, cotton), animal husbandry, and related activities. As such they played an important function in supplying the town of Kazerun with its needs, because "The cultivated land about town appears insufficient to support even the few inhabitants here: horses, camels, sheep, and goats, find, however, a scanty pasture of the plain; and a few date trees are the only productions of food for man."[236]

Table 3.3: Names of the villages in the Kazerun jurisdiction

RMM 1913	Fasa'i 1378	Motaharrizadeh 1381
1. Ab-kenaran	Ab-kenaran – 4.5 farsakh south-east	Ab-kenaran
2. Abu `Ali	Abu `Ali – 2 farsakh south-east	Abu `Ali
3. Alif	Alif – 2 farsakh south-west	Alif
4. -	·	Emam-abad
5. Papuni	Papuni – 4.5 farsakh north	Papuni
6. Pareh	Pareh – 4.5 farsakh north-west	Pareh
7. Pareskan	Pa'uskan · <3 farsakh south	Pa'uskan
8. Parishan	Parishan -2.5 farsakh east	Parishan
9. -	·	Parishuyeh
10. -	·	Panj Mahall
11. Balyan	Balyan – 1.5 farsakh south-east	Balyan
12. Benaf	Benaf – 3 farsakh west	Benaf
13. Buranjan	Buranjan – 5 farsakh east	Buranjan
14. Bushegan	Bushegan – 5 farsakh north-west	Bushegan
15. Bu'l-Hayat	Bu'l-Hayat – 6 farsakh north	Bu'l-Hayat
16. Talli-Gavak	Tel-e Gavak – 4 farsakh north-west	Tel-e Gavak
17. -	·	Qal`eh-ye Taba'i

233. Fasa'i 1378, vol. 2, p. 1430, 1448, 1450. For other locations in Fars named Kuh-e marreh, see Ibid., p. 1499; Houtum-Schindler 1911.

234. Kazeruni 1381, pp. 75-76.

235. RMM 23/1913, pp. 26-27; see also Khurmuji 1380, p. 99.

236. Buckingham 1971, pp. 329-30.

RMM 1913	Fasa'i 1378	Motaharrizadeh 1381
18. -	-	Towfiq-abad
19. Jadeseh	Jades — 2.5 farsakh north-west	Jades
20. Chenar-e Shahijan	Chenar-e Shahijan - >5 farsakh north-west	Chenar-e Shahijan
21. Chukak	Chukak — 5.5 farsakh north	Chukak
22. Hoseyn-abad	Hoseyn-abad — 5 farsakh north-west	Hoseyn-abad
23. Khoda-abad	Khoda-abad — 3 farsakh north-west	Khoda-abad
24. Dariseh	Daris — 2 farsakh north-west	Daris
25. Dadan	Davan 2.5 farsakh north	Davan
26. Do-Siran	Do-Siran >7 farsakh north	Do-Siran
27. Deh-Dasht	Deh-Dasht 4 farsakh east	Deh-Dasht
28. Dekanat	Dikanak ? 4 farsakh north	Dikanak ?
29. Robat*	-	-
30. -	-	Zedestan
31. Sartabeh	Sartabeh — 6 farsakh east	Sartabeh
32. Sarhad-e Kalati	Sarhad-e Kalani — 7.5 farsakh north-east	Sarhad-e Kalani
33. Sa`d-abad	Sa`d-abad — 3.5 farsakh north-west	Sa`d-abad
34. Semghan	Somghan — 7 farsakh north	Somghan
35. Sayyed Naseri	Sayyed Nasiri -5 farsakh north-west	Sayyed Nasiri
36. Seyf-abad	Seyf-abad — 1.5 farsakh south-east	Seyf-abad
37. -	Shapur = district	Shapur
38. -	-	Shahkhosrow
39. -	-	Sadra-bad
40. `Abdu'i	`Abdu'i — 3 farsakh north-east	`Abdu'i
41. `Amu'i	`Amu'i — 4.5 farsakh north-west	`Amu'i
42. -	-	Famur
43. -	-	Fath-abad
44. Qal`eh-Sayyed	Qal`eh ye Sayyed — 1 farsakh west	Borj-e Sayyed Nasri
45. Kasseh-Kan	Kasseh-Kan — west	Kasseh-Kan
46. Kalani	Kalani - >3 farsakh north-east	Qal`eh-ye Kalati
47. Gaveh-gond	Gav-e Kashk — 3.5 farsakh north-east	Gav-e Kashk
48. -	Gorgi dan - 5 farsakh north	Gorgi dan
49. Kaman-keshi	Kaman-keshi - <1 farsakh south-east	Kaman-keshi
50. Kindeh-Nazari	Kindeh-Nazari — 5 farsakh north-east	Kindeh-Nazari
51. -	-	Mahvari
52. Moshtan	Moshtan — >1 farsakh south	Moshtan
53. Molleh-arreh	Molleh-arreh — 3 farsakh north	Molleh-arreh
54. Mowded-khvajeh	Mowded-khvajeh — 7 farsakh east	Mowded
55. Murdak	Murdak — 4.5 farsakh north	Murdak
56. Mehrenjan	Mehrenjan — 1.5 farsakh south	Mehrenjan
57. Minbadi	Meybadi - <6 farsakh east	Meybadi
58. -	-	Miyan-rud
59. Nowdan	Nowdan — 5 farsakh north	Nowdan

RMM 1913	Fasa'i 1378	Motaharrizadeh 1381
60. -	.	Nesf-e Niyan
61. -	.	Haft-pareh
62. Vark	Vark - 4.5 farsakh east	Vark
63. Yahleh	Vahleh = the same as Benaf, nr. 12	Yahleh
64. -	.	Boneh-ye Hajj Mirza ' Ali Akbar
65. -	.	Boneh-ye Hajj Sayyed ' Abed
66. -	.	Boneh-ye Hajj Sayyed Hoseyn

Source: RMM 23/1913, p. 27; Fasa'i 1378, vol. 2, pp. 1448-49; Kazeruni 1381, pp. 75-76. In 1911, the village of Davan (Davun) was farmed to the Parsi bankers Jamshidian. Administration Report 1911, p. 15. "Deris is a large village, with some 100 tufangchis, ruled by Derodar Rajab." Administration Report 1911, p. 16. * Robat, "a collection of huts and hovels, near which are two neatly-built stone forts, occupied by the families of Shah Hussein and Shah Kuchek, two Seyeds, chiefs of the village, who, I was told, claim and obtain exemption from taxation in consideration of their descent." Abbott 1857, p. 183.

The rural population lived in villages situated at elevated locations.[237] This was different in the past, for according to the twelfth century historian Ibn Balkhi, "the farms round about are populous, and their homesteads are not [mere cabins] like those of other hamlets in these parts, but are strongly built houses, well fortified, as a defence against the Shabankarah [Kurds], who are numerous throughout this district. Each farmstead here stands separate one from another, and they are not built together [in groups of villages]."[238] Despite living in villages in later centuries, by the twentieth century and most likely much earlier, most rural people made dwellings from a kind of reed called *lamban*, without doors and shapeless, and surrounded by hedges of sharp branches of the cedar tree.[239]

Water was, as elsewhere in Iran, the major constraint on agricultural yield. Traveling through the valley in 1824, Alexander noticed its important role. "Leaving the town (which, by the way, is one of the hottest in Persia), we marched along an excellent road, and constantly passed runs of water on the surface, and innumerable kanauts below it. The soil seemed to be uncommonly rich, and extensive fields of ripe gendoom, or wheat, were seen in every direction. The sides of the road were lined with the white caper."[240] Water was not the only enabling or disabling factor of agricultural production. Kinneir reported that "the crops in this valley are therefore in general abundant, but not infrequently destroyed by locusts."[241] If neither of these impediments interfered, the return from a given quantity of seed yielded at least ten fold.[242]

---

237. RMM 23/1913, p. 27; Abbott 1857, p. 181.

238. Ibn al-Balkhi 1912, p. 55.

239. Mostafavi 1978, p. 247; Abbott 1857, pp. 181, 183 ("mud houses and keppehs, or long cylindrical looking huts, built of branches, matting, and reeds"); Boehm 1904, p. 86.

240. Alexander 1826, p. 119

241. Kinneir 1973, p. 65; Abbott 1857, p. 180; Sirjani 1361, pp. 485, 540. It also happened that a hail storm or heavy rains destroyed the crops such as in April 1888 and September 1898. Sirjani 1361, pp. 311, 553, or lack of rain such as in March-April 1897. Ibid., p. 424.

242. Stirling 1991, pp. 23, 32-33 (up to fifty fold); Abbott 1857, p. 180 (if manured 30-40 fold).

Ibn Balkhi observed that "Their corn-lands entirely lack irrigation and depend on the rains."[243] That remained the case until recent times, for *seyfi* crops and vegetables (i.e. crops sown in summer and harvested in autumn) were irrigated by *qanat* water. All other crops were rain-fed.[244] The destruction that had laid the town of Kazerun in ruins in 1790 also had devastated much of its district's irrigation system, although not its main three *qanat*s. This is suggested by Rich, who observed that "The plain of Kauzeroon was formerly well cultivated, and there are remains of many water-courses."[245] Nevertheless, by that time things were looking better and demand for products was rising. This required irrigation, which mostly meant underground canals or *qanat*s. I write mostly, because "the different streams that descend from the adjoining hills are profitably used by the agricultural part of the population."[246] As irrigation was extensively used, this required a source of water that was secure. Consequently, "Several new one have been lately made in the Kauzeroon valley; and some notion may be formed of the value of such property, when it is understood that the small stream at Dalakee brings in a revenue of four thousand rupees a year; and that one cannaut lately opened by Kulb Allee Khan, governor of Kauzeroon, afford stream at least five or six times more considerable." It was used to irrigate a garden with "some of the finest orange trees, both bitter and sweet, shaddock, lime, and pomegranate trees."[247] Despite this investment, there was still a long way to go before better conditions could be achieved. According to Stirling in 1828, "The valley of Kazeroon is doubtless very fertile and would be more populous and more cultivated were there a better government. As it is grain is very dear, and what sells at almost eight pounds for the rupee, and everything else in proportion. It is astonishing how the people can exist and afford to purchase provisions."[248] Fortunately, over time the situation improved as indicated by higher agricultural production. Because of the limited use of *qanat*s in many southern part of Iran, Kazerun with its long-time tradition had experienced *qanat* builders, who in 1866, were even used in Behbahan.[249]

In the very fertile Kazerun plain the chief products cultivated around 1900 were grain, opium, tobacco and beans.[250] "Cultivated bits of grounds are fenced round with hedges of dried branches stuck into the ground, affording protection from wandering donkeys, mules, goats, and sheep."[251] Both men and women worked in most aspects and stages of agricultural production. "Women and girls-half naked under their dust-coloured rags- are at work among the golden grain."[252] The production of wheat and barley was, of course, vital for people's survival and, therefore, was a major crop. Although the plain often "looked parched and arid,"

---

243. Ibn al-Balkhi 1912, p. 55; Mustawfi 1919, p. 125.

244. Kazeruni 1381, p. 40; Pirzadeh 1343, vol. 2, p. 419.

245. Rich 1839, p. 213

246. Stirling 1991, p. 25.

247. Fraser 1984, p. 79.

248. Stirling 1991, p. 25

249. Fasa'i 1378, vol. 1, p. 828.

250. Administration Report 1911, Appendix II, p. 16.

251. Boehm 1904, p. 85.

252. Moore 1915, pp. 419-20. In the tenth century, much grain was produced in Kazerun. Schwarz 1993, vol. 1, p. 33.

in the right season there was much cultivation of wheat and barley.[253] At that time, the valley was a pleasure to behold, because not only grains were there to be seen. "All the plains are covered with corn, mingled with flowers; the valleys are refreshed by streams of water."[254] However, Houtum-Schindler reported that very little corn was produced in the valley of Kazerun, and, therefore, "bread made of the flour of acorns is a staple of food in many villages."[255] This contradicts the fact that apparently most of its taxes were paid in grain (see below). Moreover, according to Chick, "towards the Shahpur end are rice swamps, and a large amount of rice is imported to Kazerun from Shulistan and the Mamasenni district."[256]

Other crops that were cultivated in Kazerun district included cotton, according to Yaqut, which in light of the production of *kerbas*, a coarse cotton fabric, of which was much exported, seems logical. It was still cultivated in the nineteenth and twentieth century.[257] The cultivation of flax, oddly enough, is not mentioned at all as a crop after 1400, despite Kazerun's weaving output of linen (see above). Its dates were excellent, in particular the kind known as *jilan* or *jilandar*, which were cultivated nowhere else, according to Istakhri.[258]

In the fourteenth century Kazerun was a center of the fruit trade.[259] Therefore, it is odd that in later times the production of dates is implied, but never mentioned as crop of major importance. Perhaps this is due to the fact that it seems to have been a mostly urban cultivation.[260] The same holds true for fruit trees, which are almost exclusively mentioned as part of the urban context, although they were already part of the rural economy in the tenth century. Mustawfi mentions that "Oranges, shaddocks, lemons and all the fruits grow here."[261] Wild almonds which grew in the mountains were harvested and, like other fruits, exported.[262] Figs were sold strung up with wires in the form of animals, while beets were sold at one cent (*ochavo*) per pound. The lotus plant grew in abundance and its pulverized skin without its branches was used by dyers instead of gall-nuts, because it was cheaper.[263]

---

253. Fraser 1984, p. 79; Amanat 1983, p. 185; Lycklama 1873, vol. 3, p. 25. Good quality rice was also produced. Amanat 1983, p. 185; RMM 23/1913, p. 26; Houtum-Schindler 1911; Fasa'i 1378, vol. 2, p. 1431 (wheat, barley, rice, beans, grass peas, melons); Khurmuji 1380, p. 99 (grains, rice).

254. Johnson 1818, p. 49.

255. Houtum-Schindler 1911. They called acorn flour *kalg*. Fasa'i 1378, vol. 2, p. 1430. This is an indication of the people's poverty because you only ate acorn bread if you had no other choice, see Floor 2003, p. 148.

256. Administration Report 1911, Appendix II, p. 16.

257. Spuler 1952, p. 395, n. 19; Le Strange 1905, p. 267; Rivadeneyra 1880, vol. 3, p. 21 (in 1875, cotton was 15 riyals per *arroba*, a Spanish weight equal to 11.5 kg); Amanat 1983, p. 185; Houtum-Schindler 1911.

258. Schwarz 1935, vol. 2, p. 71; Le Strange 1905, p. 267; Mustawfi 1919, p. 125.

259. Mongolen 1985, p. 358.

260. Moore 1915, p. 419 (groves of date palms).

261. Schwarz 1993, vol. 1, p. 33 (it produces many fruits); RMM 23/1913, p. 26; Mustawfi 1919, p. 125. Rivadeneyra 1880, vol. 3, p. 21 (the price of attar was three *duros* (or 15 *pesetas*) per *cuartillo*, a Spanish measure equal to 0.5 liter; Fasa'i 1378, vol. 2, p. 1430.

262. Houtum-Schindler 1911.

263. Rivadeneyra 1880, vol. 3, p. 21.

In the Safavid period, tobacco was a new crop that was introduced about 1600. As a result, many villages between Kazerun and Bandar-e Rig cultivated tobacco.[264] The best opium was produced at Lenjan, near Isfahan, while others held that of Kazerun in great esteem.[265] "They have a great many Grapes and Melons here and make Wine that may be made use of."[266] Instead of wine, large quantities of raisins were produced by the village of Davan, which was situated at higher elevation.[267] Although wine is not mentioned anymore as an output in the nineteenth century, tobacco was; this, in fact, was Kazerun district's staple produce, the esteemed Shiraz tobacco.[268] This remained so for the rest of the century and the tobacco fields surrounded the town.[269]

A great part of the plain, lying between, is planted with tobacco of a coarse kind, called khooshka, of which, great quantities are annually sent from Bushehr, to Arabia, Egypt and Turkey, where it is sold under the name of Sheerauz tobacco, though of a very inferior quality to the latter. It is very cheap, and costs, at Kauzeroon, about a keroonee (ten pence) for a man of seven pounds."[270]

As an agricultural crop, opium was not a newcomer such as tobacco. However, before the 1860s, it had never been a major cash crop. In 1786, Francklin reported that near Kazerun "great quantities of opium are produced, but the Persians do not make this very valuable commodity an article of trade; I should imagine they did in former times, as the opium of Kazeroon is much spoken of in the East."[271] It was still produced in the 1840s and 1850s,[272] but still in small qantities. This changed when there was a growing demand for Persian opium. As a result, "Much more noteworthy is the encouragement recently given to the cultivation of the poppy." This meant that the government exempted poppy fields from the payment of taxes.[273] Opium continued to be cultivated to the 1930s, when peasants were seen weeding the plants, "not throwing the weeds away, but collecting them, to be dried for fodder."[274]

264. Thevenot 1971, vol. 2, p. 150. On the introduction of tobacco, see Willem Floor, "The Art of Smoking in Iran and other uses of tobacco," in *Iranian Studies* 35 (2002), pp. 47-86.

265. Olearius 1971, p. 597; Kaempfer 1976, pp. 642-47; Thevenot 1971, vol. 2, p. 126 (Shiraz); Chardin 1811, vol. 3, pp. 300-01.

266. Thevenot 1971, vol. 2, p. 149; Khurmuji 1380, p. 99.

267. Administration Report 1911, Appendix II, p. 16.

268. Rich 1839, p. 214; Amanat 1983, p. 185; Lycklama 1873, vol. 3, p. 25; Curzon 1892, vol. 2, 205; Houtum-Schindler 1911.

269. Alexander 1826, p. 119; de Windt 1891, p. 206; RMM 23/1913, p. 26; Fasa'i 1378, vol. 2, p. 1431; Khurmuji 1380, p. 99.

270. Binning 1857, vol. 1, pp. 176-77.

271. Francklin 1976, p. 256.

272. Amanat 1983, p. 116; Abbott 1857, p. 184 (in 1850, the price was 8 *tuman*s per 10.5 lbs); Rivadeneyra 1880, vol. 3, p. 21; Stirling 1991, p. 32 (not irrigated).

273. Stack 1882, vol. 1, p. 37-38; Fasa'i 1378, vol. 2, p. 874; Khurmuji 1380, p. 99; Appendix 3.2 to this chapter. On opium production in general, see Floor 2003.

274. Merrit-Hawkes 1935, p. 41; Curzon 1892, vol. 2, 205 ff; Moore 1915, p. 419; RMM 23/1913,

Other products that farmers marketed were honey and wax, which were cheap in Kazerun in the twelfth century.[275] It was still a product of the valley of Kazerun in the 1860s, when the Dutch traveler Lycklama remarked that the most sought after agricultural product of Kazerun was not grain or tobacco, but its honey that had an exquisite taste, which he ascribed to the presence of the orange trees. Both honey and wax were exported to Java.[276] Peasant also had flocks of sheep and goats, which they kept for their milk, skins and wool. Sheep's wool was generally used for carpet manufacturing, while goat wool was turned into ropes and coarse cloth.[277] Many of these products were exported to Bushehr via a road passing through the villages of Guire [?] and Pahmur.[278]

As noted above, peasants in the Kazerun valley were poor, having to eat acorn bread. In addition, they seem to have been oppressed by their landlords, a situation that was endemic in Iran.[279] In mid-August 1890, peasants from Shahchini and Bahmanyari fled from Ja`far Qoli Khan and went to Kazerun. At 12 km from the town the landlord with 60 horsemen caught up with them and took all their possessions, both in money and in kind. He further wounded seven of them and took them shackled with him. During the fracass Ja`far Qoli Khan's brother was killed. The remaining peasants and some wounded ones sought refuge in the Imamzadeh.[280] How representative this type of happening was is unclear. According to Motahharizadeh, Naser-e Divan displayed a more benevolent attitude to the people of Kazerun, *even* towards his peasants. The fact that he stresses this point implies that such an attitude was exceptional.[281]

Transhumant Population

An aspect often ignored in urban studies is the important role that the transhumant or nomadic population played in providing market towns with a fair share of its trade goods and means of transportation. In addition, this part of the rural population played an important role in being responsible for violence in the area or for providing protection against it, for "the nomads are warlike."[282]

---

p. 26; Houtum-Schindler 1911.

275.   Ibn al-Balkhi 1912, p. 51.

276.   Lycklama 1873, vol. 3, p. 25; Rivadeneyra 1880, vol. 3, p. 21.

277.   Stirling 1991, p. 33 (two to four sheep yielded 8-10 pounds of long-fiber wool per year).

278.   Dupré 1819, vol. 2, p. 59.

279.   On this issue, see Lambton 1953 and Floor 2003.

280.   `Abbasi and Badi`i 1372, p. 49. The usual place to seek *bast* or sanctuary was in the bazaar quarter (Kazeruni 1381, p. 27), but the new mosque, imamzadeh, and telegraph office were also used as such. Motahharizadeh 1383, p. 10.

281.   Motahharizadeh 1383, p. 93, doc. 113 (my italics). For landlord behavior towards their peasants including forced return to the land, see Floor 2003.

282.   Stirling 1991, p. 25.

Before the Islamic era the transhumant population probably did not play such an important role in the economy of Iran as it did under Islamic rule. A fact is that after the year 1000 the Kazerun valley was the target of the Shabankareh Kurds, who alternatively ruled or plundered it. In the thirteenth century the Karzuvi Kurds dominated the Kazerun district.[283] With the advent of the Safavids in the sixteenth century, first the Dhu'l-Qadrs and after 1550 the Afshar tribe dominated life in Kazerun. In 1696, Kazerun was a center for recruiting troops as well as for collecting provisions for an invasion army of Muscat.[284] Many of the tribes in and adjacent to the Kazerun valley were among the main supporters of Karim Khan Zand.[285]

The following is a list of the different tribes who reside in the neighbourhood of Kazeroon.

Pharsee Maidoon[286] us esteemd the most wealthy tribe; its members are rich in cattle and individually in easy circumstances. They are likewise industrious and far the most well-behaved. Their number is from five to six thousand, and they can muster from two to two thousand five hundred fighting men – foot and horse. They own Mohamad Ali Khan for their chief, who constantly resides at Sheeraz. He has the title of *Eelkhany*

Mymun Seinee. The chief of this tribe is Mahomed Ruza Khan, who is in the possession of the celebrated fill fort Kalee Saffeed [*qal'eh-ye safid*], which has often been a thorn in the side of the Persian Kings. ... Mahomed Ruza Khan has several fine sons, of whom Shibass Khan and Abdool-Ruza Khan are the most promising. Walee Khan, who may be considered a rebel to the Government, lately thought proper to attack and kill Iouph [?] Khan the Vuzier of the Prince of Sheeraz, in a manner the most outrageous and perfidious. This compelled him to keep his sword unsheathed, and he now plunders such towns and villages to which his avarice and ambition lead him, being willing perhaps not to attract too much the notice of the Government by boldly stepping forward and declaring he aims at independence, as such conduct would perhaps draw upon him the full regard and energy of the King and his ministers, whom it is more easy to cajole, and gradually to dispossess of his territories and the riche sof his subjects than to meet openly in the field.

Walee Khan may be considered, as the effective head of the tribe, as possessingh a greater name and more vigour than Mahomed Ruza. The latter has put on the garb of displeasure in consequence of the culpability of his conduct, but this disguise is merely intended to deceive the government. Walee Khan is moreover nearly allied Mahomed Ruza Khan; he married his daughter and has several children by her, and his son Namdar Khan is spoken of in high terms. The members of this tribe are rated at ten thousand, but this estimate is probably too low is 10,000, as they are said to be able to bring in the field from six to seven thousand foot and from a thousand to fifteen hundred horse. All the other *sirdars* besides Mahomed Ruza Khan and Walee Khan and their children

283. Aigle 2005, p. 78.

284. Aubin 1972, pp. 47, 79.

285. Monteith 1857, p. 116.

286. Farsi Madan Qashqa'is, who lived near Kamarej. In 1875, they raided Khesht, and, after having taken booty, they lost it when pursued. Sirjani 1361, p. 30.

have been cut off or have died. ... They have no occupation except that of spoilage and plundering their neighbors, and carrying on feuds for the purpose of deriving advantage from the sacking of villages and supplying members with the means of subsistence.

Bakhtiaree. This tribe is wealthy and numerous; its members are stated at ten thousand, of whom three or four thousand horse and two thousand foot [are mustered]. The Sardar of this tribe is Assud Khan, a man much much esteemed He has a son named Hussain Khan.

Nanik Ally. This is another large tribe consisting of from six to seven thousand. It is both rich and powerful; it can bring into the field from one thousand to fifteen hundred foot, and three thousand horsemen. The names of the principal chiefs are: Nadir Klee Khan; Hussain Khan; Khan Kolee Khan; Alum Moored Khan; Khoda Moormut Khan; Golam Ruza Khan, Meer Ally Khan; Shumshair Khan; Surman Khan and Meera Khan.[287]

There are also many other tribes of which Stirling only mentioned the following:

Table 3.4: The tribes inhabiting the Kazerun district in 1828

Elyott tribes	No. of men	Soldiers	Name of the chiefs
Elyott Pyaundee	1,000	500	Kaid Jemshaud, Kaid Khoduwuree, Kaid Gemail
Elyott [?] Lema Buzoorgee	2,000	700	Hashim Khan, Kurreh Khan
Ardeh Sheerie	1,500	700	Sheerie Khan, Alikhan
Ahmedee & Mahmodee	900	400	Kaid Khoda Kerah
Bukree	900	600	Kaid Hubeeb
Byboor	6,000	4,000	Mirza Munshoor Khan
.	1,200	500 *	Moolah Hasim Khan
Keroonee	3,000	1,200	Aubeed Khan
Suroor	1,200	600	Aubed Khan, Ali Khan & Kaid Kurz Ully
.	3,000	900	Afraushar Khan
Zungunee	2,200	1,000	Dushtee Khan
Saolee	2,200	500	Moolah Hussain Khan
Geeray	1,700	600	Kaid Abdool Kaseem Khan
Total	26,800	12,200	

* The Journal has the figures 12,000 and 6,000 respectively for the size of this tribe. This is not only too large when compared with the other figures given, but does not reconcile with the cumulative figure given at the bottom of Stirling's table. I have therefore corrected the error.

Source: Stirling 1991, p. 28.

The Qashqa'i tribe dominated in the district. In particular, the Farsi Madan (Kamarej area) and the Kashkuli (Shapur area) sections of the Qashqa'i tribe operated in the Kazerun area.[288] However, there were still tribes of Kurdish origin as well (e.g., Zanganeh). Rich fur-

287. Stirling 1991, p. 27.

288. Mokhber al-Saltaneh called Kazerun the *mahall-e tama`-e Qashqa'i* (coveted place of the Qashqa'is). Ranjbar 1389, p. 239, doc. 296 (28 May 1913).

ther noted that in 1821, he met a few families in "the Teng-e Turkoom transporting their effects on cows, which is almost a characteristic of Koord."[289] In 1880, the Kashkulis were under Najafqoli Khan, `Abdollah Beg and Khezr Beg and numbered 2,000 families. The Darashuris under Hajji Baba Khan also numbered 2,000 families, while the Farsi Madan were under Ja`farqoli Khan, Mohammad Taher Khan, Hasan Khan and Felamerz Khan numbered 2,000 families as well.[290]

Like tribes elsewhere in Iran, these transhumant groups moved each year between their summer and winter quarters with their herds of sheep, goat, donkeys, horses, mules, and cows. For example, the Qashqa'i tribe wintered in the warmer regions near Firuzabad, Kazerun, Jerreh, and Farashband.[291] It seems that they were not much engaged in agricultural activities, although it is quite likely that tribal leaders owned villages in their migration zone. The women of the Lali tribe that Stirling visited prepared cakes, generally from half barley and half wheat flour, rather than from acorn flour, which was the common fare of tribes elsewhere as well as the peasants of Kazerun. Apart from their husbandry activities producing dairy products, wool and skins, probably their most remunerative activity was that of horse and mule breeding. Further, they further made "cheese, ghee, curds and sour milk daily." The women also made carpets, felt covers (namads), and worsted fabrics.[292]

These activities were common to all transhumant groups, but it would seem that given the good pasturage in the Kazerun area, it was possible to raise a considerable number of horses and mules. In 1875, MacGregor noted that "There is very excellent grazing in this valley, and a considerable number of excellent mules and Galloways are bred in it, in fact it is the home of most of the muleteers round." At that time, the price for mule varied between 80 to 150 rupees and 3,000 to 4,000 might be obtained.[293] Each year, mules, when one or more years old, were brought for sale to Kazerun, many of which were exported.[294] To breed mules, you needed donkeys and horses, which the transhumant groups also raised and sold in Kazerun. As discussed above, many horses were reared in the area, which perhaps were not the superior kind, but as Col. Pelly put it, they were "good serviceable horses."[295] The breeding and trading of horses and mules was badly hurt after 1907, because of disturbances and fights among and between tribal groups. By 1913, the scarcity of mules was such that the British Residency in Bushehr commented that because no mules were bred anymore in Iran that it would take years to bring back production to its old level. However, Iran had more pressing needs and probably would not be able to afford the luxury of mule breeding, while it was further expected that motorized traffic would replace pack animals. Therefore, the British Residency at Bushehr rightly raised the question whether it was really worthwhile to start

---

289. Rich 1839, p. 212.

290. Administration Report 1879-80, p. 23. For a detailed overview of the tribal groups, their chiefs, strengths and activities around 1914, see Wilson 1916.

291. Sirjani 1361, p. 489; see also Akhgar 1366, pp. 119-21.

292. For a description of these activities in the Kazerun area, see Stirling 1991, pp. 29-30; in general, see Floor 2003, chapter eight.

293. Mac Gregor 1879, vol. 1, pp. 20-21 (drawing of Kazerun).

294. Pelly 1865 b, p. 147.

295. Stirling 1991, p. 25; Pelly 1865 b, p. 147.

mule breeding again. It goes without saying that this development hurt the financial position of the tribes.[296]

Thus, the tribal population played a vital role in providing Kazerun with its provisions and part of its export products, and thus a part of the town's wealth. Assessing the supply situation of Kazerun in 1863, Col. Pelly concluded, "Fruit and supplies, whether grain or meat, can be procured at Kauzeroon in good quantity, but these could not be depended on by a force entering Persia, unless the tribes were for you."[297] This gave the transhumant population, or rather its leaders, considerable leverage in dealing with the town. Stirling and others understood this, because although in terms of trade he considered Kazerun of no importance, he opined:

> This town may nevertheless be considered as the chief city in these parts, and as there are several tribes of the Elyotts [Iliyat or tribes] who reside in the neighbourhood, it deserves some attention in consequence.[298]

GOVERNORS OF KAZERUN

It is not known who governed Kazerun prior to the Safavid period, when, for the first time, we have data on governors in charge of this jurisdiction. However, it may be assumed that also under earlier dynasties, Kazerun was under a governor or *hakem* or some other government official, because around 1000 there was a Zoroastrian governor, named Khurshid. We may assume that he was succeeded by other governors, as this was the usual method of administrating towns such as Kazerun during that period as well as later. The governor's tasks were threefold: (a) maintenance of law and order: (b) the provision of public services; and (c) revenue collection necessary to carry out the first two tasks.

(a) The maintenance of law and order

As far as security in the town of Kazerun was concerned the governor relied on local officials such as the *kalantar*, who was in charge of the entire town, and who was assisted by the chiefs of the four main quarters (*kadkhoda*). They were responsible not only for keeping law and order in the town, but also for the collection of the urban taxes.[299] However, in practice, according to Stirling, "there is no police establishment whatever in the town, every man is left to

---

296. Administration Report 1913, p. 33. Indeed, 20 years later most goods were transported by lorries.

297. Pelly 1865 b, p. 148; see also Monteith 1857, p. 116.

298. Stirling 1991, p. 25; de Windt 1891, p. 206 ("Kazeroon is, next to Shiraz, the most important place in the province of Fars.") However, Abbott 1857, p. 184, reported in 1850 that the governor "considered Jehrum the second town in Fars."

299. Motahharizadeh 1383, p. 12.

protect his own house and premises the best way he may. He can expect no help either from the government or his neighbours. The Prince when present, it is true, now and then amuses himself by amputating the hands and ears of robbers, who are caught, but as there exists no establishment for catching thieves, such occurrences must be very infrequent."[300] This situation may explain why the houses of Kazerun looked like forts and why there were so many fortified towers and houses in its rural area (see above).

We do not know since when this local system was in place in Kazerun, but we may assume that it was a system with a long historical pedigree.[301] De Thevenot, in 1665, is the first who refers to the *kalantar* of Kazerun. He reported that Kazerun:

> is Commanded by a *Kelontar*. ... Here they would have seized our Mules to carry Provisions for the King to *Ispahan*, but the Reverend Father Provincial, going to wait upon the *Kelontar* to represent to him that we were *Franks*; so soon as the *Kelontar* saw him, he ordered that our Mules should not be taken, because we were strangers.[302]

The *kalantar*s, just like the *kadkhoda*s, were selected from among the notables of the town quarters. The function was often hereditary. For example, Khvajeh Yusof, the Naser-e Divan's grandfather, was the chief (*kadkhoda*) of Gonbad quarter. He was succeeded in this post by his son Khvajeh Hasan ʿAli, who made such an impression on his contemporaries that at the end of the nineteenth century he became *kalantar*. When he died in about 1903, he was succeeded by his son Khvajeh Ebrahim, the brother of Khvajeh ʿAbdollah (Naser-e Divan). The latter succeeded his brother as *kalantar* of Kazerun in 1908.[303] By the end of 1919, a beginning was made to establish a modern police force (*nazmiyeh*) in Kazerun.[304]

Because the valley of Kazerun sometimes was an unsafe place, the governor of Kazerun employed *tofangchi*s to take action against raiders and robbers as well as to try and impose his will on certain sections of the town's people.[305] Sometimes, the governor had to retreat when the robbers were more numerous than his own force.[306] When the governor was also a tribal chief, as was the case with the Afshar governors (see above) he would use his own tribesmen to enforce law and order. In 1816, the governor of Kazerun maintained "some show of consequence, and has a considerable armed retinue, both horse and foot."[307] In 1841, the governor was Mohammad Hasan Khan who hailed from Tabriz. He was a general (*sartip*) with "one

---

300. Stirling 1991, p. 34.

301. On the functions of the *kalantar* and *kadkhoda*, see Floor 1992 a and Ibid., 1992 b, available at http://www.iranica.com.

302. Thevenot 1971, vol. 2, p. 149.

303. Motahharizadeh 1383, p. 13. Hajj Aqa Babay was *kalantar* of Kazerun in 1298/1881. Sirjani 1361, p. 152.

304. Mafi and Saʿvandiyan 1366, vol. 3, pp. 858, 867-68.

305. Abbott 1857, p. 184; Sirjani 1361, p. 152 (when a merchant was robbed the governor arrested the thief).

306. Sirjani 1361, pp. 34-35.

307. Johnson 1818, pp. 47-48; Sirjani 1361, pp. 14, 21-22.

regiment of infantry of 400 men from Faraghun, Kesoz, and Meloir, with 2 fieldpieces and 40-50 well-appointed cavalry."[308] In 1874, there was still a *sartip* in Kazerun, who was "in charge of the Kazeroon division. This officer, we were informed, is paid by the Persian government for maintaining five hundred mounted guards for protecting the road and keeping order, but nevertheless only employs about thirty poorly appointed horsemen for that nominal purpose."[309] For the same reason, the governor had established so-called road-guards post along the road. Between Daleki and Dasht-e Arzhan, basically the Kazerun jurisdiction along the commercial road, these were to be found at the following locations:

> Sar-e Kotal-e Malu, Daghuni, Ja`farjun, Konar-e Takhteh, Durah Khesht, Chorum, Kotal-e Kamarej, Karavansara-ye Hakim-bashi, Tang-e Torkan, Karavansara-ye Rahdar, Deris, Qahvahkhaneh, Bagh-e Sheikh Hajji, Bagh-e Sayyed Mohammad, Kazerun, Qal`eh-ye Sho`a` al-Saltaneh, Pol-e Abgineh, Zir-e Kotal-e Dokhtar, `Abu'i, Dasht-e Baram, Karavansara-ye Miyan-e Kotal, Sarchang, Qal`eh-ye Moshiri, and Borj-e Sineh-ye safid.[310]

The governor also needed armed men to collect the revenue from tribal leaders and big landowners. In 1828,

> The prince [Timur Mirza] had left to Kist because Jamal Khan had not paid his taxes. He had about 100 men, who were not very willing to go. Before they left they had demonstrated because they had no money and had not received their wages and could not take to the field. He said that provisions would be made. In total he has 100 horse and 100 foot, but other chiefs come to assist him with their men. The prince left no protection at Kazeroon despite the proximity of Vali Khan, the terror of travelers and carried out depredations as far as Shiraz. He had offered his services if he would receive a robe of honor but the prince refused.[311]

(b) The provision of public services.

Not much is known about this subject beyond a few facts (see also the section 'water' above). For example, Imam Qoli Khan, the Safavid governor-general of Fars built a parapet on the dangerous mountain road from Kazerun-Shiraz.[312] Kalb `Ali Khan, the governor of Kazerun in 1786, allotted a supply of water to a piece of land just outside town, to irrigate the Bagh-e

---

308. De Bode 1845, vol. 1, p. 205. See also, the suppression of Vali Khan Mamasani by Timur Mirza.

309. Waters 1876, pp. 196-97 (he was indeed unable to recuperate goods stolen from the British party nor find the robbers who had shot and wounded Capt. Napier and some of his suite.)

310. Motahharizadeh 1383, p. 16, n. 26. On the institution of road-guards, see Floor 1998, pp. 384f and Emerson and Floor 1971.

311. Stirling 1991, pp. 23-24.

312. Le Bruyn 1737, vol. 2, p. 67; Tavernier 1930, pp. 163, 299, 307, 324-5 (private sector); Thevenot 1971, vol. 2, p. 134; Chardin 1811, vol. 8, pp. 498-9. For its existence in 1786, see Francklin 1976, p. 47.

Nazar, a garden with "some of the finest orange trees, both bitter and sweet, shaddock, lime, and pomegranate trees."[313] Another governor, Imam Qoli Khan, constructed the pleasure house in the Bagh-e Nazar, a garden that was much appreciated by the Kazerunis, who were proud of it.[314] In addition to the Indian-European Telegraph Department office, there also was a Persian telegraph office as well as a post office, which in 1896 was under Mirza Moham-mad ʿAli.[315]

(c) The revenue collection

It is not exactly known what the precise jurisdiction of the governorship of Kazerun was, also because it changed over time (see above). When the governor-general of Fars, Hoseyn ʿAli Mirza assigned Kazerun as source of income to one of his wives, Timur Mirza one of her sons, became its governor.[316] However, in this case it seems that his jurisdiction was much larger than of governor of Kazerun before and after him. In 1828, according to Stirling:

> The principality of Kazeroon has the following dependencies: Kunor Tukhta, the chief of whom is Roshun Khan; Delakee, the chief of which is Mokum Khan; Barrusjoon, the chief of which is Selim Khan; Thungistan, the chief of which is Mahomed Khan; and Khist of which is Jemal Khan. These, together with the villages around Kazeroon, yield an annual revenue of 41,000 toomans in the following proportions:

The villages around Kazeroon	20,000
The villages of Barrusjoon under Selim Khan	3,000
The villages under Roshun Khan at Kunor Tukhta	3,000
The villages of Khist under Jemal Khan	8,000
The villages of Thungistan under Mahomed Khan	5,000
The villages of Delakee under Mokun Khan	2,000

> The above sums include everything in them, all *abwalis* [water dues from irrigated lands], customs and duties, which the exception of occasional presents when in the presence of the Prince, which are supposed to be regulated by some unknown customs which have hitherto prevailed. Each of these districts may be considered as the most considerable and wealthy of the local proprietors of the

313. Fraser 1984, p. 79. "The governor's garden, to the left, is tastily planted with orange trees and cypresses, and is watered by a machine worked by oxen." Price 1832, p. 9.

314. Buckingham 1971, p. 326.

315. Sadid al-Saltaneh 1362, p. 37.

316. Fasa'i 1378, vol. 1, p. 754.

land; these estates from time immemorial have been in the possession of their families.[317]

However, in the second half of the nineteenth century, Kazerun's jurisdiction extended from the Arzhan plain to the Khesht *sarhadd*. It included twenty villages, except for Davan, which belonged to Mo'tamad al-Dowleh, the rest were in the hands of Shirazis. Its taxes were recorded as some 10,000 odd *tuman*s.[318] This means that this jurisdiction was considerably reduced in size. The taxes of Kazerun in 1821, when it was still held by Afshar khans, amounted to 20,000 *tuman*s just as under Timur Mirza a few years later, an increase compared with 1808 when the annual tax burden was 8,000 *tuman*s.[319] Around 1850, "the *maliyat* or annual revenue of this town and all the lands attached to it, amounts to 18,000 tomans."[320] Pelly found that in 1863, "The district of Kauzeroon pays a lump sum of some 25,000 tomans.[321] This indicates that the reduction in size of the Kazerun jurisdiction must have taken place much later. In 1875, the Spanish traveler Rivadeneyra reported the taxes to be 12,000 *tuman*s.[322] In mid-June 1882, most of the people of Kazerun fled, because of a hundred percent increase in taxes.[323] This must have been an incidental and short-lived increase, because the amount of 10,000 *tuman*s was still paid by Kazerun in 1908, according to Kazeruni.[324] However, in 1912, according to a report by the government of Iran, Kazerun's revenues amounted to 29,147 *tuman*s, which is more in the line with the trend.[325] The tax on crops traditionally was 10% ('*oshr*), although the actual rate was higher. The rate on *khaleseh* land (crown land) was 11% and on *arbabi* land (private land) 22%.[326] Morier reported that in 1812 he asked a peasant near Kazerun "what he paid yearly to the government; in the way of tribute or tax; 'Yearly?,' said he, 'why we pay monthly, and frequently twice a month'- 'And upon what objects are the taxes levied?'- 'Upon what we possess,' added he; 'and when they can find nothing else to tax they take our children.'"[327] The agricultural revenues were collected in the same manner as elsewhere in Iran.

---

317. Stirling 1991, pp. 22-23.

318. Kazeruni 1381, p. 40.

319. Rich 1839, p. 214. Of this amount 100 *tuman*s was contributed by the capitation tax paid by the Jews. Dupré 1819, vol. 2, p. 22.

320. Binning 1857, vol. 1, p. 177.

321. Pelly 1865 b, p. 147.

322. Rivadeneyra 1880, p. 22.

323. Sirjani 1361, p. 164.

324. Kazeruni 1381, p. 40. This book was printed in 1909.

325. RMM 23/1913, p. 27. Most of these taxes were paid in kind, some 700,000 lbs. of grain. Administration Report 1911, Appendix II, p. 15.

326. Motahharizadeh 1383, pp. 109-110 (doc. 5) (Naser-e Divan was then [acting?] governor). On the level and manner of the collecting of agricultural taxes in Iran, see Floor 1999a.

327. Morier 1818, p. 52. See also Dupré 1819, vol. 2, p. 23, who asked the governor's secretary what the country's products were. He replied: "We have everything, save money, because the king takes care of that by taking it from us."

At Kazeroon and the neighbourhood the rent of the government is levied in kind and not in money. The government is always at the expense of transportation to its own granaries where it is disposed of. The assessment is made by a *zabita* [a tax official who assesses the land tax dues] who measures the quantity of the land in the possession of each individual. The *zabita* is paid by the government and is an officer employed by it for this purpose, and levying the quantity of produce and superintending the interests of the government whenever the corn [i.e., grain] is prepared and separated from the husk.[328]

For the collection of urban taxes, mostly from traders and craftsmen, the governor relied on the *kalantar* and *kadkhoda*s. The guilds (*asnaf*) of Kazerun paid one *qran* and seven *shahi*s per *tuman*, presumably of their income, while the muleteers paid a tax known as *sar-qateri*. In 1912, the central government transferred the task of tax collection to the newly created Finance Department (*edareh-ye maliyat*). This department was led by Mirza ʿAbbas Khan and he, together with Naser-e Divan, as *kalantar* and member of the Finance Department, was responsible for the revenue collection. However, the former was killed during the fight that broke out between Naser-e Divan and the gendarmerie in 1914. As a result, Naser-e Divan had to flee from Kazerun and for a few months no taxes were collected. After a few months, when the situation in Kazerun had quieted down Naser-e Divan was allowed to return on condition that he stayed in his house and did not interfere in government affairs. When later in 1915, the state of military government in Kazerun was discontinued the civilian governor Nazem al-Molk appointed Naser-e Divan once again to collect the taxes as member of the Finance Department. It was on an earlier occasion that the governor-general of Fars, Nezam al-Saltaneh, awarded Khvajeh ʿAbdollah the title of Naser-e Divan, because of his collaboration.[329] In 1922 a new fiscal system and organization was introduced, which, among other things, meant the abolition of the payment of *darughegi*.[330]

---

328. Stirling 1991, p. 23. The taxes of the village of Buranjan, e.g., was entirely paid in dried figs, walnuts, almonds, grape syrup, raisins, pomegranates, dried apricots, and wild almonds (*aluk* or *bekhrak*). Fasa'i 1378, vol. 2, p. 1340; see also Motahharizadeh 1383, p. 179 (doc. 113).

329. Motahharizadeh 1383, pp. 96, 110.

330. Motahharizadeh 1383, pp. 178-79 (doc. 112).

HISTORY OF KAZERUN

Until 1500

The conquest of Fars by the Arab invaders was not easy and opposition was fierce, and even after the conquest there were uprisings. In 694-95 a Moslem force was annihilated at Kazerun, which was the scene of three-year battle between the Khavarej and Mohlab.[331] But the Arabs were able to impose their will in the end. Later, fights and battles also occurred, but now these were fought between groups that were (nominally) Moslem. In 934, the Buyid ruler Rokn al-Dowleh occupied the Kazerun district.[332] In 1108, Kazerun was sacked and plundered, while in 1113 it was the scene of war again.[333] At the end of the twelfth century, taking advantage of Seljuq weakness, the Shabankareh Kurds ravaged Fars, in particular the Kazerun district. The Seljuqs then took steps to repair the damage and develop Kazerun.[334] In 1262-63, Kazerun was the scene of a fight between Atabeg Seljuq and the Mongol general Altaju.[335] Altaju killed many of the Atabeg's followers in Kazerun as well as its inhabitants. Atabeg Saljuq had sought refuge at the tomb of Morshed al-Din Abu Eshaq al-Kazeruni. He allegedly threw a stone onto the sheikh's tomb to get his intercession, but this did not have the desired result.[336] In 1300, Chaghatay attackers penetrated as far as Kazerun, which they destroyed and plundered, taking the herds from the fields.[337]

On 17 January 1343, there were fights in Shiraz between partisans of Yagha-Basti, a Chupanid outsider and Sheikh Abu Eshaq, a former Injuid governor with local roots. The latter was supported by part of the notables of Shiraz and their followers. After a few days of battle the partisans of Abu Eshaq went to Kazerun to seek help. Its religious authority was Amin al-Din al-Balyani, a disciple of Morshed al-Din Abu Eshaq al-Kazeruni. Balyani was member of the ruling Inju family, and given his spiritual role, the Kazerunis supported the Injuids. Amir Deylam Shah came to Kazerun with some adherents and attacked the palace of the Atabegs, where Yaghi-Basti had made his residence, and forced him to flee and thus, the region remained in the hands of Sheikh Abu Eshaq.[338]

---

331. Spuler 1952, pp. 16, 22; Fasa'i 1378, vol. 1, p. 189.

332. Spuler 1952, p. 91; Fasa'i 1378, vol. 1, p. 216.

333. Fasa'i 1378, vol. 1, pp. 238, 240.

334. Aigle 2005, p. 98f.

335. Spuler 1985, p. 120, Fasa'i 1378, vol. 1, pp. 265-66.

336. Aigle 2005, p. 117.

337. Spuler 1985, p. 89; Fasa'i 1378, vol. 1, p. 285.

338. Aigle 2005, pp. 179-80.

After 1500: Safavid – Qajar period

In 1503, Kazerun was once again the staging area for troops, when Soltan Morad entered the town just before his flight to Baghdad. He was followed by Safavid forces in 1504, who killed all the preachers of Kazerun, because they were Sunni. Kachal Beg was nominated head of the tribes there.[339] From the Safavid conquest of Kazerun in about 1504 until 1548, the governorship was held by members of the Dhu'l-Qadr tribe, more in particular by Elyas Beg and his descendants. Members of the same tribe also held the function of governor-general of Fars as well as of other governorships.[340] For unknown reasons, the Dhu'l-Qadrs lost control of the governorship of Kazerun. It may have been due to the fact that in 1548 Elqas Mirza penetrated Iran as far as Kazerun and besieged the brother of the governor of Kazerun in nearby Qal`eh-ye Safid.[341] Whatever the reason, from 1548 until 1834, or for 286 years, the governorship of Kazerun was held by Khans of the Afshar tribe (see Table 3.5), be it with some interruptions. In a Safavid geography text from about 1680, the town is therefore listed as Kazerun-e Afshar.[342] The first of the Afshar tribe who held this function was Kepek Soltan Afshar, who became governor in 1548. The post seems to have been held by members of one family, at least since about 1620, when Khvajeh Pir Budaq Afshar was appointed by Shah `Abbas I. He was succeeded by his son Khvajeh Pir Vali, and then by Khvajeh Hoseyn `Ali. He governed probably around 1660.[343] At that time, de Thevenot visited Kazerun and reported "it depends on the *Vizir* of *Schiras*."[344] This does not mean that there was no governor of Kazerun, but rather that the province of Fars was not governed any more by a governor-general (*begler-begi*), from whom the lower-ranking governors in his province depended, but by a royal vizier. This situation had come into being in 1632.[345] The governors in Fars province, like the one of Kazerun, were his subordinates and that is what de Thevenot meant.

In the aftermath of the fall of Isfahan and the Safavid dynasty in October 1722, riflemen (*tofangchis*) of Semghan (a village in Kazerun's jurisdiction) and other Sunnis from Fars supported the invading Afghans to respectively take Shiraz in 1723 and, in 1729, defend Shiraz and Fars against the returning Safavids.[346] During the reign of Nader Shah (r. 1736-1747), Khesht was separated from Kazerun.[347] At that time Khvajeh Hoseyn `Ali was governor of Kazerun. He had two sons: Khvajeh Hosam al-Din and Khvajeh Hoseyn `Ali, the former governed after his father, and then later appointed his younger brother as his deputy, when he went to Isfahan. Apparently the situation in Kazerun was unsettled at that time, because at one time there were rebels in the bazaar quarter, who invited Khvajeh Hoseyn `Ali for a

---

339. Qomi 1359, vol. 1, pp. 76, 80; Nasiri 2008, p. 214.

340. Nasiri 2008, p. 214.

341. Fasa'i 1378, vol. 1, p. 401.

342. Mostowfi 1989, p. 345.

343. Fasa'i 1378, vol. 2, p. 1440.

344. Thevenot 1971, vol. 2, p. 149; Kazeruni 1381, p. 44.

345. Naseri 2008, p. 280.

346. Fasa'i 1378, vol. 1, pp. 502, 511.

347. Fasa'i 1378, vol. 1, p. 586.

bridal party. When he entered the house he saw that the men had formed a circle and in the middle a group of men with bare swords were playing the sword game. The men in the circle did not allow Khvajeh Hoseyn 'Ali to pass and the sword players then hacked him to pieces. When his older brother heard this he rode from Isfahan to Kazerun with some men and killed many in the rebellious quarter. He then regretted his action and deeded some farms as an endowment to maintain Koran readers to read the Koran for the spiritual rewards of the bazaar quarter people; he also gave the survivors money, clothes, and food. Some of the endowments were still extant in about 1900. Later he built a madraseh, and endowed it with many thousands of books, some villages and farms. Two water mills in the center of Kazerun were also among his good deeds. He then went to Mecca and his brother's son Khvajeh Mohammad Reza b. Khvajeh Hoseyn 'Ali became governor around 1734. He was succeeded by Khvajeh Abu'l-Hasan the sister's son of Mohammad Reza. After him, the post was held by Khvajeh 'Ali Qoli for many years, who received the title of Khan in 1149/1736. [348]

After the fall of Nader Shah in 1747 and the dissolution of the Afsharid state under his successors, one of the contenders for power, 'Ali Mardan Khan, plundered Kazerun in 1753 before being stopped at Khesht by the riflemen of Khesht and Abdu'i, as a result of which he lost all his booty. In 1754, his former partner, Karim Khan Zand, set up his headquarters at Kazerun, being on the run from another contender for power, Azad Khan Afghan, because its people under 'Ali Qoli Khan Kazeruni supported him. Learning of the approach of Ahmad Khan, 'Ali Qoli Khan abandoned Kazerun and went to Fort Pa'uskan and joined Karim Khan at Khesht. Karim Khan Zand received additional support from the coastal areas. Azad Khan's troops advanced under Fath 'Ali Khan and in mid-September 1754 massacred the remaining inhabitants of Kazerun for having sheltered the Zands. But Azad Khan was defeated in the Kamarej pass and thereafter Karim Khan Zand (r. 1754-1779) established his rule over most of Iran. [349]

During the dissolution of Zand rule, Kazerun once again was sacked due to the vagaries of political life. 'Ali Qoli Khan Kazeruni, a loyal Zand partisan, was sent by Ja'far Khan (r. 1785-1789) to quell a revolt in Kashan. He did so by granting terms to the rebels, of which Ja'far Khan did not agree. He imprisoned the rebels and 'Ali Qoli Khan Kazeruni returned home. Ja'far Khan lured him back to Shiraz and threw him into prison. This triggered a coup against Ja'far Khan in January 1789, who was murdered by some of his courtiers. [350] Kazerun's troubles were not over yet, for Lotf 'Ali Khan, Ja'far Khan's son was engaged in a losing war against Aqa Mohammad Khan Qajar. In 1791, Lotf 'Ali Khan fled to Bushehr to seek help. To that end he stayed in Khesht for some time. There he was attacked by 'Ali Qoli Khan Kazeruni, but escaped. After he returned from the coast, Lotf 'Ali Khan attacked and took Kazerun and had 'Ali Qoli Khan Kazeruni and his son 'Ali Naqi Khan blinded. [351] In 1792,

348. Fasa'i 1378, vol. 2, p. 1440-41; Kazeruni 1381, pp. 44-45.

349. Perry 1979, pp. 58-59; Kalantar 1325, pp. 44-46; Fasa'i 1378, vol. 1, pp. 207 or 590, 595; Khurmuji 1380, pp. 426-28, 450.

350. Khurmuji 1380, pp. 482, 484; Fasa'i 1378, vol. 1, pp. 637.

351. Khurmuji 1380, p. 487; Fasa'i 1378, vol. 1, p. 649.

when pursuing the Zand leaders, Aqa Mohammad Shah stayed for some time in Kazerun; he later recruited troops among the Mamasanis.[352]

Khvajeh `Ali Qoli was among the Khans who were imprisoned by Ja`far Khan Zand in 1788. Because he had no sons, he was succeeded by his brother's son, Reza Qoli Khan, the son of Hoseyn `Ali Khan, who was blinded with his son by Lotf `Ali Khan Zand in 1792. After his death, his other son Mohammad Qoli Khan, was governor of Kazerun for ten years. Because he had no son, his brother Kalb `Ali Khan succeeded him, who was governor for 14 years until about 1824.[353] After an Afsharless period of about ten years as of 1834, `Abbas Qoli Khan Afshar, the son `Ali Taqi Khan Afshar, the son who was blinded in 1792, became governor and he remained so until 1844. Then the Afshar tribe lost the governorship, which it held for almost 286 years. There were still a number of them around in Kazerun at the turn of the twentieth century such as `Ali Qoli Khan, and his brother Mohammad Qoli Khan, who managed *vaqf* property.[354]

This Afshar hold on the governorship may have been interrupted between 1682 and 1691, when Saru Khan Sahandlu, the *qurchi-bashi* was reported to be governor of Kazerun. The likelihood of this appointment is borne out by the *Dastur al-Moluk* that states that Kazerun was the *qurchi-bashi*'s revenue assignment or *teyul*, be it that this is reported for this single case only.[355] It is likely that an Afshar khan continued to be the *de facto* governor, only sharing a part of the revenues of Kazerun with a powerful courtier such as the *qurchi-bashi*. This is suggested by the *Dastur-e Shahriyar* that states that in 1694 the *qurchi-bashi* had a revenue (*teyul*) in Kazerun.[356] This seems to have been a standard procedure, for thirty years earlier, in 1073/1662-63, Imamverdi Beg, the *amir shekar-bashi* had a share of 1,000 *tuman*s in Kazerun's revenues.[357] Such an interruption in Afshar control over the governorship of Kazerun once again took place between 1826 and 1834, when Kazerun was given to the mother of Reza Qoli Mirza as a revenue source. Her other son, "Timoor Mirza, one of the sons of the Prince of Sheeraz, is the resident governor here; as he is however a young man more given to play than business, the affairs of the district are chiefly entrusted to the *Vuzier*, who is by all accounts an able man."[358] In 1834, when his father lost the bid for the throne and had to flee, Timur Mirza also left Iran.

There are some problems with the list of Afshar governors provided by Fasa'i, which probably is based on local information. For example, Buckingham reported that the house in the *Bagh-e Nazar* had been constructed by a certain Imam Qoli Khan, "who was governor of Kazerun some 15 years ago." As Buckingham was in Kazerun in 1816, this means that he was governor in about 1800. After his death his son Mohammad Qoli Khan succeeded him. The

---

352. Roschanzamir 1970, p. 115. Ironically, in 1792 Qajar troops were sent against Lotf `Ali Khan from Kazerun.

353. Fasa'i 1378, vol. 2, p. 1440-41; Kazeruni 1381, pp. 44-45. According to Brydges-Jones who visited Kazerun in 1809, he reported that its governor was "universally well spoken of, as a generous, and charitable man." Brydges-Jones 1976, p. 79.

354. Fasa'i 1378, vol. 2, pp. 1441-42; Kazeruni 1381, pp. 44-45.

355. Ansari 2007, p. 22.

356. Nasiri 1383, p. 20.

357. Vahid-e Qazvini 1383, p. 750.

358. Stirling 1991, p. 19.

young man lived a hedonistic life and was surrounded by horses, servants, slaves and beautiful women in his harem. When a dervish visited him one day, he became so convinced by his philosophy that he resigned his government to another and made a vow of poverty and piety, accoding to Buckingham.[359] Fasa'i's list has a Mohammad Qoli Khan, who was governor until 1811; however, he gives his father's name as Reza Qoli Khan. One of the sources, Fasa'i or Buckingham, must have made a mistake or received erroneous information. Fasa'i and Buckingham provide conflicting information in yet another case. According to Fasa'i, Kalb `Ali Khan Afshar was governor of Kazerun between 1811 and 1824. However, according to Buckingham, when he visited the town in 1816 the name of its governor was Kazem Beg. A possible explanation is that Kazem Beg was a deputy-governor, who officiated in the absence of Kalb `Ali Khan, otherwise Fasa'i must have made a mistake. Fasa'i's list is also at odds with yet another contemporary observer. According to Fasa'i, `Abbas Qoli Khan Afshar was governor of Kazerun between 1834 and 1844. But, when de Bode visited the town in 1841, he reported that Mohammad Hasan Khan was its governor. This means that either `Abbas Qoli Khan Afshar's tenure did not last ten years, or that Fasa'i had the wrong name.[360] After the Afshar khans lost control over Kazerun in 1844, the governors selected by Tehran were mostly 'regulars', i.e. bureaucrats who often had functioned as governor elsewhere. Also, there were deputy-governors, who acted as governor *pro-tem*, if need be.[361]

Kazerun was not a quiet district. The construction of its fort-like houses is an indication that people felt insecure and that fights occurred in the town. The fights were not necessarily only between quarters, but often with the governor. In 1850, "The population of the lower quarter had revolted against its governor, Abbass Kuly Khan, and had just killed five of his people and two of the inhabitants of the upper division; this has occasioned a blood-feud between the two quarters. A discharge of small arms was maintained on either side at night during my stay."[362] This was neither the first nor the last time this happened. In 1863, Col. Pelly witnessed that a fight was going on between the governor and his retainers and certain other tribesmen; fights took place daily and finally the governor had to go into hiding. The reason was revenue collection.

> It happened there was a change of Governors taking place, the one newly appointed had not arrived from Shirauz. Meantime none of the corn [i.e., grain] long reaped and stacked could be housed, because no division of crop could take place. Meantime, also the old Governor was endeavouring to collect all he could of old debts, hence the uproar. I noticed too, that the youths of the town, following the example of their elders, turned out to the number of fifty or so, and had a battle royal with slings and stones."[363]

359. Buckingham 1971, pp. 326-27.

360. De Bode 1845, vol. 1, p. 205.

361. Sirjani 1361, p. 373.

362. Abbott 1857, p. 184.

363. Pelly 1865 b, p. 148.

At that time, people told Pelly that in the past their situation was better, and the decline was due to government tyranny. Pelly, however, was not convinced. "I find, however, that the revenue now paid is that which has long been paid, and that the population has long been what it is now."[364]

However, people were unhappy with their governors in particular during the last quarter of the nineteenth century. This seemingly higher fractious frequency is likely due to the fact that more information is available for that period rather than that there was a real increase in people's opposition to their governors, because governance before 1875 was certainly not better than thereafter. The fact is, however, that as 1875 the people of Kazerun regularly complained about their governors, such as in 1875 about Ebrahim Fasa'i.[365]

In 1879, people killed Mirza Nasrollah Sardezeki who had been appointed governor of Kazerun in 1877.[366] When in 1879 Mirza Nasrollah was on his way to Kazerun to assume its governorship he was killed at Chenar-e Faryab by two people from Kuh-marreh, who shot him on 15 May 1879 and he died the next day.[367] The governorship was taken care of by Mirza Aqa Khan Vakil. However, he was not acceptable for unknown reasons, for the *lutis* (toughs) of Kazerun wanted to kill him. Fights broke out and there were casualties on both sides, but the result was that the governor went into hiding.[368] When the people of Kazerun complained about him after the fights, he was immediately dismissed. He, as well as some of the rioters, was summoned to Shiraz.[369] In June 1882 most of the people fled Kazerun, because their tax burden had been arbitrarily increased and the governor was dismissed.[370] As a result, the *kalantar* of Kazerun, Hajj Aqa Babay officiated as temporary governor. However that was not a good choice. He oppressed the people of Kazerun such that they affixed a letter on the door of the *Saheb Divan* or vizier of Fars, stating that "the deputy-governor Hajji Aqa Babay is so oppressing us that you either dismiss or execute him." The vizier of Fars had a problem, because he had accepted payment from Hajji Aqa Babay and, moreover, no new governor was found.[371] Apparently, some accommodation was reached as he remained in office. However, when some time later Hajj Aqa Babay had a man bastinadoed so much that he died, the people of Kazerun rioted in the streets and took refuge (*bast*) in the telegraph office and mosque and complained much about him. He was summoned to Shiraz with some of the elders (*rish-safidan*) of Kazerun. Hajj Aqa Babay posed a problem for the vizier in Shiraz, because he had done an excellent job, and each year he had paid twice as much as was normal. However, all this additional money he had taken from the people to have clear accounts. He added 10-12,000 *tumans* to the normal tax burden as *ta'arof* for himself. Despite his regular payments, Shiraz had no choice but to dismiss him as deputy-governor around 20 May 1883.[372]

---

364. Pelly 1865 b, p. 147.

365. Sirjani 1361, p. 27.

366. Fasa'i 1378, vol. 2, p. 1066; Sirjani 1361, p. 109.

367. Sirjani 1361, pp. 108-09 (23 Jomadi I 1296).

368. Sirjani 1361, p. 131 (Rabi` II 1298). He perhaps is the governor, who received Stack and gave him a chair to sit on. Stack 1882, vol. 1, p. 38.

369. Sirjani 1361, p. 151 (Rabi` II 1299).

370. Sirjani 1361, p. 164 (Sha`ban 1299).

371. Sirjani 1361, p. 183 (early March 1883). Hajj Aqa Babay had given a promissory note (*tamassok*) to obtain the government of Kazerun. Sirjani 1361, p. 187.

372. Sirjani 1361, pp. 190-91 (May 1883).

The people of Kazerun were not happy with the selection of Soleyman Khan Jahromi as the new governor in Sha`ban 1300/June 1883 and, therefore, staged a sit-in (*bast*) in the mosque. The reason that Hajji Aqa Babay had been dismissed, was beause he took each month 2,000 *tuman*s more than was usual. As a result, many people had fled Kazerun. However, the government in Shiraz had taken a promissory note (*tamassok*) from Soleyman Khan that stated he had to pay nearly 30,000 *tuman*s per year, exclusive of operational cost and his *haqq al-hokumeh*. This was double the amount that was paid when Farhad Mirza Mo`tamed al-Dowleh was governor-general (1876-80), when it was 16,000 *tuman*s including *pishkesh*. In this respect the situation in Kazerun was not unlike other towns in Fars where also too much was demanded.[373] Hajj Aqa Babay confirmed that what the people of Kazerun said was true, but he had not kept the money for himself, because he paid it all to the vizier of Fars.[374] As a result of the complaints, the Shiraz government did not know whether it would appoint Soleyman Khan as governor and was considering Nowzar Mirza as an alternative.[375]

In 1888, the situation was totally confused, because the Shiraz government first appointed Nasir al-Dowleh as governor of Kazerun and then had second thoughts and two weeks later appointed Mirza Aqa Khan. Zell al-Soltan, the governor-general of Fars, who resided in Isfahan, was upset about this and asked why they had selected these two persons, when the new governor should be Mirza Hoseyn Khan. In fact, he was also appointed governor of Bushehr, where he made his residence. He appointed Mirza Yusof as his deputy-governor of Kazerun, Khesht and Kamarej.[376]

Despite complaints about a governor this did not mean that after their dismissal they were not appointed governor elsewhere or even were reappointed to Kazerun at a later date. This was, for example, the case with Mohammad Qasem Khan who was again appointed in March 1878.[377] In early August 1887, Hajj Aqa Babay was once again appointed governor of Kazerun. In Shiraz he put on his robe of honor, paid the first installment of the revenues and went to Kazerun, where the Kazerunis shot him on arrival.[378]

The telegraph office played an important role in these events; in fact it often functioned as "the nerve center for protest" in Kazerun as elsewhere in Iran.[379] On 8 December 1892, for example, 500 men and women entered the telegraph office to complain about the governor of Kazerun.[380] In August 1895, the entire population of Kazerun took sanctuary in the telegraph office to signal that they did not want Nasrollah Mirza, a son of Rokn al-Dowleh, as their governor. The governor-general of Fars, Rokn al-Dowleh then sent another son to Kazerun to find out what oppression had been committed and to settle the matter.[381]

---

373. Fasa'i 1378, vol. 2, 1281; Sirjani 1361, p. 192.

374. Sirjani 1361, p. 193.

375. Sirjani 1361, p. 194.

376. Sirjani 1361, pp. 216-17.

377. Sirjani 1361, p. 89 (Rabi` I, 1295).

378. Sirjani 1361, p. 295.

379. Rubin 1999, chapter 11.

380. Sirjani 1361, p. 421.

381. Sirjani 1361, p. 491.

In mid-March 1897, the people of Kazerun were rioting, and gathered around the telegraph office, because bread was expensive and there was no wheat to be had, even at 3 *qran*s per Tabriz *man*; no action was taken to investigate the matter.[382] In August 1903, the people of Kazerun rioted and went en masse to the telegraph office and sent a message stating: "we do not want Mas'ud al-Dowleh." In fact, they wanted to kill him. Montaser al-Dowleh was sent posthaste from Shiraz and was able to settle matters between the parties.[383] Such arbitration was not always successful. For example, when there was rioting in Kazerun in June 1899 the governor-general in Shiraz sent one of his top officials to settle the grievances, but the people of Kazerun beat and imprisoned the official. Shortly thereafter he was liberated. The leaders of the rioters were taken to Shiraz, where they were beaten As a result, the people of Kazerun protested against this and took sanctuary at the telegraph office.[384]

From the above it is clear that governors of Kazerun needed to be tough individuals, who literally risked their life, when their actions were perceived to be oppressive and detrimental to people's interests. People increasingly used violence as a weapon of protest, which was not out of character with the behavior displayed by local leaders towards each other.[385]

Table 3.5: Names of governors of Kazerun (1504 - 1925)

Name	Year	Observations	Source
Elyas Beyg Dhu'l-Qadr aka Kachal Beyg	909/1504	Hakem of Kazerun	Nasiri 2008, p. 214
Names unknown	909-955/1504-1548	Hakem of Kazerun; governed by Kachal Beyg's descendents	Nasiri 2008, p. 214
Ebrahim Khan Dhu'l-Qadr	Jomadi II 955/July 1548	Hakem of Kazerun	Fasa'i 1378, vol. 1, p. 400-01
Kepek Soltan Afshar	955-?/1548-?	Hakem of Kazerun	Nasiri 2008, p. 214
Morad Soltan	998/1590	Hakem of Kazerun	Nasiri 2008, p. 214
Amir Khan Afshar	999-1003/1591-1595	Hakem of Kazerun	Fasa'i 1378, vol. 1, p. 438; Nasiri 2008, p. 214
Esma'il Khan Alplu Afshar	1003-?/1595-?	Hakem of Kazerun + Kerman	Nasiri 2008, p. 214
Khvajeh Pir Budaq Afshar	ca. 1620	Hakem of Kazerun	Kazeruni 1381, p. 44
Khvajeh Pir Vali Afshar	?	Hakem of Kazerun	Kazeruni 1381, p. 44
Khvajeh Hoseyn 'Ali Afshar	?	Hakem of Kazerun	Kazeruni 1381, p. 44
Saru Khan Sahandlu	1093?-1103/1682?-1691	Hakem of Hamadan + Semnan + Kazerun (Cazran)	Nasiri 2008, p. 214
Khvajeh Hesam al-Din Afshar	?	Hakem of Kazerun	Kazeruni 1381, p. 44; his brother Khvajeh Hoseyn 'Ali as deputy
Khvajeh Mohammad Reza b. Khvajeh Hoseyn 'Ali Afshar	?	Hakem of Kazerun	Kazeruni 1381, p. 45

382. Sirjani 1361, p. 423 bread also got more expensive at Shiraz Ibid. p. 424. The increased bread price was due to drought; shortly thereafter the price dropped somewhat, but it still could not to be had at 2 *qran* per *man*. Ibid., p. 426 (May 1897).

383. Sirjani 1361, p. 717 (August 1903).

384. Sirjani 1361, p. 572.

385. Sayyed Mahmud Kazeruni, one of the notables of Kazerun, was accused of having been involved with Naser al-Din Shah's assassination and was taken to Tehran. Sirjani 1361, p. 425.

Name	Year	Observations	Source
Khvajeh Abu'l-Hasan Afshar	?	Hakem of Kazerun	Kazeruni 1381, p. 45; the sister's son of Mohammad Reza
Khvajeh `Ali Qoli Afshar	? 1767	Hakem of Kazerun	Kazeruni 1381, p. 45
Hasan `Ali Khan Afshar	?	Hakem of Kazerun	Kazeruni 1381, p. 45
Hoseyn `Ali Khan Afshar	?	Hakem of Kazerun	Kazeruni 1381, p. 45
Reza Qoli Khan son of Hoseyn `Ali Khan Afshar	?	Hakem of Kazerun	Kazeruni 1381, p. 45
Mohammad Qoli Khan Afshar	? 1808	Hakem of Kazerun	Kazeruni 1381, p. 45; Buckingham 1971, pp. 326-27; Dupré 1819, vol. 2, p. 22
Kalb `Ali Khan Afshar	1226-1229/1811-14	Hakem of Kazerun	Kazeruni 1381, p. 45
Mirza Baqer Famuri	1229/1814	*Zabet* Kazerun	Fasa'i 1378, vol. 1, p. 711
Kazem Khan	1231/1816	Hakem of Kazerun	Buckingham 1971, pp. 326-27
Kalb `Ali Khan Afshar	?-1240/?-1824	Hakem of Kazerun	Kazeruni 1381, p. 45; Fraser 1984, pp. 80-81
Timur Mirza	1240-1250/1824-34	Hakem of Kazerun	Kazeruni 1381, p. 45
`Abbas Qoli Khan Afshar	1250-1260/1834-44	Hakem of Kazerun	Kazeruni 1381, p. 45
Mohammad Hasan Khan	1841?	Hakem of *navahi-ye* Kazerun	de Bode 1848, 1, 205
Mirza Mohammad Fasa'i	1263-64/1847-48	Hakem of Kazerun, Dashti, Dashtestan, Khesht, Mamasani, Kuhgiluyeh, Behbahan	Fasa'i 1378, vol. 2, p. 931
`Abbas Qoli Khan	1850	Hakem of Kazerun	Abbott 1857, p. 184
Mirza `Ali Mohammad Khan Qavam al-Molk	1267/1850	Hakem of *navahi-ye* Kazerun	Fasa'i 1378, vol. 2, p. 967
Mirza `Ali Mohammad Khan Nazem al-Molk	1268-1272/1851-56	Hakem of Kazerun, Darab, Jahrom, Qir, Jevim, Bidshahr	Sepehr 1377, 3, p. 1384; Fasa'i 1378, vol. 1, p. 808
Mirza Na`im Nuri	1272/1856	Hakem of Kazerun, Darab, Jahrom, Qir, Jevim, Bidshahr	Fasa'i 1378, vol. 1, p. 808
Mirza Mahmud Kazeruni	1857	Hakem of Kazerun	Clerk 1861, p. 63
Mir Heydar Khan-e Talesh	1275-?/1858-?	Hakem of Kazerun	Fasa'i 1378, vol. 1, p. 820
Jamal al-Din Mirza	1280/1864	Hakem of Kazerun	Fasa'i 1378, vol. 1, p. 1095
Soleyman Mirza, Sho`a al-Dowleh	1282-85/1865-68	Hakem of Kazerun	Fasa'i 1378, vol. 1, 827, 832; nephew of Hosam al-Saltaneh
Hajj Gholam Reza	?	Hakem of Kazerun	Motahharizadeh 1381, p. 59
Mirza Ebrahim Fasa'i	1291 Rabi` II-1292/May 1874-March 1875	Hakem of Kazerun	Sirjani 1361, pp. 14, 25
Mohammad Taqi Khan	Rabi` I 1292/ April 1875	Hakem of Kazerun, Khesht, Kamarej	Sirjani 1361, p. 28
Mohamad Qasem Khan Beyza'i	1294/1877-78	Hakem of Kazerun	Sirjani 1361, p. 89
Mirza Asadollah	Jomadi I 1295/May 1878	Withdrew?	Sirjani 1361, p. 89
Mohamad Qasem Khan Beyza'i	1295/1878-	Hakem of Kazerun	Sirjani 1361, p. 89
Mirza Nasrollah Sardezeki	11-24 Jomadi I 1296/3-15 May 1879	Hakem of Kazerun	Fasa'i 1378, vol. 2, p. 1066; Sirjani 1361, p. 108-09

Name	Year	Observations	Source
Mirza Nasrollah Sardezeki's son	Rajab 1296/June 1879	Under tutelage of Mirza Moh. Reza Mostowfi, his maternal grandfather	Sirjani 1361, p. 109
Mirza Aqa Khan Vakil	Jomadi II 1298- end Rabi II 1299/May 1881-21 March 1882	Hakem of Kazerun, Kamarej + Khesht	Sirjani 1361, 131, 151
Hajj Aqa Babay	March 1882-May 1883	Caretaker	Sirjani 1361, p. 183, 190-91
Soleyman Khan Jahromi	1300/1883	Hakem of Kazerun	Sirjani 1361, 192. However, Fasa'i 1378, vol. 2, p. 966 has Mirza Hoseyn Khan Mo'tamen al-Molk
Hajj Nasir al-Molk	April 1884	Hakem of Kazerun, Behbahan, Mamasani/withdrawn?	Sirjani 1361, p. 215
Mirza Aqa Khan, nephew of Saheb Divan	end May 1884	Hakem of Kazerun/withdrawn?	Sirjani 1361, p. 215
Mirza Hoseyn Khan Mo'tamen al-Molk	1301/May 1884	Haken of *navahi-ye* Kazerun; deputy Kazerun Mirza Yusof	Sirjani 1361, pp. 216-17
Hajj Nasir al-Molk	Rajab 1303 — April 1887 as people protested he was withdrawn	Hakem of Bushehr, Dashti, Dastestan, Khest, Kamarej, Kazerun	Mafi et al. 1361, vol. 1, p. 164
Hajj Aqa Babay	August 1887 killed on arrival	Hakem of Kazerun	Sirjani 1361, p. 295
Mohammad Ebrahim Khan	1889	Hakem of Kazerun	Pirzadeh 2, 417
Nasir al-Molk	1889	Hakem of Kazerun	Sirjani 1361, p. 357
Hajj `Abbas `Ali Beg	April 1890-	Hakem of Kazerun	Sirjani 1361, p. 357
Nasir al-Molk	April 1893	Hakem of Kazerun, Fasa, Mamasani	Sirjani 1361, p. 431
Mohammad Sadeq Khan	April 1894	Hakem of Kazerun, Qir, Jahrom/refused	Sirjani 1361, p. 453
Qavam al-Molk	April 1894	Hakem of Kazerun, Dashti, Dashtestan, Banader, Khamseh, Darab	Sirjani 1361, p. 453
Mo'ed al-Molk, Saheb Divan's nephew	d. August 1894	Hakem of Kazerun, Estanabat, larestan	Sirjani 1361, p. 463
Nasrollah Mirza, Rokn al-Dowleh's son	April 1895	Hakem of Kazerun	Administration Report 1895-96, p. 6; Sirjani 1361, pp. 482, 491
Mohammad Khan Mir Panjeh	April 1895-	Hakem of Kazerun	Sadid al-Saltaneh 1362, p. 36
Mohammad Karim Khan Kashkuli	1320/1901	Hakem of Kazerun	Sirjani 1361, p. 702
Mas`ud al-Dowleh	1321/1903	Hakem of Kazerun	Sirjani 1361, p. 717
Mohammad Karim Khan Kashkuli	1323/1905	Hakem of Kazerun	Motahharizadeh 1383, p. 15, n. 10; Qa'emmaqami 1359, p. 130
Mirza Ebrahim Fasa'i	?-1906	Hakem of Kazerun	Motahharizadeh 1383, p. 10
Hajj Zargham al-Shari`eh	1907-08	Hakem of Kazerun	Administration Report 1907-08, p. 23; Fasa'i 2, p. 987
Mohammad Karim Khan Kashkuli	?-1327/end September 1909	Hakem of Kazerun	Administration Report 1909, p. 17; Motahharizadeh 1383, pp. 21-22; few months
Mo`in al-Shari`eh	1327/end 1909	Hakem of Kazerun	Motahharizadeh 1383, p. 23
Mo`aven al-Mamalek	1910	Hakem of Kazerun	Ranjbar 1389, p. 161

Name	Year	Observations	Source
Mohammad `Ali Khan Kashkuli	1911	By Nezam al-Saltaneh	Administration Report 1911, p. 23; Motahharizadeh 1383, p. 25
Naser-e Divan	1329/1911	By Nezam al-Saltaneh	Motahharizadeh 1383, p. 11, doc. 7
Mazhar al-Dowleh	1331/1913	By Mokhber al-Saltaneh	Motahharizadeh 1383, p. 30, 114, doc. 15
Ahmad Khan Daryabegi	1331/1913 — short period only	By Mokhber al-Saltaneh	Motahharizadeh 1383, p. 31
Col. Merrill	March-June 1914	Military governor	Administration Report 1914, p. 7
Major Lundberg	June-September 1914	Military governor	Akhgar 1366, p. 115
Captain Akhgar	October-December 1914	Military governor during 3 months	Akhgar 1366, p. 115
Salar-e Heshmat or Salar-e Nosrat	1916	Hakem of Kazerun	Safiri 134; Akhgar 1366, p. 204
Fath al-Molk	End 1916	Military governor; did not arrive	Administration Report 1916, p. 7
Naser-e Divan	End 1916-?	acting Hakem of Kazerun by default	
Naser al-Dowleh	February 1917	Hakem of Kazerun	Mafi 1366, vol. 1,304
Naser-e Divan	1917-January 1919	acting Hakem of Kazerun by default	
Salar-e Mo`tazed	22 January 1919- November 1920	Hakem of Kazerun	Administration Report 1919, p. 2
Jalal al-Molk	End November 1920-?	Deputy governor	Administration Report 1920, p. 4
Naser-e Divan	January 1922	Deputy governor	Motahharizadeh 1383, p. 177, 180f
`Ata al-Dowleh	1922	Hakem of Kazerun	Administration Report 1922, p. 3
N.N.	1923	Military governor	Administration Report 1923, p. 1
N.N.	as of July 1924	Military governor	Administration Report 1924, p. 12
N.N.	1925	Military governor	Administration Report 1925, p. 13

Observation: Mirza Ebrahim is listed as governor of Kazerun prior to 1293/1876. Fasa'i 1378, vol. 2, p. 932.

Security on the Trade Route

The history of Kazerun during the nineteenth and the early twentieth century is character-ized by two main themes. The first one is oppression of the people by many of the successive governors of the town and people's opposition against them. The second one is the security of the trade route between Bushehr and Shiraz, the major trade artery for the economy of much of southern Iran. This second theme may be divided into two sub-themes; one, during which the route was made unsafe by the Mamasani tribe and other tribal elements in the nineteenth century. The other, where the weakening of the central government's authority and power after 1905 caused by and coincided with the growth of nationalism and increased foreign (in particular British) interference, which gave the concomitant lawlessness a sheen of moral rectitude. The first theme was discussed above in the section on governors. Here I discuss the second theme that of insecurity of the trade route and its consequences.

Due to the civil wars in the second part of the eighteenth century, "the rapacity and tyranny of their rulers" increased as did insecurity in the area.[386] A member of the Malcolm embassy noted that the road between Khesht and Kazerun was "in many parts difficult and unpleasant. The country between this and the former stage is infested with a tribe of robbers or bandits called Mamasunnee, which renders it requisite for the traveller to be constantly upon his guard."[387] The Mamasani tribal group was the one that acquired a very bad reputa-tion, because its members were the main culprits of raids on caravans and travelers. In 1821, according to the British traveler James Bailie Fraser:

> They are divided, I was informed, into four separate *teers*, or smaller tribes;
> the Dushman-Zeearees, the Iowees, the Pehwendeh, and the Roostumees.
> Mahomed Reza Khan is the chief of the whole, and Wullee Khan is the next
> in importance. The former resides in Faaleeoon, near Ardacoon, the latter at,
> or in close vicinity of the Quilla Suffeed [Qal`eh-ye safid]. A bloody feud exists
> between them and the Kauzeroonees, of which tribe Kulb Allee Khan, the
> governor, is chief: and this has lately been aggravated by the murther of Shums-
> u-Deen, a person of importance in the latter tribe, who was treacherously
> shot by Moolla Mahmood, a Mahmood sunnie [Mamasani], not far from
> Kauzeroon, because he was obnoxious to that tribe on account of the activity he
> had shewn in repressing their disposition to plunder.[388]

---

386. Ouseley 1819, vol. 1, p. 272.

387. Hollingberry 1976, p. 24. Monteith 1857, p. 116 qualified all the tribes near Kazerun as lawless, great plunderers and wretchedly poor.

388. Fraser 1984, pp. 80-81. For the *qal`eh-ye safid* or white fort, see Anonymous 1368, p. 59ff. Lumsden, who had been the guest of the murdered Shams al-Din at Shapur on 4 May 1820, learnt of the murder of "Meershumes ud Deen" on 20 May. It happened "while this chief was riding out with Moolah Shah Mahomed, this man first shot him through the back, and then finished by cutting the ill-fated chief with his sword. The cause of the destruction of Meershumes ud Deen, is said to have been an improper or unnamed intimacy between him and a member of the murderers family. He was not, perhaps, much to be regretted, having usurped the estate of an elder brother, and recently put several men to death. The prince of Shirauz had, however, ordered the murderer to be apprehended." Lumsden 2010, p. 44

The murderer fled to Shiraz where he was killed by a servant of the murdered man. Shams al-Din's kin came to Shiraz and asked the prince-governor for the killer, who agreed to do so and they killed him on the spot. However, this did not improve the situation, for there was unrevenged blood between the two tribes. As a result, "The Kauzeroonees view their enemies with a fearful as well as a jealous eye; for a predatory tribe like theirs have it in their power to inflict upon their more settled neighbours much serious loss; and at all events to keep them most disagreeably on the alert." Therefore, about one year later, the prince-governor sent some troops, took three of the Mamasani perpetrators prisoner, including their women and children. This almost immediately resulted in the return to more peaceful conditions. The Mamasanis even restored some cattle stolen from Kalb ʿAli Khan, the governor of Kazerun and asked him to intercede with the prince for them. They pledged to not to plunder the roads anymore.[389]

It would seem that this measure, as well as follow-up military measures, indeed had a salutary effect, because Fasa'i implies that Vali Khan Mamasani plunder raids were something of the past by 1835.[390] Nevertheless, in 1841, Vali Khan was still very much on people's mind.[391] However, a decade later Binning reported that when traveling to Kazerun no more armed guards were needed now that the Mamasani had been dispersed.[392] In 1873-74, the roads between Shiraz and Bushehr were very unsafe and robberies were common and trade was often suspended. Another problem was the demand of toll or transit duties from foreign merchants. Incidence of robberies dropped during the winter due to its severity.[393] The situation seems really to have improved so much that in 1875, according to MacGregor, "people generally do not go about armed, some have inferior matchlocks."[394] This sentiment is echoed by the British authorities who noted that in 1875-76 caravan routes between Bushehr and Shiraz were pretty clear of robbers.[395] This remarkable improvement was due to Moʿtamed al-Dowleh, the new governor-general of Fars, who maintained security on the roads "in a unprecedented manner."[396] As long as he remained in office the security was maintained on the roads.[397] This changed when Moʿtamed al-Dowleh was replaced as governor-general. As a result, insecurity in general increased, because of the infighting among the Qavam al-Molk family clique in charge of the administration of Fars.[398] In 1886 there were many robberies, and the insecurity was made worse by internal dissent among the Qashqai leadership.[399] In-

---

389. Fraser 1984, p. 81.

390. Fasa'i 1378, vol. 1, p. 768.

391. De Bode 1845, vol. 1, p. 210.

392. Binning 1857, vol. 1, p.178.

393. Administration 1873-74, p. 7.

394. Mac Gregor 1879, vol. 1, p. 22

395. Administration Report 1875-76, p. 5.

396. Administration Report 1877-78, p. 5.

397. Administration Report 1878-79, p. 8; Administration Report 1879-80, p. 6; Administration Report 1880-81, p. 8.

398. Administration Report 1884-85, p. 8.

399. Administration Report 1886-87, p. 8.

security increased because of maladministration of Fars, lawlessness and defiance of government authority by the tribes, in particular by the Qashqa'is.[400] In 1897-99, several robberies occurred on the trade route, but these were recompensed by the government of Iran.[401] Under Asaf al-Dowleh's administration (1902-03) roads were generally unsafe and highway robberies frequent, and the same held for 1904-05, when also *rahdari* was collected.[402]

Attacks on caravans and travelers continued to take place, and sometimes people were killed. In one case this concerned an Armenian and but it was not considered of major importance as he was but an unbeliever.[403] Sometimes no action was taken as in 1875, when there was no governor in Kazerun. However, in November 1890, troops were sent along the route Kazerun-Bushehr to provide protection.[404] In August 1899, when the governor-general of Fars sent troops to Kazerun to reclaim goods stolen from foreign merchants the soldiers were opposed by armed Kazerunis, who threatened to kill them. The latter believed it was wiser to avoid confrontation and returned to Shiraz, much to the chagrin of the governor-general.[405]

Table 3.6: Selected occurrences of high-way robbery near Kazerun (1875-1902)

Year	Nature of crime	Source
1875	Attack on a caravan between Kamarej and Kazerun	Sirjani 1361, p. 34 (Jomadi I 1292)
1875	Attack on caravan near Kazerun	Sirjani 1361, pp. 42-43
1881	Highway robbery near Kazerun	Sirjani 1361, p. 131 (Rabi` II 1298)
1885	At Kotal-e Dokhtar *hajj* pilgrims robbed of all they had	Sirjani 1361, p. 244
1886	Mail robbed near Kazerun	Sirjani 1361, p. 277
1887	Two caravans plundered near Kazerun	Sirjani 1361, p. 294
1896	Robbery near Kazerun in September	Sirjani 1361, p. 513
1899	Goods plundered from foreign merchants in September	Sirjani 1361, p. 584
1902	Qashqa'is stole much property in November	Sirjani 1361, p. 489

Table 3.6 suggests that the incidence of robbery and raids was much reduced as compared with the first quarter of the nineteenth century when the Mamasani raids gave the area a bad name. However, what the above also tells is that the Kazerun area had a latent problem of violence. As long as there was a government that had the will and the power to enforce security, the incidents of robberies remained relatively low. But, as is clear from the period between 1905 and 1918, when Iran had a government that became weaker and more irrelevant by the day, these latent violent forces manifested themselves with a vengeance. It was fortuitous that this unleasing of violence coincided with the growth of nationalism, so that the one often could be perpetrated under the guise of the other.

400. Administration Report 1894-95, p. 10; Administration Report 1895-96, p. 7.

401. Administration Report 1897-98, p. 6; Administration Report 1897-98, p. 9; Administration Report 1898-99, p. 8.

402. Administration Report 1902-1903, p. 4; Administration Report 1904-1905, pp. 1, 12.

403. Sirjani 1361, p. 678.

404. Sirjani 1361, p. 345; Ibid., p. 369 (November 1890).

405. Sirjani 1361, p. 584.

The Nationalist Period

The period from 1905 to 1920 was a pivotal one in the history of Iran, one that still evokes very strong feelings. It all started with the constitutional movement, which demanded the establishment of a constitutional monarchy, in which people enjoyed equal and shared political rights, and of a country that was independent of foreign powers. The movement wanted to establish a more just society, one that was not based on ethnicity. The fact that the creation of this new society was impeded by, among other things, the reality that most people in Iran still held a strong allegiance to their ethnic group, village or town and not to forget Islam, rather than to these civic ideals, thus standing in direct contradiction of the very ideals the nationalist movement strove after, did not douse people's enthusiasm. Being human, they not only did not (want to) see the contradictions; they also selected those elements that fit their own ideals or needs to be able to share in the revolutionary enthusiasm. The nationalist movement thus provided a political and philosophical cover for those who wanted to challenge authority, an attitude and activity which were endemic to the political scene of Kazerun, as shown above. Whereas in the past opposition was expressed in terms of injustice and oppression, now the need to fight despotism and foreign domination was added to the political menu.

The next fifteen years, Kazerun was part, and sometimes at the center of the main problem between Bushehr and Shiraz, i.e., of the insecurity of the trade route between these two towns. The main route from Bushehr went via Ahmadi, Borazjan, Daleki, and Kazerun to Shiraz. Because the telegraph line followed this same route, this road, therefore, was known as the Telegraph road. It was also referred to as the 'postal road', because the mail was carried along it as well as the 'royal road', probably to please the shah or to indicate its commercial importance. Until 1905 this route had been rather safe and although travelers and caravans were robbed or plundered this was not a regular occurrence, but this was to change.

In 1905 the Telegraph road to Shiraz became unsafe due to attacks by local chiefs and for some time, therefore, the less convenient road via Firuzabad was used. After pressure by the British, the governor-general of Fars, Sho`a` al-Saltaneh, son of Mozaffar al-Din Shah arrested and punished several of the roadguards, which temporarily led to an improvement. However, by September 1905 the situation reverted to the previous situation where travelers were subjected to the collection of illegal imposts. A string of 100 British-owned mules were held up at Pol-e Abgineh and had to pay 10 *shahi*s per mules. The British demanded action from Sho`a` al-Saltaneh who promised to replace the roadguards with guards of the regular infantry and to station in between them mounted soldiers or *sovar*s. However, although 3-4 soldiers were sent to support the post of each roadguard station, the *sovar*s were never sent. Initially this plan worked well, but as of December 1905 the soldiers and roadguards started blackmailing travelers and caravans again, in particular between Kazerun and Borazjan. In early 1906, the situation was totally out of control and the Shiraz government claimed it could do nothing due to the disturbed situation of Fars, the result of the oppression by the dismissed Sho`a` al-Saltaneh. His dismissal in September 1905 had nothing to do with his failure to improve safety on the Telegraph road, but rather with his large-scale property thefts all over Fars, against which people protested vociferously.[406]

---

406. Administration Report 1905-06, pp. 21-22.

The land grabs perpetrated by Sho'a' al-Saltaneh also occurred in Kazerun in 1905. He already had landed property there and tried to extend his holdings by usurping other people's land. Allegedly to further and protect his interests, he had appointed Mohammad Karim Khan Kashkuli as governor of Kazerun. People closed their shops to protest against this appointment.[407] There is no evidence, however, that the Kashkuli chief was involved in the governor-general's landgrabs. It is more likely that local notables resented the fact that a chief of a section of the powerful Qashqa'i tribe acquired more influence than he had already in the Kazerun valley. The leader of the local protest movement was Khvajeh Ebrahim, the *kalantar* of Kazerun, who until then was the main power in Kazerun, be it under the control of Heydar Khan of Kamarej (see below). Like his younger brother Khvajeh 'Abdollah, who later gained fame and notoriety under the name of Naser-e Divan, he belonged to the town's upper class. Their grandfather Khvajeh Yusof lived in the Gonbad quarter. Due to his economic and social position he was chosen as *kadkhoda* of that quarter. He probably died in 1280/1863-64. He was succeeded by his son Khvajeh Hasan 'Ali, who, due to his qualities, succeeded in becoming *kalantar* of Kazerun. He died about 1321/1903 and was succeeded by his son Khvajeh Ebrahim.[408]

It is understandable that the British blamed the various chiefs along the Telegraph road for all the problems. After all, the government of Iran, of which local governors were its representatives, was responsible for the maintenance of law and order on the road. When they saw that the authority of those governors was totally undermined and challenged by local chiefs, who then used their new-found unchecked power to rob, steal and plunder, who else were they to blame? From the very beginning of the political troubles in Iran, the local chiefs along the Telegraph road from Bushehr via Borazjan, Daleki, and Kazerun to Shiraz smelled political and financial opportunity. The power and authority of the central government as well as that of the governor-general of Fars had weakened significantly due to the political disorder in the country after 1906. As a result, these local chiefs behaved as if they were independent of the governor-general of Fars and were constantly fighting with each other and preying on commercial traffic. To provide themselves with additional cash income, they imposed and levied illegal fees on travelers and caravans passing through their territory.[409] Because these chiefs were operating outside the law and order, they did not care that the collection of *rahdari* and other similar fees was prohibited by article 3 of the commercial convention of 1903. The cause of the problem was nicely encapsulated by the British commercial counselor in Bushehr:

---

407. Qa'emmaqami 1359, pp. 38, 130; Motahharizadeh 1383, p. 21; Kazeruni 1381, p. 43.

408. Motahharizadeh 1383, pp. 10, n. 6 (Naser-e Divan was born about 1290/1873), 13. Consul Chick reported about Naser-e Divan's family the following: "Three generations ago this family emigrated from the Khwajeh family of the Haft Lang branch of the Bakhtiaris. He is connected by marriage with the Sardar-i-Nedun." Administration Report 1911, Appendix II, p. 16.

409. The newspaper *Jonub* 1371, year 1, 19 Rajab 1329 (16 July 1911), p. 7 agreed, and stated that while the *tofangchi*/robber levied 1 to 2 *qran*s per animal at his chief's orders, the level of greed at Kazerun was much lower where much smaller amounts were demanded. All this changed when Heydar Beg of Kamarej took over. The lower level of extortion at Kazerun probably was due to the fact that many muleteers were from Kazerun (see above).

It being a well known fact that a road constitutes a source of revenue to the chieftains, large and small, through whose territory it passes, speculation in roads became at one time a serious business pursuit for this gentry, every Khan between here [Bushehr] and Shiraz within a radius of 70 miles dreaming of the happy day when a regularly paid douceur or the expenditure of one lump sum judiciously placed he might ensure a steady stream of muleteers setting through his country and perpetually replenishing his empty coffers. Intrigues innumerable took place for the attainment of this object and competition ran so high that if caravans were induced for a time to follow a new line of march, the roadguards of the disappointed chieftain, whose livelihood was affected by the change, not infrequently crossed over the rival track with the deliberate intention of rendering it so thoroughly unsafe for all and sundry that traffic would speedily be diverted again to its former channel.[410]

The problems began right at Bushehr's gate. There were two routes for goods to leave Bushehr: (a) on animals by the town gate and land (Ahmadi) route leading past Borazjan to Kazerun and Shiraz, which was the principal caravan road for all trade entering Persia via the Gulf; and (b) by lighter to Shif and then by animals over land to Borazjan, which was mainly used for local traffic. The problem started already at the gate of Bushehr where 1 *qran* was collected by the *kalantar*, despite protests from the British government. The local governor justified its collection by referring to the fact that the Minister of Finance included this fee in the *kalantar's* revenue schedule. The Shif road was avoided by all British and the principal Persian merchants due to its inconvenience and pilferage. However, the Khan of Angali wanted caravans to pass through his territory. He tried to obtain this exclusive right since 1906 by offering large sums to the governor of Bushehr. In the absence of a legal way, he, when he could, collected fees or detained mules, to force caravans to use the Daleki-Shif road.[411]

By March 1906 road conditions were better,[412] but they did not remain that way. The situation soon deteriorated again. Imposition of fees and robberies were frequent. In particular between Kazerun and Daleki the road was unsafe due to raids carried out by Mullah Mansur and Malek Manaf. The roadguards claimed *tofangchi-giri* and sometimes assaulted travelers. The Fars authorities claimed that they could not do anything to stop this, but nevertheless included these revenues in those to be collected and paid by district governors. Also, further down the road there were problems. By December 1906, travelers preferred to take the Ahmadi route from Borazjan to Bushehr.[413]

In the past, when the passes were in a bad condition (e.g., due to snow) or when fighting had broken out among local chiefs, and thus the Telegraph road had become unsafe, caravans often used the alternative route via Firuzabad. However, it had not been used for a number of years; while it had become less attractive as an alternative route in 1907. According to the British, the countryside which had to be traversed was insecure and lacked all the amenities and accommodations that a trade route required. "Every man's hand seemed to

410. Trade Report 1909-10, p. 1.

411. Persia no. 1 (1910), p. 87 (In July 1909, he collected 50 *tuman*s from an unprotected 70 mule caravan approaching Bushehr); Administration Report 1907-1908, p. 7.

412. Administration Report 1905-06, pp. 21-22.

413. Administration Report 1906-07, pp. 15, 19.

be against his neighbour; no one dared stay abroad after dark; peasants who formerly kept transport animals for hire have sold them; ground has gone out of cultivation as there is no security for the gathering of the crop and the country generally is at the mercy of the most lawless element of the peasant population." At the same time, the normal route to Kazerun was also insecure, and caravan trade came to a halt occasionally. At many locations illegal imposts were collected, while the local chiefs concerned tried to force traffic to either travel the Bushehr-Ahmadi-Borazjan route or via the Shif-Borazjan route. Given the total lack of control of the Shiraz authorities over the outlying parts of Fars province it was a wonder that the road to Bushehr was open at all.[414]

Another important source of insecurity was the chaotic situation in Kazerun in 1907-08, due to "intestine feuds and the absence of all authority, and the standing quarrel between Hyder Khan of Kamarij and Nur Muhammad Khan of Daliki, each of whom had his candidate for the post of Kadkhuda of Konartakhteh."[415] Heydar Beg or Khan was the son of Mullah Mohammad Shafi`, the chief (*zabet*) of Kamarej. His father had been executed because of his criminal activities by Hosam al-Saltaneh, who was governor-general of Fars from 1865 to 1868. According to another version, he had been killed by some of his retainers in 1871. He had five sons, of whom Mullah Hasan Qoli succeeded his father. The sons were engaged in highway robbery like their father. Mullah Hasan Qoli was killed in Daleki in 1891, and in October 1896, his successor, Mullah `Abbas Qoli Kamareji, who had killed a few people, sought refuge in the New Mosque (*Masjed-e now*) in Kazerun. Before a plan was put in motion to arrest him he fled, and as a result both the town and its environs were in uproar, because he continued his raids on caravans. He later was caught and imprisoned[416] and apparently released, because he was then killed by retainers in 1895. His youngest brother, Heydar Beg succeeded

---

414. Administration Report 1907-08, pp. 8-10. Both roads were used in the eighteenth century. "From Bushehr to Scherauze, there are two different direct Routes, the one passing through Kaseroon, the other through Firouzabad. The merchants as well as the Chelmadars [sic; *chavardars*], of the Caravans, give the Preference to the former of these Routes, as abounding less with difficult Passes amongst the Mountains, and with greater Plenty of Forage for the Cattle of the Caravan." Saldanha 1986, vol. 1, p. 424 (Jones-Manesty Report 15/08/1790); see also Dupré 1819, vol. p. 52f who took this road against the wishes of his *mehmendar*. In April 1875, Col. Ross traveled the road via Firuzabad and reported that it was "somewhat longer, but from the gradients being greater, it is considered more capable of being made practible for wheeled conveyances or artillery. At present this road is not used as regards the seaport traffic." Administration Report 1875-76, pp. 13-14. This was also the opinion of Col. Stewart who traveled the road in the 1860s. Moreover, he added that it had "poor supply of water, timber and forage" reason why the road via Kazerun was chosen to extend the telegraph. Goldsmid 1874, p. 183. In 1883, the Firuzabad road was surveyed by a French engineer "in connection with a project for construction of a railway between the Caspian Sea and the Persian Gulf." Administration Report 1883-84, p. 8. In 1906, Mr. Grahame, British consul in Shiraz, inspected this road and concluded that it was superior to the Kazerun road, there was water, and there was only insecurity on the leg between Ahram and Firzubad that "was in a lawless condition, every man's hand being apparently against his neighbour, and the villagers as a rule not venturing outside their immediate stretch of land." Administration Report 1906-1907, p. 21.

415. Administration Report 1907-08, p. 23; Appendix 3.4. Even an unabashed and ardent supporter of Kazerun like Akhgar 1366, p. 124 had to admit that the people of Kazerun were a feuding lot, who were always fighting among themselves, and so were there neighbors. Ibid., p. 104. These feuds were a way of life between the communities living along the Telegraph road, see, e.g., Anderson 1880, p. 48.

416. Motahharizadeh 1383, pp. 23-24; Sirjani 1361, pp. 14, 555; Sadid al-Saltaneh 1362, p. 36.

him.[417] When in January 1900 a major fight broke out between those of Daleki and Kamarej the chief of Daleki lost, while there were casualties on both sides. Shiraz sent troops to arrest Heydar Beg, who was taken into custody in December 1901 and imprisoned in Shiraz. It was believed that he would be freed when he gave a large present. The merchants of Shiraz commented that if that happened, the road to Bushehr would become unsafe for their caravans. What everybody expected indeed happened. The governor-general Sho'a' al-Saltaneh after having received an appropriate gift allowed Heydar Beg to escape. He gathered his followers and after having killed four people he took Kamarej. Heydar Beg then telegraphed the acting governor-general, Mo'tamed al-Saltaneh that he had arrived at Kamarej (Sho'a' al-Saltaneh had been recalled to Tehran in February 1902). As Mo'tamed al-Saltaneh had no power to subdue him, he made a virtue of a necessity, and in March 1902 sent Heydar Beg a robe of honor, bestowed on him the title of Khan and made him responsible for the safety on the road in the Kamarej area. One year later he was back plundering traffic on the road. Heydar Beg also started to throw his weight around and took Kazerun and forced the *kalantar* Khvajeh Ebrahim to give his daughter in marriage. To further cement their new-found family unity Heydar Beg gave his daughter to the *kalantar*'s younger brother, Khvajeh 'Abdollah, the later Naser-e Divan. The governor-general then charged Heydar Beg with the security of the road from Daleki to Kazerun.[418] As stated above, the feud between Daleki and Kamarej which had been dormant in 1907 exploded in January 1908 when a small war broke out in and around Konar Takhteh. Many people were killed and the road was closed between mid-January and mid-February 1908. There also were the usual robberies, while raider plundered a caravan; seven more caravans were waiting in Daleki for the violence to subside and relative safety to return.[419]

In the town of Kazerun there was no peace and quiet either. After a provincial *anjoman* was formed in Shiraz in 1907, other towns likewise wanted to create local ones, as did the people of Kazerun. However, the local religious leader, Hajj Sayyed Mahmud opposed this. The people then wrote to Mo'eyed al-Dowleh, governor-general of Fars, asking him to support them in creating an *anjoman*.[420] It is not clear whether the *anjoman* was established in Kazerun or not. Nevertheless, this event is an indication of the level of the tense nature of political life in Kazerun. As a result, the governor of Kazerun in 1907-08, Hajji Zargham al-Shari'eh, son of the Imam-e Jom'eh of Shiraz, who owned much land there, had no authority. The real power was in the hands of the *kalantar* of Kazerun, Khvajeh Ebrahim, "who

---

417. On this family's history and Kamarej, see Appendix 3.4.

418. Motahharizadeh 1383, pp. 23-24; Sirjani 1361, pp. 627, 658, 664, 723; *Jonub* 1371, year 1, 19 Rajab 1329 (16 July 1911), p. 7; Appendix IV.

419. Administration Report 1907-08, pp. 23-24; Bashiri 1367, vol. 1, p. 127. According to Motahharizadeh, Khvajeh Ebrahim was appointed as governor after Mohammad Karim Khan Kashkuli had been dismissed. But he then was detained, and a local rich landowner, Mo'in al-Shari'eh was appointed governor by Qavam al-Molk, the acting governor-general of Fars. When he was dismissed as acting governor-general, Khvajeh Ebrahim was freed and re-appointed by Nezam al-Saltaneh Mafi, the new governor-general. Motahharizadeh does neither mention any dates nor any sources, while the dates for the governors-general (acting or not) do not agree with those of the governors. Motahharizadeh 1383, p. 23.

420. Sarvestani 1383, p. 88.

used his powers for the extermination of his numerous private enemies. This naturally led to frequent fighting in and around the town."[421]

What did not help to improve matters in Fars either was the rapidity with which governors-general of Fars changed and how ineffective most of them were. After Sho'a' al-Saltaneh had left Shiraz on 30 September 1905, it was only on 8 December 1905 that Eqbal al-Saltaneh was appointed as governor-general.[422] He lasted till February 1906; thereafter from February to June 1906 Vazir-e Mahkhus and from July to November 1906 'Ala al-Dowleh served in that capacity. Then followed from November 1906 to February 1907 a period during which the sons of Qavam al-Molk were acting governor-general. In February 1907, Mo'eyed al-Dowleh was appointed governor-general, who arrived on 15 April 1907.[423] However, he was weak and sickly and left already on 13 June 1907, and was succeeded by Ne-zam al-Saltaneh, who resigned on 3 November 1907. Khabir al-Dowleh, the telegraph chief, officiated until 8 February 1908, when Vazir-e Makhsus, with the title of Saheb-Ekhtiyar be-came governor-general. He remained in office until 17 March 1908, when the appointment of Zell al-Soltan was announced.[424] During the short tenure of Zell al-Soltan (March-July 1908) as governor-general, security reigned on the roads, thereafter, there was none. Such was his reputation that even when he was not yet in Shiraz (he only arrived there on 8 May 1908) the roads were safe. The situation changed after his departure. Robberies were frequent in particular during the fall migration of the Qashqa'is. Fighting between Heydar Khan of Ka-marej and the Khan of Daleki also resumed after Zell al-Soltan's departure. Kazerun, which had become quiet during Zell al-Soltan governorship, "relapsed into its usual anarchy." This lasted until the appointment of Mohammad Karim Khan, a Kashkuli Qashqa'i chief as gov-ernor of Kazerun at the end of September 1908.[425]

One of the new governor's first actions was to dismiss the *kalantar* Khvajeh Ebrahim, the source of all trouble in Kazerun, according to the British. He with his brother Khva-jeh 'Abdollah (the later Naser-e Divan), mobilized armed supporters to resist the governor Mohammad Karim Khan Kashkuli. On 9 November 1908 Khvajeh Ebrahim was treacher-ously murdered. This did not resolve matters, of course. It was but a symptom of what was happening all along the Telegraph road. The people of Kazerun rose up against the governor and there was fighting in the town. Tehran sent a special vizier, Gholam Hoseyn Ghaffari to

---

421. Administration Report 1907-08, p. 23. "The Kura'i-Khamseh were owned by the Imam Juma of Shiraz, both the Kashkuli and Farsimedan Khans forcibly took possession of them in the autumn of 1911." Administration Report 1911, Appendix II, p. 16. It is possible that at that time Khvajeh Ebrahim was for a few weeks twice governor of Kazerun, although the timing given by Motahharizadeh 1383, p. 23 does not seem to be correct.

422. Administration Report 1905-06, p. 25. For the chaotic situation in Fars, see Ranjbar 1389, p. 17, doc. 24 (24 December 1905).

423. Administration Report 1906-07, p. 16. "Two brigands, Mullah Mansour and Malek Manaf, infested the district between Kazeroon and Daliki. British firms suffered excessively. The Persian post was not spared." Also, *tofangchi-giri* or guard duties were levied from muleteers by road guards between Kazerun and Borazjan. Ibid., p. 19. Travelers on the road between Kazerun and Shiraz were regularly divested of their possessions by Darashu'i Qashqa'i tribesmen, who also sacked Dasht-arzhan. Ranjbar 1389, p. 53, doc. 62 (6 November 1907).

424. Administration Report 1907-08, p. 20.

425. Administration Report 1908, p. 17; Kazeruni 1381, p. 94.

Shiraz to investigate the matter and settle the problems. Ghaffari was upset by the violent behavior of the Kazerunis as well as the shooting that went on and in his telegram to the Kazerunis he asked whether Khvajeh `Abdollah (Naser-e Divan) had gone mad? Therefore, on 7 December 1908 he ordered Khvajeh `Abdollah to stop his untoward activities.[426] The telegraph chief of Kazerun was ordered to inform the business community to open the shops so that matters would quieten down. Those who had complaints were invited to come to Shiraz to explain them. The artisans and shopkeepers then opened their shops again, but the ulama and merchants sought refuge in the Imamzadeh. On 11 December 1908, encouraged by their example, a group of Turks (i.e., Turkic speakers) wanted to join them, which led to scuffles with the governor's people (who, being Qashqa'is, were also Turkic speakers) who wanted to prevent this and five people were wounded. Because of the continuing unsettled and tumultuous situation, the ulama and merchants of Kazerun sent a telegram to Sayyed `Abdollah Behbahani, an influential religious scholar and one of the major leaders of the Constutitonal movement in Tehran, to ask his support for their plight. They accused Mohammad Karim Khan Kashkuli of oppression, property theft, and of imposition of a new tax on opium and on leased land (*moqate`eh-ye molki*). Behbahani replied on 5 March 1909, and the result was that the governor was sacked after having been in office for a few months.[427] The town was besieged for a while by local khans in 1909.[428]

During the summer of 1909, traders took the Firuzabad road, which was controlled by Sowlat al-Dowleh, the paramount chief of the Qashqa'i tribe. It was rather safe, but unfit for any but summer travel, due to lack of accommodation. However, Sowlat al-Dowleh had tasted money and was unlikely to let this morsel drop from his and his tribe's mouth. For the route chosen ran through the land of Sowlat al-Dowleh own tribal group, that of the `Amaleh.[429] Sowlat al-Dowleh had entered into an agreement with the merchants of Shiraz, guaranteeing "the safety of merchandise dispatched by a roundabout route from the coast to Shiraz, against a small fee for each load."[430] Nevertheless, robberies were still numerous that year. This was because "British merchants cannot avail themselves of this arrangement [with Sowlat al-Dowleh], for the insurance companies will have nothing to do with any but the regular routes; the Persian Government declines responsibility on the same account; while in case of loss it would be easier to obtain compensation from the man in the moon than from the Solat."[431] Also, there was fighting for control of stretches of the trade road, such as that part controlled by Kazerun. In July 1909, the Bushehr-Borazjan, Daleki-Kazerun road had been blocked for two months because of a feud between the Khan of Kamarej and the headman of Daleki and the Khan of Borazjan. The cause of the feud was the control over the road and there was heavy fighting in the narrow mountain passes.[432] When Heydar Beg of

426. Motahharizadeh 1383, p. 21, docs. 3-4; Qa'emmaqam 1359, pp. 129-30 (13 Dhi Qa`deh [1326]); Administration Report 1908, p. 17.

427. Motahharizadeh 1383, pp. 21-23, docs. 3-4; Qa'emmaqam 1359, pp. 129-30, 155, 273-74.

428. Sarvestani 1383, p. 141 quoting *Habl al-Matin* nr. 25, 1327 (March 1909).

429. Administration Report 1909, p. 26.

430. Fraser 1910, p. 265.

431. Administration Report 1909, p. 26; Fraser 1910, p. 265.

432. Persia no. 1 (1910), pp. 87-88.

Kamarej was killed by one of his men in September 1909, Khurshid Khan, his confidant and the guardian of his infant son, succeeded him, but Kamarej lost its control over Kazerun,[433] which by then was firmly in the hands of Khvajeh ʿAbdollah (Naser-e Divan).[434] In June 1909, a Russian caravan with consul Kabloubousky en route to Shiraz was attacked at Kazerun; one Cossack was seriously wounded. When the Russian consul-general Passek wanted to return to Bushehr his caravan was attacked near Khan-Zenan on 26 November and, therefore, he returned to Shiraz. As a result of these events the Kazerun route was closed altogether.[435]

These continuous fights and robberies had their impact on the direction of commercial traffic, because in 1909 no less than five different routes were used to travel from Bushehr to Shiraz, namely via:

(i) Kazerun;

(ii) Firuzabad;

(iii) Jerreh, Haft Mellah-Miyan-Menzil-Jerreh;

(iv) Jerreh (Borazjun, Tang-e Ram Jerreh); and

(v) Jerreh (Borazjan, Daleki, Sar Mashhad, Jerreh).[436]

433. Motahharizadeh 1383, p. 24; *Jonub* 1371, year 1, 19 Rajab 1329 (16 July 1911), p. 7.

434. Administration Report 1911, Appendix II, p. 16.

435. Administration Report 1909, p. 9; Administration Report 1909, p. 2; Ranjbar 1389, doc. 101 (26 November 1909).

436. Trade Report 1909-10, p. 1.

SKETCH MAP TO ACCOMPANY REPORT ON TRADE OF
BUSHIRE CONSULAR DISTRICT,

N

Scale

0   50   100 Miles

Ispahan

Bebahan

To Mahommerah

Bunder Dilam

DASHTISTAN

Kazeroon

Shiraz

To Kerman

L. Niriz

Borazjoon

JIRRCHC

Shif

Bushire

TANGISTAN

Firuzabad

DASHTI

PERSIAN

GULF

Bahrein

F A R S

KERMAN

LARISTAN

Map of various routes, Trade Report 1910

The endemic feuding, raiding and robbing not only had its impact on which route trade took, but also on its volume. Trade via the Bushehr-Shiraz route had declined since 1907 due to fighting between the Arab, Lor, and Qashqa'i tribes. Because of the resulting insecurity, goods could not be shipped and this led to congestion. Because Persian merchants depended mainly on British credit, bills were not paid as merchants either could not sell or had to sell goods at a loss. This led to bankruptcies among Persian traders, while British firms had large sums outstanding which they were unable to settle. Imports via the Telegraph road dropped from £439,937 in 1907-08 to £328,375 in 1908-09 or a reduction of about 30%. Prospects for the next year looked even worse. What made matters worse was that the local khans along the trade route acted totally independent from the governor-general of Fars. Their constant fighting caused the road to be unsafe or entirely blocked for months, while they also exacted illegal imposts. Moreover, because of ill-treatment by the 'road-guards' many muleteers refused to travel this route causing a shortage of transport capacity and thus higher rates. In 1905, some 5-7,000 mules traveled the road, while in 1909 their number was estimated to be only 2-3,000. Transport rates per 737 lbs. for Bushehr-Shiraz route rose from 80-90 qrans during 1900-05, to double that rate in 1909, and even to 200-300 qrans in 1909-10. As a result, insurance premiums also rose from 15s per £100 in 1905, to 30s. in 1907, 40s. in 1908, while in 1909 hardly any insurance was offered at all, unless at war risk premiums (£5 per £100), or 250% higher.[437]

Not only Persian traders and transporters as well as British merchants and insurers suffered losses, but it also reduced the level of their operations or closed them down, and some even went bankrupt. These higher costs of doing business as well as the losses had to be paid by somebody, and, as usual, it was the consumer; in this case the Persian consumer.

> A sugar famine in Shiraz had raised the price so high that fancy rates are being paid for transport. ... The unfortunate Bushire merchant has large quantities of sugar ready for dispatch to the scene of shortage, but robbery is a certainty on the *rah-i-Shah*, and on the road guaranteed by the Sowlat there are no caravanserais, and hence no protection for the sugar, which will surely melt in the rain, or otherwise suffer damage from the weather.[438]

The road problem was not made easier by the continuous high turnover of governor-generals of Fars. After Zell al-Soltan had been dismissed and left on 6 July 1908, he was succeeded by Asaf al-Dowleh who arrived on 21 September 1908. He remained in office until July 1909, when Zell al-Soltan once again was appointed. However, the Bakhtiyari victory at Tehran and the abdication of Mohammad `Ali Shah put a stop to that appointment and `Ala al-Dowleh was appointed instead. However, Sowlat al-Dowleh did not allow him to

437. Persia no. 1 (1910), pp. 87-89, 90 (list of imposts collected and where); Persia no. 1, 1911, pp. 23 (January 1910 – road blocked for one month), 38 (April 1910 – road between Kazerun and Daleki was very unsafe). Bushehr's reduced trade was Ahwaz's gain, whence it was transported to Isfahan. Administration Report 1909, p. 15. See also Bayat 1381, p. 204 (complaint by Persian merchants about insecurity at Kazerun/Kamarej and the substantial losses they suffered).

438. Fraser 1910, p. 266.

enter Fars, who wanted his puppet ʿEyn al-Dowleh to be appointed. Tehran gave in to his blackmail, but then Taqizadeh, a leading *Majles* deputy of the Democratic Party, torpedoed this sweet deal, and finally on 21 September 1909 Saham al-Dowleh was appointed, who remained in office till January 1910.[439] As a result, the two men could not collaborate, which made for a delicate political situation and contributed to the continued insecurity. In January 1910, the Telegraph road was blocked due to a disagreement between Sowlat al-Dowleh and the governor-general of Fars, Saham al-Dowleh. The former demanded governorships in return for guaranteeing security on the Shiraz-Kazerun stretch of the Telegraph road. This was refused; he then proposed that the route via Jerreh be used as he guaranteed its safety. As the governor-general refused, merchants did not take this road. However, this led to his resignation. Tehran appointed Farmanfarma as his successor, but he remained in Tehran.[440] Because the merchants did not want to wait, they started to use the route via Jerreh in February 1910.[441] They were right not to wait, because Farmanfarma resigned after one month, and Zafar al-Saltaneh was appointed as the new governor-general. However, everybody knew that the real governor-general was Sowlat al-Dowleh, and because he wanted caravans to use the Jerreh route, they did.[442] However, as time would tell, Sowlat al-Dowleh was not a reliable partner. The routes were suddenly and arbitrarily changed. In January 1910, he made a commitment to a number of merchants in Shiraz to make roads safe in his territory. However, "he altered the route to be used by muleteers three times within a few weeks, to tracks via the Tang-e Kalimeh, then via Husseinabad and Tang-i-Ram respectively, and finally fixed on the Jirreh-Sar Mashhad-Daliki road. The Firuzabad road was also used a little." [443]

Meanwhile, the route between Kazerun and Daleki was unsafe, and numerous robberies occurred there. The Jerreh route remained open under Sowlat al-Dowleh's protection, but it lacked caravanserais or arrangements for fodder at various stages. Moreover, the muleteers resented Sowlat al-Dowleh's recent agreement with the Khans of Daleki and Borazjan to divert the trade through their territories. This meant that caravans had to make two long marches on a bad road without supplies being available. Meanwhile, the khans of Tangestan and Chahkuteh also tried to have trade pass through their territory, thus creating more uncertainty and insecurity. As there was no other choice and the central government assumed the responsibility for the Jerreh route the Iranian and foreign merchants gave up their opposition.[444]

439. Administration Report 1908, p. 13; Administration Report 1909, p. 19.

440. Persia no. 1 (1911), p. 23 (January 1910). The Buyer Ahmadi were also robbing caravans in 1910. Persia 1 (1911), pp. 18-21.

441. Persia no. 1 (1911), p. 29 (February 1910).

442. Persia no. 1 (1911), p. 31 (February-March 1910); Administration Report 1910, p. 4 (Saham al-Dowleh left Shiraz on 5 February 1910. Zafar al-Saltaneh reached Shiraz on 29 May, "with 800 infantry and 200 sowars; all, however, armed with obsolete rifles, and none supplied with cartridges"). Sowlat al-Dowleh also engineered the appointment of Qashqa'i (-friendly) governors elsewhere in Fars, including in Kazerun. Ranjbar 1389, p. 161, doc. 209 (22 May 1911).

443. Administration Report 1910, p. 17.

444. Persia no. 1 (1911), p. 38 (February 1910); Administration Report 1910, p. 2. For a discussion of these two Khans, see Administration Report 1911, Appendix II, pp. 1-2 (Chahkuteh), 11-13 (Tangestan).

Sowlat al-Dowleh

KAZERUN—HALFWAY STATION TO SHIRAZ • 141

Because of the insecurity of the trade routes, there was increased congestion of goods at certain locations, which spoiled prices. It also caused the Russian Odessa Line, which had the land and maritime transport contract for Iranian tobacco, to have this sent from Isfahan to Ahvaz rather than to Bushehr for transshipment.[445] In May 1910, Sowlat al-Dowleh all-of-a-sudden informed the merchants of Shiraz that he was no longer responsible for any new caravans on the until then safe Jerreh route. As a result all trade stopped. Merchants therefore were in discussion with Sowlat al-Dowleh to find a solution. It was said that he wanted caravans to take the route via Firuzabad.[446] To everybody's surprise, in June 1910, the Bushehr-Kazerun route was open without problem,[447] but that was a temporary phenomenon, because the only route that was safe was the one for which Sowlat al-Dowleh provided guards.[448] On 8 July 1910, the governor-general said that the governor of Kazerun assumed responsibility for the Telegraph route to Bushehr, but Sowlat al-Dowleh opposed this, and thus caravans were afraid to use the normal trade route.[449] Because the Firuzabad road was safe, caravans used it. Nevertheless, the Qashqa'is still blackmailed the muleteers by raiding the Telegraph road to make sure that it was unsafe.[450] This had a negative impact on transport rates, which went up to 310 *qran*s for 775 lbs, although they dropped to 200 *qran*s in June and to 150 *qran*s at end of the year. Throughout this period mules were hard to get.[451] In September 1910, the road from Kazerun to Bushehr remained closed, and caravans continued to use the Firuzabad road.[452] However, towards the end of the year that road also became unsafe, for by that time, "The roads in Fars are all unsafe, and traffic is almost entirely suspended."[453] On 14 October 1910, the British protested against the continuing robberies to Tehran. As a result, Tehran made a deal with Sowlat al-Dowleh, viz. that he was put in charge of the Telegraph road, which was declared open and its safety guaranteed by Sowlat al-Dowleh. However, by that time the passes were blocked with snow, so it was unclear how he was going to realize his commitment.[454]

Zafar al-Saltaneh was dismissed as governor-general of Fars at the end of 1910, and Ne-zam al-Saltaneh was appointed in his stead; he arrived in Shiraz in the beginning of January

445. Administration Report 1910, p. 17.

446. Persia no. 1 (1911), p. 59.

447. Persia no. 1 (1911), p. 62.

448. Persia no. 1 (1911), p. 74 (July 1910).

449. Persia no. 1 (1911), p. 85.

450. Persia no. 1 (1911), p. 96 (August 1910).

451. Administration Report 1910, p. 17.

452. Persia no. 1 (1911), p. 101.

453. Persia no. 1 (1911), p. 111; see also Ranjbar 1389, pp. 119-20, doc. 153 (4 October 1910).

454. Administration Report 1910, p. 17; see further Tayyebi 1389, p. 90, doc. 78 (21 November 1910) where Sowlat al-Dowleh offers the *Majles* and the government of Iran to guarantee safety on the road between Shiraz and Bushehr; and Ranjbar 1389, p. 124, doc. 156 (7 November 1910), where the government of Iran announces the road security agreement with Sowlat al-Dowleh, and Ibid., pp. 126-27, doc. 161 (28 December 1910) where Sowlat al-Dowleh reports on some of his activities and asks for military equipment and ammunition.

1911.[455] Initially, the Telegraph road was safe in 1911, although it was occasionally closed due to Nezam al-Saltaneh's actions at Kamarej. This was because the various tribal groups were afraid of action by Nezam al-Saltaneh and therefore, did not raid.[456] Nezam al-Saltaneh's actions near Kamarej were due to the fact that Khurshid Khan until the spring of 1911 held Tang-e Torkan, Rahdar and the adjacent Shapur district, plus the Kamarej valley. According, to the British, he kept admirable order, although he levied *rahdari*. However, he was ousted by Nezam al-Saltaneh, and his place was taken by Mohammad `Ali Khan Kashkuli, the governor of Kazerun.[457] This change had come about due to the machinations of Sowlat al-Dowleh. He was unable to control the Telegraph road, because the stretch Shiraz-Tang-e Torkan was under the Kashkuli Khans, and Kazerun was under Mohammad `Ali Khan Kashkuli. Sowlat al-Dowleh, therefore, wanted control over a longer stretch of the route, but Khurshid Khan controlled Kamarej, and of old he was hostile to the Qashqa'is. Sowlat al-Dowleh then convinced Nezam al-Saltaneh that Khurshid Khan was but a highwayman. Nezam al-Saltaneh ordered Sowlat al-Dowleh to arrest Khurshid Khan and to take possession of Kamarej. After some fighting, Khurshid Khan fled into the mountains. Mohammad `Ali Khan Kashkuli took Kamarej as part of his territory. Thereafter, Khurshid Khan and his followers carried out raids. As a result, safety on the road grew worse rather than better, so that Nezam al-Saltaneh was required to send a force to suppress the violence. Because these troops were unsuccessfull in taking Khurshid Khan and through intercession, Khurshid Khan was given amnesty and his old road stretch at Kamarej. This development increased the enmity between Mohammad `Ali Khan Kashkuli and Khurshid Khan. Naser-e Divan, the *kalantar* of Kazerun took the side of Khurshid Khan.[458]

---

455. Administration Report 1910, pp. 12, 15.

456. Administration Report 1911, p. 20. This insecure situation induced Naser-e Divan to write to the journal *Jonub* expressing the hope that Mohammad Qoli Khan Kashkuli would exert himself to suppress highway robbery. The Qashqa'i representative replied that he did his best to prevent the Mamasani and Buyer Ahmadi from raiding, as a result of which the road between Shiraz and Kazerun was safe. *Jonub* 1371, year 1, 20 Moharram 1229 (21 January 1911), p. 7. This was followed up by a report from the Ilkhani with more details of what action Mohammad Qoli Khan Kashkuli had undertaken, and what the Qashqa'is were doing assisting the government against the robbers of Tangestan. No action against Khurshid Khan or Kamarej, however, is mentioned. Ibid., year 1, 4 Safar 1229 (4 February 1911), p. 7.

457. Persia no. 1, 1912, p. 143 (15 July 1912). *Jonub* 1371, year 1, 19 Rajab 1329 (16 July 1911), p. 7, also reported that Khurshid Khan had kept good order. When he was attacked with cannon and his village besieged, Khurshid Khan sent a plea to the *Majles* and government of Iran to assist him against the attack by the Qashqa'i tribe, whose leaders had misled the governor-general of Fars. Tayyebi 1389, p. 114 (doc. 89 8 April 1911). Later the government of Iran also acknowledged that Khurshid Khan's activities had been beneficial to trade. Ranjbar 1389, p. 161, doc. 209 (21 May or 20 June 1911), 189, doc. 233 (8 November 1911).

458. Motahharizadeh 1383, p. 25; Appendix 3.4; *Jonub* 1371, year 1, 19 Rajab 1329 (16 July 1911), pp. 7-8; Ibid., 5 Ramazan 1329 (30 August 1911), p. 6 (also details about the role played by E`temad al-Tojjar Behbahani and the return of all the robbed goods by Khurshid Khan). The Qashqa'i leadership criticized the violent behavior of Sheikh Hoseyn Chahkutahi and of Za'er Khezr. *Jonub* 1371, year 1, 18 Rabi` II 1229 (18 April 1911), p. 4.

Mohammad Karim Khan Kashkuli on the left

In mid-1911 the road became unsafe again due to troubles in Shiraz. Trade came to a total standstill, for although the road was open, goods could not be distributed from the market towns, due to anarchy in their hinterland. In October and November 1911, the Bushehr-Shiraz road was partially and then entirely closed. When it was opened again robberies immediately took place and two Japanese merchants were robbed. The situation of the road was so bad that in October 1910 the British warned Tehran that "unless order was restored within three months," they would themselves police the Bushehr-Isfahan road, hinting that a 1,200 local force under British officers would do that. The announcement of the formation of a Swedish-officered gendarmerie by the government of Iran in September 1911 gave Tehran some respite. However, when robberies continued to increase, the British government decided to reinforce the mounted escorts for the Shiraz consulate and other areas. However, matters were delayed and finally only the consular guards in Bushehr, Shiraz, and Isfahan were reinforced. Because there was a strong resentment against Russia due to its military occupation of the north, and less so against Great Britain in the south, a resentment reinforced by agitation by mullahs and newspapers like *Habl al-Matin*, even acquiring overtones of anti-Christian sentiments, the British were apprehensive about the reception of the landing of Indian troops as they wanted to avoid the impression that they had territorial or other sinister designs towards the south. Therefore, London informed Tehran that these escorts would not patrol the roads, if Tehran implemented a good alternative solution. On 27 October 1911, a force of 160 and on 2 January 1912 another 100 British-Indian troops landed at Bushehr, unfortunately this coincided with Russia reinforcing its forces in the north, the Russian threat to occupy Tehran, the outbreak of hostilities in Tabriz, and Italy's declaration of war against the Ottoman government in Tripoli. Moreover, the British consulate had given refuge to Qavam al-Molk, which made Sowlat al-Molk (the former's bitter enemy) believe that these troops were to attack the Qashqa'is and curb their lawless activities. Ghazanfar al-Saltaneh, the chief of Borazjan wanted to oppose the landing, because the caravans refused to pay *rahdari* and because of inflammatory telegrams from Najaf and elsewhere. However, he finally did nothing, although the British suspected him of having engineered the hostile attitude of the tribes and an attack on 24 December 1911 further up the road.[459]

---

459. Administration Report 1911, pp. 2, 14-15, 19-23. "The normal escort of the Shiraz Consulate, as in most of our Consulates in Persia, consists of ten or twelve Sawars from an Indian Cavalry regiment, who keep guard at the Consulate gate, and accompany the Consul on visits of ceremony and tours in the country, etc. But when I arrived at Shiraz in December 1912 I found that besides the usual escort of Sawars there were six squadrons of an Indian Cavalry regiment and seventy to eighty Indian infantrymen as well." O'Connor 1931, p. 193. Likewise, at Bushehr the British Residency only had a small guard of Indian soldiers hence the soldiers for Shiraz had to be sent from India. Douglas 1923, p. 105.

Photo of the British consular guard in Shiraz, Nystrøm 1925, p. 86

In late 1911, Mahallati, an influential religious leader in Shiraz and supporter of the Democratic Party, issued a *fatwa* to oppose foreign troops and people followed suit when other ulama concurred with Mahallati. According to Motahharizadeh, Naser-e Divan with the support of some people from Bushehr was part of the group that attacked a group of British subjects and wounded Consul Smart and killed two men of his Indian escort in December 1911.[460] According to British sources, when Smart traveled from Shiraz to Bushehr to take up his new post, his party was attacked about 12 miles west of Kazerun (Kotal-e Dokhtar) and the attacks continued until he arrived in town. At every village they passed the attack was renewed and it looked as if the entire Kazerun valley participated in the attack.[461] Mohammad ʿAli Khan Kashkuli, who saved the slightly wounded Smart and took him to his camp, maintained that he was not responsible for the attack. He told Smart: "the common people were no longer properly under constraint; they had been much excited by the priests against our troops; he had given orders to the tofangchis to let me pass, but the people were out of hand."[462] Despite his claim of innocence, the British were convinced that Mohammad

---

460. Motahharizadeh 1383, p. 26 quoting Adamiyat 1370, p. 25. In response to the ulama's call, Sowlat al-Dowleh also had sent tribesmen to Jerreh and Kazerun in December 1911 to stop British troops, which did not come. Ranjbar 1389, p. 206, doc. 254 (22 January 1912).

461. Persia no. 1, 1912, p. 11 (26 December 1911).

462. Persia no. 1, 1912, p. 11 (13 January 1912).

`Ali Khan Kashkuli was responsible for the attack and they insisted on the arrest of the persons responsible.[463]

Photo of Mohammad `Ali Khan Kashkuli

Because Nezam al-Saltaneh was unable to secure the road to Bushehr he was dismissed in October 1911. Initially, Rokn al-Dowleh and then Farmanfarma were named as

---

463. Administration Report 1911, pp. 23-24. However, in 1914 it is reported that Ali Mohammad Kamareji, the "notorious outlaw, chief culprit in the attack on Consul Smart lost his life towards the end of October in a local fight near Kazerun." Administration Report 1913, p. 8.

replacements but neither man was interested to accept the post. Early November 1911, `Ala al-Dowleh was appointed, but before he left for Shiraz he was assassinated in Tehran in December. Qavam al-Molk was then appointed temporarily against his wishes. He was relieved by Mokhber al-Saltaneh, the new governor-general, who arrived in Shiraz on 16 October 1912.[464] The English demanded the arrest of those who had wounded Smart and punishment of Mohammad `Ali Khan Kashkuli, who had become the main source of insecurity on the road.[465]

In 1912, traffic on the road was interrupted for prolonged periods and was forcibly diverted "to execrable and little used tracks" to avoid infighting by the various khans, such as:

Zair Khadhar of Tangistan in alliance with Ahmed Khan of Angali against Sheikh Husein of Chahkutah.

Agha Haidar and brothers of Chaghadak and Tul-i-Siah against the inhabitants of Buneh-i-Gaz who were aided by Zair Khadhar of Tangistan.

Ghazanfar-es-Sultaneh of Borasjun in alliance with Nur Muhammad Khan of Daliki against Ismail Khan of Shabankareh, father-in-law of the former.

Nur Muhammad Khan of Daliki and brother Husein Beg of Kunar Takhteh against Mulla Kuli of Kumarij supported by Ismail Khan of Shabankareh.

Ismail Khan of Shabankareh and Muhammad Khan, Kashkuli, against Agha Sardar of Khisht and other Khisht elements supported by the Daliki Khan.

The late Khurshid Beg of Kumarij against Ali Muhammad the Kumarij outlaw aided by Muhammad Ali Khan, Kashkuli.

Nasir-ud-Diwan, Kalantar of Kazerun, against Muhammad Ali Khan, Kashkuli.

Sowlet-ed-Dowleh, Kashgai, with Ayyaz Kikha Darashuri, against the former's half brother Zeigham-ed-Dowleh supported by other Kashgai Kalantars and Kawam-ul-Mulk.[466]

The situation in Fars had grown so uncertain that Smart, the British consul in Shiraz raised the necessity to evacuate all Europeans from Shiraz. This was discussed with London, which rejected such a move, because the need might be there and then it might not. Moreover, London feared loss of face among the Moslem population, while it would give Russia a pretext to take further action in the north. It was, therefore, suggested to open negotiations with the tribal chiefs to each guard a section of the road, assuring them a subsidy and monthly pay for the guards and imply that the reinforced garrison of Bushehr, if need be, might be used against them. However, before negotiations were to start the Khan of Borazjan had to be eliminated or punished and a strict blockade of the littoral to be maintained. The cost of the subsidy to be paid to the various Khans had to come out of the customs revenues. In exchange the Khans had to pay compensation for all British goods robbed within their section of the road. London wanted to go ahead with this scheme as the formation of the

---

464. Administration Report 1911, p. 12; Administration Report 1912, p. 14.

465. Mokhber al-Saltaneh 1344, p. 268.

466. Administration Report 1912, pp. 17-18.

Gendarmerie had not yet taken place. However, when the Persian government learnt of this plan it protested strongly, because this would weaken its authority among the tribal chiefs.[467]

The reasons for proposing to take some action, to improve security on the Telegraph road, was that London considered that the situation was growing worse. During the period between 1908 and 1911 there had been a total of 64 attacks on caravans, which resulted in a loss of 738,165 qrans to British subjects. The losses were higher if those of non-British subjects would be taken into account.[468] Moreover, the combination of the levying of rahdari, the shortage of mules, and the hostilities along the route (mainly between Borazjan and Kazerun) had increased mule hire from 110 qrans in March 1907 to 170 in 1910 and to 420-440 in October 1912. Rates eventually rose to 50 tumans, and rahdari continued to be levied.[469] In fact, the increase of illegal imposts rose as well from 3 qrans 70 shahis in June 1907 to 27 qrans 50 shahis per mule in May 1912.[470] As a result of all these developments traffic on the Telegraph road decreased. On 8 June 1912, it was reported that since mid-April only 4,024 mules had entered Bushehr, and only 1,070 in the last 18 days. "This is totally insufficient," the British reported.[471]

Nothing came of this proposal to pay the tribal chief in exchange for security on the Telegraph road, however. London decided to abandon the planned negotiations, because it needed the Persian government's support and approval. Moreover, because by August 1912 an as yet untested gendarmerie force had been formed, whose presence was desperately needed.[472] Although the road situation was somewhat better than in 1911, there still were many robberies between Daleki and Kazerun. Moreover, the Kashkuli chiefs put stretches of the roads up for auction. "The right to fleece and blackmail is now being bought and sold openly. Kashkulis have deflected road to Kadun valley to avoid passing via Kazerun. They have entrusted ill-famed [Khvajeh Ebrahim] caravanserai mentioned to Ali Mohammad [Kamareji] who is at enmity with Khan of Kamarej, next stage." At the end of April 1911, traffic stopped altogether due to tribal fighting at Khaneh Zenyan.[473] By June 1912, the unauthhorized Shif route had also been brought in use again.[474]

Because Mohammad `Ali Khan Kashkuli tried to stop the passage of caravans through Tang-e Torkan it united the chiefs of Kazerun and Kamarej, who led caravans via the steeper

467. Administration Report 1912, pp. 20-25.

468. Persia no. 1, 1912, pp. 92-94.

469. Persia no. 1, 1912, p. 286; see also Jonub 1371, year 1, 19 Rajab 1329 (16 July 1911), p. 8; Administration Report 1912, p. 29. According to Yate 1917, p. 173, n. 1, "A tufangchi (Mousquetaire) is a living embodiment of the motto 'set a thief to catch a thief,' only – he does not catch him. Thief and tufangchi understand each other thouroughly in Persia."

470. Persia no. 1, 1912, p. 148 (August 1912).

471. Persia no. 1 (1913), p. 78-79 (Smart to Townley 8 June 1912, p. 78-79).

472. Administration Report 1912, pp. 24-25.

473. Persia no. 1 (1913), pp. 78-79 (Smart to Townley 8 June 1912). The Qashqa'is were responsible for many of the raids enabled, among other reasons, by the large number of modern arms that had become available to the tribesmen. Jonub 1371, year 1, 20 Ramazan 1329 (14 September 1911), p. 3.

474. Persia no. 1 (1913), p. 78-79 (Smart to Townley 8 June 1912, p. 78-79).

Bardon pass.[475] "Some caravans to escape ruffianly roadguards, Mohammed Ali Khan's dependents at Rahdar, make short cut from Kamarij over precipitous pass to Kazerun via Bardun, this track being at present efficiently guarded by Khurshid Khan of Kamarij and Kalantar of Kazerun."[476] Caravans north of Kazerun were even more harassed and blackmailed by Qashqa'i roadguards for not having taken the Nowdan route. Khurshid Khan, therefore, wanted to retake Rahdar and Shapur from Mohammad 'Ali Khan Kashkuli, and asked for British help to do so.[477]

Such help was not given, of course. Not so much because shortly thereafter Khurshid Khan was killed, but, more importantly, the British did not want to police the road themselves. Therefore, they had agreed to finance the creation and operation of the Swedish-officered gendarmerie in the previous year. A large number of the newly created gendarmerie arrived on 14 April 1912 in Shiraz.[478] In October 1912, Mokhber al-Saltaneh, the governor-general of Fars decided to put the Shiraz-Kazerun road under the control of a force consisting of 150 gendarmes and 110 local riflemen, who would be paid by the gendarmerie. Henceforth no *rahdari* would be collected.[479] The gendarmerie force had to fight its way to Kazerun, for there was strong resistance at Tang-e Torkan and elsewhere, resulting in dead and wounded on both sides.[480] Mokhber al-Saltaneh came down hard on Mohammad 'Ali Khan Kashkuli. In addition, he ordered Ahmad Khan Daryabegi, the governor of the Gulf Ports, to march from Bushehr to Kazerun with two aims: to secure the Telegraph road with the gendarmerie and to take serious action against Mohammad 'Ali Khan Kashkuli and other recalcitrant Qashqa'i Khans. The result was a somewhat safer road near Kazerun, but the fire was not put out, for it remained smoldering. In an unrelated event, on 11 December 1912, Capt. Eckford was killed at Dasht-e Arjan, when his hunting party ran into a group of Buyer Ahmadi marauders. They were just lying in wait for a caravan and were not targeting British military; it was just a case of bad luck. On 25 January 1913, Daryabegi escaped an ambush by Mohammad 'Ali Khan Kashkuli at Tang-e Torkan. Traffic continued, but heavy tolls were levied between Kazerun and Tang-e Torkan.[481] On 14 February 1914, a donkey caravan was taken

475. Motahharizadeh 1383, pp. 26-27.

476. Persia no. 1, 1912, pp. 79-80 (9 June 1912); Appendix 3.4. In the valley of Kamarij, "I observed a path along the rocks on our right hand, which led to Kauzeroon by a shorter but more difficult cut, only used in troublesome times, or by foot messengers." Rich 1839, p. 211; see also Curzon 1892, vol. 2, p. 220.

477. Persia no. 1, 1912, p. 79-80 (9 June 1912). The Kashkulis, whose Khans controlled the villages of Shapur and its valley, camped on the banks of the Shapur river in spring and fall. Administration Report 1911, Appendix II, p. 16.

478. Persia no. 1 (1913), p. 38. For a picture of their arrival in Shiraz, see Nyström 1925, p. 79. For an analysis of the role and functioning of the gendarmerie, see Cronin 1996; see also Ineichen 2002.

479. Persia no. 1, 1912, p. 195 (22 October 1912); Mokhber al-Saltaneh 1344, pp. 248, 254 (he was not convinced that Swedish officers were needed).

480. Motahharizadrh 1383, p. 112 (doc. 10)

481. Persia 1914, no. 1, p. 25; Mokhber al-Saltaneh 1344, p. 251; O'Connor 1931, pp. 194-95; Demorgny 1914, pp. 95-97. According to Motahharizadeh 1383, p. 27, the Kashkulis had given up their interference and the road was free again, which in light of their continued exactions either is erroneous or refers to a later date. Villagers also suffered as the marauders stole their sheep. Persia 1914, no. 1, p. 67.

near Kazerun, but it was recovered by Daryabegi. On 27 and 28 February 1913, Bolvardis, sedentarized Qashqa'is, stole sheep and donkeys near Kazerun.[482]

With the gendarmerie force in place, it was found that the men from the north were unable to police the road in the south; it was too hot for them. Mokhber al-Saltaneh then arranged with chiefs on the road south of Kazerun that their men would act as roadguard. No *rahdari* would be collected in lieu of a monthly payment to the Khans, while some of his men would be hired as roadguards. The British opposed this plan as the Khans would consider the subsidy a permanent payment. Although road security remained bad, some progress was made. The collection of *rahdari* was kept in check, and the rates of transport were reduced through pressure of a combination of Bushehr forwarding merchants. Transport rates had risen to 500 *qrans* in 1912, but in March 1913 they had already been reduced to 300 *qrans*; for certain commodities they even went down to 225 (piece-goods) and 270 *qrans* (sugar).[483] It would seem that the governor-general of Fars indeed paid the chiefs of Chenarak, Ahmadi, Borazjan, Daleki and Konar Takhteh a subvention, which in the case of the chief of Borazjan allegedly amounted to more than 7,000 *tumans*. As a result, the chiefs of Dashti and Dashtestan also asked a subvention as did Naser-e Divan of Kazerun.[484] Given the good results that the gendarmerie had achieved and the adequacy of their number O'Connor saw no need to keep the British-Indian troops in Shiraz. They marched without any problem to Bushehr and returned to India, while O'Connor was left with an escort of only ten Indian horsemen.[485]

Although there were those who opposed the gendarmerie, this was not the case in Kazerun, according to Motahharizadeh. He does not provide any evidence for this statement, apart from pointing out that Mohammad ʿAli Khan Kashkuli, who held Shapur temporarily, vacated this area when confronted with a superior force of gendarmes. However, that force treacherously attacked his stronghold of Tul-e Kolah, while he was negotiating with Major Uggla on the arrangement of his withdrawal from the district.[486] Moreover, the Swedish officers, whether Major Oscar Ohlson or his collegue Per Nyström, all were convinced that

---

482. Persia 1914, no. 1, p. 47. In mid-March 1913, Mohammad ʿAli Khan Kashkuli's followers destroyed the telegraph line near Kazerun; they prevented staff to repair it for some time. Persia 1914, no. 1, p. 60.

483. Administration Report 1913, pp. 23, 32; O'Connor 1931, p. 200. On the heat suffered by the gendarmes and not feeling 'at home', see Akhgar 1366, pp. 112, 116.

484. Nava'i 1385, pp. 126-27. In 1913, "the Governor-General made an arrangement with certain headmen on the road south of Kazerun under which rahdari was to be abolished, in return for a monthly stipend paid to the Khan, and the enrolment of a certain number of his men as road guards. The scheme entailed an expenditure of about £150 a month or rather less than it was estimated would have to be paid for similar services under a scheme drawn up by the gendarmerie." Administration Report 1913, p. 23.

485. O'Connor 1931, p. 2001; Administration Report 1913, p. 16 ("the regiment was shown every civility and attention by the headmen of Daliki, Borasjun and Ahmadi"). For a picture of the gendarmes in front of the British consulate in Shiraz, see Nyström 1925, p. 86. In the early fall of 1913, Mokhber al-Saltaneh, governor-general of Fars reported that the road between Shiraz and Bushehr was completely safe even on stretches of the road where as yet no gendarmes were posted. Ranjbar 1389, p. 249, doc. 309 (fall 1913).

486. Motahharizadeh 1383, p. 29, 113 (doc. 13); Appendix 3.2; Mokhber al-Saltaneh 1344, p. 254; Administration Report 1913, pp. 24-25 (gives a detailed description of the gendarmerie action). South of Kazerun the gendarmerie did not feel welcome, see Akhgar 1366, p. 113.

Naser-e Divan was hostile and involved in the robberies of caravans.[487] Since there were at least five Swedish officers at the end of 1913 in Kazerun, they had first-hand knowledge of the situation there, including that concerning Naser-e Divan's attitude, role and activities. Therefore, it was irrelevant, as Motahharizadeh has it, that the Armenian telegrapher in Kazerun was conspiring against Naser-e Divan by sending untrue information to O'Connor to blacken his name and to have him declared a rebel so that the gendarmes would also arrest him. Moreover, Mokhber al-Saltaneh, the governor-general of Fars had no faith in any of his reports. Naser-e Divan was returning to Kazerun with his men, when, allegedly at the instigation of the telegrapher, officers of gendarmerie surrounded him half-way and asked that he surrender his arms, but he refused. `Ali Mohammad Kamareji openly opposed the gendarmerie and skirmished with them and then fled to the fort (qal`eh) in Tang-e Torkan.[488]

Meanwhile, in mid-November 1913, a large gendarmerie force surrounded the fort where `Ali Mohammad Kamareji had sought refuge, but he was able, or rather he was allowed, to escape. After the failed attempt to capture `Ali Mohammad Kamareji the gendarmerie force destroyed many towers and disarmed villagers in the area. As a result, the villagers poured into Kazerun. The bulk of the gendarmerie force had marched down to Borazjan, its intended base, while a small detachment remained in Kazerun. When a column of 32 gendarmes left Kazerun on 21 November 1913, it was attacked by tribesmen, probably those of `Ali Mohammad Kamareji. After losing two men the gendarmes returned to their barracks in Kazerun. Having arrived there they were attacked at sunset by the peasants they had displaced a few days earlier. `Ali Mohammad Kamareji, who had been hiding in the neighborhood, joined the attack. Some people were killed, and fear took hold of the inhabitants including Mazhar al-Dowleh the governor, who sought refuge in the telegraph office. At midnight, the 32 gendarmes fled from the barracks to the telegraph building, where the telegraphist disarmed them to avoid an armed encounter. `Ali Mohammad Kamareji surrounded the telegraph building and plundered the goods of the gendarmes in the barracks.[489]

On learning about the attack, Colonel Uggla immediately sent 500 men from Bushehr to Kazerun under Major Lundberg, while Mokhber al-Saltaneh sent Daryabegi with 100 cavalry and 200 foot to assist the gendarmerie. At that time, it was further reported that `Ali Mohammad Kamareji's *tofangchi*s had killed a finance agent at Dehris. After a brisk fight from

487.   Nyström 1925, pp. 183-88 (which also contains notes from Ohlson diary); Appendix 3.1.

488.   Motahharizadeh 1383, pp. 29, 114; Administration Report 1913, pp. 24-25, 29; Appendix 3.2; Ranjbar 1389, p. 252, doc. 314 (26 November 1913). It is true, of course, that none of the Swedish officers spoke or understood Persian, while they also were said to be insensitive to local susceptibilities. They, therefore, relied much on, if not were guided by, their Persian colleague officers, most of whom were from the North and for whom the tribal south was also a foreign country. However, the latter, many of whom were sympathetic to the local chiefs, were certainly able to gauge whether they were welcome, tolerated, or considered to be a hostile force and whether Naser-e Divan was engaged in road exactions or not. Cronin 1996, pp. 110, 119.

489.   Administration Report 1913, pp. 24-25; Motahharizadeh 1383, pp. 29-30, 38 n. 62; Oberling 1974, p. 122; Appendix 3.1. Mokhber al-Saltaneh 1344, pp. 258-59 disapproved of the gendarmerie operation against Mohammad `Ali Khan and later against Naser-e Divan, which he blamed on the European officials in Shiraz (Stas the head of the Treasury, Merrill and Uggla in league with O'Connor), who had sent the troops without his approval. If true, this is telling as to the degree of institutional anarchy that reigned in Shiraz. Mokhber al-Saltaneh from the beginning of his tenure as governor-general had made it clear that he distrusted and disliked the Belgian officials and did not want them to be employed as financial agents. Administration Report 1912, p. 15.

29 November to 1 December 1913, the gendarmes were able to take Kazerun and restore order. The siege was broken and ʻAli Mohammad Kamareji and his men fled into the hills. The gendarmes had suffered five dead and 26 wounded, among whom were three Persian officers. The other side had lost 29 dead and an unknown number of wounded. Three ringleaders were hanged,[490] among whom Gholam ʻAli Beg, a follower of Naser-e Divan. During these events Naser-e Divan was but an observer and did not interfere, according to Motahharizadeh. He allegedly had stayed at home, but had his men at a ready. However, why is it that the Swedish officers of the gendarmerie believed that he was involved in the attack and instigator of the troubles, which led to killing of the tax official? Also, why did Naser-e Divan flee after the fight? Moreover, Gholam ʻAli Beg, and one of his men together with other followers were arrested for participation in the attack and executed. The government of Iran also believed that Naser-e Divan was involved and ordered his expulsion from Kazerun.[491]

Mazhar al-Dowleh, the governor of Kazerun was recalled to Shiraz and allegedly had to account for the many complaints against him. However, Mokhber al-Saltaneh does not make any mention of this or the governor himself in his memoirs, when discussing the attack and its aftermath, although he continued to employ him. Daryabegi was appointed governor of Kazerun and Mokhber al-Saltaneh asked him to accord Naser-e Divan amnesty, as his guilt was not proven, and take him to Shiraz. Naser-e Divan then returned unarmed to Kazerun and lived quietly in his house. However, he nourished resentment concerning the gendarmerie; and each party was waiting for the next move by the other.[492]

---

490. Ranjbar 1389, pp. 253, doc. 315 (1? December 1913), 254, doc. 316 (2 December 1913); Administration Report 1913, p. 25. Later it was claimed that the finance agent was a Baha'i, an often used and convenient argument to escape punishment for a crime committed, as Baha'is were and are beyond the pale in Iran and may be killed at will. Motahharizadeh 1383, p. 38, n. 60, 114 (doc. 15).

491. Motahharizadeh 1383, pp. 30, 115 (doc. 17). *The Times* (5 December 1913), first reported that ʻAli Mohammad was behind the attack, who was dissatisfied "at the restitution to the rightful owners of the lands in the Shahpur district by Mohammad Ali Kashkuli," but later (28 February 1914), wrote that Naser-e Divan was suspected to have been "the ring leader." Oberling 1974, p. 122. However, the gendarmerie suspected that Mokhber al-Saltaneh was implicated in the uprising. Cronin 1996, p. 111.

492. Motahharizadeh 1383, pp. 30-31, 124, doc. 35; *Fars* year 1, nr. 35, p. 2, which expressed the hope that he would not fall into his old and bad ways.

Photo of the front of the house where Major Ohlson died, Nystrøm 1925, p. 188

On 26 February 1914, a small gendarmerie force attacked the house and tower of Naser-e Divan, "the late [sic] Kadkhuda of Kazerun, who had adopted a menacing attitude."[493] The British consul in Shiraz, Major O'Connor, described Naser-e Divan as a semi-independent, semi-robber chieftain, "finding his time-honoured privileges and perquisites were being curtailed and indeed threatened with complete extinction, assumed a threatening attitude towards the gendarmerie."[494] However, according to Motahharizadeh, O'Connor had asked the gendarmerie to arrest Naser-e Divan in his house, for which assertion he provides no evidence.[495] At 3 a.m. in the morning, Major Ohlson and his gendarmes went to Naser-e Divan's fortlike compound. Because he did not expect him to surrender voluntarily, Major Ohlson believed that the best way to gain access to the compound was to blow up the gate with a mine. While doing so he was shot and killed, which suggests that the defenders had advance warning of his action, despite the steps he had taken to prevent this. His party withdrew to the barracks, where the gendarmes were almost immediately surrounded and besieged. The town was in uproar and stood behind Naser-e Divan, while the ulama issued a *fatwa* against the gendarmes. Naser-e Divan attacked the barracks immediately with "all his own 'tufang-chis,' and any local tribesmen and scallywags who thought fit to join in." The gendarmes were

493. Administration Report 1914, p. 7.

494. O'Connor 1931, p. 207.

495. Motahharizadeh 1883, p. 31. Moreover, Nyström 1925, p. 186 does not bear this out. It is also highly unlikely that the neutral Swedish officers, some of whom were actually anti-British, would have danced to the tune of a British official, although Mokhber al-Saltaneh 1344, p. 259 blames O'Connor and Uggla for the attack. In 1916, the Swedish officers published a declaration in which they made it clear that they were not only neutral, but working for the interest of Iran just like Shuster had done before them to bring about Iran's freedom and independence. Cronin 1996, pp. 118-19; see also Ineichen 2002, pp. 145ff.

in big trouble and it was feared that all would be killed. Mme Ohlson took command until the arrival of Major Rimbeau, who was employed by Col. Merrill, an American officer, who had been 'requested' by Mokhber al-Saltaneh in June 1913 to organize a military force for Fars to maintain peace and order in the province under the command of the governorgeneral.[496] Col. Uggla in Shiraz on hearing this news immediately sent reinforcements, but the attacking force had become so strong that although the relief force was able to reach the barracks it could not raise the siege. Col. Merrill, who was raising men for his new force was then sent to their relief.[497]

When Major Rimbeau arrived at Kazerun he helped the besieged in stiffening their resolve. The arrival of reinforcements also helped and on 2 March 1914 Col. Merrill with his troops arrived. As a result, on 5 March 1914 the town was re-occupied and Naser-e Divan fled with his men into the hills. According to O'Connor, "There was some looting in the town by the gendarmerie and the other miscellaneous elements, but this was put a stop to with a firm hand by the Swedish officers and Merrill."[498] However, the official British Residency report states that Merill, who acted as military governor, could do little to restrain the gendarmes to take revenge and plunder as his force was too weak to do so, while the Swedish officers offered no help at all. The gendarmes looted the whole town, including the bazaar. Some 30 to 40 prisoners were about to be executed, were not it for Col. Merrill's intervention.[499] During the siege Naser-e Divan's men had behaved in a similar manner when they plundered the Jewish quarter, "and five Jews [were] abducted by rioters, who ask [a] large ransom for their release."[500] All merchants, craftsmen and ulama were arrested and imprisoned because of their collaboration with Naser-e Divan. According to the *kargozar* of Fars, the conflict resulted in more than 300 wounded and killed on both sides, amongst which were non-combattants. Many Kazerunis migrated to neighboring towns as well as to Bushehr. The merchants of Bushehr collected money to help the refugees.[501]

---

496. Administration Report 1913, p. 21; *Fars* year 1, nr. 35, p. 2 announced Merrill's arrival in Shiraz. Capt. Merrill had been with Shuster, but remained in Iran after his departure and then became a police instructor in Shiraz. As provincial army chief he was promoted to colonel, while 20-year old Lt. Rimbeau, a St. Cyr graduate who had fled France following a duel, became Merrill's assistant and a major. O'Connor 1931, pp. 206-07; Anonymous 1917, pp. 68, 73. Mokhber al-Saltaneh 1344, pp. 257-59, 262 was not so enamored with Merrill and Rimbeau, who had been foisted upon him, or with any European working in his governorship for that matter. He also wanted to reduce the gendarmerie force by half. Ranjbar 1389, p. 254, doc. 316 (19 May 1914). The ulama of Shiraz also had misgivings about Col. Merrill. Tayyebi 1389, p. 122, doc. 93 (6 February 1915).

497. O'Connor, pp. 207-08; Nyström 1925, pp. 187-88; Motahharizadeh 1883, p. 31.

498. O'Connor 1931, p. 209. Major Ohlson's bullet-riddled body was later found in a *qanat*, where it had been dumped. Nyström 1925, p. 191.

499. Administration Report 1914, p. 7; Mokhber al-Saltaneh 1344, p. 259; see also Administration Report 1913, p. 23 about an earlier case of looting by the gendarmes. An unknown British [?] journal blamed the gendarmerie for the plundering of Kazerun and declared the behavior of the Swedish officers to be shameful. It further suggested that they be replaced by Persian speaking British officers. Ranjbar 1389, p. 264, doc. 327 (10 April 1914). The ulama intervened for some close adherents, shopkeepers mostly, and asked the authorities to restore the plundered goods to them. Ranjbar 1389, pp. 354-55, doc.316 (no date), 262, doc. 325 (21 May 1914).

500. American Jewish Yearbook (July 1, 1913, to June 30, 1914), p. 202 (March 1914). http://www.ajcarchives.org/AJC_DATA/Files/1914_1915_4_YearReview.pdf

501. Motahharizadeh 1383, p. 32. The gendarmerie losses were 50 killed and missing and 25

Mme Helen Ohlson, Nystrøm 1925, p. 189

Henceforth the gendarmerie maintained law and order at Kazerun and on the Shiraz-Bushehr road and initially, assisted by Qashqa'is (presumably Kashkulis), they continued

wounded. Oberling 1974, p. 123. A Russian newspaper reported that 1,000 Kazeruni refugees allegedly had asked the Ottoman government for asylum. Ranjbar 1389, p. 265, doc. 328 (9 May 1914).

searching for and fighting with Naser-e Divan and his men.[502] It took time to re-establish peace and quiet. When Moore traveled through Kazerun on 2 May 1914, he reported that "The valley of Kazarun had recently been the site of much fighting, and is still the haunt of brigands, our captain divides his ten men into two columns, which he heads rifle in hand."[503] The town still bore the scars of war. Again Moore: "We pass the ruins of houses blown up by the gendarmerie after an attack on them in which the Swedish commander was killed. "Poor people! First the brigands pillage them, then retire, leaving the more or less innocent to be punished for the misdeeds of the others." A fortified telegraph station with bullet holes was another memento to the recent attack.[504]

Col. Uggla and the Shiraz government discussed what to do in the aftermath. It was decided to arrest Naser-e Divan and ban him, while plundered goods were returned to their owners. But as Naser-e Divan was not to be found, it was realized that without him peace would not return.[505] Moore, who passed through Kazerun one month after the conclusion of the fight, opined that although the road was protected by gendarme posts, they could do little against a large armed mounted group of robbers.[506] Apparently others agreed, because it was decided to contact Naser-e Divan and offer him amnesty. Col. Uggla reached agreement with Naser-e Divan in early June 1914, who, to the dismay of the British, "entered their service!" On his return Naser-e Divan was appointed *kalantar* of Kazerun as well as the agent for the Finance Department.[507] There was, however, good news for the British, because Mohammad `Ali Kamareji was killed in October 1914, in a local fight near Kazerun.[508]

---

502. O'Connor 1931, p. 209; *The Times* (25 March 1914), p. 7; Oberling 1974, p. 123.

503. Moore 1915, p. 419.

504. Moore 1915, p. 420.

505. Motahharizadeh 1383, p. 32.

506. Moore 1915, p. 421.

507. Administration Report 1914, p. 7 (Therefore, O'Connor raised the usefulness of gendarmerie; it cost £150,000 per year, more than the revenues of Fars); Motahharizadeh 1383, p. 32. Mokhber al-Saltaneh 1344, p. 259, states that he instructed Daryabegi to give amnesty to Naser-e Divan as he was not convinced of his guilt. On his return, his men did not bother travelers.

508. Administration Report 1914, p. 8. It is not clear whether Naser-e Divan was involved in this, but this seems likely. The British reported on 30 June 1914 that "Nasir-i-Divan is reported to have come under an arrangement with Colonel Uggla and to have arrested a brother of Ali Mahomet Kamaraji, who was conspicious for the opposition to the gendarmerie last February." Vatandoust and Pourhasan 1380, p. 24. See also Motahharizadeh 1383, p. 121 (doc. 29) where Mokhber al-Saltaneh orders Naser-e Divan to take action against the Kamareji chief and his followers.

Photo of gendarmerie post at Kazerun, Moore 1915, p. 431

In this context of greed, anarchy, and feuding, the outbreak of WW I became an additional element. Iran had declared itself neutral, but Iran was drawn willy-nilly into the war by the warring parties. The existing anti-British and anti-Russian feelings were reinforced by a number of factors. German agents inside Iran wanted to harass and damage British interests in the south, "by embarrassing us and drawing off troops from the more important theatre."[509] By distributing money and propaganda they found fertile soil, in particular among those who were hurt by British efforts to curb their illegal exactions and raiding of caravans and/or who were anti-British.[510] Many of those were found among the members of the Democratic Party that stood for a nationalist policy and complete independence of Iran; one free from foreign influence. What helped these currents in political life was the issuance of *fatwas* by ulama in Najaf and elsewhere declaring holy war or *jihad* against Russia and Great Britain. It was this argument that, e.g. Sowlat al-Dowleh and others used to maintain their innocence of rebellion and the illegal use of violence by claiming they had just followed the orders of the ulama and the government of Iran. The problem with this argument is that on many occasions Sowlat al-Dowleh, Naser-e Divan and others chose to ignore the orders of the government of Iran, when it did not fit their own particular personal agenda.[511] Also, the Democrats who during WW I actively opposed British interests, on many occasions had sought the help and protection of Great Britain, a state whose very presence in Iran they professed to abhor. Even local holy men, such as Hajj ʿAli Agha Dhuʾl-Riyasateyn (*raʾis-e anjoman-e eslami-ye Shiraz*) "the leading priest in the extreme constitutional party," sought refuge in British consulate in May 1909, while others of the same party followed his example.[512] He still was a leading

---

509. Douglas 1923, p. 105. Anticipating the outbreak of WW I, Great Britain sent a brigade from India to Bushehr. When a few days later war was declared this force was moved immediately to Basra. One battalion was left behind in Bushehr as a garrison, which was a violation of Iran's neutrality.

510. Cronin 1996, p. 117.

511. For Sowlat al-Dowleh's reasons, see Oberling 1974, p. 139.

512. Persia no. 1 (1910), p. 47 (May 1909).

member of the Democratic Party in Shiraz in November 1915, when it arrested the British consul and his compatriots.[513]

Photo of guard tower, Moore 1915, p. 431

After a bad start, the gendarmerie had been quite effective in bringing security to the Telegraph road in 1914, according to the British. "Rahdari had ceased, caravans and travelers have passed practically unmolested and credit must be given to the Gendarmerie for having brought about, for the moment, this satisfactory state of affairs."[514] In June 1914, Mokhber al-Saltaneh dismissed Merrill fom his service, ostensibly for spying on him, or more likely that he was too supportive of British interests and because he was a nuisance.[515] It is somewhat theatrical and exaggerated when the British commented that Mokhber al-Saltaneh undid everything Col. Merrill had achieved, and thus "the so-called 'Army' had relapsed into its former condition of inefficiency."[516] Indeed, Merrill had tilted the balance of power in favor of the gendarmerie force in Kazerun through his arrival and he had brought some measure of tranquility to the town as its military governor, but these were no great achievements. Moreover, his rag tag force was just that, a collection of irregulars, and there is no indication that this force had become a more effective one. In fact, when at the end of 1913 Merrill was sent to Bushehr to assist its governor collecting the revenue his force achieved little success, there were many desertions and the local chiefs were not impressed.[517] Now that his force was left to its own resources, Mokhber al-Saltaneh accepted or engineered that control over Kazerun and other locations outside Shiraz reverted to local chiefs. By not punishing Naser-e Divan, but by granting him amnesty Mokhber al-Saltaneh to all intents and purposes had abdicated any responsibility for that part of Fars. This became crystal clear after Mokhber al-Saltaneh

---

513. Farashbandi 1359, p. 24.

514. Administration Report 1914, p. 9; Cronin 1996, p. 111.

515. Anonymous 1917, p. 73; Mokhber al-Saltaneh 1344, p. 264, did not care much for the qualities of Merrill.

516. Administration Report 1914, p. 8.

517. Administration Report 1914, p. 10 (Movaqqar al-Dowleh, the governor of Bushehr stated that the force was "recruited from the dregs of the Shiraz populace").

was replaced as governor-general on 14 September 1915.[518] At that time Naser-e Divan, according to Christopher Sykes, was "short, bow-legged (as becoming a race of muleteers), a trifle overdressed, and with an immense moustache dyed the colour of fire. His head was filled with images of war, and once on a visit to Shiraz he had been photographs astride a horse, slaying a fancied gazelle. Many prints of this photograph were nailed to the walls of his great house, and it is common in Shiraz to this day."[519]

Until early 1915, Kazerun had been under a military governor, because the situation was still insecure. Naser-e Divan lived in Kazerun with his armed men, while the entire countryside around the town was up in arms and supported him. The gendarmerie, therefore, had a force of 800 foot and horse to maintain law and order. The post of military governor was first held by Col. Merrill, then by Major Lundberg, and, when he left for Sweden, he was replaced by Captain Akhgar. The latter complained that immediately 200 men of his force were recalled to Shiraz, which he blamed on his being an Iranian. He was not too much upset by this but tried to compensate for this weakening of his force by improving the relations between his force and the local population. Akhgar invited the ulama, to whom he explained his mission, while he stressed the fact that they had common objectives; he further changed the gendarmerie's behavior in the area. Akhgar also contacted Naser-e Divan, who until that time allegedly had not dared to leave his fortified house to seek contact with government officials. This had the desired result in that the people of Kazerun abandoned their hostile attitude towards the gendarmes. Akhgar also established friendly relations with Mohammad 'Ali Kashkuli, who promised his support. Meanwhile, the loyalty of the gendarmerie force came under pressure when their monthly wages were not paid, which Akhgar ascribed to the hostility that Leleux, the financial officer of Fars and his assistant Moses Khan bore the gendarmerie. When Akhgar left after a three-month's stint as commander and military governor he found that everybody loved the gendarmerie and recognized Akhgar as a fellow-patriot, whom they thanked for his services.[520] It seemed as if the events leading up to the clash with Naser-e Divan in February 1914 had never happened, or if they did, in another country. Akhgar wants us to believe that all that was needed was to be a nice guy and treat people correctly and they gave up their untoward activities. Unfortunately, the reality was different, as detailed hereunder. After Akhgar left Kazerun by early 1915, Naser-e Divan and his supporters (which now included the gendarmerie) had complete control of the town and its valley. It was probably after that time that Kazerun acquired a municipal council (hey'at-e baladiyeh)

---

518. Mokhber al-Saltaneh was disappointed and had asked to be dismissed. He blamed the events at Kazerun on the gendarmerie force and stated that they were not needed to enforce payment of the taxes, which should be left to the local government officials. Ranjbar 1389, p. 262, doc. 324 (19 May 1914), 263, doc. 326 (16 March 1914).

519. Sykes 1936, p. 74.

520. Akhgar 1366, pp. 115-19, 123-24. LeLeux in his turn complained about the gendarmerie that collected taxes without permission from the financial authorities, see Ineichen 2002, p. 137. Akhgar's version of the events does not mention at all the agreement between Uggla and Naser-e Divan and the latter's appointment as kalantar of Kazerun and financial agent in June 1914 and, therefore, his statement that Naser-e Divan was cloistered in house and afraid to meet government officials in the last quarter of 1914 doesn't ring true and makes the reliability of his report suspect. See also Motahharizadeh 1383, p. 119 (doc. 24) that shows that Naser-e Divan was in correspondence with the governor-general of Fars in July 1914.

that consisted of five persons, who insisted that their council only became legitimate after its charter had been signed by Naser-e Divan.[521]

Meanwhile, German agents were active in Iran to induce Persian nationalists to cooperate with them and like-minded persons to cause damage to British interests. The most famous and effective of these agents was Wassmuss, who after his arrest in Bushehr by the British had been able to escape. He went via Borazjan and Kazerun to Shiraz, and in each of these locations he was helped and protected by the gendarmerie. Wassmuss was in Kazerun on 12 March 1915 and asked Naser-e Divan to support him with his *tofangchi*s against the British. According to O'Connor, the chaplain (mullah) of the gendarmerie in Kazerun, Sheikh Hamadani had gone to the homes of the *mojtahed*s there and was presented with an announcement calling for the *jihad*. Furthermore, Mirza Hasan, the brother of Habl al-Matin had come to Kazerun and was engaged in secret planning sessions. Moreover, he brought letters from the ulama of Borazjan for their colleagues in Kazerun to join them in their opposition to the British. However, in his *Memoirs*, Mokhber al-Saltaneh asserts that Naser-e Divan would not take any action against the British.[522] Wassmuss continued his journey to Shiraz where he was warmly welcomed by the Swedish officers commanding the gendarmerie regiment. These also arranged for him to be received the next day by Mokhber al-Saltaneh who sent a rented coach to fetch Wassmuss. He told the German agent to submit his ideas to the government in Tehran as he did not have the authority to take a decision in this matter. After their discussions he allowed Wassmuss to meet Qavam al-Molk and Sowlat al-Dowleh. Wasmuss tried to induce the latter to support the anti-British activities in the Garmsirat given his enmity towards the British.[523]

---

521. Motahharizadeh 1383, p. 120 (doc. 27).

522. Mokhber al-Saltaneh 1344, pp. 277-78; Nezam-Mafi 1363, pp. 131, 136, 183; Sepehr 1336, p. 76; Sykes 1936, pp. 74-75. The British opined that Mokhber al-Saltaneh "being an ardent pro-German, entered into the business [with Wassmuss's anti-British activities] heart and soul." He was alleged to have established close contacts with Ghazanfar al-Saltaneh of Borazjan, while the Gendarmerie officers in Borazjan and Kazerun whole-heartedly joined the anti-British movement. Administration Report 1914, p. 4; see also Ibid., 1915, p. 7.

523. Sepehr 1336, p. 76; Mokhber al-Saltaneh 1344, p. 277; Sykes 1936, pp. 77-79; von Mikusch 1937, pp. 114-21.

Nasr Diwan and his Son

Photo of Naser-e Divan

On 15 May 1915, the *fatwa* of the Shi'ite ulama declaring *jihad* against the English was made public in Shiraz. This order made it incumbent on every Moslem to work together and attack the British.[524] This did not happen, although with German help, plans were being made to do so. Naser-e Divan had sought contact with the Tangestani chiefs as well as the German agent Wassmuss to improve and coordinate their opposition to British interests. On 11 June 1915, another meeting took place in Kazerun, which was hosted by Naser-e Divan and attended by Sowlat al-Dowleh, Hajj Reza, one of Kazerun's notables, Wassmuss, and Nilstrom, a Swedish gendarmerie officer. The subject of the meeting was a joint attack on Bushehr by the coastal khans. Wassmuss made it clear that this should be their show and that those attending the meeting would not participate.[525] According to the British, by that time the gendarmerie force at Kazerun had become a center of pro-German intrigue. The gendarmes expelled the *kalantar* of Kamarej, because he was not willing to collaborate with them and wanted to remain neutral.[526]

When the German 'consul' in Shiraz, Wüstrov, learnt in early November 1915 that O'Connor had asked that 300 British-Indian soldiers be sent to protect the British consulate in Shiraz, he convinced the Democrats in Shiraz to take action. As a result, supported by the gendarmerie under the command of Major 'Ali Qoli Khan Pesiyan, they arrested all British subjects on 10 November 1915 and took the males to Ahram in Tangestan; the British females were released and sent to Bushehr where they arrived on 20 November 1915. The Democrats were assured of strong support from Kazerun. When O'Connor and other Europeans arrived in Kazerun on 13 November 1915, they were welcomed by an angry mob, organized by Naser-e Divan who, together with the senior gendarmerie officer, rode next to O'Connor.[527] Margaret Ferguson, who was a teenage girl at that time, described her experience of the welcoming party in Kazerun as follows:

> The crowd closed in about us like an angry sea, cutting each member of the
> party off from the other, and it seemed to us that our guards melted away into
> the background by some prearranged scheme. The crowd took up a vociferous
> chant of 'Down with England,' 'Long Live Persia,' and-by some enthusiast
> whose voice was stronger than his intelligence-'Zandibad Jarge Panjum'-'Long
> Live George the Fifth'-of England! The women had also been well coached in
> their part and clustering like hordes of crows on the town roofs, they loosed

---

524. Nilstrom 1372, p. 23. For the text of Ayatollah Shirazi's *fatwa*, see Sepehr 1336, pp. 72-73.

525. Nilstrom 1372, p. 28. Nilstrom was based in Tehran and charged with liaising between the Fars regiment and the rest of the gendarmerie force.

526. Administration Report 1915, p. 4.

527. Administration Report 1915, pp. 7-8; O'Connor 1931, pp. 223, 231-33; Oberling 1974, pp. 135-36. According to von Blücher 1949, p. 22, Wüstrow master-minded the arrest of the British colony and implies that the Persian Democrats and other nationalists were guided by the various German agents, who played on their extreme nationalist sentiments. The fact also that pay was in arrears for months and German gold was flowing, may also have nudged the rank-and-file of the gendarmerie force to become 'pro-German.' Cronin 1996, p. 116; see also Candler 1919, p. 189; Motahharizadeh 1383, p. 127 (doc. 39). Sepehr 1336, pp. 79-80 doesn't even mention German involvement in the Shiraz events and presents it as an entirely Persian affair.

upon us that horrid, warbling cry produced by yelling and smacking the palm of
the hand against the lips. It's an eerie, bloodthirsty sound.[528]

Shortly thereafter, Magardich, the IETD Armenian telegrapher of Kazerun was executed by the Democrats who had taken over Shiraz, allegedly because he had sent false and
misleading reports about Naser-e Divan to O'Connor.[529] Not only were the British consul
O'Connor and his compatriots driven out of Shiraz by the Democrats, but so was Qavam al-
Molk, only one month later in December 1915, who after Mokhber al-Saltaneh's departure
had been appointed acting governor-general and was friendly towards Great Britain. The
Democrats appointed Nasir al-Molk as acting governor-general, but, according to the British,
it was the German 'consul' Wüstrov who was the real power in Shiraz. This 'rebellious' situation lasted until 8 April 1916, when Fath al-Molk, a captain of the gendarmerie, on behalf
of Qavam al-Molk, who had received arms and funds from the British, took Shiraz and did
away with the short-lived Democrat party's rule. The new Qavam al-Molk and Sowlat al-
Dowleh entered Shiraz on 24 April 1916, the old Qavam al-Molk having died when he fell
off his horse on 21 April when hunting. They imprisoned a number of Germans, Austrians
and Democrats and executed some of Qavam al-Molk's former servants, who had joined his
enemies. Tehran appointed ʿAbdol-Hoseyn Mirza Farmanfarma as governor-general, against
the armed opposition of Qavam al-Molk and Sowlat al-Dowleh. However, British pressure
won out and Farfamfarma arrived on 15 October 1916 in Shiraz after his opponents had
relented.[530]

By that time a column of the recently formed South Persian Rifles (SPR) under Sykes
had arrived in Shiraz. In early 1916, Percy Sykes was sent from India to Bandar Abbas with 6
officers, 20 Indian NCOs and 25 *sovar*s to create a local, but British-officered force to restore
law and order in Southern Iran, taking the place of the disbanded Swedish-led gendarmerie.
It was in this area where the Nationalists and German agents had dealt a severe blow to the
British position and prestige. On 16 March 1916, Percy Sykes started to recruit in Bandar
Abbas for the South Persian Rifles (SPR) as he called this new force. The SPR headquarters

528. Ferguson 1941, pp. 84-85; see also O'Connor 1931, p. 238, who relates a similar story.

529. Motahharizadeh 1383, p. 37, n. 56. Bayat 1381, p. 178, n. 1, 185; Mokhber al-Saltaneh
1344, p. 278, had wanted to replace Magardich, because he never believed any report he sent. He
also had little faith in the reports sent by the Persian telegrapher! Ibid., p. 273; Nezam-Mafi 1363,
p. 137; Bayat 1381, p. 178.

530. Administration Report 1915, p. 2 (first Nosrat al-Soltan, a son of Mozaffar al-Din Shah, was
appointed to replace Qavam al-Molk, but he never proceeded beyond Isfahan); Administration
Report 1916, pp. 5-6. On 6 April 1916, Nyström, the commander of the national Gendarmerie, who
had come from Tehran, assisted by other neutral Swedish officers, launched a counter-coup against
their pro-German compatriots and arrested all rebel officers and took control of Shiraz and handed
it over to Qavam al-Molk's representative. Oberling 1974, p. 136; Ineichen 2002, p. 155. Nyström
1925, p. 256 hardly mentions this event, and, therefore, Cronin's take on this event is the more
likely one, who argues that due to a drop in support for the Democrats, Qavam al-Molk was able to
convince Captain Mohammad Hasan Khan Fath al-Molk to join his side. With some British-supplied
arms and money and the help of a group of NCO's he was able to take Shiraz after a few days of
fighting. Nyström then formally handed over the command of the Fars regiment to him. Cronin
1996, p. 124; see also Akhgar 1366, pp. 210-15.

were moved from Bandar Abbas at the end of 1916. Henceforth there were two centers, one at Shiraz and the other at Kerman that took over that function.[531]

After his arrival at Shiraz, Sykes incorporated the remaining Fars gendarmerie[532] regiment into the SPR and thus provided an armed fist to the governor-general. Farmanfarma wanted to go with Sykes to Kazerun at the end of the year to resolve the road question. To that end a detachment of the SPR had already gone to Kazerun and had taken over the gendarmerie barracks in early December. As the road between Shiraz and Bushehr had been opened after August and traffic had resumed the British and other observers were totally surprised what happened next. On 17 December 1916, Naser-e Divan, whom the British referred to as hereditary *kalantar* of Kazerun, by treachery gained entry into the gendarmerie barracks, captured guns and some machine-guns, and imprisoned the local governor. He then expelled the SPR from the town. It then also became clear that Naser-e Divan, until then unbeknownst to the British, had been in close contact with the hostile khans of Tangestan and Dashtestan whom he asked for reinforcements. Farmanfarma sent some troops from Shiraz with Fath al-Molk, the head of the gendarmerie, as military governor of Kazerun. They occupied the Miyan-e Kotal caravanserai and Dasht-e Arjan, but Kotal-e Pir-e Zan was held by Naser-e Divan's forces, which they were unable to dislodge. Some men of the SPR were wounded. Before and after these events, Naser-e Divan sent messages to the anti-British Khans of Daleki, Borazjan, Chahkutah and Tangestan asking for help. Not much help was given, but the road to Shiraz was blocked again, with Kazerun rather than Borazjan as the center of the troubles. Naser-e Divan then took Miyan-e Kotal and on 21 December 1916, after some fighting, he took the SPR post of Dasht-e Arjan and its garrison prisoner. Sykes sent new troops to retake Kazerun and Dasht-e Arjan, but they met with strong opposition, suffered casualties, failed to achieve their objectives and withdrew.[533]

With Naser-e Divan in open rebellion, action needed to be taken. The British believed that Wassmuss and his rebel Dashtestan khans were behind the attack on the SPR at Kazerun and Dasht-e Arjan, if not Sowlat al-Dowleh and others. Whether this is true or not cannot be ascertained, but a fact is that Wassmuss visited Naser-e Divan in Kazerun toward the end of 1916 and that shortly therafter he had taken the barracks, as described above.[534] It was also suggested that the plan was one by an advisor of Qavam al-Molk, though without his knowledge. Another possible instigator was Mokhber al-Saltaneh, who was said to have incited the tribes to attack the SPR and the Kazerunis were among those willing to do so. Later, it appeared that Sowlat al-Dowleh was indeed the instigator, not because he was hostile towards the SPR, but as a counter-measure against intrigues by Farmanfarma against him. Sowlat al-Dowleh was suspicious of the British after they had accepted an offer of help against Kazerun in April 1917, from Mohammad 'Ali Khan, chief of the Kashkuli section of the Qashaqa'is and, at that time, an enemy of Sowlat al-Dowleh. However, when Sykes met

---

531. For the history of the SPR, see Safiri 1364.

532. After the Shiraz events the government of Iran dismissed most Swedish officers, only four remained. At the insistence of Russia the weakened gendarmerie was renamed *Amniyeh* in the spring of 1916. Ineichen 2002, p. 156.

533. Administration Report 1916, pp. 3, 7-8; Safiri 1364, p. 134; Sykes 1936, pp. 192-94; Moberly 1987, pp. 211-12, 217-21 (detailed description of the battle); Sykes 1969, vol. 2, pp. 472-75.

534. Sykes 1936, pp. 116-17, 186-88.

Sowlat al-Dowleh on 25 May 1917 they had an amiable meeting and the latter agreed to the following:[535]

to guard the Shahi road from Tang-i-Turkan (one stage below Kazerun) to Dastarjin [Dasht-e Arjan] with his own men;

to guard the Shahi road from Dastarjin to Chenar Rahdar jointly with the South Persian Rifles;

to provide 450 men for the above two purposes, these men to be paid from Shiraz at the rate of Tomans 5,050 per mensem; these arrangements to last for three months at least;

to keep Naser-i-Diwan out of Kazerun for six months and put in his own Deputy-Governor;

to capture or expel Muhammad Reza Dirisi, the notorious anti-British pamphleteer, from Kazerun;

to be responsible for the good behaviour of his tribe and pay revenue, in return for which he would be supported in his position as Ilkhani.[536]

This agreement temporarily led to better relations between Sowlat al-Dowleh and Farmanfarma, after the latter was prodded by the British.[537] The result of the agreement was not impressive, although Sowlat al-Dowleh, without using force, was able to make Naser-e Divan leave Kazerun for a few weeks. The government of Iran disapproved of the agreement, while the Qashqa'i guards immediately starting collecting *rahdari*. Sowlat al-Dowleh justified this by stating that he needed 300 *tumans* more money to compensate for the loss of *rahdari*. Later Farmanfarma met with Sowlat al-Dowleh and discussed the pardoning of Naser-e Divan. One main issue in Kazerun was the feud between Naser-e Divan and Mohammad 'Ali Khan Kashkuli. The latter wanted to enlarge his territory beyond the village of Shapur that he owned, or as the British put it, "while he can hold it." He extended his sway north and south and took the Rahdar caravanserai and the Tang-e Torkan, thus commanding the main road to Kazerun. His Kashkuli rival, Mohammad Khan, had similar ambitions regarding villages in Kamarej and Khesht and tried to take Deris near Kazerun. Naser-e Divan supported the latter, but at a certain moment Mohammad 'Ali Khan succeeded in taking Miyan-e Kotal in April 1917. He offered it to Sykes, who declined accept it. From then onwards his career went into a downward spiral. By the end of June 1917, Naser-e Divan had taken the village of Shapur, and by the end of the year Sowlat al-Dowleh had taken the *kalantar*ship from Mohammad 'Ali Khan Kashkuli and pursued him into Kuhgiluyeh. He also imprisoned Mohammad 'Ali Khan and thus controlled the Kashkuli section of his tribe, which had been such a thorn in his side for a long time.[538]

---

535. Moberley 1987, p. 296.

536. Administration Report 1917, p. 2.

537. Moberley 1987, pp. 212, 296, 298.

538. Administration Report 1918, pp. 2-3; Mafi and Sa`vandiyan 1366, vol. 1, p. 398.

Photo of Farmanfarma, Qavam, and Sykes

There was the usual infighting on the lower part of the road, which was disputed between the *kalantars* of Khesht (pro-British, or so they believed), Nur Mohammad Khan of Daleki (originally anti-British, later chastened, or so they believed) and the rival league of Tangestan on the one hand and that of the Hayat Da'ud confederacy on the other hand. The main news item was the expulsion of Nur Mohammad Khan from the Konar Takhteh plain and the occupation of the Kotal-e Malu by a loyal *kadkhoda* of Konar Takhteh. These events were followed by a serious quarrel between Borazjan and Daleki in September 1917. In consequence, Nur Mohammad Khan of Daleki started to divert traffic via the Shabankareh-Shif route; he finally made an agreement with the Khans of Shabankareh and Angali to oppose the Tangestan league and protect trade on the Shif-Daleki stretch. This was a serious blow to the rebel confederates.[539]

The Kazerunis led by Naser-e Divan tried to play a leadership role among the anti-British Khans of the Telegraph road and even tried to lecture the other Khans. The British cited "An amusing instance of Satan rebuking sin was a circular letter from Nasir-i-Diwan to the rebel Khans threatening them with his hostility if they did not moderate their exactions on the muleteers."[540] Most of these muleteers were Kazerunis hence Naser-e Divan's interest. No need to say that his appeal fell on deaf ears. To advertise their cause, the Kazerun Nationalists gave their revolutionary message a medium by intercepting all mail passing between Bushehr and Shiraz and affixing Persian stamps with the hand stamped overprint *Mellat-e Kazerun 1335* (The Nation of Kazerun 1335 [1917]). The envelopes also received a censor stamp in violet ink (*dar Kazerun taftish shod*, or 'inspected in Kazerun').[541] Naser-e Divan allegedly also struck his own coins. Christopher Sykes, who reported this, commented "and perhaps his name will always be held in honour by collectors of rare specimens of money."[542] In addition, a gelatin-printed newspaper, named *Neda-ye Haqq* (Voice of Truth) was published by the Bushehri native, Sayyed Mohammad Reza Eslah in Kazerun.[543]

Sowlet al-Dowleh who had been talking to and playing all sides, finally decided to oppose Farmanfarma and his pro-British party in April 1918 and began a *jihad* one month later. On 25 May 1918, Khaneh Zenyan, which was held by the SPR, was taken by treachery by a mixed force of Qashqa'is and Kazerunis, who killed Capt. Will and Sgt. Coomber in cold blood. The 1,500 Kazerunis who poured into the fort, "in their furor turned upon their new allies [i.e. the SPR], robbed them, and turned them out." Thereafter, the Qashqa'is only

---

539. Administration Report 1917, pp. 2-3; Akhgar 1366, p. 108.

540. Administration Report 1917, p. 3. Douglas 1923, p. 107, wrote that transport costs from Bushehr to Shiraz were prohibitive and amounted to more than £50 per ton, so that trade had come to a standstill.

541. Sadri 2002, pp. 178-79. This probably was inspired by the example of Lar in 1327/1909, see Ibid., pp. 172-73; Vothuqi 1375, p. 142. Because some mail did not arrive Farmanfarma urged Naser-e Divan to see to it that the people's mail was not interfered with, as the English did not need the Telegraph road to send mail, as they had the mail route with Bandar Abbas, which was operating efficiently. Motahharizadeh 1383, p. 162 (doc. 83).

542. Sykes 1936, p. 182. As far as I know this is the only source that mentions the minting of coins. It seems unlikely, although Naser-e Divan collected the government taxes for which he was admonished by Farmanfarma who asked him to respect the rules in this respect. Motahharizadeh 1383, p. 163 (doc. 84).

543. *Fars*, year 2, nr. 19 (1336/1917), p. 9.

met with defeat in other engagements. In June and July 1918, the Qashqa'is and their allies (amongst whom Kazerunis) attacked the British-Indian troops at Shiraz, which had arrived in April 1917. However, despite the defection of the SPR force, this offensive led to nowhere. Nevertheless, the 2,000 men British-Indian force in Shiraz was in a precarious position, the more so since "a third had died of influenza and others from cholera, in addition to the casualties sustained in action."[544]

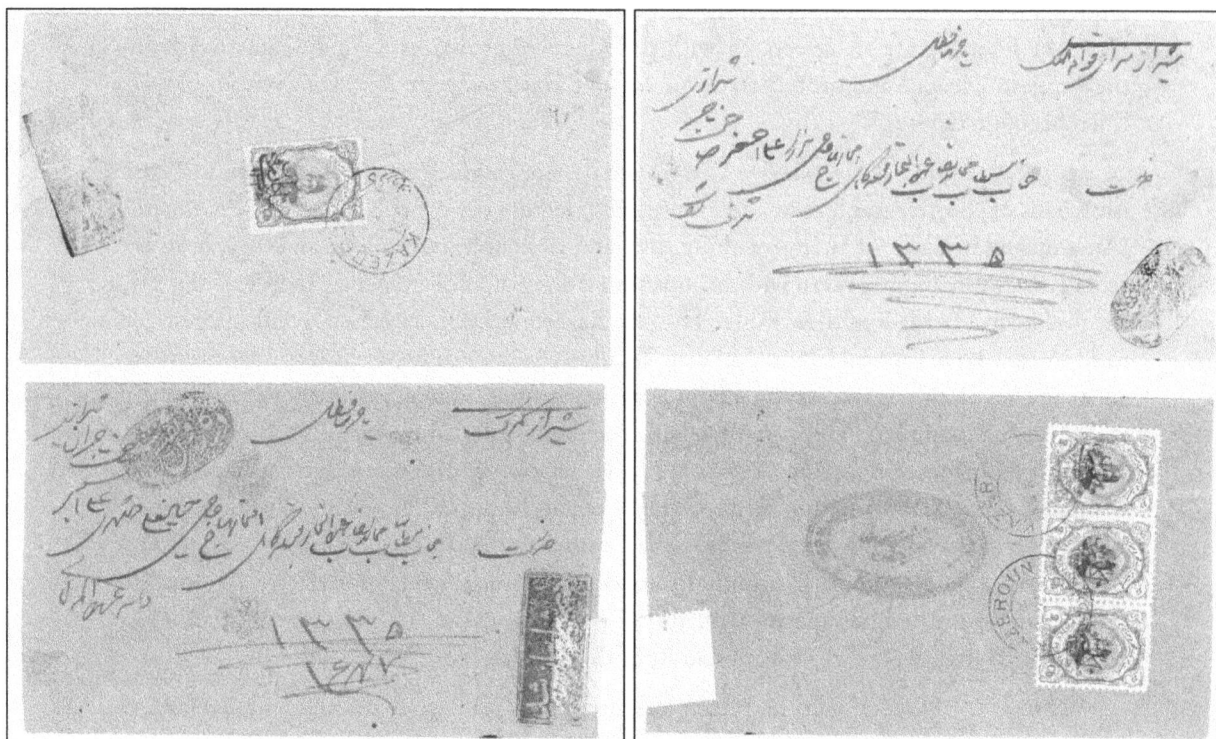

Photo of censored envelop with stamp overprinted with Kazerun 1337 as well as the censor's stamp, *dar Kazerun taftish shod*

To secure its hinterland and in particular the road to Shiraz as well as to deal with the hostile actions by Sowlat al-Dowleh and Naser-e Divan the British decided to reinforce their garrison in Bushehr.[545] To do so required the construction of a light-gauge railway to Daleki. The reason being that until Daleki camels could be used, but only mules could tra-

544. Administration Report 1918, pp. 2-3; Sykes 1969, vol. 2, pp. 476, 503-08; Oberling 1974, pp. 140, 142; Douglas 1923, p. 107; Balfour 1922, p. 107; Sykes 1936, pp. 203-09. Despite *fatwas* and exhortations by the Lari and Shirazi ulama to rise up against the British there was hardly any effective reaction by the population at large, which probably was too sick and tired of the politicking and high prices. Motahharizadeh 1383, pp. 150-52, 154 (docs. 676-69, 72).

545. In August 1918, the additional so-called Strike Force consisted of one squadron of the 15th Lancers, the 35th Mountain Battery less one section, two 15-pounder field guns, No.3 Indian Machine Gun Company (less 2 sections), a local machine gun section, the 54th Company Sappers and Miners, the 81st Pioneers, the 71st Punjabis and the 2/113th Infantry. Douglas 1923, p. 108. This dashed the hopes of Farmanfarma to settle the road problem without the intervention of foreign troops. Mafi and Sa`vandiyan 1366, vol. 1, p. 399.

verse the difficult passes that followed thereafter. However, the number of mules available was small and hence the decision to construct a railway was taken. Originally, the intention was to construct the railway as far as Daleki, but given greater than expected terrain difficulties and to avoid delays it went only as far as Borazjan. Instead a cart road was made between Borazjan and Daleki, while goods were transported by light Ford lorries from the railhead to the foothills. This freed up the pack animals for use beyond Daleki, after completion of the road and railway.[546]

This plan was opposed by Ghazanfar al-Saltaneh of Borazjan, Sheikh Hoseyn of Chahkutah, and Za'er Khezr of Tangestan, who had been "passively hostile" since 10 August 1916, when O'Connor and the other British hostages were released. Therefore, they were worried when Great Britain started to make preparations in July – August 1918 to send a strike force to Shiraz to deal with the Qashqa'i question and that of Fars in general. On 20 June they asked what the purpose was of the additional troops and were told that these were to deal with Sowlat al-Dowleh and Naser-e Divan.[547] On 21 September 1918 they assembled a force of about 600 men at Chaghadak, because the railway threatened their independence, or least they felt that way. After vain attempts to negotiate a peaceful passage the British-Indian Strike Force routed the opponents on 29 September 1918. The 600 men force fled after one hour engagement suffering 30 casualties, leaving 30,000 rounds of ammunition, other supplies and some animals behind, and fled into the mountains. Ghazanfar al-Saltaneh rode 44 km to Borazjan without even stopping. The Strike Force then occupied Chahkutah, Ahram and Borazjan (23 October). Ghazanfar al-Saltaneh had made a deal with the governor of Bushehr to surrender and go into exile, but he changed his mind and fled into the Gisehkan hills. Once Ghazanfar al-Saltaneh and the other two local chiefs had been dislodged and had become fugitives, they were "attacked by their private enemies," according to Moberly. He was chased away and his cousin, Agha Khan, whom he had kept in chains for seven years, was freed and appointed in his place as chief of Borazjan. Daleki was occupied on 30 October 1918. Thereafter, the Strike Force was everywhere well received. First, by Baba Khan, chief of Konar Takhteh and later by the joint *kalantar*s of Khesht, 'Ali Weys Khan and Sardar Khan. The area between Borazjan and Khesht was totally impoverished despite the fact that for years no revenues had been collected. This was because the chiefs had to spend much money on arms and ammunition and because of the damage done to the fields by hostilities among themselves. On 17 November 1918, Nur Mohammad Khan of Daleki and his brother were arrested; his three nephews had fled into the hills and were sniping at the Strike Force. They were, therefore, removed to Bushehr and Kal 'Ali Khan, a former headman, was appointed in his place by the governor of Bushehr, which, like other appointments, were later confirmed by Farmanfarma. Only Ghazanfar al-Saltaneh was a hereditary chief, the others were usurpers or temporary agents appointed by absentee landowners, and thus the British rightly did not expect much opposition against these appointments. Nur Mohammad Khan, e.g., was a Borazjani appointed by Nezam al-Saltaneh, the owner of the village. He had acquired his importance by the levying of illegal imposts, which enabled him to pay *tofangchi*s. His adherents Baba Khan and Gholam Reza fled to Konar Takhteh, where Mullah Fathollah, the son of the previous chief was appointed. The Strike Force moved to the Kamarej pass, which was said

546. Douglas 1923, p. 108.

547. Administration Report 1918, p.3.

to be held by Kazerunis under Mohammad Ebrahim, Naser-e Divan's *farrash-bashi*, and his principal supporter. However, he was not there when the Strike Force attacked, but Mullah ʿEvaz, the headman of Kamarej appointed by Naser-e Divan was. After the taking of Kamarej it was given to Mullah Qoli as guardian of the infant son of Heydar Khan of Kamarej.[548]

The Strike Force entered Kazerun on 27 January 1919.[549] According to the newspaper *Fars*, the Kazeruni rebels and Turks (presumably Qashqa'is) had abandoned their barricades just outside the town, which they plundered before they fled into the hills. A few days earlier Salar-e Moʿtazed, who had been appointed deputy-governor, had already safely entered Kazerun. The British constructed a very modern fort at Kazerun and also established a string of posts of *tofangchi*s along the Telegraph road to maintain security. Before they left Kazerun in the spring of 1919, the British had constructed a motor road from Borazjan to Rudak, 9.5 km from Kamarej, but the rest remained unfinished as the Labor Corps had departed, because of the end of WW I. The unfinished part was a well-graded camel path over which a car could travel and actually had done so all the way to Shiraz. However, in the following years there was no road maintenance and thus the road deteriorated. It took a number of years before a new motor road was constructed. Until 1922, when it was dismantled, trade also benefited from the railway between Bushehr and Daleki.[550] After the departure of the Strike Force the Telegraph road was taken over by the newly formed SPR, which, for a short while, were assisted by Indian troops. At the end of November 1920, Jalal al-Molk became deputy-governor of Kazerun.[551]

---

548. Administration Report 1918, pp. 3-6; Douglas 1923, p. 108; Barrow, Hirtzel, Napier and Yate 1921, p. 166; Safiri 1364, pp. 234 (re events leading up to the attack on Khaneh Zenyan), 236-37; Sykes 1936, pp. 214-15. Moberly 1987, pp. 409, 452 (The chiefs of Khesht after having welcomed the Strike Force on 13 November went to Naser-e Divan to assist him stopping the British advance). On Nur Mohammad Khan and Daleki, see Appendix 3.5. Kal ʿAli Khan was not an effective headman and in March 1919 was replaced by Kal Esmaʿil Hakim. Administration Report 1919, p. 3. Naser-e Divan had already sent arms on September 1918 and thereafter to defend Qalʿeh-ye Dokhtar and the pass leading to Kazerun. Motahharizadeh 1383, pOp. 164-65 (docs. 86, 88, 89, 90, 91).

549. The British informed the population that they were there to bring order and support the government and all those who did not undertake any hostile activities had nothing to fear. Motahharizadeh 1383, p. 165-66 (doc. 92).

550. Administration Report 1919, pp. 2-3; Administration Report 1918, p. 6; *Fars*, year 2, nr. 27 (1918); Ibid., year 3, nr. 20, p. 7; Ibid., year 3, nr. 28, p. 10 (1919). Barrow, Hirtzel, Napier and Yate 1921, p. 166. Thus a Persian wish had been realized, for in 1913 Chick reported that "the desire of Persian circles here [in Bushehr is] to obtain motor traction between here and Daliki, 3 stages distant of Shiraz." Anonymous 1917, pp. 140, 151-52, 157. In 1919, less than 50 light passenger cars, mostly Fords, were able to use this road, which was then just completed. However, by 1923 the road was in need of significant repairs. Despite this fact the government began collecting tolls on animal transport on the Shiraz-Kazerun section of the road as of early January 1923. The British protested that this was in contravention of art. 4 of the 1903 Anglo-Persian Commercial Convention, which allowed such tolls only on "carriagable" roads and only after these had been completed. Muleteers broke up the toll gates when first erected and like Iranian merchants forcefully protested to Tehran, because they feared that the money would not be used for road repairs or other transportation improvements. However, Tehran ignored these protests and most of the collected money was indeed transferred to the Ministry of Finance, only some money being used for scanty road repairs. Administration Report 1923, p. 21. For a description on how difficult it was to drive a lorry over this road in 1924, see Braunnagel 1925.

551. *Fars*, year 3, nr. 20, p. 6 (1919); Administration Report 1920, p. 4; Douglas 1923, p. 113; Mafi and Saʿvandiyan 1366, vol. 2, p. 690.

The progress made by the Strike Force, apart from its superior firepower and discipline, was due to the fact that all hostile chiefs with some followers fled into the hills. Moreover, many people in the south were sick and tired of the decade-long violence and insecurity. Also, it was helpful that the 1918 influenza epidemic had weakened people (as it did the British Indian troops); in fact, the southerly migration of the Qashqa'is in that year had stopped due to the influenza. Moreover, it was difficult to buy ammunition, while artillery fire did wonders for the Strike Force. Despite the hostilities, people showed no real anti-British feeling and gladly did business with the invading army. Wassmuss had gone to Kazerun when the situation became too hot in Dashtestan, but he was not well received by Naser-e Divan or by Sowlat al-Dowleh, who was deposed and succeeded by his half-brother Sardar-e Ehtesham.[552]

After the British Strike Force had defeated the Kazerunis at Kamarej, on about 20 January 1919 Naser-e Divan with some 100 followers fled to Jerreh, 32 km south-east of Kazerun. There Naser-e Divan was attacked by airplanes and he then fled into the hills, where he stayed with Masih Khan Farsi-Madan; he took no further hostile action. Naser-e Divan, Mohammad Ebrahim his *farrash-bashi*, and party arrived in Shiraz on 12 April 1919 and took refuge with Qavam al-Molk, while Ghazanfar al-Saltaneh gave himself up to Farmanfarma on 1 June 1919. Naser-e Divan was banished to Darab for two years and Qavam al-Molk stood guarantee that he would not leave. Mohammad Ebrahim, the *farrash-bashi* was imprisoned and put on trial for the murder of Capt. Will and Sgt. Coomber.[553] In December 1920, he was released on condition "that a suitable security was deposited that he did not return to Kazerun and that he took no retaliatory measures against the witnesses in the case."[554] After his two year banishment, Naser-e Divan asked to be allowed to return to Kazerun. Qavam al-Molk pressed the British consul at Shiraz to agree, because he himself was unable to prevent his return. It would be better, he argued, to acquiesce, the more so since the SPR were about to be disbanded and Great Britian could do nothing then. The consul accepted that logic, but insisted that Naser-e Divan sign an undertaking, which was kept at the consulate, "to behave correctly and in a friendly manner to British subjects and interests, and not seek revenge on Persians who had rendered services to the Indian Troops and the South Persia Rifles." Qavam al-Molk personally pledged that if Naser-e Divan reneged on his undertaking he would expel him from Kazerun and punish him.[555]

552. Administration Report 1918, pp. 6-7 (Wassmuss and Oertl were informed by the government of Iran that the Armistice had been signed and they could be repatriated or be treated as prisoners of war. They sent evasive replies); Moberly 1987, p. 453; Akhgar 1366, pp. 225-28 expressed a negative opinion about Wassmuss, whose role was exaggerated by Europeans, while that of the real actors, Iranians, was ignored and he, therefore, set the record straight, or so he believed. Sowlat al-Dowleh blamed the British for the course of events because, among other things, they had not respected the agreement he had made with Sykes in 1917, see Motahharizadeh 1383, p. 173 (doc. 99).

553. Administration Report 1919, pp. 2-3, 5; Moberly 1987, pp. 457-58; Bayat 1381, p. 265; Sykes 1936, p. 218; Mafi and Sa`vandiyan 1366, vol. 2, p. 613 (has details about the bombing, number of bombs, casualties, and the damage done to the Farsimadan); Fars, year 2, nr. 37, p. 8; nr. 38, p. 6; nr. 39, p. 6, nr. 39, p. 13 (1918) has details of the pursuit of the rebels by the Persian army under Qavam al-Molk. Concerning the pursuit of Naser-e Divan, see also Fars, year 3, nr. 20, pp. 6-7 (1919). For Farmanfarma's accusations against Naser-e Divan and the latter's reply, see Motahharizadeh 1383, pp. 166-68 (doc. 93), 169-70 (doc. 96). Farmanfarma urged him to surrender. Ibid., p. 168 (doc. 94). The British impounded all Naser-e Divan's properties, which they listed. Ibid., p. 171 (doc. 97).

554. Administration Report 1920, p. 5.

555. Administration Report 1921, pp. 4-5. The fiscal department of Fars immediately asked

Meanwhile, what had been feared after the disbandment of the SPR became reality. Immediately after the flight of the rebels the SPR (and for a shorter while also Indian troops) had put guards along the Telegraph road to guarantee safe passage for caravans and to give warning of any enemy gatherings. The 160 SPR guards were replaced by 23 road guards and seven *sowars* and as a result the governor of Kazerun, `Ata al-Dowleh reported in February 1922 that the Telegraph road was becoming insecure due to robberies. Reza Khan, the Minister of War then increased the number of guards to 130 on this road.[556] The situation remained insecure, however, as was the case throughout the countryside of Fars, and robberies were rife. As a result, a military governor was appointed for Kazerun as in many other places in Fars, which had the effect that local chiefs lost influence and were constantly harassed by the authorities. Moreover, as of 1923 the road was guarded by Cossacks of the regular army. No more irregularly paid *Amniyeh* roadguards, which in 1923 were commanded by Naser-e Divan, were employed as during the previous year, as they were only a little better than robbers. The entire mercantile and muleteer community was pleased, although here and there fees like `alafi*, *rahdari*, etc. were still collected. However, this was a temporary military intervention, because in subseqent years the *Amniyeh* guards were guarding the road again.[557] In July 1924 a new military governor appointed at Kazerun. In November 1924, Reza Khan came to Kazerun on his way to Khuzestan to suppress the revolt of Sheikh Khaz`al. During his short stay in Kazerun, Naser-e Divan offered his services as well as that of his *tofangchis*, which was accepted. He then marched with his men to Khuzestan and participated in the show of strength that brought down the powerful ruler of south Khuzestan.[558]

Despite the service rendered in Khuzestan, Naser-e Divan was not trusted by Reza Khan's government, although it bestowed the title of Naser-e Lashkar on him.[559] His son-in-law, Khvajeh Bashi, who for years had disturbed the town and valley of Kazerun, was immediately deported when, after his return from Khuzestan, he caused difficulties for the military governor in April 1925. He was still kept in detention in early 1926 in Shiraz, with numerous claims outstanding against him. Because the military considered the presence of Naser-e

Naser-e Divan to assist in the payment of tax arrears of Shapur. Motahharizadeh 1383, p. p. 174 (doc. 101). His action to restore order in Kazerun, where disorder had broken out in early January 1922, was also much appreciated by the government of Fars and the Iranian army. At that time or shortly thereafter he was deputy-governor of Kazerun. Motahharizadeh 1383, pp. 175-66 (docs. 103-06, 108).

556. Administration Report 1922, p. 3; *Fars*, year 3, nr. 41, pp. 6-7, 13 (Shawwal 1337/1919).

557. Administration Report 1923, pp. 1, 7, 10, 16, 2; Ibid., 1925, p. 14; Motahharizadeh 1383, pp. 182, 185-87 (doc. 121, 124, 127, 130). The British consul in Shiraz was much more positive about the *Amniyeh*, which had mostly suppressed the illegal imposts and blackmail by local armed men by the end of 1923. "Posts of four to five uniformed men are now established every 4 to 8 miles from Bushehr to Isfahan, and regulations issued repudiating responsibility for the loss of merchandise at halting-places other than these posts." The recovery of stolen goods or fines imposed also had a salutary effect on the security of the road. There was still some 'blackmail' in the form of limiting the places where fodder was sold, with a view to benefit the local headman or the *Amniyeh* itself. Ibid., 1923, p. 15. His remarks, therefore, must concern the road between Shiraz and Isfahan.

558. Administration Report 1924, pp. 12-13. Despite the report of the alleged bravery of Khvajeh-bashi (Motaharrizadeh 1383, p. 103, n. 56), there was no fighting in Khuzestan; it was an entirely peaceful surrender of power. The only skirmishes that took place were with troops coming from the direction of Isfahan. Administration Report 1924, p. 51.

559. Motahharizadeh 1383, pp. 97, 189 (doc. 135).

Divan in Kazerun potentially undermining their authority, he was also removed to Shiraz in July 1925. From there he was given permission to make a pilgrimage to Mashhad. Naser-e Divan was allowed to return in November 1925 much to the annoyance of the military governor, for the former *kalantar* still enjoyed much local support. According to the commander of the *Amniyeh*, Amir Lashkar Aqa Khan, "local politicians prevented him from obtaining compensation from Nasir Diwan and other Kazerunis [who] proved to have benefited from robberies." In that year, the valley of Kazerun was still much disturbed by several bands of marauders, who terrorized the people of the town and thus diminished the authority of the military governor, who, with his few men could do little to put a stop to this marauding. There were also several instances of robberies on the Telegraph road.[560] This road remained unsafe for some years to come, being raided by Buyer Ahmadis, Qashqa'is, and Banawis as well as rendered unsafe by conflicts about the chieftainship of Daleki. The *Amniyeh* was not capable of suppressing the banditry and even the military, despite very costly operations, initially had little success. By 1930, however, the road had become safe and few robberies occurred.[561] Naser-e Divan did not engage in any of the rebellious activities that arose in Fars (Borazjan, Daleki) in the late 1920s, because he realized that another era had arrived in which the type of behavior that he and his class of notables had engaged in for centuries was no longer tolerated by the powers that be. He, therefore, spent the rest of his days at home and on his agricultural properties. According to Christopher Sykes, who met Naser-e Divan around 1934, "his great moustaches are cut to a more contemporary shape, and his picturesqueness is marred by a tweed suit and a porter's cap. But on his breast there flops a great medal, and he is still the subject for extempore verse and long-chanted Persian tales."[562] Naser-e Divan died in 1942 and was buried in his hometown in the Golbon-Kazeruni cemetery.[563]

Discussion

Once in a while Kazerun is mentioned in historial chronicles, because some war lord plundered it. In the early Islamic period it also attracted some attention because of its high quality linen fabrics and as the birth place of the founder of the Kazeruniyeh order. But usually Kazerun is absent from their pages, because it was off the beaten track. It does not seem to have recovered from the Mongol onslaught and became a quiet rural market town. It was located

---

560. Administration Report 1925, pp. 13-14. In January 1925, Esma`il Mehrinjani was killed outside Kazerun; in April Fazlollah was arrested, tried in Shiraz and executed. In May, Mir Mazkur of Homeyjan was captured and hung, but his brother Mir Gholam was still attacking soldiers and caravans. Other robbers were also active, such as a gang from Dahleh, who killed several soldiers and made the area unsafe. Administration Report 1925, p. 13. In mid-1926, military governors were replaced by civilians throughout the country. Administration Report 1926, p. 3.

561. Administration Report 1926, pp. 4, 10; Administration Report 1927, pp. 2, 5; Administration Report 1928, pp. 18-19; Administration Report 1930, p. 9.

562. Sykes 1936, pp. 182-83. For a list of Naser-e Divan's property, see Motahharizadrh 1383, p. 239.

563. Motahharizadeh 1383, p. 98.

in a tough neighborhood, tough because its neighbors were various tribal groups. At times, these made life difficult with their raids, in particular of caravans.

The nineteenth century is a period where apart from tribal marauding and attacks on caravans there often was a conflict between the population of Kazerun and its governor. Such conflicts are usually characterized as being the result of oppression. There is no doubt that there was oppression. However, there also was intense infighting and jockeying for power among the leading notables, both within and outside Kazerun and the accusation of 'oppression' was a sometimes convenient label to hide other, more selfish partisan differences. During most of the nineteenth century, the government of Fars was able to 'manage' this violence and keep it within bounds. However, even then, the government sometimes had to overlook certain behavior, as the cost of suppressing it was high and the results uncertain.

When one of the major parameters changed in the early twentieth century (viz. the breakdown of central government authority and power) the latent violence manifested itself and focused on two objectives. First, to get control over the routes of commercial traffic to be able to tax it; second, to prevent old enemies from doing the same. Given the lucrative nature of taxing trade, the traditional feuds, acquired an additional financial nature and became more and more accentuated. As a result, mini-wars between various local chiefs were fought and many people, on both sides, were killed, just to control more stretches of road.

After 1907, the levying of illegal imposts of trade caravans passing from Bushehr to Shiraz and beyond, and even raiding and plundering those caravans, was justified by its perpetrators as harming British interests. There is no doubt that some British firms suffered damage, but tens of thousands of Iranians, who were the buyers and/or sellers of those goods or who transported them were the ones who paid the real price. Often, they lost their goods and animals, while consumers were confronted with ever higher prices. They, therefore, were less appreciative of this enforced contribution to 'the anti-British effort,' which only benefited a number of local chiefs. The latter were engaged in the same plunder and looting business that they had been in before they found out that they were nationalists and that robbing caravans was the proper nationalist thing to do.[564] I am leaving aside here the damage done to the rural areas adjacent to the road, which became impoverished, because of the constant fights between the Khans that drained their resources.

These sentiments allowed the various political players to pursue policies and follow actions and commit deeds that were neither in the interest of Iran nor of its people. Naser-e Divan, the *kalantar* of Kazerun also falls into this category, because he and his family were partly responsible for the insecurity within and outside Kazerun. It is difficult to form a balanced opinion about him when feelings and sentiments were and still are so strong, either negative or positive. According to the British, he was "probably the most cruel scoundrel in Fars,"[565] According to the pro-British newspaper *Fars*, which was published in Shiraz, Naser-e Divan was an artificial patriot (*vatan-khvah-e masnu'i*) and only sought his own benefit. Those who counseled him not to ally himself with Nur Mohammad, Ghazanfar al-Saltaneh and others like them he accused of being dissentors and traitors.[566] There is no doubt in my

---

564. See, e.g., *Jonub* 1371, year 1, 20 Ramazan 1329 (14 September 1911), p. 3.

565. Administration Report 1921, p. 5.

566. *Fars*, year 3, nr. 14 (1918).

mind that Naser-e Divan was trying to defend his traditional prerogatives, as he saw them. At the same time, it was genuine patriotism that drove him and others like him to attack what they believed were British interests.[567] The fact that in 1914 various ulama issued *fatwas* that it was incumbent on Moslems to oppose and combat the British, provided futher incentives and political cover for his otherwise negative and reactive activities. I use these negative qualifiers on purpose, because rather than being part of the solution, Naser-e Divan and the other icons of the anti-British armed opposition were part of the problem.

It is ironic that those who wanted to be free of British interference with Iran's affairs were the main cause that Great Britain increasingly felt it had to interfere. If the petty chiefs along the Telegraph road had not robbed and raided caravans and collected illegal imposts, Great Britain would never have landed one additional soldier in Bushehr, where it had only a small consular guard until 1914, or pressured the government of Iran to take steps that were deemed unpopular. After all, Great Britain had been importing and exporting goods via Bushehr since 1763 and prior to 1916 it had never used military force to protect the road, because there was no need to! It was the failure of the government of Iran to control raiding by the petty chiefs, which resulted in the growing lack of safety and security of the road after 1905, that made Great Britain increasingly worried. In fact, it became so worried that it felt that if the government of Iran did nothing it had to do something itself, although it did not want to. In this connection it is further instructive that the same scenario did not manifest itself on the Bandar Abbas-Kerman road, another major trade artery, this one linking the Persian Gulf with S.E. Iran. Here also there was increasing insecurity on the road and a rising number of robberies. However, these were mostly committed by migrating Baharlus and other pastoralists rather than by petty chiefs along the trade route. There too, of course, there was the occasional *kalantar*, who was greedy, but in comparison to the Bushehr-Shiraz route it was not a chronic problem. There was no infighting among them, and the problem of robberies remained manageable although costly to the economy of Iran, but no British troops were landed there. However, the greed of the Khans and *kalantar*s along the Telegraph road was such that it became an obstacle to trade, which dropped significantly, part of which was rerouted via Bandar Abbas! Great Britain had an interest that trade was not impeded because it was out of the customs revenues that Iran reimbursed it for the loans it received from Great Britain. In short, if these patriotic Khans and their followers had just been good law-abiding citizens, who did not steal and rob, commit violence, thus enabling their compatriots to carry on with their lives in commerce, the whole 'British' problem might not have arisen.[568]

What changed the dynamic, of course, was British violation of Iran's neutrality during World War I. German agitators found fertile soil to spread their anti-British message as well as willing partners to inflict damage on British interests. Those Persian Khans who opposed

---

567. A British journalist traveling in Iran during the Great War opined: "Nearly every Persian is, first at all, a nationalist. He would not be human if he were not. His hatred of interference and dictation is a very natural and genuine passion." However, he then spoils his argument by suggesting that whereas the Persians shrunk from "the hug of the Russian bear," their only quarrel with the British was "that we had ranged ourselves with the Russians," as of 1907. Candler 1919, pp. 189-90. It is true that unlike Russia, Great Britain had no occupation troops stationed in Iran, but it was also engaged in political interference to protect and promoting its own interests.

568. In this connection, see also Mafi and Sa`vandiyan 1366, vol. 2, pp. 592-93; Motahharizadeh 1383, p. 125 (doc. 38) where similar sentiments are voiced.

Britain because of its interference with their smuggling and highway robbery activities now could continue to engage in these predatory activities under the cover of acting against British interests. The British, of course, made no distinction between these two forces that drove these Khans to act; to them they were rebels, German collaborators, and criminals. They never questioned their own actions, which were seen as righteous, in the interest of Iran, and, therefore, necessary. Nevertheless, once the war was over the British withdrew their troops, as promised, despite the fact that the road to Shiraz and beyond was still insecure. It left the security of the road to the government of Iran, which needed a decade to make it secure, facing the same problems that had exasperated the British for more than a decade.

APPENDIX 3.1

FAMINE IN KAZERUN IN 1871

The British traveler Brittlebank visited Iran during the 1871 famine and left a vivid description of the people's suffering, which was alleviated in many places, such as Kazerun, by British charity.

Our next halt was Kazeroon. ... Here, too, I had the satisfaction of seeing the starving people fed by English charity. The morning after our arrival, a crowd of emaciated natives poured into the yard of the [telegraph] station. Some sat on their heels, some propped themselves up against the wall, others lay wearily at full length on the ground. They numbered in all-men, women, and children-a couple of hundred. They were all in rags or more than half naked, and the effluvia from them was so fetid, that although standing on the top of the station, about twelve or fourteen yards off, I could scarcely bear it. They were of all ages; but their suffering semed to have told most on the children. The girls looked like hags, the boys like aged dwarfs. Two of three Persian 'gholam'- men who, when the telegraphic communication is interrupted, go down the line until they discover the place at fault-stood at the gate, in order that the very poor and starving might alone enter. I could not make out what test they applied to discriminate between the famished and the half-famished, but I noticed that they rejected very miserable-looking women who supplicated for admittance. Another 'gholam' assisted the Armenian [telegrapher] in distributing the dates, the form in which the relief was given. When the dates were brought in, every device was resorted to in order to obtain a double supply; and the crowd sometimes became so wild that the trays on which the fruit was placed were upset, and what might in truth be term a life and death fight was fought over it. The distribution over, the unhappy beings got back as they best could to their hovels to pine and suffer, sustained only by the hope of a future dole at the station.[569]

---

569. Brittlebank 1873, pp. 132-34.

APPENDIX 3.2

AGRICULTURE IN KAZERUN

ADMINISTRATION REPORT 1878-79, pp. 36–38

Shatwee or Autumn Sowings

The land in Kazeroon is private property. If the cultivation be undertaken by the landowner himself he has to provide seed for an area of one gao (i.e., an ox) of cultivation, *viz.*, 1,000 lbs. wheat and 1,000 lbs. barley, and pay about 14 krans for the labour of ploughing and sowing. He pays in kind 11 per cent. of the yield of his harvest to Government and 20 per cent. to the reapers who have to undertake all the duties appertaining to the collection of the harvest and the carriage into the stores of the landlord. The landowner also pays 2 to 4 per cent. for threshing or treading the corn.

Other than a landowner undertaking a cultivation has to pay to the landowner 9 per cent. in kind, from the outturn of his harvest as rent for one gao of ground and 14 per cent. to Government as tax. His other expenses are the same as above.

The agriculturists of Kazeroon are of two classes, *viz.*, the ryot-i-padishah and the non-ryot, the former being always looked down upon by all classes and subjected to Government to more oppression than the others. The ryot cultivator thus not only pays more taxes to Government, but has to pay his taxes in cash instead of in kind and at 30 per cent. above market value. He is also obliged to give a certain quantity of straw to Government officials whenever required.

A ryot when a landowner, and cultivating his own grounds, has to pay 15½ per cent. on his harvest in cash at the above enhanced valuation.

A poor ryot pays about 60 krans annually in cash to Government. There is another class of ryots who are obliged to buy at 30 per cent. above market value a certain portion of the produce received by Government as taxes. A wealthy ryot is entirely at the mercy of the authorities, a sum of about 1,000 krans being annually levied from him.

The value of one gao of land is from 100 krans to 600 krans according to locality.

To start a cultivation an expense of about fifteen tomans is necessary, *viz.*:-

One ox valuing	50 krans	
Seed	60	"
Labour about	14	"
Straw and cotton seeds	16	"
Sundries	10	"

One donkey is also maintained by a ryot when undertaking four or more gaos of cultivation.

About 2,000 lbs. of grain are sufficient to cultivating one gao of ground at Kazeroon.

In the case of saifee cultivation, no distinction is made by Government between a ryot and a non-ryot.

Saifee sowings are always undertaken by proprietors of water and agriculturalists conjointly, the proprietor providing the water and the ground, and the agriculturalist finding the seed, labour, implements, &c.

Should the waterowner, however, not be a landowner as well, any other landowner would be but too glad to permit his lands to be used for saifee cultivation gratis, inasmuch as the soil becomes enriched, by manuring which the saifee cultivation necessitates.

The time taken up for saifee sowings is about seven months, the following being cultivated: tobacco, watermelon, mashmelon, vegetables, cotton, sesame seeds, lentils, &c., rice, gram.

A tax of 20 percent. *ad valorem* on the outturn is levied by Government, three-fifths of which is payable by the proprietor of the water and two-fifths by the cultivator, and the balance is equally divided beteen the proprietor and cultivator.

Rice and gram, however, form an exception, and are cultivated under the following conditions:-

The agriculturalist recoups himself for the quantity of seed supplied by him, after the harvest. He then goes into equal shares with the waterowner who alone pays Government taxes as follows: if a ryot, he pays three-fifths of his share to Government; if a non-ryot, he pays only half, the agriculturalist paying no tax on his share.

In all cases the Government share of the produce is to be carried to Government stores at the cultivator's expense.

The approximate value of the produce on the spot is-

Wheat	at 40 to 60 cents per Kazeroon maund				
Barley	" 25 " 30 "	"	"	"
Gram	" 50 " 80 "	"	"	"
Sesame	" 70 " 100 "	"	"	"
Maithee	" 15 " 20 "	"	"	"
Dholl	" 15 " 20 "	"	"	"
Cotton	" 2½ " 3 "	"	"	"
Rice	" 50 " 80 "	"	"	"

The expenses of a ryot cultivator in Kazeroon, supposed to have one wife and two children, are ten tomans per annum.

The yield of wheat and barley is from ten to twelve-fold in a good year and three to four in a bad one.

Rice in a bad year yields twenty-fold and in a very good year sixty-fold. Cotton five-fold is a bad year and ten-fold in a good year.

Irrigation in Kazeroon is generally conducted by means of kanats, and the water thereof should in all cases be allowed free passage across grounds, even though not belonging to the proprietor of the kanat.

Should the proprietir of a kanat not wish to undertake any saifee cultivation, he would still be made liable by Government to such taxes as may be due by cultivation.

The land in Kazeroon is sown every alternate year. The portions remaining fallow are ploughed.

No taxes whatever are levied by Government on gardens at Kazeroon.

In the cultivation of poppy at Kazeroon, the proprietor provides the land, seed and expenses of sowing; the cultivation is then made over to the ryot who undertakes all the labour necessary for the tending of the crop till the season of collection, when the proprietor pays for the labour of incision, say one kran per man per day. The outturn is then equally divided between the landowner and the ryots. No taxes are levied by Government on the cultivation of opium at Kazeroon.

APPENDIX 3.3

GENDARMERIE OPERATION AGAINST MOHAMMAD `ALI KAMAREJI IN NOVEMBER 1913

The following, with some minor changes, is taken from the report of His Majesty's Consul, Shiraz, on the attempt of the gendarmerie to punish the notorious brigand, `Ali Muhammad Kamareji.

"On the morning of the 15ᵗʰ a force of all arms, about 600 to 700 strong, with its five Swedish officers (Majors Uggla and Lundberg, and Captains Killander, Pousette and Lundberg), marched out towards Shapur district which lies to the north of the Bushehr road extending from about the village of Dehris to the Rahdar Caravanserai, and bounded by the hills about five or six miles to the north.

"As far as concerned Muhammad Ali Khan no difficulty was experienced. Major Uggla sent an advance guard of cavalry to cut off his retreat in case he meditated any treachery, and himself proceeded directly to his fort of Fatehabad. Here he was courteously received by Muhammad Ali Khan, who appeared to in a wholesome state of apprehension, and who agreed to quit the district with all his men, on the 17ᵗʰ, leaving only (by arrangement with Major Uggla) some 30 tufangchis to act as joint guards to various towers together with the gendarmerie.

"Whilst negotiations were in progress, Captain Pousette had advanced with a few men to the Tul-i-Kuhah fort (these various places will be found marked on sheet No. 100 of the degree sheets published by the Survey Department of India), occupied by Ali Muhammad and his band, and called upon him to surrender. On his refusing to do so, a force of all arms advanced against the fort, and at 2 P.M. began the attack upon it. These operations lasted until sunset and were continued during the night. As far as could be gathered from the accounts of the Swedish officers, the attacks was well pressed forward, the two small 7 centimetre mountain guns advancing eventually to within 50 to 100 yards on the walls of the fort, and the gendarmes in general behaving very well and courageously. The brigands (estimated at about 50 in number) kept themselves well hidden, and maintained a brisk and accurate fire on the attackers.

"The fort is an exceedingly strong one, standing on a small rise, built of solid stone, and with two tiers of fire.

"After nightfall (according to the accounts of the Swedish officers on the spot) the troops entirely surrounded the fort, and a storming party was held in readiness to rush in as soon as a breach was effected. But just after midnight it was found that the fort had been quietly evacuated, and when the gendarmeres rushed in there was no one there. It is impossible to understand how, except through gross negligence on the part of the attackers, or the connivance of some of the gendarmes. The brigands effected their escape. It was a bright moonlight night, and a dog would have been plainly visible at 100 yards. The ground immediately surrounding the fort is open. There were four Swedish officers on the spot, and a sufficient force of gendarmes to surround the place entirely. With ordinary vigilance and care not a man should have escaped alive. And yet Ali Muhammad, 50 men, 5 women, and some donkeys laden with ammunition, etc, succeeded in getting away without anyone seeing them or knowing in which direction they had gone. It was a most deplorable blunder, and has been the direct cause of all subsequent troubles at and near Kazerun."[570]

---

570. Administration Report 1913, pp. 24-25.

APPENDIX 3.4

A Woman's Bravery
Mme. Ohlson's Defence of Kazerun Barracks

A Stirring Account
London, April 30 [1914]

Poverty Bay Herald, XLI, 13406. 13 June 1914, p. 10.[571]

The death of Major Ohlson, the commander of the Persian gendarmerie at Kazerun, was reported in brief messages received at the end of February. Major Ohlson was killed while attempting to lay a mine under the gateway of the fortified house of Nasr Diwan, Kalantar of Kazerun. Nasr Diwan had been suspected for some time of disloyalty and of being the ringleader of an attack on Kazerun at the end of November. After the death of their leader the gendarmerie were compelled to retire to their fortified barracks. There they were commanded by the widow of Major Ohlson. We have now received the following stirring account of Mme/ Ohlson's experiences: -

An Unsatisfactory Situation

I joined my husband about the beginning of February in Kazerun, where he was in commend of the gendarmerie force for the protection of the Bushehr-Shiraz road. He expressed as being extremely dissatisfied with the situation in Kazerun and district, and was determined to take action to re-establish the supremacy of the gendarmerie there and throughout the entire length of the road. Nasr Diwan, Kalantar of Kazerun, being most accessible, it was decided that he should be captured, and arrangements to this end were in preparation.

A Schneider gun was sent from the Mamasenni country, and this was expected to reach Kazerun on the afternoon of February 26. Nasr Diwan and his followers were aware that this gun was on its way, and anticipated an attack on them as soon as it arrived. The night before its arrival, therefore, was chosen for the execution of the design, as it was anticipated that the enemy might then be taken by surprise. The plan in detail was as follows: Major Ohlson with two Swedish non-commissioned officers and 10 native gendarmes was to proceed to Nasr Diwan's house, and blow up the entrance gate with guncotton. A storming party of 30 gendarmes was to set out simultaneously by another road to surround the house; and 60 more were to take up position in support of the

---

571. See also the *New York Times* of 14 February 1914.

high ground in the vicinity. In addition to this all the main exists from the town were to be guarded to prevent any escape.

The Command of a Gun

An eight-centimetre gun was in readiness to take up position on a hill commanding the town, and I was to await orders from my husband, and then proceed with it to the place assigned. At 1.30 a.m. on the 27th my husband got up and informed the native officers of his plan, which up to that moment he had kept a profound secret. Major Ohlson set out from the barracks at about 3 a.m., and I remained awaiting orders to start off with the big gun.

Not long after my husband's departure we found ourselves surrounded and hotly attacked by the enemy. The suddenness of the attack led me to suspect treachery. The maxims were by my orders carried on to the roof of the barracks, and from there we opened a brisk fire on our assailants. Shortly after this, and while the fighting was still in progress, the men forming the parties sent out for the capture of Nasr Diwan, returned to the barracks by twos and threes. Major Ohlson, however, had not yet put in an appearance, but as I had no idea what had happened I was not alarmed for his safety, and fully expected him to return at nightfall. In the afternoon the Schneider gun, escorted by 50 mounted gendarmes, arrived at Bagh-i-Nazar, and started a bombardment on the town.

For six days and nights the fight continued almost incessantly, and I was during that time unable to disrobe, and had to take what rest I could in the room occupied by the native officers. Many of the gendarmes were badly wounded, and I had to witness the terrible sufferings of these men awaiting surgical aid. I attended to them with the help of a native surgeon, and provided them with food and saw to their comfort generally.

Threats of the Enemy

The yelling and shouting of our enemies during the lulls in the firing, especially at night, was terrifying, and resembles more the howling of wild beasts than anything human. Those occupying positions near the barracks would scream threats at us, such as "When we get hold of you we shall gnaw the flesh from your bones." Our supplies became exhausted, and for nearly two days we had to subsist almost entirely upon tea. One of the native officers, however, by a stratagem succeeded in seizing a quantity of rice and meat, which reached us only just in time.

On the fifth day intense excitement was aroused by the discovery that an attempt was being made to mine the barracks. This was detected by one of the gendarmes, who reported hearing some sounds as of digging under the floor of a room in which he had been sleeping. After the reinforcements had arrived the matter was investigated, and it was found that our foes had tunneled up to within a few yards of the barrack wall from a caravanserai nearly 200 yards away.

No news having been received of the fate of my husband, I concluded that he was still alive and a prisoner in the hands of Nasr Diwan. My sole thought was to effect his rescue, and with this end in view I used every effort to stimulate and encourage the gendarmerie to fight on.

APPENDIX 3.5

KUMARIJ

The principal portion of the Kumarij district consists of a level plain stretching beyond the top of the Kotal-i-Kumarij to the southern end of the Tang-i-Turkan, and measuring some four miles by three miles. But the actual boundaries are on the –

North: the southern end of the Tang-i-Turkan.

South: the village of Cheroom on the banks of the Shapur river, beyond the foot of the Kumarij Kotal.

East: the mountains of Kuh-i-Mast and Kuh-i-Gunjishk, which separate the district from the Kazerun plain.

West: the river Shapur at Rudak, which belongs to Kumarij.

Only five villages are in the district: --
Kumarij (about 150 houses inhabited).
Rudak.
Banaft.
Cheroom.
Caravanserai (Deh Kuhne).

It was formerly part of the sub-government of Khisht, but is now owned by Mushar-ud-Dowleh, to whom the revenue amounting to [blank] tomans is paid.

Qashgai clans are neighbours to the district on three sides; the kashkuli and Chahar Bunicheh tribes outside the further extremity of the Tang-i-Turkan and near Bushakun; the Farsimedan about four miles the further side of the Kuh-i-Mast; the Kashkuli again about seven miles to the west of Rudak.

There are two alternative routes between Kazerun, Kumarij and Konar Takhteh. One, the Rah-i-Bardun, over the Kuh-i-Mast, is often used by Khurshid Khan for caravans to Kazerun, when he is at strife with the kashkulis. The other route from Kazerun leaves the main track at the caravanserai and passes by the Kuh-i-Surkh road to the north of Kumarij till it descends on to the Konar Takhteh plain, thus avoiding the Tang-i-Turkan, Kumarij and the Kotal-i-Kumarij altogether.

About 1905, in the time of Haidar Khan, its late chief, the district of Kumarij was more important than today: Haidar Khan, by force of arms, obtained unlimited control from the top of the Kotal-i-Malu to Kazerun, where he established himself as Deputy Governor, turned out and defeated Khwajeh Ibrahim, Kalantar of Kazerun. Haidar Khan died of wounds inflicted by a slave at Kazerun in September 1909, leaving an infant son, Farajullah Khan, in the guardianship of a black confidant, Khurshid.

The latter possesses considerable talents, and great bravery: he has had to repel attacks by a brother of the late Haidar Khan, and constant aggression from men whom he has outlawed from Kumarij, including the well-known Ali Mohammad. The Kashkulis are bitter enemies of his, and covet the district. In the spring of 1911 Nizam-us-Sultaneh determined to attack Kumarij, urged on by Soulet-ud-Douleh: several hundred Qashgais with other partisans of Nizam bombarded the village, and Khurshid, after shutting himself up in the Khan's fort on which many of his own villagers fired, escaped to the Kuh-i-Mast. He was gradually joined by his adherents, and returned in June 1911 to Kumarij, when he destroyed most of the houses in the village to prevent the inhabitants opposing him again. He makes a great show of ruling not in his own right but on behalf of Farajullah Khan. He is on friendly terms with the Kalantar of Kazerun, Khwajeh Abdulla, Nasir-ud-Diwan, but not very well disposed towards Hussein Beg of Daliki. He pays his own tufangchis (who probably do not number more than 150) well. The outstanding feature of Khurshid's politics is enmity with the Kashgais. The Tang-i-Turkan is a no-man's land, neither Qashqais nor Kumarijis venture beyond their respective ends.

Previous rulers of Kumarij

Mulla Mohammad Sheffi (killed by retainers about 1871: married 3 wives: had 10 sons).

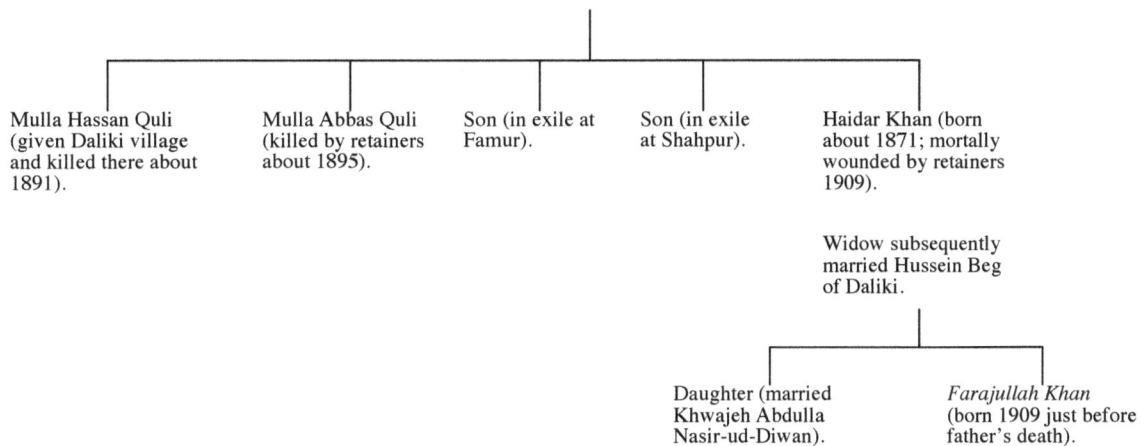

Mulla Hassan Quli (given Daliki village and killed there about 1891).

Mulla Abbas Quli (killed by retainers about 1895).

Son (in exile at Famur).

Son (in exile at Shahpur).

Haidar Khan (born about 1871; mortally wounded by retainers 1909).

Widow subsequently married Hussein Beg of Daliki.

Daughter (married Khwajeh Abdulla Nasir-ud-Diwan).

Farajullah Khan (born 1909 just before father's death).

N.B. – Since the above was written, Khurshid Beg had been accidentally killed: and the political future of the district becomes still more uncertain.

Source: Administration Report 1911, Appendix II, pp. 14-15. (Notes by Mr. H.G. Chick, commercial adviser to the political residency in the Persian Gulf, upon various districts of Fars and of the Gulf Ports).

APPENDIX 3.6

DALIKI

This small district, containing 3 villages only, is bounded on the –

East: by the mountains.

South: by the Borazjun frontier passing about 3 miles north of Qaraoul Khane.

West: boundary lies along the Zira border to the west of a narrow strip containing the large date plantations of Sarkeverdun and continues about ¾ mile to the west of the Shur river till it reaches the mountains behind Behbera and Mazarai.

North: by the bridge of Daliki: there is nothing but montains each side of this.

Daliki is the property of Nizam-us-Sultaneh, the Khan paying some 8,200 tomans each year to Nizam-us-Sultaneh, and 500 tomans to Mughis-ud-Douleh, his 'peshkar.'

Its revenue consists of about 8,000 tomans from the date gardens, and many thousands tomans from taxation of caravans, and the monopoly of the sale of grain to them.

The villages of Daliki district are:-

Daliki (with about 400 houses).

Sarkeverdun (west of the river).

Qaleh-i-Sefid

Muhammad Reza Beg, grandfather of the present Khan, was killed in 1856 at the gate of Bushehr: he originally was Kedkhuda of Ziaret in Borazjun.

Habibullah Beg, his son, was powerless and the district was taken by the Khans of Borazjun. He was in the service of the Khan for some years, and then transferred to Daliki as Kalantar under the Fars Government.

After his death, Muhammad Reza Beg ruled as Kalantar of Daliki, and was killed at Kumarij by Haidar Khan some 11 years ago, his wife having been a cousin of Haidar Khan. Nur Muhammad Khan succeeded him, and the district was sold by the Shah to the Nizam-us-Sultaneh. Nur Muhammad was later given the title of Khan. He is on terms of enmity with the Khans of Shabancara, and an ally of Ghazanfer-us-Sultaneh of Borazjun.

The genealogy of the ruling family is as follows: --

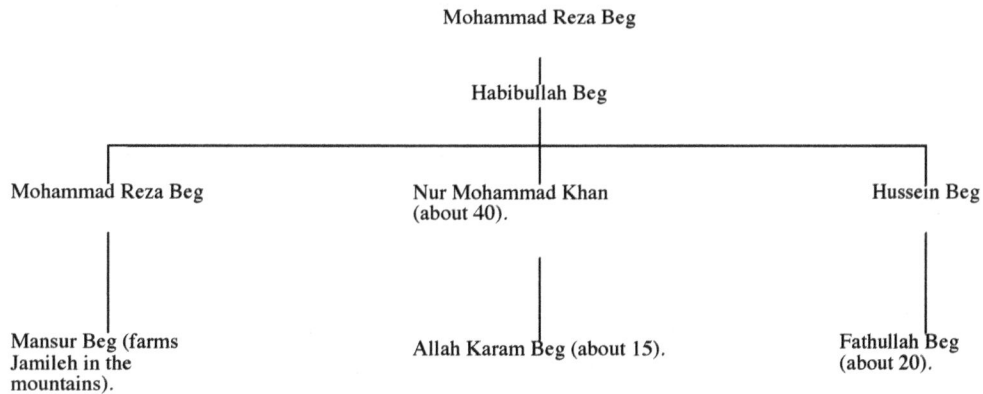

```
                         Mohammad Reza Beg
                                |
                         Habibullah Beg
        ┌───────────────────────┼───────────────────────┐
Mohammad Reza Beg        Nur Mohammad Khan          Hussein Beg
                         (about 40).
        │                        │                         │
Mansur Beg (farms        Allah Karam Beg (about 15).  Fathullah Beg
Jamileh in the                                        (about 20).
mountains).
```

Owing to his close relations, as tenant, with Nizam-us-Sultaneh, Nur Muhammad Khan has succeeded in getting the control of the villages of Dawaguni and Banaki on the Khisht plain given to him, and his brother Hussein Beg generally resides at Banaki. Thus the Kotal-i-Malu pass is wholly under the control of the Daliki Khans. His nephew Mansur Beg farmed from Mushar-ud-Douleh in 1911 the village of Jamileh, in the mountainsup the Daliki river, and district.

Extortion of the large revenue from caravans is the all-important object of the Khan's policy. He is considered ill-disposed towards the British.

Source: Administration Report 1911, Appendix II, pp. 10-11 (Notes by Mr. H.G. Chick, commercial adviser to the political residency in the Persian Gulf, upon various districts of Fars and of the Gulf Ports).

APPENDIX 3.7

Enclosure 1 in No. 226.

Acting Consul Knox to Sir G. Barclay.

Sir,   *Shiraz, December 26, 1911.*
IN compliance with instructions contained in your circular telegram of the 8t
December, I have the honour to transmit herewith a return of attacks and robberies o
British subjects and of robberies of British goods which have taken place in thi
consular district within the past four years. This return is confined to those attack
and robberies that have occurred on the main roads.

I have treated the subject-matter in two forms, the first dealing with the date c
the robbery, the locality, the aggressors, and the persons prejudiced ; in the second
have noted the nature of the attack or robbery, the value of the property robbed, an
the amount recovered by the Persian authorities. It has also seemed not inappropriat
to append a statement of wilful damage to the lines of the Indo-European Telegrap
Department during the last three years for which figures are at present available.

I have, &c.
G. G. KNOX.

Enclosure 2 in No. 226.

RETURN of Attacks on and Robberies from British Subjects for 1908–12.

Form I.

No.	Date.	Locality.	Aggressors.	Persons or Firm Prejudiced.
	1908.			
1	January 12 ..	Kotal-i-Malu ..	Villagers ..	His Majesty's Government.
2	February 5 ..	Sivand ..	Arabs ..	Messrs. Haji Ali Akbar, of Man chester.
3	March (?) ..	Ab Barik ..	Basiri ..	Messrs. Dixon
4	„ 18 .	Mian Kotal ..	Kashgais ..	„ „
5	July 8 ..	„ ..	Kaloonis ..	„ Ziegler.
6	August 10 ..	Dalaki ..	Villagers ..	„ Somech.
				„ Isaacs.
7	„ 18 ..	Near Dalaki ..	„ ..	„ Dixon.
8	„ 20 ..	Zarghun ..	Arabs ..	„ Ziegler.
				„ Zeitoon.
9	„ 20 ..	Kazerun ..	Road guards ..	„ Dixon.
10	„ 23 ..	Tang-i-Turkan ..	Villagers ..	„ D. Sassoon.
11	September 6 ..	Mian Kotal ..	„ „ ..	„ Dixon.
12	„ 9 ..	Shulgistan..	Boir Ahmad ..	Imperial Bank.
13	„ 9 ..	Khaneh Khorreh ..	Arabs ..	Egyptian subject.
14	October 3 ..	Shulgistan..	Boir Ahmad ..	Tehran Club.
15	November 7 ..	„ ..	„ ..	Messrs. Ziegler.
16	„ 10 ..	Ahmadi ..	Unknown ..	Bombay Parsi firm. Major Ducat.
17	„ 17 ..	Shulgistan ..	Boir Ahmad ..	Messrs. Dixon.
18	December 7 ..	Deh Sheikh ..	Masermi (?) ..	„ Zeitoon Khalil.
	1909.			
19	February 15 ..	Zinian ..	Unknown ..	Messrs. Somech.
20	March 17 ..	Kurdshul ..	Lashanis ..	Mr. E. Gentleman.
21	„ 30 ..	Abbasabad ..	Villagers ..	Rev. J. C. Linton.
22	April 6 ..	Sivand ..	Arabs ..	Messrs. Ziegler.
23	„ 9 ..	Behbehan ..	Lurs ..	Mr. J. C. Smith (Indo-Europea Telegraph Department).
24	May 16 ..	Chenar Rahdar ..	Masermi ..	Messrs Ziegler.
25	„ 18 ..	Abdui ..	Road guards ..	„ Dixon.
26	„ 22 ..	Deh Sheikh ..	Masermis ..	„ Ziegler.
27	June 3 ..	Haft Mullah ..	Villagers ..	„ Dixon.
28	„ 7 ..	Zinian ..	Kashgais ..	„ Mowla, of Bombay.
29	August 16 ..	Pul-i-Khan..	Arabs ..	Mr. G. Middleton.
30	October 28 ..	Khaneh Kergun ..	Boir Ahmad ..	Messrs. D. Sassoon.
31	November 28 ..	Sineh Safid ..	Kashgai ..	„ Andrew Weir.
32	„ 18 ..	Konar Takhteh ..	Villagers ..	„ Ziegler.
	1910.			
33	January (?) ..	Chenar Rahdar ..	Masermis ..	Messrs. Ziegler.
34	April 12 ..	Kaderabad..	Villagers ..	Clerk, His Majesty's consulate.
35	„ 17 ..	Shulgistan..	Boir Ahmad (?) ..	Mr. J. H. Bill, His Majesty' consul.

No.	Date.	Locality.	Aggressors.	Persons or Firm Prejudiced.
	1910.			
36	May 30 ..	Near Siakh ..	Sorkhis	Messrs. Ziegler.
37	August 13 ..	,, ...	Kashgais	,, ,,
38	November 14 ..	Ag. Cheshmeh ..	Kashgai and Lur (?)..	,, Dixon.
				,, Somech.
				,, Service Reeve.
				,, D. Sassoon.
				,, H. S. Mohammed Kazeruni, of Bombay.
39	August (?) ..	Gerdeneh Imamzadeh Ismail	Kashgai	British Indian subject.
40	November (?) ..	,, ,,	Boir Ahmad ..	Two British Indian subjects.
	1911.			
41	February 22 ..	Ab Barik	Arabs	Messrs. Ziegler.
42	,, 15 ..	Khaneh Kergun ..	Kurdshulir.. ..	,, ,,
43	March 13 ..	Surmek	Villagers	,, ,,
44	April 1 ..	God-i-Narm ..	Kurdshulis.. ..	,, Dixon.
45	February 12 ..	Khaneh Kergun ..	,, ...	,, D. Sassoon.
46	June 20 ..	Kamarej	Kashgais	,, Livingstone.
47	July 7 ..	Dastarjin	Villagers	,, Dixon.
48	,, 17 ..	Morghab	Unknown	,, Ziegler.
49	,, 27 ..	Khosrow Shirin ..	Kashgais	Imperial Bank of Persia.
50	August 22 ..	Kazerun	Villagers	Messrs. Livingstone,
51	,, 26 ..	Tang-i-Turkan ..	Kamarejis	,, Somech.
52	September 7 ..	Konar Takhteh ..	Villagers	,, Ziegler.
53	,, 9 ..	Tang-i-Turkan ..	Kashkulis	,, Sassoon
54	,, 17 ..	,, ..	Road guards ..	British Indian subject.
55	,, 26 ..	Pul-i-Fesa.. ..	Kashgai	Lieutenant A. T. Wilson, I.A.
56	October 1 ..	Pulabguineh ..	Villagers	Messrs. Ziegler.
57	,, 3 ..	Tang-i-Turkan ..	Kashkulis (?) .	,, Andrew Weir.
58	,, 12 ..	Shulgistan.. ..	Boir Ahmad ..	(a.) Miss Ross.
				(b.) Messrs. Ziegler.
				,, Dixon.
				Lloyd's (insured opium).
59	,, 13 ..	Deh Sheikh ..	Kashgai	Messrs. Ziegler.
60	,, 29 ..	Khaneh Khorreh ..	Uncertain	Miss Ross.
61	November 19 ..	Pul-i-Karagach ..	Boir Ahmad ..	Japanese merchants under British protection.
62	,, 30 ..	Shulgistan.. ..	Kuhgelus (?) ..	One squadron 39th C.I. Horse.
63	December 20 ..	Dastarjin	Villagers	Messrs. Ziegler.
64	,, 24 ..	Kotal Dakhter ..	Kashkulis	Fifty men 39th C.I. Horse.

NOTE.—It seems worthy of note that only one British subject has travelled between Shiraz and Ispahan in the interval between the attack on Mr. Bill in April 1909 (No. 35) and that on Miss Ross on the 12th October, 1911.

No. 62 was an attack on a caravan near the squadron of Central India Horse proceeding to reinforce the consular escort at Ispahan; in the ensuing skirmish the rissaldar major of that regiment was severely wounded.

No. 64 was a treacherous attack by road guards, in which one sowar was killed, one wounded, and two horses killed.

Form II.

No. in Form I.	Nature of Robbery.	Value Robbed.	Amount Recovered.
		Krans.	Krans.
1	Escort sowar held up	2,360·00	Nil.
2	Caravan robbery	630·00	,,
3	,, ,, ...	2,615·00	,,
4	,, ,, ...	4,398·00	,,
5	,, ,, ...	350·00	,,
6	,, ,, ...	1,470·00	,,
7	,, ,, ...	2,300·C0	,,
8	,, ,, ...	9,768·00	5,255·00
9	,, ,, ...	2,745·00	Nil.
10	,, ,, ...	7,800·00	,,
11	,, ,, ...	2,785·00	,,
12	,, ,, ...	2,550·00	,,
13	,, ,, ...	1,150·00	,,
14	,, ,, ...	2,730·00	,,
15	,, ,, ...	2,650·00	,.

No. in Form I.	Nature of Robbery.			Value Robbed.	Amount Recovered.
				Krans.	Krans.
16	Caravan robbery	..	..	1,220·00	Nil.
17	,, ,,	..	..	31,368·25	,,
18	,, ,,	..	..	2,065·75	,,
19	,, ,,	..	..	2,396·00	,,
20	Robbery and assault	..	..	10,600·00	,,
21	,, ,,	..	..	6,194·00	,,
22	Caravan robbery	..	..	651·00	651·00
23	Attack	..	..	5,800·00	5,800·00
24	Caravan robbery	..	..	18,888·00	Nil.
25	,, ,,	..	..	1,749·00	,,
26	,, ,,	..	..	1,800·00	,,
27	,, ,,	..	..	2,332·00	,,
28	,, ,,	..	..	5,800·00	,,
29	Robbery and assault	..	..	2,110·00	,,
30	Caravan robbery	..	..	23,072·00	,,
31	,, ,,	..	..	28,080·00	,,
32	,, ,,	..	..	1,119·00	,,
33	,, ,,	..	..	21,792·00	4,196·00
34	Robbery and assault	..		5,600·00	600·00
35	Attack on His Majesty's consul (two sowars of escort killed)		..	..	..
36	Caravan robbery	..	..	565·00	Nil
37	,, ,,	..	..	2,941·00	1,373·85
38	,, ,,	..	..	54,277·00	Nil.
39	Attack	..	..	398·00	,,
40	,,	..	..	346·00	,,
41	Caravan robbery	..	..	5,673·00	,,
42	,, ,,	..	..	1,320·00	,,
43	,, ,,	..	..	835·00	,,
44	,, ,,	..	..	4,510·00	,,
45	,, ,,	..	..	3,500·00	,,
46	,, ,,	..	..	4,698·00	,,
47	,, ,,	..	..	1,300·00	,,
48	,, ,,	..	..	15,515·00	,,
49	,, ,,	..	..	15,000·00	,,
50	,, ,,	..	..	750·00	,,
51	,, ,,	..	..	2,057·00	,,
52	,, ,,	..	..	280·00	,,
53	,, ,,	..	..	2,500·00	,,
54	,, ,,	..	..	1,349·00	,,
55	Robbery and assault	..	..	..	Property restored.
56	Caravan robbery	..		600·00	Nil.
57	,, ,,	..	..	21,600·00	,,
58	(a.) Robbery and assault		..	13,515·00 (255l.)	13,515·00
	(b.) Caravan robbery	..	..	359,100·00 (approximate)	Nil.
59	Caravan robbery	..	..	5,115·00	,,
60	Attack	..	..	633·00	,,
61	Robbery and assault	..		..	..
62	Skirmish	..		..	..
63	Caravan robbery	..	..	850·00	850·00
64	Attack	..	..	..	..
	Total..	..	..	738,165·00	32,240·85

NOTE.—The designation of caravan robbery includes in some cases simple thefts of merchandise on the road.

STATEMENT of Wilful Damage to the Lines of the Indo-European Telegraph Department between Bushire and Abadeh.

						Krans.
Year ended the 1st January, 1909	..	..	..	..	..	16,726
,, ,, ,, 1910	..	..	..	..	..	33,893
,, ,, ,, 1911	..	..	..	..	..	47,323
Total	..	..	..	..	..	97,942

G. G. KNOX.

CHAPTER FOUR

THE RISE AND FALL OF THE BANU KAʿB
A BORDER STATE IN SOUTHERN KHUZESTAN[1]

Summary: This study discusses the efforts of the Banu Kaʿb, a tribal confederacy straddling two countries (Iraq, Iran), to maintain their independence between 1740-1840. In doing so, they had to fight not only two powerful external foreign centers (Baghdad, Tehran), but also its own periphery (particularly Mohammareh). As a result the Banu Kaʿb lost their independence to the new nation-state of Iran with which it had nothing in common but for a claim to the same piece of land.

INTRODUCTION

This is a case-study of the rise and fall of a group of borderers. With this term I refer to mainly tribal groups whose abode straddled the 'border' between Iran and its neighboring states. One such group of borderers was that of the Kaʿb tribal confederacy, the largest Arab group in Southern Khuzestan and one that did not at all identify with either the Safavid-Qajar or the Ottoman state and its aspirations. This and other similar groups rather preferred to remain independent and on their own; they felt no affinity whatsoever to the larger states that surrounded and laid claim to them. Throughout the centuries borderers like the Kaʿb had been able to carve out a quasi-independent status, only paying obligatory recognition to the surrounding larger states when it could not be avoided. Usually, the people lived in relatively

---

1. First published in the journal *IRAN* XLIV (2006), pp. 277-315 and translated into Persian by Mostafa Namdari Monfared to be published by Shadegan (Tehran).

inaccessible areas where the central government, in this case, of Safavid-Zand-Qajar Iran and the Ottoman Empire, only had at best nominal control and oftentimes no control at all.

These tribal borderers felt no allegiance to anyone with the exception of their immediate clan leader. Even within the tribal confederacy the supreme Sheikh's authority was not always recognized and had to be sustained by both positive and negative inducements. These borderers therefore did not acknowledge any central state and its individual members had not even an understanding of such a phenomenon. The only thing that they acknowledged was force and clan loyalty. Government interference with such tribes depended on the level of their nuisance value and the relative strength or weakness of the central government. If the tribes became too strong, i.e. too unruly and 'forgot' to pay their tribute, the central government either sent troops, when negotiations had failed, or it ignored the situation. Sending troops might be a hazardous undertaking for the government troops might be defeated in which case the problem usually grew larger and so did its nuisance value. In case of borderers the problem had an additional dimension, viz. that of borders. Borderers did not recognize them, but if these served their purpose they used borders to their own advantage when threatened by one of the states in which they lived. This did not always work, of course. Borders between states were but cease-fire lines and at any given time one of the neighboring governments might exercise its 'right' to claim territory on whatever spurious entitlement it preferred to base its land grab. As a result, border wars might threaten or really break out due to actions of borderers on the 'other' side of the border. This is also what happened in the case of the Ka`b and this threat of war led to (i) the first modern attempt to delineate an international recognized border between the Ottoman Empire and the Kingdom of Qajar Iran and to (ii) the end of the Ka`b's independence.

The Ka`b (Cha`b) (sing. Ka`bi; Cha`bi) was the largest and most important Arab tribal confederacy in S. Khuzestan.[2] Despite their sometimes pivotal role in regional politics the Danish traveler Niebuhr wrote in 1764 that "The Kiab or Tsjab were of no importance before Sheikh Soliman."[3] Under the paramount chief Soleyman or Salman (r. 1737-68) the Ka`b indeed became something of a regional household name, although Niebuhr was wrong in implying that they were unknown and unimportant before that time. However, people's memory is short, if not fickle, and about 90 years later the Russian traveler de Bode implied that the once notorious Ka`b had been forgotten. He wrote that "Their name became known due to Ali pasha's attack in 1837 and subsequent negotiations between Persia and Turkey."[4] Each time the Ka`b came into the news this was because some outside power interfered with them and the result was invariably an attack on their freedom.

In what follows I discuss the juggling act of the Ka`b, who, between 1740 and 1840 and even thereafter, tried to maintain their independence from both the Ottoman Empire and Safavid-Zand and Qajar Iran. Within this international power play there was yet another factor. In addition to the sometimes murderous infighting between leading members of the ruling family, there was the additional power play between the K`ab's center at Falahiyah

---

2. The *kaf* is velarized in S. Iraq and Ka`b therefore becomes Cha`b. The form Ja`b is also found. Golestaneh 2536, p. 332. The Ka`b were also known in eastern Arabia and southern Iraq as Ku`ub. Abu Hakimah 1960.

3. Niebuhr 1772, p. 319.

4. De Bode 1845, vol. 2, p. 110.

and its periphery at Mohammareh, which it was unable to control after 1830. Whereas the first power play between the two foreign centers was won by Qajar Iran, as far as the Ka`b related problems were concerned, the second power play within the Ka`b confederacy was won by its own periphery. What it meant was that the Qajar authorities established control over the Ka`b, while, in a reversal of roles, the latter became the vassals of the Sheikh of Mohammareh, who until the 1840s had been a vassal of the supreme chief of the Ka`b.

The relations between the two states (the Ottoman Empire and Safavid-Zand Iran) and the Ka`b as well as between Falahiyeh and Mohammareh has been analyzed so far in two studies that exclusively deal with the Ka`b and their history. Kasravi, relying mostly on the *Tarikh-e Ka`b* by Sheikh Fathollah Ka`bi, described the tribe's history within Khuzestan's history with a broad brush. He was followed by John Perry some 50 years later, who, building on Kasravi's work, focused on the period of the Ka`b under Sheikh Salman and his conflict with the English East India Company, the Ottoman government of Basra and the Zand government in Shiraz. However, the history of the Ka`b did not end there, although Perry suggests as much, for history would almost repeat itself. Furthermore, additional data puts the rise of the Ka`b in a slightly different light than has been propounded by these two earlier studies. After the epoch-making reign of Sheikh Salman (r. 1738-68), when the Ka`b carved out a quasi-independent territory for themselves, the case of the Ka`b became once again a burning issue for its neighbors in the 1840s, because of claims made by both the Ottoman government and the Qajar government on some tracts of land in the Shatt al-Arab estuary as well as on the 'nationality' of the tribe itself. Once again the Ka`b had to defend their territory and this time they lost.

Origins

Before I discuss the events that led to the Ka`b's notoriety and problems I need to say something about their origin. For tribes apparently need to have an origin, which most of the time, like in the case of important people, is an invented one. As Abu Hakimah has observed, Arab authors and genealogists do not speak of the Ka`b in detail but usually list them under Ka`b b. Rabi`a. "They are said to belong to Qays `Aylan, a major central and eastern Arabian tribe."[5] The same story was apparently also current among the nineteenth century Ka`b who claimed descent "from the `Avamir or Bani `Amir, descended from a certain Ka`ab b. Rabi` b. `Amir, allegedly the 24[th] in descent from Ishmael. Their original home was in the Nejd and there is a remnant of them still there at a place called Bishauraniyyah." However, nobody has been able to identify the latter place.[6] According to Sheikh Fathollah Ka`bi, the tribal historian, the Ka`b are a branch of the Banu Khafaja, a large tribe that had emigrated from the Arabian peninsula into Iraq prior to the foundation of Islam and had taken up its abode between Baghdad and Basra. During the early Islamic period they were known as proverbial highwaymen. Although at times the authorities tried induce the Banu Khafaja, as they did

---

5. Abu Hakimah 1960.

6. Lorimer 1915, p. 961.

with other tribes, to be in charge of road security this worked at best temporarily. The Persian poet Saʻdi related how the caravan he was traveling with was picked clean by the Banu Khafaja, the supposed road guards, in the thirteenth century.[7] Therefore, it seems safe to assume that the Kaʻb hailed from the Najd, whether that was in the seventeenth century as some have it or 17 centuries earlier, according to another source.[8]

The Political Lay of the Land in the Sixteenth-Seventeenth Century

Because in the 1840s the Ottoman government claimed that the Mohammareh area where the Kaʻb were residing had been granted by Sultan Selim (r. 1512-20) in 1512 to four holy men of Basra, and that therefore the area was Ottoman territory, it is useful to take a closer look at that claim. The Ottoman government did not produce any documents to provide evidence for its claim, while historically speaking it seems highly unlikely that such a grant actually took place.[9] In 1512, Basra was ruled by an independent Arab dynasty of the Muntafiq, an Arab tribe that has politically and militarily dominated that area until the beginning of the twentieth century. Nominally, Shah Esmaʻil I not Sultan Selim I claimed suzerainty over the area, but the former never enforced it. Only after the conquest of Baghdad by Sultan Soleyman (r. 1520-66) in 1534 did the Muntafiq ruler of Basra offer his *pro forma* allegiance to the Ottoman Sultan. However, for the next 12 years nothing changed, although Ottoman coins were struck at Basra during that time. It was only in December 1546 that Basra was incorporated into the Ottoman Empire. However, Ottoman rule never was really accepted in southern Iraq and for the next 60 years or so the Ottoman governors of Basra had to almost constantly fight the rebellious Arab tribes around their city. The Ottomans finally lost this war of attrition and in 1612 or thereabouts an Ottoman official with local ties, Afrasiyab, founded an independent dynasty that ruled Basra till 1669. He paid no tribute to the Ottoman Sultan, although the latter confirmed the investiture of every new Afrasiyabid Pasha with a robe of honor after having received some presents. The re-establishment of Ottoman rule in 1669 resulted in ten years of relative peace and quiet, but as of 1680 the running war with the Arab tribes, in particular the Muntafiq, started again and lasted until the mid- nineteenth century.[10] In short, the head of the Ottoman governor of Basra was always lying very uneasily.

---

7. Kasravi 1333, p. 98. The Kaʻb were also known in those days as the Banu Hazan. Zarrabi 1342, p. 282.

8. Chrikov 1989, vol. 2, p. 471.

9. Rawlinson 1989, vol. 1, p. 293. ("The dependence of Bussorah ... upon Turkey, of the lands on the left bank of the Shatt-el-Arab, from the sea as far as Girdelan, has been acknowledged and recorded, the famous Sultan Selim, in about A.D. 1512, having conferred the lands in question in free grant upon four holy men of Bussorah-Sheikh Abd-el-Salam, Sheikh Ahmed-el-Befahee, Sheikh Habeeb Ollah, and Sheikh Ibrahim Roodhein-and a great part of the original patents, passed under the Sultan's seal, being, as it is affirmed, still in existence.").

10. For the history of Basra during the period of 1600-1730 see Floor 2006, chapter 8. For the rest of the eighteenth and the nineteenth century see Abdullah 2001; Fattah 1997; Longrigg 1925.

On the Safavid side of the 'border' things were better in that there was not that much opposition to Safavid and later to Afshar, Zand, and Qajar rule as there was against Ottoman rule on the other side of the river. The main power in southern Khuzestan (or `Arabistan as it was then usually referred to) was the chief of the Musha`sha` confederacy. He resided at Hoveyzeh and claimed descent from the prophet Mohammad. After their defeat in 1508 against Shah Esma`il I, the Musha`sha` accepted Safavid rule and only occasionally was there need for central government forces to intervene in Khuzestan. The Musha`sha` chief was appointed *Vali* or governor of Hoveyzeh by the Safavids and he wielded considerable influence in Khuzestan affairs. This influence was curtailed by the presence of the Afshars in Dowraq, with whom they were on a hostile footing. The Musha`sha`, like other Arab tribal groups, held lands on both sides of the 'border', in S. Iraq in particular at Zakiyyeh. The Musha`sha` therefore were involved in local politics in southern Iraq as were S. Iraqi tribal groups in southern Khuzestan.[11] It was thus not a strange thing that the Ka`b likewise had a foot in both S. Iraq and S. Khuzestan.

The Ka`b Move from Wasit to Qobban

Whatever the alleged origin of the Ka`b may be, it would seem that during the sixteenth century they lived in the Wasit area at the confluence of the Tigris and Euphrates rivers. According to Rawlinson, "In the early part of seventeenth century Chaabs were in the marshes of Wasit and paid "Meer-i-Kalameyah" a tribute for the right of pasturing their buffaloes."[12] Rawlinson and others place their migration from that area to Qobban on the banks of the Karun River in the late seventeenth century. About 1680, due to a drought, the Ka`b emigrated to the delta of the Karun and twelve years later to Qobban.[13] However, according to the Ka`b's own history they were already settled at Qobban at the end of the sixteenth century. They later received the right to remain there for services rendered to Afrasiyab Pasha, the man who ousted the Ottomans around 1612 with their help as well as from other Arab tribes. Afrasiyab Pasha also ousted the forces of the *Vali* of Hoveyzeh from Basra province as well as those of another Safavid official, Bektash Agha Afshar, from the Qobban area. When Safavid forces under Emamqoli Khan attacked Basra in the late 1620s, it were the Ka`b under Sheikh Badr b. `Othman who at Qobban opposed the Safavid troops. As a reward for their valor the Ka`b allegedly received title to the islands of the estuary.[14]

It seems that further penetration into Safavid controlled lands had begun already by the mid-seventeenth century. For example, Sheikh Fathollah Ka`bi, the tribal historian, wrote that

---

11. Caskel 1929, pp. 48-93; Ibid. 1934, pp. 415-34; Mazzaoui 1981, pp. 139-62; Scarcia 1971, pp. 633-37; Kasravi 1333.

12. Rawlinson 1989, vol. 1, p. 281; Layard 1846, p. 41.

13. Rawlinson 1989, vol. 1, p. 281; Chirikov 1989, vol. 2, p. 471; Schofield 1989, vol. 1, p. 268 (Memorandum by Mr. Taylor Thomson).

14. Kasravi 1333, p. 101. For the rise of Afrasiyab Pasha and the wars with the Safavids see Floor 2006, pp. 544-47.

when it became known that Hoseyn Pasha had been ousted from his government of Basra in 1668 he loaded his family into boats and went to Ma`shur. It was also in those days that under influence of the Musha`sha` the Ka`b became Shi`ites through their vassalage to the *Vali* of Hoveyzeh.[15] Although `Azzawi states that the Ka`b do not figure among a 1696 list of tribes of the Musha`sha` confederacy[16] that had dominated Southern Khuzestan since the late fifteenth century, a contemporary Persian source explicitly mentions that the Ka`b were the vassals of Sayyed Farajollah, the chief of the Musha`sha` and *Vali* of Hoveyzeh. The latter conquered Basra in 1694 with the help of amongst others the Ka`b.[17] However, vassalage is a relative term and a borderer tribe like the Ka`b only remained a vassal when it was in its interest or when it could be enforced. In short, the Ka`b only looked after their own immediate interest and felt no allegiance to any outside force or political system. A decade later the Ka`b began, or rather continued, with their policy of switching allegiance between Ottomans and Safavids depending on how advantageous that was for them. After the departure of the Safavids from Basra in 1701, the Ka`b helped restore Ottoman rule over the city by ousting the Muntafiq, who had replaced the Safavids as the occupying power of the city. On November 25, 1705, when Khalil Pasha entered Basra, Sheikh Sarhan (Serahan), of the Ka`b (Shiahab) tribe, an enemy of Sheikh Mughamis and his Muntafiq, entered Basra with 2,000 men on that same day.[18]

In the years preceding and following the fall of the Safavid dynasty in 1722, the Ka`b slowly extended their sphere of influence towards the North, to the Jarrahi River, where later they would settle. Nami ascribes their expansion into Khuzestan as the result of the pressure from the governors of Basra.[19] This is quite likely, given the behavior of the Ottoman governors towards the Arab tribes at that time. Having already made the first steps into Safavid territory, the ones that followed thereafter were made easier, when Ottoman behavior became oppressive. Hamilton has left the following account of his experience of about 1721 that is emblematic for the Ottoman-Arab tribal relationship.

> While I was at *Bassora*, a Parcel of Janisaries were sent to the Island of *Gabon*, which lies between the City and the Mouth of the River Euphrates. ... It being pretty well inhabited, and the Bashaw imposing exorbitant taxes on those poor Islanders, which they either would not, or could not pay, sent the aforementioned Janisaries to dragoon them into Compliance. They first built a sconce, and fortified it, both to secure themselves from sudden Attacks or Surprize, as well as to hold what they might distrain from the poor Peasants.[20]

---

15. Kasravi 1333, p. 102.

16. al-`Azzawi 1956, vol. 4, p. 184 quoting Sayyid Ni`matallah al-Jaza'iri's *Zuhar al-Rabi`* written in 1107/1696-97.

17. Nasiri 1373, p. 241.

18. Gollancz 1927, pp. 525-26. On the Persian occupation of Basra see Floor 2006, pp. 578-84.

19. Nami Isfahan 1363, p. 126.

20. Hamilton 1930, vol. 1, p. 57.

The Arabs concerned, given that they resided at Qobban, must have been the Ka'b; they did not tolerate such treatment and fought back of which Hamilton gives a lively account.

Sheikh Fathollah Ka'bi mentions in his *Tarikh-e Ka'b* that the tribe went through a difficult and very violent period between 1694 and 1722. This is also indicated by the fact that the tribe had four chiefs during that time, who all were killed, some by their own tribesmen. In 1694 'Ali b. Nasir b. Mohammad was tribal chief; he was killed by the Ka'b. 'Abdollah b. Nasir replaced him, but he was also killed and was succeeded by Sarhan, who again was killed. This must have happened in 1722, because Sarhan was replaced by Mir Rahmah, who was killed in 1722 after a few days after the succession.[21] The fact that the Ka'b were exposed to this type of oppression and violence may have induced tribal leadership to seek a safer haven inland. The fact that the *Vali* of Hoveyzeh regarded them as his vassals may have facilitated their decision to migrate to Khuzestan. Under their new chief Sheikh Farajollah (r. 1722-34), the Ka'b went raiding in the Dowraq area during the Mohammad Baluch Khan revolt of 1734. It is through this drive northward that the Ka'b came to the notice of Nader Shah Afshar during his pacification of Khuzestan in 1734, as part of the suppression of that revolt. According to Kasravi, Nader Shah sent Mohammad Hoseyn Khan Qajar to Qobban, which he besieged and forced the Ka'b to subject themselves to the new ruler of Iran. But, this is not borne out by contemporary sources that only mention that Arab forces allied with and/or vassals of the *Vali* of Hoveyzeh submitted themselves to Nader Shah's punitive force.[22]

However, on 14 January 1734 the Dutch factory at Basra recorded in its journal that, "Molla Mhamed prince of Havize [sic; Hoveyzeh] received information that Tamas Chan [sic; Tahmasp Khan, i.e. the later Nader Shah] had arrived there [i.e., Hoveyzeh], and marches on Shushtar and then on the Gaab [sic; Cha'b or Ka'b Arabs], to enforce their obedience on the inhabitants of the island of Gaban [sic; Qobban] as well as on other Arabs." On 20 January 1734 the same source reported that, "according to information from merchants from Suster [sic; Shushtar], Tamas Chan has pardoned the rebels with the exception of the Tjaabs [Cha'b Arabs] against whom he has sent a certain Chan Kasom Chan [sic; Khan Qasem Khan] with 5,000 men to destroy their Sheikh Farajollah (sjeeg Ferae houla)." Nadir Shah also sent a letter to the *mutasallim* of Basra, which was received on 26 January, warning him not to give protection to any of the Arabs whom he was pursuing. Also to send him five galleys well-equipped with crews and military supplies. In reply the *mutasallim* sent on 26 January 1734 a certain Galiff Evendi [sic; Khalifa Efendi] with five galleys towards Haffar where Nader's troops were said to be. On 31 January the *mutasallim* sent the grains and butter that Nader Shah had demanded. On 5 February 1734 a vessel from Bushehr brought news of the total defeat of Mohammad Khan Baluch and his supporters. Two days later the Persian general at Qobban sent a letter to the *mutasallim* asking him for food and fodder. On 10 February 1734 five galleys left Basra for Qobban with food supplies and fodder. On 13 and 14 February news was received in Basra that the Persian troops had chased the Tjaabs

---

21. Kasravi 1333, p. 103; Zarrabi 1342, p. 282.

22. Kasravi 1333, p. 103; see e.g., Marvi 1369, vol. 1, p. 344. This and other contemporary sources make no mention either of Mohammad Khan Qajar in connection with this campaign. On the revolt of Mohammad Khan Baluch see Floor 1983, pp. 63-93.

(Cha'b) and other Arabs into a castle on Qobban, where they were besieged. The Arabs had released Persian prisoners of war.[23]

However, the Ka'b were living in an area where the concept of border had no meaning. They also did not feel themselves beholden either to the Afshar Shah or the Ottoman Sultan. Therefore, because they had economic bonds with Basra (trade, land, houses and other property) they were in regular contact with the authorities and notables of that city. When in 1734 the governor of Basra needed troops to fight the Muntafiq tribe, their old rival and enemy, he appealed to the Ka'b, whom Nader Shah believed were his subjects. During the fighting, the tribal chief Sheikh Farajollah was killed and he was succeeded by Sheikh Tahmaz Khanfar, but before the year was out he was challenged by Sheikh Salman and his brother Sheikh 'Othman. They killed Sheikh Tahmaz in 1737-38 and his son Bandar replaced him.[24] But after two months Salman killed him also; as a result he and his brother became supreme chiefs of the Ka'b. It was this fraternal duo that would guide the fortunes of the Ka'b for the next 30 years and they would make the Ka'b a force that everybody in the region had to reckon with.[25] It is not clear whether Salman and 'Othman belonged to the Al Bu Nasir family that until then had produced the supreme Sheikhs of the Ka'b. If not, we have here a case not of family infighting, but of agents of the periphery imposing themselves on the Ka'b's center, a situation similar to that of the nineteenth century.

It would seem that the Ka'b continued to pay pasturage rights to the Ottoman government once they were at Qobban as they had done at Wasit, "and the annual dress of investiture from Bussorah was continued to the Sheikh without any reference to this change of residence." This situation of the Ka'b paying taxes to and receiving the dress of investiture from Basra apparently continued until at least 1740. The only relationship with Afsharid Iran was that the Ka'b paid the Afshar chief of Dowraq annual presents of horses, butter, etc. as compensation for pasturage "on the immediate banks of the Gobun [sic; Qobban] branch of the Karun." Prior to the arrival of Ka'b Afshar clans had used the land, but these had retreated to their kinsmen on the banks of the Jarrahi.[26] In 1743 the Ka'b supported Nader Shah's general Khvajeh Khan in his campaign against Basra. Sheikh Salman joined Khvajeh Khan's army in Gordalan in the Shatt al-Arab opposite Basra. The three-month siege and its aftermath had a negative impact on the economy of Basra.[27]

---

23. NA, VOC 2323, Extract Bassouras dagverhaal, f. 2041-51.

24. Administration Report 1889-90, p. 13 and Curzon 1892, vol. 2, p. 328 suggest that Tahmaz was a brother of Salman and 'Othman, but Kasravi, who had access to the *Tarikh-e Ka'b* does not and therefore it is unlikely that they were.

25. Administration Report 1889-90, p. 13. Sheikh Salman is also often referred to as Sheikh Soleyman (Soliman), but Kasravi, based on Ka'b tribal history, attests that his name in fact was Salman, as does Ghaffari, which name I therefore prefer. Kasravi 1333, pp. 104, 169-71. The name of Sheikh 'Othman seems to indicate that the tribe had not as yet completed the Shi'itization process as it seems unlikely that a Shi'ite would bear the name of one of the accursed caliphs who, according to his partisans, had denied 'Ali his rightful inheritance.

26. Rawlinson 1989, vol. 1, p. 282.

27. Perry 1979, p. 161; Abdullah 2001, p. 49; al-Shushstari 1924, p. 96.

The Ka'b Move from Qobban to Dowraq

Between 1740 and 1750 major changes took place. Until 1747, the year of Nader Shah's death, the Ka'b remained in Qobban, but already, they had started to move northward. The Karun had until around 1745 a second outlet to the Persian Gulf called the Qobban, which was parallel to and about 10 miles east of its present outlet the Bahmanshir. When around 1745 the course of the Qobban canal became obstructed the Karun poured into the Bahmanshir and the Haffar channels, "and the lands along the old or eastern bed of the river were thrown almost entirely out of cultivation." The Ka'b had to look for new habitations. Already, they had cast covetous eyes at Dowraq a decade earlier and that is where they went this time. The main body of the Ka'b under Sheikh Salman crossed the Qobban canal to the Jarrahi River and expelled the Afshars from Dowraq and its dependencies and settled there. Some Ka'b also settled along the Haffar and Shatt al-Arab and became sharecroppers of the Ottoman land owners.[28]

The thrust northward was not as sudden as Rawlinson and others have implied. Niebuhr reported that Sheikh Salman had first begun subduing smaller neighbors, then he subdued some small districts in Khuzestan and promised tribute to the warring khans who were contending Nader Shah's throne.[29] The more paced migration is also suggested by the fact that the Ka'b had first settled at the Sabla, some 2.5 miles above the present mouth. At that time there were allegedly only 40 families.[30] Sabla was on the right bank of the Karun opposite the island of Deyr and the Marid creek.[31] On learning the news of Nader Shah's death, the Ka'b moved with all their goods into the direction of Dowraq. Because the news of his death had not yet been confirmed and as they were still afraid of him they stayed at a place called Shakha al-Khan. When the news of his death was confirmed, they moved ahead to Dowraq and ousted the Afshars and turned it into the flourishing town of Falahiyeh.[32]

Even the ouster of the Afshars was not achieved in one sudden move, but was brought about in easy non-threatening stages until the final mortal blow. The land they newly occupied was held by the Afshars whose center was at Dowraq and who still held these lands in 1750.[33] The Afshars allowed the Ka'b to settle in the lower part of the country paying a tribute of butter and other animal products. The Ka'b also paid the Ottoman government an annual sum for the occupation of lands near the Euphrates and the Ka'b supreme Sheikh probably received his investiture from the governor of Basra. Qobban then at one arm of the

---

28. Rawlinson 1989, vol. 1, pp. 282-83, 313. According to Kunke 1991, pp. 74, 85, 147 the Ka'b were already settled at Dowraq at the beginning of the seventeenth century. However, this is based on the mistaken assumption that the manuscript translated by Kunke really dates from 1716, which is highly improbable. A more likely date for the writing of the manuscript is around 1800.

29. Niebuhr 1772, p. 319.

30. Chirikov 1989, vol. 2, p. 471.

31. Lorimer 1915, p. 961.

32. Kasravi 1333, pp. 104-05. According to Fasa'i, in 1170/1756-57, after a conflict with governor of Baghdad, Sheikh Salman moved away with 2,000 families, and settled down near Dowraq. Later he calls the Ka'b Iraqi Arabs who came in 1187/1773-74 under Sheikh Salman to Dowraq. Fasa'i 1378, vol. 2, pp. 1413, 1616. See also Hedayat 1339, vol. 9, p. 79, which may have been Fasa'i's source.

33. al-Shushstari 1925, p. 99.

Karun was their principal place and of some importance. They soon ascended the Jarrahi and pitched their tents near a small hill or artificial mound on which the modern town of Falahiyeh arose. The Afshars opposed this encroachment of their lands, but the Ka`b told them that the pasture was better there for buffaloes than at Qobban where they did not prosper. They were allowed to remain, but when they dug a moat around the mound the Afshars protested. The Ka`b said the ditch was to protect their buffaloes against rustlers who came every night. The Afshars accepted this, but not when the next year a stout mud-wall had been built within the ditch so that the Ka`b could defend themselves against an attacking enemy. The Afshars fearing that the Ka`b would no longer respect their authority, invited a chief of a neighboring tribe to expel them. Because this unnamed chief fell ill in spring the expedition was postponed to the fall. Meanwhile, the Afshars concluded a peace with the Ka`b, which the former intended to break as soon as they could receive outside assistance. The Ka`b then invited the Afshars to a feast; while they were eating the Ka`b attacked and killed 14 of them, all chiefs of the Dowraq Afshars. They then asked the *Vali* of Hoveyzeh, who was the major power in Khuzestan at that time, to help them drive out the "Persians". They told him: "We are Arabs, and consequently the Walis' [sic] brothers. It is better that we should be his subjects; we are willing to render him the same services and pay the same tribute as the Afshars." The *Vali* agreed and marched with the Ka`b against Dowraq, which was completely destroyed. The Afshars fled to Lehrowi [sic; Liravi?] where they built a castle. A few years later the governor of Fars tried to retake the land, but after a few encounters the Afshars were forced to leave the Dowraq area altogether.[34]

Within Khuzestan, the Ka`b first kept a low profile, because after the ouster of the Afshars they for a time paid the *Vali* of Hoveyzeh "the same amount of revenue which had been realized from the former occupants."[35] Towards Basra the Ka`b pursued a more aggressive policy with piracy at the mouth of the Shatt al-Arab as well as the seizure of Dawasir and islands west of the delta. Although in 1749, Soleyman Pasha put a stop to the Ka`b attacks,[36] Sheikh Salman had been able to reinforce his control over both banks of the Shatt al-Arab, thus covering an area as far north as Ahvaz, east to the Hendiyan and west at Bubiyan Island. Until then, the Ka`b chief resided at Qobban, "situated on the left bank of the eastern branch of the Karun" and the tribe's chief strength was there. This was made possible by (i) the Ka`b's attachment to their hereditary chief, and (ii) the growth in number, of which Sheikh Salman made use. Once established at the Jarrahi he again took interest in Qobban. He built a dam across the Karun at Sabla, "at the point of its bifurcation and thus forcing part of the water into the old channel restoring fertility to the deserted lands." At the same time he expanded his territory by acquiring lands east of the Hendiyan River and northward along the Karun near Band-e Kir. From Basra he took the Island of Abadan by threat and bribery, the territory of Dawasir on the right bank of the Shatt al-Arab, also a tract of land north of the Haffar Canal and along the course of the Shatt al-Arab comprising the districts of Mohammareh,

34. Layard 1846, pp. 41-42; Lorimer 1915, p. 961.

35. Rawlinson 1989, vol. 1, 285. The staged acquisition of Dowraq is also suggested by Kasravi 1333, pp. 104, 106, n. 1, for he writes that until 1160/1747 the Ka`b were still at Qobban and that only two years later they obtained and started developing Dowraq.

36. Longrigg 1925, pp. 168-69.

Haffar and Tamar.[37] The building of the big irrigation dam must have required much time and manpower not allowing more adventurous schemes. To the north of the Ka'b, the tribes did not much intervene for fear of a regional war between those of Hoveyzeh and the Al Kathir and the succession war in Afsharid Iran at large. After their move to Dowraq, the Ka'b paid no taxes to either the Ottoman or Zand government, claiming exactions by the one as an excuse for the other. Cultivation of dates, rice and wheat, pasture and trade yielded much revenue, however.[38] The principal Ka'b 'towns' were Dowraq, Haffar and Qobban.[39] The Ka'b enjoyed some 10 years of relative peace and Shushtari remarked on the safety in the Sheikh's domain and contrasted this with the fighting and insecurity in northern Khuzestan.[40]

As mentioned above, the Ka'b paid no taxes to outside authorities at that time. Probably, it was this 'oversight' that induced Karim Khan Zand to try and obtain tribute from Sheikh Salman. He had won the succession war that erupted after Nadir Shah's death and he aimed to make all previous Safavid territories subject and tributary again to his central government that was based in Shiraz. Therefore, in 1757, Karim Khan invaded the territory of the Ka'b. The latter vacated their fort at Falahiyeh and flooded their land. Karim Khan having been there for three months, and not having been able to cross the canals, then had to cope with an outbreak of plague in his army. He beat a hasty retreat leaving his artillery behind that the Ka'b acquired.[41] The accounts differ about the financial result of this campaign. According to Fathollah Ka'bi, the Ka'b paid nothing, while Niebuhr reported that Karim Khan was satisfied with the payment of a small sum. Ghaffari reported that the Ka'b were punished, plundered and brought to heel. According to the East India Company (EIC), the Ka'b bought Karim Khan off with a payment of 15,000 *tumans* three times more than the original demand to make him stop the devastation of the land.[42]

Whatever amount he may have paid, Sheikh Salman was not cowed by this Zand invasion. He still wanted to play a major role in the upper Persian Gulf, both politically and commercially. Sheikh Salman therefore tried to get Basra on his side. He made friends with the "Ajals" [=rijal or notables], the chief people of those parts and occupied all the isles the Shatt al-Arab's delta. Sheikh Salman then started building a naval force; his first vessel was built in 1758 and by 1765 he had 10 large (*galvats*) and 70 small ones (*daniq*). The Ka'b vessels not only moved around their territory, but also got involved in Persian Gulf politics such as with Bushehr and Bahrain in February 1761.[43] In that month Sheikh Salman tried in vain to conquer Bahrain that was held by Sheikh Sa'dun of Bushehr. The latter was helped by the 'Utbis of Kuwait and they in their turn attacked Sheikh Salman; the result was a stalemate. The *mutasallim* of Basra wanted to mediate between the parties, because their conflict was an obstacle to trade, an important source of revenue to Basra. Sheikh Salman sent him a haughty

---

37. Rawlinson 1989, vol. 1, p. 283; Longrigg 1925, pp. 168-69; Nami 1363, p. 126.

38. Kasravi 1333, pp. 143-52; Niebuhr 1772, p. 320; Perry 1979, pp. 161-62.

39. Niebuhr 1772, p. 320.

40. Perry 1971, p. 135.

41. Layard 1846, p. 43; Niebuhr 1772, p. 319.

42. Niebuhr 1772, p. 319; Perry 1979, p. 163; Ghaffari Kashani, p. 255; Olivier 1802, vol. 6, pp. 106-07.

43. Niebuhr 1772, p. 319.

reply, which angered the *mutasallim* who then supported Sheikh Sa'dun. The *mutasallim* started to attack the Ka'b by land and he finally besieged Sheikh Salman in his fort by the end of July 1761. On 30 September 1761 the *mutasallim* of Basra and Sheikh Salman concluded an agreement, which led to the end of the siege, but not of the hostilities between the parties concerned.[44] In 1762, 'Ali Aqa, the *mutasallim* of Basra, wanted to collect the taxes due to him. He was assisted by Sayyed Mutallib, the *Vali* of Hoveyzeh and also, be it reluctantly, the EIC, which blocked the Jarrahi and Khur Musa. The *Vali* of Hoveyzeh wanted to put an end to Ka'b encroachment of his territory as well as enforce their submission to him, but he died in a battle against Karim Khan Zand and thus he could not participate in the operations against the Ka'b. Sheikh Salman withdrew to his stronghold of Falahiyeh, and bought off the blockade with a present to the Pasha of Baghdad. When the blockade was lifted a new opportunity arose in May 1762 with the death of Soleyman Pasha. Sheikh Salman counterattacked in August 1762 and blocked Basra with his vessels, which the obsolete and immobile Ottoman galleys could not match.[45]

After the death of Soleyman Pasha the situation at Basra was in total confusion until August when 'Ali Pasha, until then *mutasallim* of Basra, took over in Baghdad. Sheikh Salman with his Ka'b tribesmen continued to blockade the Shatt al-Arab; ostensibly to protect merchants coming to Basra, but in reality he wanted to be independent from Basra and draw trade to Qobban and Dowraq. He invited the Dutch on Khark Island to conclude an offensive and defensive treaty; he offered to buy all their goods and asked them to intercede with Sheikh Sa'dun of Bushehr to make peace with him. The Dutch sent senior assistant Tam to Qobban to inform Sheikh Salman that they were not able to do as he wished, although they would intercede with Sheikh Sa'dun to make peace with him. This indeed happened and trade resumed with Basra with Sheikh Salman coming to an understanding with 'Ali Pasha in 1763. In October 1763 a grateful Sheikh Salman sent the Dutch a *galvat* to strengthen their ties. The Dutch accepted the vessel, because they needed it against Mir Mohanna of Rig, who had been attacking their position.[46] In October 1763, the Ka'b drove out peasants from the Dawasir area. The EIC had an interest in some date groves there and therefore wanted to take punitive action. The *mutasallim* of Basra who had just made peace with the Ka'b did not want to begin hostile action and therefore wrote to Sheikh Salman asking him to take corrective measures. The EIC agent did not like this and started moving ships to block Ka'b navigation. 'Ali Pasha came down from Baghdad with an army to join the English operation, but the Ka'b withdrew into the marshes and the engagement remained inconclusive. Sheikh Salman then sought and obtained peace without further fighting.[47]

The Ka'b were still felt to be a major nuisance. In 1764 'Omar Pasha, the new governor of Baghdad, proposed that Karim Khan Zand carry out a joint pincer movement to

---

44. Floor 1994, pp. 180-81.

45. Kasravi 1333, pp. 107-08; Lorimer 1915, pp. 161-66, 1217-18; Longrigg 1925, p. 173; Golestaneh 2536, pp. 332-33 even mentions that the *Vali* of Hoveyzeh was the chief of the Ka'b. Maybe Golestaneh meant that they were his vassals, as they indeed had been in the past, who would do his bidding once again after he had subdued them, as had been the *Vali*'s intention. See for a different explanation Perry 1979, p. 107, n. 47.

46. Floor 1994, pp. 184-84.

47. Lorimer 1915, p. 1218; Longrigg 1925, p. 173.

attack the Ka`b, whom he considered to be his, albeit rebellious, subjects. The *mutasallim* of Basra would provide troops, supplies and vessels. Karim Khan accepted the proposal. At the end of 1764 Zand troops moved into Dashtestan and entered Ka`b territory in April, 1765. Because the Zand troops were too strong to oppose, the Ka`b fled and were difficult to find in the marshes. As the Zand army advanced the Ka`b hopped from island to island, each time staying one step ahead of it. They abandoned Falahiyeh and moved to Haffar. The Zand army waited for the Basra force to arrive; meanwhile the Ka`b were on Abadan island. When the Zand army arrived at Haffar it was found abandoned and so it built a fort there. Karim Khan wrote to the *mutasallim* of Basra to ask where the promised troops and vessels were. The *mutasallim* did not have his army ready made his excuses and only sent two vessels. Niebuhr states that the Ka`b had bribed him, while the EIC reported that he really wanted to supply the troops and vessels, but had problems in doing so. When the Zand army moved to Abadan island with some vessels supplied by the *Vali* of Hoveyzeh, the Ka`b took to the open sea, where the Zand troops could not follow as they had no fleet. After six weeks the Zand army returned in May 1765 just as the *mutasallim* of Basra was embarking his promised troops. The returning Zand army destroyed the Falahiyeh area and most importantly the major dam at Sabla, but not the date groves. Sheikh Salman then opened negotiations to avoid further destruction of his lands and made peace with Karim Khan Zand in July 1765. He paid a large sum as a present, sent his son as a hostage to Shiraz and promised to pay an annual tribute of 3,000 *tuman*s.[48]

The Ka`b were not yet scot-free, however, for the mutassalim of Basra led a campaign on the right side of the river with a view to expel the Ka`b from Dawasir. He sent troops against them with some naval assistance from the English, who wanted revenge. A naval battle took place at the mouth of the Haffar Canal; the Basra force was outmaneuvered by the Ka`b who defeated it. At the same time, the Ka`b continued their raiding operations and plundered the Basra date groves in August 1765 and took three ships from the qaputan bashi. The mutassalim "then purchased present and future impunity for a small sum." The whole affair lasted three weeks. The threat from the Omani fleet to attack the Ka`b on which the mutassalim had counted did not materialize.[49]

In the aftermath of Karim Khan's attack, Sheikh Salman's residence was moved from Qobban to the Jarrahi River. This was because Karim Khan, to weaken Sheikh Salman had destroyed the Sabla dam across the Karun, which divided its waters, and the Qobban channel became for a second time almost dry. Sheikh Salman after the withdrawal of the Zand troops found his capital in ruins and the lands around it without the means of irrigation; he could either rebuild the dam at great cost, which might once again be destroyed by invading enemies or relocate to a more favorable spot where water would be his protection rather than his ruin, and thus he moved to Falahiyeh or Dowraq-Falahiyeh as it was then called.[50]

48. Floor 1994, p. 185; Perry 1979, pp. 163-64, 169; Niebuhr 1772, p. 320; Ghaffari 1369, p. 257; Olivier 1802, vol. 6, pp. 109-10.

49. Longrigg 1925, p. 175; Perry 1979, p. 164. Like the EIC the Omanis had offered naval support, because they were interested to secure the shipping lanes to and from Basra as their main interest in Basra was trade. On Omani policy and activities at that time see Risso 1986.

50. Rawlinson 1989, vol. 1, pp. 284-85. Sabla was then abandoned and only a few people still lived there at the end of the nineteenth century. Lorimer 1915, p. 961.

Although Sheikh Salman had been forced to pay tribute, neither the Zand army nor the joint Basra-English force had been able to subdue the Ka'b. Sheikh Salman did not only retake his abandoned lands but "extended his conquests farther over the territory bordering on Basra (although in the dominions of the Sultan) and- he showed more courage in attacking- he made himself master of two English vessels."[51] In July 1765, the Ka'b took two EIC vessels in revenge for their assistance to Basra. Although Sheikh Salman returned the crews after an agreement of sorts had been reached, this did not result in peace. The EIC Council at Bombay and the EIC agent at Basra wanted revenge. Bombay sent four vessels in March 1766 with more than 400 soldiers. The governor of Basra promised help, but did not deliver. The EIC force then sailed into the creeks leading to Dowraq, but got stuck. It needed the support of the Basra mutassalim and threatened to leave by July 1, if none would be forthcoming. The Ka'b had secured their rear by having given rich presents to Karim Khan. An English attack in June did not resolve much nor did negotiations thereafter. In fact, they made things worse, for during a parley the English killed a number of Ka'b Sheikhs and wounded Sheikh Ghanim, Sheikh Salman's oldest son. At the end of June 1766 the Basra force finally arrived, but this did not change the situation much. In September the Ka'b attacked and burnt seven of the 12 vessels of the Basra force. On 23 September 1766 the EIC force attacked the fort of Dowraq and was defeated, with heavy losses in men and material; it withdrew in September. The Basra force remained at Dowraq doing nothing. Induced by rich presents sent by Sheikh Salman, Karim Khan wrote in September to the EIC at Basra and the Pasha at Baghdad demanding that they leave his territory, which they did. The result of the punitive campaign was: the loss of seven Basra vessels as well as of three EIC ships with their cargo; many men killed and wounded; and many guns as well as reputations lost.[52]

Despite Karim Khan's peremptory order to leave his lands he was not averse to cooperating with the EIC, including against the Ka'b, when it suited him. In early 1767 Karim Khan needed naval assistance against Mir Mohanna of Bandar-e Rig. He asked the EIC for naval support, offering the British to make the Ka'b pay compensation for their losses, but nothing came of this. The EIC was not very proactive in pursuing the matter, while the Ka'b gave Karim Khan presents to desist from this path. The EIC had neither forgotten nor forgiven their loss and imposed a blockade on the Ka'b in 1767-68, but this was abandoned as ineffective. In 1768 the *mutasallim* of Basra negotiated a peace agreement with the Ka'b.[53] Thereafter, in August 1768 Sheikh Salman died after a long illness.[54]

---

51. Anonymous 1939, vol. 1, p. 666; Longrigg 1925, p. 175.

52. Perry 1971, pp. 143-46; Longrigg 1925, p. 175. In 1765, EIC had stored coffee with the Dutch on Khark to avoid the Ka'b; Lorimer 1915, p. 411.

53. Perry 1971, p. 149; Abdullah 2001, p. 104.

54. Perry 1979, p. 165; Administration Report 1889-90, p. 13.

The Ka`b under the Sons of Sheikh `Othman

Perry has argued that after the death of Sheikh Salman in 1768 the Ka`b's energies were spent and eventually sputtered out.[55] However, Ka`b history presents a different record. Sheikh Salman's son Ghanim who had already been guiding operations prior to his father's death was mainly occupied with fighting Omani pirates. In 1768 he also assisted the *mutasallim* Basra against the Muntafiq tribe, after the EIC had promised free passage, which shortly thereafter ended its futile blockade against the Ka`b altogether. Sheikh Ghanim was then killed by his own men in 1769 for reasons unknown.[56] Sheikh Ghanim's brother Davud succeeded him, but he lasted only one year and suffered the same fate as his brother.[57] Sheikh Barakat, son of `Othman, was the next ruling Ka`b Sheikh; he continued his uncle's aggressive external policy. At the end of July 1773 when the plague was over in Basra, the Ka`b, who also had been struck by the plague, but less so, immediately attacked and plundered two quarters of the town and burnt the *qaputan basha*'s house with some of his boats. The *mutasallim* of Basra had to buy peace at a high price.[58]

Although peace had been bought, the situation remained tense and explosive. When in April 1774 the *mutasallim* of Basra executed a Ka`b tribesman, they attacked the city and plundered and burnt several bazaars. This prompted the EIC to help the government of Basra against Ka`b.[59] In 1774 the Ka`b promised support to both the Zands and Ottomans, and then captured an Ottoman vessel, which was rescued by the British. They then withdrew all their tribesmen from Basra, which was perceived as a threatening gesture. Indeed, midwinter Ka`b raids showed the weakness of the Basra government.[60] These raids were followed by the siege of the Zand army that lasted more than one year. On March 16, 1775 some 30,000 Zand troops were at Suwayb commanded by Sadeq Khan Zand. The Ka`b supported the Zand army with their vessels; the qaputan bashi had an equal number, but these were not equal to the Ka`b vessels.[61] Because of the cooperation with the Ka`b, the Zand army had the fleet they lacked to move around in the marshes and canals. Parsons, a member of the EIC staff at Basra, then suggested to put a boom in the channel to Basra to deny the Ka`b access and it worked.[62]

The Basra mutassalim hoped for relief from Masqat that had a commercial interest in Basra. When the Omani fleet arrived September 1775 at the Shatt al-Arab it found the

---

55. Perry 1979, p. 165.

56. Perry 1979, p. 150; Abdullah 2001, p. 51; Administration Report 1889-90, p. 13. On a detailed discussion of this entire campaign, see Floor 2007.

57. Administration Report 1889-90, p. 13 does not mention Davud's rule and lists Barakat as the next ruler, but one year later.

58. Perry 1979, p. 170; Lorimer 1915, p. 1221; Anonymous 1939, vol. 1, p. 673; Abdullah 2001, p. 53.

59. Parsons 1808, p. 162; Abdullah 2001, p. 36.

60. Longrigg 1925, p. 188.

61. Longrigg 1925, pp. 190-91.

62. Perry 1979, pp. 174, 177; Nami 1363, pp. 134-39; Hedayat 1339, vol. 9, p. 79; Parsons 1808, p. 166.

entrance blocked by a chain bridge. Karim Khan had the chain made in Shiraz and with it a pontoon bridge had been constructed with the help of the Ka'b and Sheikh Sa'dun of Bush-ehr. The Ka'b guarded one end of this chain bridge. When a heavy storm broke the chain bridge, the Omani fleet sailed to Basra.[63] The presence of the Omani fleet made no difference for Basra fell to the Zand invaders in April 1776. The available sources do not mention that the Ka'b played a major role during the siege and later during the occupation of Basra. Nevertheless, their assistance must have been appreciated, because Kasravi stated that Karim Khan rewarded the tribe with the town and district of Hendiyan with an annual tax of 1,000 *tumans*.[64]

After the departure of the Zand occupation force in March 1779, Sheikh Barakat of the Ka'b seized the large and fertile district of Bujidi from the Ottomans (between Tamar and Haffar) and gave it to the Bawi Arabs, into which tribe he had married. This tribe became part of the Ka'b confederacy. In 1780 there were again warnings against raids by the Ka'b fleet.[65] Sheikh Barakat was murdered in 1782-83. His legacy included that he added Ramhormuz to Ka'b territory, had fought with Bushehr and Oman for control of the upper Persian Gulf and had collected toll at the Shatt al-Arab.[66] His successor and brother, Sheikh Ghazban, took possession of the entire left bank of the Shatt al-Arab until Gordalan and he even colonized the right bank of the Shatt al-Arab from the sea to 10 miles of Basra. He did not take Basra itself, feeling that he would overextend himself.[67] Originally the land on the left bank was owned by one of the leading notables of Basra, the grandfather of Sheikh Darwish al-Kawazi Bash-A'yan al-Basra, according to Hajji Ahmad, one of his descendents:[68]

> Some Chaabis hired the land for the purpose of planting it, on the usual terms, the produce or proceeds of the sale to be shared equally by the lord and the cultivator of the soil, previous to the deduction of the Government tax [levied by the Governor of Bussorah], which was paid by the latter. For some years during the lifetime of the father and grandfather, the half was duly paid, but shortly after the death of the former, the Chaabis rebelling, for two years gave Sheikh Dervish nothing, who, having then obtained assistance from the Governor of Bussorah and the Montafik Arabs, attacked the Sheikh of Chaab, Ghuzban, defeated him, and took possession of Durak and Fellahieh. The matter was arranged by the Chaabis agreeing to give up half the produce of the soil, according to custom. Sheikh Dervish, who possessed much land around Bussorah returned to that place, continued to receive half the produce until the day of his death (about forty years since).

63. Perry 1979, pp. 180-81; Nami 1363, p. 196f.

64. De Bode 1845, vol. 2, pp. 115-16; Kasravi 1333, p. 187. The Ka'b must have played a role in the occupation of Basra, because in 1774 they gave the Carmelites in Basra (who were French) a passport of protection, because the French were the friends of Karim Khan Zand. Anonymous 1939, vol. 2, p. 1211.

65. Abdullah 2001, pp. 74, 85 (examples of booty taken).

66. Kasravi 1333, p. 114; Administration Report 1889-90, p. 13.

67. Rawlinson 1989, vol. 1, p. 287.

68. On Sheikh Darwish al-Kawazi see Abdullah 2001, p. 33.

The Chaabis, having now by degrees become powerful, took forcible possession
of the soil as far as Gerdelan (opposite to Bussorah), refusing to pay rent
to the heirs of Sheikh Dervish, or any tax to the Governors of Bussorah.
Mohammarah was not a place worthy of attention till the latter end of Sheikh
Dervish's lifetime.[69]

Sheikh Ghazban had to fight Soleyman Pasha of Baghdad and the Muntafiq. Then
Basra and people from various ports in the Persian Gulf and Aden banded together against
the Ka'b, who won. He took Ramhormuz and Hendiyan back, but these victories came at a
price for much blood flowed.[70]

In March 1783 the Ka'b were in open warfare with the *mutasallim* at Basra; they
crossed the river every night to pillage the bazaars and houses of Basra. The French botanist
Michaux was taken in a vessel from Qurna to Basra by a Ka'b boatman and therefore he was
able to get through. The English consul at Basra believed that he was a friend of "Sheikh Ali-
Khalfan" (sic; must be Ghazban) of the Ka'b and with his recommendation Michaux and his
party might leave Basra. Armed with this recommendation Michaux left and was met at the
entrance of the river by eight Ka'b *galvat*s and despite the promises, he and his party were
plundered. The Ka'b Sheikh was camped at the confluence of the Karun. There was a total of
15 Ka'b vessels to attack the Basra fleet. Michaux was set free and the tribesmen returned his
money and guns, the result of a letter from the English consul, but other stuff that he needed
was lost. Meanwhile the two fleets were fighting. According to Michaux, "the wild Arabs had
a belt, and band around the hair and the lance, that was all their accouterment."[71]

The Muntafiq had supported Basra against the Ka'b in 1783-84. The next year this
situation was reversed. In 1785, Soleyman Pasha of Baghdad had asked for Ka'b support
against the Muntafiq whose chief Thuwayni was the Ka'b's chief's bitter enemy. Sheikh Thuwayni was deposed by rivals working with the *mutasallim* of Basra and he fled to the Ka'b for
protection.[72] "The Montafik Sheikh Twiney and Sheikh Gathban of the Chab were enemies
to such a degree, and for so long a time that it became a proverb in Bussorah, when one would
express the violent hatred of another, to say: 'It was like the hatred of Twiney to Gathban.'
Twiney was ousted from his Sheikhdom and fled to his enemy and was received with honor
and given Gathban's signet ring as a sign of total safety in his domain. Because of this refuge
he was able to regain his chiefship" Thereafter the enmity between the two Sheikhs continued as before.[73] In 1791, bad relations between the government of Basra and the Ka'b led to
the construction of riverain forts, increased piracy, and indecisive naval battles.[74]

69. Schofield 1989, vol. 1, p. 129 (Statement of Hadji Ahmed).

70. Kasravi 1333, p. 114.

71. Hamy 1911, pp. 26-29.

72. Longrigg 1925, pp. 204-05.

73. Buckingham 1971, pp. 397-98.

74. Longrigg 1925, p. 206.

The Ka`b and Qajar Iran: Early Contacts

The Ka`b had much less trouble with the Zand government than they had with the Ottomans. After Karim Khan Zand's death in March 1779, once again a succession war broke out, mainly between Zand and Qajar contenders. The new unsettled situation meant that the Ka`b were left to their own devices until well into Fath `Ali Shah's reign (r. 1797-1834), with one exception. In the winter of 1786/87 Ja`far Khan Zand marched against the Ka`b, because Sheikh Ghazban had been disobedient. He attacked and plundered them and obtained a rich booty in herds.[75] The situation was not unlike the one after 1747 when the Ka`b were able to thrive, being left undisturbed by the warring parties vying for the succession to the throne until finally Karim Khan Zand had won. After the latter's death in 1779 another succession war started that was finally settled in 1794 with the death of the last Zand pretender to the throne. Thereafter it still took some years for the new Qajar dynasty to pacify various warlords as well as to settle inter-Qajar problems.

Sheikh Ghazban was killed in 1793; he was succeeded by Mobarak son of Barakat, who was ousted by the Ka`b in 1794-95, when Faris son of Davud replaced him. He was deposed one year later and was succeeded by Mohammad another son of Barakat. `Alwan b. Mohammad b. Shinawa b. Farajollah then became Sheikh of the Ka`b for a while, but was replaced by his predecessor Mohammad, son of Barakat in 1801-02. Kinneir wrote that the situation in Khuzestan was in turmoil and general insecurity reigned. The Ka`b did not pay any taxes to the Qajar government at that time. During the reign of Fath `Ali Shah southern Khuzestan (Ramhormuz, Falahiyeh, Hendiyan) became part of Fars province and northern Khuzestan became part of Kirmanshah province. Although in 1806 Mohammad `Ali Mirza Dowlatshah, the governor of Kermanshah, marched to Shushtar but, this time he did not proceed any farther.[76] The Wahhabis who had launched an attack on southern Iraq in 1806 had little success in the marsh lands; the Muntafiq and Ka`b expelled them and retook their villages.[77]

In 1812, Sheikh Mohammad died and Sheikh Gheyth son of Ghazban succeeded him. In that same year, the governor of Fars sent an army of 30,000 men led by Mirza Behbahan against the Ka`b. They clashed near Deh Mullah and the Ka`b defeated the Qajar army.[78] Sheikh Gheyth the son of Ghazban, building on his father's land acquisitions, restored the ancient limits of Ka`b territory as they had existed under Sheikh Salman, holding nothing higher up the Shatt al-Arab than Tamar district. He did not go farther to avoid a conflict with the Muntafiq who were growing in power and by worries about Qajar designs on his territory. Shortly thereafter he built a fort on either side of the Haffar Canal to protect his border

---

75. Nami 1363, p. 296f; Shirazi 1888, p. 36f; Fasa'i 1378, vol. 1, p. 637.

76. Kasravi 1333, pp. 113-17; de Bode 1845, vol. 2, p. 116; Administration Report 1889-90, p. 13, which does not list Mohammad b. Barakat as ruler. In 1801 it lists Barakat b. `Othman b. Soltan as ruyler until 1812.

77. Longrigg 1925, p. 230.

78. Kasravi 1333, p. 118; Administration Report 1889-90, p. 13 (he was "the first Chief who took the appellation of Sheikh, by which his successors have been known since.")

against the Muntafiq and entrusted this fort to his slave Mirdow. Under the rule of Mirdow's son, Hajj Yusof, the insignificant place attracted commerce because of its favorable location and became Mohammareh, as discussed in what follows.[79]

Shaikh Gheyth's concern about the Qajars had to do with the fact that he did not pay any tribute and he realized that the day would come when the government in Tehran would demand its due, whether he agreed or not. From the beginning of the Qajar government, payment of the Ka`b was counted as part of the annual revenue of Fars, although the Ka`b paid irregularly and the level is unknown. The Qajar government had fixed it at 4,000 *tuman*s, which was the original assessment of the Afshars on the Jarrahi. But it would seem that the Ka`b may have paid not more than 25% of this.[80] The Ka`b Sheikhs did not pay tribute but *pishkesh* to Shiraz in the form of a fixed number of Arab horses, cash, etc, and sometimes even resisted the Qajar authorities.[81] Fath `Ali Shah was the first to insist on a regular payment of a fixed amount; the salary of Hasan Khan, an official at the Shiraz court was drawn per barat on the chief of Falahiyeh, but whether it was regularly paid and at what level is uncertain. Independently of Hasan Khan's salary, gifts were sent to Shiraz and when Mohammad `Ali Mirza, not the governor of Fars, but of Kermanshah and northern Khuzestan, marched against Falahiyeh in 1816 he received 13,000 *tuman*s from Sheikh Gheyth "on account, it as alleged, of accumulated arrears of revenue."[82] Layard estimated that the Ka`b Sheikh only paid 3,400 *tuman*s (£1,700) to the governor of Shiraz, which he considered to be a small sum given his revenues. There always was some pretext to demand more and Mo`tamed al-Dowleh received 5,000 *tuman*s from the Sheikh, plus horses and presents in 1839. Originally the Ka`b only paid 1,000 *tuman*s yearly which was considered as a kind of *pishkesh* rather than as an annual tribute. They did not consider themselves Qajar subjects and there was no government agent at Falahiyeh.[83]

The Qajar government never made an effort to appoint a governor of the tribe, levy troops for the defense of the state or the legitimate functions of sovereignty before 1841. The Qajar government was satisfied just to receive the *pishkesh*, which Sheikh Thamir during the Erzerum talks of 1849, asserted was just in lieu of the rent of the lands they owned in Qajar Iran. Since the accession of Mohammad Shah (r. 1834-48) the government in Tehran became more pro-active.[84] When in 1835, Manuchehr Khan attacked Fort Goli-Golab near Hendiyan he summoned the nearby Ka`b to provide the Qajar troops with provisions. The Sheikh answered that there was no precedent for this and thus, he could not do so, but after the fall of the fort he changed his mind and send the supplies plus several thousand *tuman*s.[85]

Until Mo`tamed al-Dowleh gave them a devastating blow in 1841 the Ka`b lived in relative peace and independence from outside forces. This did not mean that they had no

79. Rawlinson 1989, vol. 1, pp. 287-88.

80. Rawlinson 1989, vol. 1, p. 289.

81. De Bode 1845, vol. 2, p. 116; Schofield 1989, vol. 1, pp. 128-29.

82. Layard 1846, p. 43; Kasravi 1333, p. 118.

83. Layard 1846, p. 44.

84. Rawlinson 1989, vol. 1, pp. 289-90.

85. De Bode 1845, vol. 2, pp. 116-17.

problems, but these were internal and of their own making. Sheikh Gheyth was expelled in 1816 by the Ka'b and 'Abdollah son of Mohammad replaced him. But he lasted only seven months when Gheyth took over again. The Ka'b killed Sheikh Gheyth in 1828-29; his brother Mobader took over and killed all the murderers of his brother. In 1829-30 Fath 'Ali Shah came to Khuzestan. He went to Behbahan and Sheikh Mobader met him with *pishkesh* between Behbahan and Ramhormuz and the shah, having been satified, then went to the north.[86]

Ottoman Attack on Mohammareh and Falahi in 1837

The relationship between the Ka'b and the government in Basra continued to be an ambivalent one, based more on perceived advantage than on the relationship between an obedient subject and its government. Around 1828 Hamud al-Thamir, the old chief of the Muntafiq, who was being threatened by Baghdad, asked the Ka'b and other Arab tribes to help him attack Basra.[87] It is not clear whether the Ka'b went along with the call to arms. It seems unlikely since the request came from the Muntafiq, but it is possible, because despite their enmity they had collaborated before. Only a few years later, in 1831 the *mutasallim* of Basra was driven out of the city by a coalition of Arab forces led by the Zubayr. He fled to Mohammareh to ask Sheikh Mobader for help, which was given. The Ka'b launched an attack against Basra. Sheikh Mobader was kept abreast regularly about the progress and he was able to restore the *mutasallim* to his city.[88] Sheikh Mobader was ousted shortly thereafter in 1831-32 and 'Abdollah son of Mohammad replaced him. In that same year the plague broke out, which killed many. Sheikh 'Abdollah did not last long and was replaced by Modaber's youngest brother, Sheikh Thamir son of Ghazban in 1832 or 1833.[89]

Despite the assistance given to the *mutasallim* of Basra and the payment of taxes, the government of Baghdad was displeased with the Ka'b and in particular about the developments around Mohammareh. The first Ottoman show of muscle occurred in 1837 by 'Ali Pasha of Baghdad and his subsequent appointment of Sheikh 'Abd al-Razzaq as chief of the Ka'b instead of Sheikh Thamir.[90] This development was something of a surprise. From

---

86. Kasravi 1333, p. 119; Sepehr 1377, vol. 1, p. 439 (according to this text, these events took place in 1244/1828-29). According to Administration Report 1889-90, p. 13, Sheikh Gheyth "united the tribe which at that time was divided in fractions."

87. Longrigg 1925, p. 248.

88. Fattah 1997. p. 97; Longrigg 1925, p. 271, n. 3; Stocqueler 1832, vol. 1, pp. 67-68, 76 ("many subordinate sheikhs reporting on measures taken to reinforce the troops at Mohammareh or to await instructions.")

89. Kasravi 1333, pp. 120-22; Administration Report 1889-90, p. 13 has 'Abdollah b. Mohammad rule during 1831-1837. According to Fasa'i 1378, vol. 2, p. 1413, Sheikh Thamir was the grandson of Sheikh Salman, while Loftus 1857, p. 282 called him Sheikh Salman's great-grandson. However, according to Sheik Thamir's own statement "Sheikh Soliman was the brother of my grandfather, who took that part of the tribe to Fellahiyeh that is now there." Schofield 1989, vol. 2, p. 175; see also the genealogical tree of the Ka'b's ruling family.

90. Rawlinson 1989, vol. 2, p. 288.

1833, Sheikh Thamir, the younger brother of Sheikh Gheyth and Sheikh Mobader, the new paramount chief of the Ka`b, maintained more friendly relations with the Ottoman government than his predecessors with a view of possible conflict with the Qajar government. He sent an annual gift of horses and cash to the *mutasallim* of Basra independent of the rent of the lands on the Shatt al-Arab and in return he received a robe of honor.[91] The Ka`b paid a fixed sum for the tribe irrespective of the districts where they lived. According to Sheikh Thamir, they paid "300 kiauras of dates. The kiaura is 20 botmauns of Bussorah, which is 6 botmauns of Bagdad, of 6 Bagdad okas each; 1 oke of Bagdad being 1½ okes of Constantinople. This makes 324,000 okes, Constantinople weight, of dates per annum paid to Turkey."[92] From another statement made by Sheikh Thamir in 1843 the schizoid fiscal relationship that the Ka`b had with Ottomans and Qajars becomes evident. He paid the miri to Basra until last year, but not regularly since 1836-37. It was "for the land that belongs to Turkey." For the part that belonged to the Qajars he had paid 1,200 *tuman*s until 33 years ago, when the sum was increased to 3,000 *tuman*s. "Last year's tribute is in the hands of a banker, but we do not know who to pay it to, as Persia and Turkey both claim the land."[93]

The root of the problem was Mohammareh. This fledgling port had been promoted by the Ka`b Sheikhs to be a free place of commerce with lower duties than at Basra, and many merchants from Basra and elsewhere thus preferred to take their goods and trade there, which was a great revenue loss for Basra.[94] Mohammareh consisted of two parts; one part was built on the northern bank of the Haffar Canal, which was invariably called Mohammareh and the other part, built on the southern bank of the Haffar, which was usually called Kut al-Sheikh. Merchants preferred northern Mohammareh to Kut al-Sheikh, because the former was on the mainland and the latter on an island, and thus it was easier to transport goods to Iran and Iraq from Mohammareh.[95] The difference in duties was not the only reason for the growth of Mohammareh, which actually may not have competed that much with Basra. Another and more important reason was the drying up of Hoveyzeh's main channel connecting it with the Shatt al-Arab through which it had maintained strong commercial ties with Basra since at least 1500. In consequence, Hoveyzeh faded away and by 1852 was almost depopulated. Its commercial role was totally taken over by Basra and Mohammareh and the decline of Hoveyzeh was thus the major reason for Mohammareh's rise as a port. Most of its trade and

---

91. Rawlinson 1989, vol. 1, p. 288. That the orientation of much of the Ka`b was more towards S. Iraq than to Iran is also clear from the fact that, according to Stocqueler 1832, vol. 1, p. 82, "the inhabitants refused Persian coin and only wanted Turkish piasters."

92. Schofield 1989, vol. 1, p. 118 (on this page is also a list of the places where the Ka`b lived).

93. Schofield 1989, vol. 1, p. 108. It was not unusual for tribal leaders to pay their annual taxes via a banker (*sarraf*) with whom they had other regular business relations, see Floor 1979 a.

94. Schofield 1989, vol. 1, p. 128; de Bode 1845, vol. 2, p. 117. "Since 1833 the authorities charge half-duty and sometimes less on goods transshipped in this port, "so I think a similar duty will be charged on the reshipment of goods landed here for into some other vessel, and this practice has more strongly been carried on since six years back." Schofield 1989, vol. 1, p. 129 (statement by J.A. Malcolm, Armenian merchant at Bushehr to Lt. A.B. Kemball, British acting resident at Bushehr 12/8/1842).

95. Rawlinson 1989, vol. 1, p. 374.

even more so of other Ka'b ports (Ma'shur, Hendiyan) was limited to southern Khuzestan and parts of Fars.[96]

Mohammareh had grown from a small village into a small town between 1830 and 1837 and had become a trade emporium. Basra allegedly suffered a loss of revenues, due to increased trade at Mohammareh. 'Ali Pasha wanted to protect Basra's interests.[97] According to Kazeruni,

> The place became so flourishing that the rent of a single room in a caravanserai amounted to 10 kurush (ain) per mensem, a sum equivalent to fifteen Shiraz rupees, and the merchants were only too glad to secure accommodation at that exorbitant rate. Wealthy and respectable merchants in fact have certified that the condition of Mohammerah was at one time so flourishing as to rival Calcutta and Bombay, not considered in regard to its actual extent, but as being more populous and celebrated than either of the above-mentioned cities in reference to the space which they relatively occupied. Agha Abdul Mahommed, a merchant who visited Mohammarah before the expedition of the Pasha of Baghdad on certain commercial affairs of his own, has taken oath also that during his residence of one month in the place, lakhs of gold and silver money were in daily circulation.[98]

However, the port's economic importance should not be exaggerated. In its most flourishing state, according to Rawlinson, Mohammareh had at most 500 houses and more than 400 of these were reed huts plastered with mud; there were four caravanserais and three temporary sheds, which were used as coffeehouses. Sheikh Jaber once brought a boatload of burnt bricks from Basra to build his own house and one caravanserai and they were the only brick constructions in the town ever, other buildings were all of mud and/or reed. "As for the lakhs of gold and silver money in daily circulation, no one that I have ever conversed with believe it possible that there could have been at any one time a lakh of rupees collected in Mohammareh. The staples of export and import were respectively dates and rice, and at all times three-fourths of the inhabitants were Arabs."[99]

The official cause of 'Ali Pasha's attack was that Mohammareh was drawing population and riches from Basra and became powerful. The Porte itself allegedly ordered 'Ali Pasha to

---

96. Fattah 1997, pp. 63, 72-73; Amanat 1983, p. 90; Pelly 1865 a, pp. 39-40; Curzon 1892, vol. 2, p. 328.

97. Rawlinson 1989, vol. 1, pp. 297-98; Bode 1845, vol. 2, p. 117. 'Ali Pasha is sometimes also referred to as 'Ali Reza Pasha.

98. Kazeruni 1367, p. 29. The two chapters on Mohammareh in this book, which the Qajar government offered as evidence for its claims to the territory and for indemnification to the Erzerum negotiations in 1844, were translated into English with critical marginal notes by Rawlinson 1989, vol. 1, pp. 373-77. (Schofield noted that "Both Sir S. Canning and Major Rawlinson treated this memorandum as having been written by Count Medem, the Russian Minister at Tehran. Colonel Sheil, however, took pains to correct the misapprehension and pointed out that the memorandum had been compiled by a Persian merchant.") Rawlinson considered the geographical part of the memorandum entirely incorrect.

99. Schofield 1989, vol. 1, pp. 374-75 (marginal note), 388 (one lac of rupees = £10-12,000).

bring it to obedience.[100] In 1837, `Ali Pasha took advantage of the fact that Mohammad Shah and the bulk of the Qajar army were engaged in the siege of Herat at the other end of the country. When news reached the Qajar court that `Ali Pasha of Baghdad was moving against Mohammareh Mo`tamed al-Dowleh governor of Kermanshah, Lurestan and Khuzestan allegedly instructed Taqi Khan Bakhtiyari to offer Sheikh Thamir assistance of 2,000 cavalry, provided the Sheikh gave the troops supplies en route and during the campaign. Sheikh Thamir is said to have replied that he did not think `Ali Pasha was going to attack him. This was due to the fact that a kinsman of his, whom the pasha had promised the chieftainship, had lulled him into a sense of false security. This relative, Sheikh `Ali Reza, had told Sheikh Thamir that the army was to march against Basra.[101]

`Ali Pasha marched his 6,000 troops from Baghdad; the supplies came by boat. At Qurna he crossed the river using a boat bridge and used Kut Gordolan as his staging area. Here he was joined by Muntafiq, Khaza'il and other Arab tribes and thus, had a force of about 20,000 men. From Gordolan it was 12 km to Mohammareh and he marched to the Darband canal situated at about two km from the town. It is not known how many defenders there were in the town. According to one source, the whole population was at most 3,000, including the Arab garrison. One thing is certain, the entire Ka`b tribal force had not been mobilized to resist the Ottoman attack. In fact, it has been reported that Sheikh Thamir withheld support from Sheikh Jaber out of jealousy. There were nevertheless many defenders, for many had to take a stand outside the town in a palm grove. `Ali Pasha ordered his artillery to start shelling the town, while the defenders shot back from the walls with guns and small arms. The Ottoman artillery was very ineffective, but incompetence of the defenders gave the Ottomans the opening they needed. One of the few cannons of which Mohammareh boasted was overloaded by its gunners which then burst and caused panic among the town's defenders, who deserted their posts. The Ottoman army was encouraged by this and `Ali Pasha immediately gave orders to attack. Once they had made a breach in the wall the Ottoman forces streamed into the town, for there were no defenders at the walls anymore. Those who could fled in vessels via the Haffar, those who could not jumped into the river and many drowned. Of those who remained many of the men were slaughtered, while women, girls and boys were raped and sold as slaves. The same thing happened to the many black slaves that were in the town. The town, including all merchandise that was found, and the surrounding villages were plundered and burnt down. The large vessels belonging to Sheikh Jaber were also taken. `Ali Pasha leveled the walls, carried off the guns and left the place defenseless.[102]

Kazeruni offers a different version of how the loss of life came about, which, in light of Chirikov's account and the sources adduced by Kasravi, does not seem to be borne out by the facts.

---

100. Schofield 1989, vol. 1, p. 129; Kasravi 1333, p. 126; Watson 1976, p. 337.

101. Bode 1845, vol. 2, pp. 118-19.

102. Rawlinson 1989, vol. 1, pp. 298, 375; Chirikov 1989, vol. 2, pp. 464, 466-68; Kasravi 1333, pp. 127-28; Kaziruni 1367, pp. 31-32; Schofield 1989, vol. 1, pp. 375-76.

Amongst the Arabs of those parts are two particular tribes, named respectively De-rissis [Idris] and Ansar, who have risen to great power, and to whom is owing the ruin of Mohammareh, Jabir having been deputed by Sheikh Thamir Khan to govern Mohammerah, appropriated to himself the entire revenues which arose from the gardens without admitting the Keab Arabs to any participation. On the arrival accordingly of the Pasha of Bagdad, and enmity having at the same time broken out between the two tribes, a project was formed for the assasissination of Jabir, who, however, obtaining information of the plot three days after the Pasha's arrival and before any slaughter had commenced, fled away in a boat [baghaleh] with his family and servants. On this intelligence getting abroad, the whole population was seized with a sort of panic and cast themselves into the waters of the Shatt; women and chil-dren unable to swim peished in the waves, about 4,000 souls were carried into slavery by the Arnaouts [selseleh-ye Arnahut] and Turkish [Rumi] soldiers, others saved themselves by flight. The Mahommedans of Bussorah purchased many of these children for 18 to 20 kurnah [qorush] a head, and restored them to their parents.[103]

The next step was that 'Ali Pasha moved against Falahiyeh, and Sheikh Thamir was forced to flee to Ramhormuz and Hendiyan and left control of the Ka'b to 'Ali Pasha. This precipitous flight thus lends credence to his being caught unawares, as reported by de Bode. 'Ali Pasha appointed Sheikh 'Ali Reza, a relative of Sheikh Thamir as his successor. Sheikh Jaber of Mohammareh had fled to Bushehr in vain to solicit help from the governor Shiraz. He then is said to have gone to Kuwait, to have begged forgiveness from 'Ali Pasha, and to have given him horses. As a result he was pardoned and received a robe of honor. Another source states that Sheikh Jaber just returned to his ruined town after the Ottoman with-drawal and relied on his own resources for protection.[104]

According to de Bode, who also reported the refused offer of military support from the Bakhtiyaris, said Sheikh Thamir was taken unawares. For if he had been aware he could have flooded the area, making it impassible for the pasha.[105] This is a reasonable argument that may well be true in light of Sheikh Thamir's total lack of preparation and even of a sem-blance of organized resistance against the attack. However, Sheikh Thamir told a different story to the Border Commission in 1843. True, he then wanted to support the Ottoman argument that Mohammareh and the Ka'b were respectively Ottoman territory and sub-jects, and that makes his statement suspect. However, he stated then that 'Ali Pasha had first threatened to come and get his due and further that he had given the Ka'b three months' notice. When 'Ali Pasha took Mohammareh the merchants had already fled and only his own people had suffered. After the conquest 'Ali Pasha had invited the merchants back be-cause he had nothing against them and so they did.[106] Sheikh Thamir's statement does not

---

103. Kazeruni 1367, p. 31; Schofield 1989, vol. 1, pp. 375-76.

104. Kasravi 1333, p. 128; Rawlinson 1989, vol. 1, p. 298. It is also reported that Sheikh Thamir fled to Mohammad Taqi Bakhtiyari, which would explain why the latter fled to Sheikh Thamir in 1841, when he was in serious trouble. Layard 1846.

105. De Bode 1845, vol. 2, p. 118-19.

106. Schofield 1989, vol. 1, p. 108.

seem to be borne out by the facts. The loss of the Shushtar merchants alone was estimated to be more 60,000 *tuman*s or £30,000, according to de Bode, while Chirikov reported it to be 1.5 million rubles.[107]

After two months, 'Ali Pasha returned to Baghdad. When the Ottoman troops left, Sheikh Thamir returned with some Arab forces and his relative Sheikh 'Abdol-Reza fled to Mohammareh and thence with his brother to Basra. Sheikh Thamir allegedly signed an agreement with 'Ali Pasha of allegiance of the Ka'b to Basra in exchange for his confirmation to the chiefship. Sheikh Jaber, who had returned, refused to go along with this and maintained his independence from Sheikh Thamir and threatened to call for Qajar help if interfered with.[108] In 1842, Lieutenant Selby observed that Mohammareh "has suffered severely, and trade for a time has declined in consequence."[109]

The Beginning of the End

Like the Ottoman attack of Mohammareh, the Qajar attack on the Ka'b stronghold of Falahiyeh in 1840 came as a surprise. The Ka'b leadership had tried not to antagonize the Qajar authorities. In that same year Captain Hennell landed at south Mohammareh. Sheikh Fares, who was its chief, admitted that he was subject to the Qajar state and that tribute was paid to the prince-governor of Shiraz.[110] Until then Qajar forces had never attacked Falahiyeh, although sometimes the governor of Shiraz sent troops against Ka'b territory to collect tribute.[111] Apart from financial reasons (tax collection) political reasons were probably the overriding motive for the campaign by Mo'tamed al-Dowleh to terminate the quasi-independence of both the Bakhtiyaris and the Ka'b. This consideration became even more sensitive in the case of the latter because of the Ottoman claims on Mohammareh and the Ka'b themselves as well as the British occupation of Khark Island. It was clear that the government in Tehran wanted to assert its property rights of both Mohammareh and the Ka'b so at to be able to oppose any Ottoman claim or British encroachment on its territory.

In March 1840 Mo'tamed al-Dowleh ostensibly marched from Isfahan to take up his new function as governor of Khuzestan. He obtained free and unhindered passage through Bakhtiyari territory after giving assurances that he had no intentions whatsoever to undertake action against this freebooting tribe. After he safely arrived with his army in Khuzestan and had secured the road through Bakhtiyari country, he turned on the tribe and defeated the forces sent against him. The tribal leadership led by its paramount chief Mohammad Taqi

---

107.   Bode 1845, vol. 2, p. 119; Chirikov 1989, vol. 2, p. 468. According to the Ottoman government, trade never reached the level of £120,000 per year at Mohammareh. Schofield 1989, vol. 1, pp. 251, 396 (which the Russians considered too low an estimate), 419.

108.   Rawlinson 1989, vol. 1, p. 298 (who has 'Abd al-Razzaq instead of 'Abd al-Riza); Kasravi 1333, p. 128.

109.   Selby 1844, pp. 224-25.

110.   Schofield 1989, vol. 1, p. 127.

111.   Schofield 1989, vol. 1, p. 128

rather than surrendering fled to Falahiyeh.[112] The main reason that Mohammad Taqi fled to Sheikh Thamir was he believed that the lands of the Ka'b were on Ottoman soil and therefore Mo'tamed al-Dowleh would not dare to invade them. Furthermore, even if he would do so, Mohammad Taqi believed that the 15,000 men strength of the Ka'b was too formidable for Mo'tamed al-Dowleh to attack.[113] The fact that Sheikh Thamir had sought refuge with him in 1837 also may have played a role.

Mo'tamed al-Dowleh was joined by the *Vali* of Hoveyzeh and the Bawi Arabs, whose chief had been promised the chieftainship of the Ka'b if Sheikh Thamir would be captured. Also, Sheikh 'Abdol-Reza one of the leading notables of the Ka'b and a relative of Sheikh Thamir, who was living in Baghdad and wanted to be chief, joined the Qajar army. Sheikh Thamir wished to avoid an invasion of his country by the Qajars. If the latter would attack he would resist, for he would not hand over Mohammad Taqi. "The country between Areiba and Fellahiyah had been placed under water by destroying the dykes and embankments of the river and of the canals, so that it was impassible by horsemen." Crops were also set on fire and there was a general flight of the population.[114]

> On the approach of an enemy, the numerous villages on the banks of Jerrahi are deserted; and the inhabitants, at an hour's notice, transforming their reed huts into rafts, float with their property into Fellahiyah. The villages in the neighbourhood of the town, immediately follow their example; and a crowd of men, women and children collect within its walls, or in the surrounding date-groves – their presence being highly inconvenient in cases of siege, particularly among Arabs, who lay up few provisions for the future. During my residence in Fellahiyah, when a siege was daily expected, the flocks collected were so numerous, and pasture so scanty, that eight to ten lambs, without the skins, were sold for one koron [sic; *qran*], or a shilling. The Sheikh has generally a considerable supply of dates, and some of this fruit, with a little flour, was daily distributed among those assembled for his defence.[115]

As intended, the flooded lands denied Qajar troops, in particular their artillery access to Falahiyeh. Mo'tamed al-Dowleh finally sent Shafi'eh Khan to Mohammad Taqi with a letter in which he threatened to kill the hostages he held (son, brother and nephew) if he did not surrender. If he would do this, all would be forgiven and forgotten. Mo'tamed al-Dowleh promised two hostages as a sign of his sincerity (his nephew and a mojtahed). After two days of negotiations, Mohammad Taqi yielded and went to Mo'tamed al-Dowleh, who also promised that his army would leave Ka'b territory. After having put Mohammad Taqi in irons, Mo'tamed al-Dowleh sent a letter to Sheikh Thamir demanding immediate payment of 12,000 *tumans* (about £6,000) as condition for the departure of his troops, which

112. Layard 1971, pp. 192-96.

113. Sepehr 1377, vol. 2, p. 770.

114. Layard 1971, pp. 240-42 (with a very vivid description of how entire village moved leading to general flight in the marshes), 255; Ibid. 1846, p. 36; Sepehr 1377, vol. 2, p. 772; Kasravi 1333, p. 132.

115. Layard 1846, p. 41.

had been further reinforced. Sheikh Thamir decided to refuse and began preparation for the defense of Falahiyeh. Moʿtamed al-Dowleh knowing how difficult it would be to invade the marsh lands opted for negotiations and sent a sayyid. If Sheikh Thamir would pay 5,000 *tumans* the troops would leave immediately. The Kaʿb leadership accepted this offer, although they believed they could defend themselves, but having lost much already in crops thought this a better alternative. When the money was paid Moʿtamed al-Dowleh refused to move until all members of Mohammad Taqi's family had been delivered to him. The Kaʿb refused to violate the rights of their guests. After the refusal the Qajar army came closer to Falahiyeh to the channel of Umm al-Zakhar (or Umm al-Sakhar). Then the Kaʿb and the Bakhtiyaris decided to make a night attack. The attack was executed, but the first wave was unsuccessful; as the soldiers were all armed and under orders and it was decided to withdraw. Aw Khan Baba was liberated however. Moʿtamed al-Dowleh then tried to make a bridge over one of the canals but this failed due to strong Arab resistance. After three days realizing that he would be unable to take the town, he left and returned to Dezful.[116] According to Kasravi, Moʿtamed al-Dowleh's departure was made possible by an agreement that henceforth Sheikh Thamir would pay henceforth his arrears over a number of years. Sheikh Thamir also sent two hostages, Sheikhs Morid and Fadʿam, as security for the agreement's implementation.[117]

According to Kasravi, later Sheikh Thamir killed the remaining Bakhtiyari chiefs under his protection and delivered their womenfolk as well as those of Mohammad Taqi to Moʿtamed al-Dowleh. The latter was so upset about this, which seems somewhat out of character, that he ordered the two Sheikhs that were hostages to be killed, but the ulama of Dezful interceded. Layard lays the blame for the killing and capture of the concerned Bakhtiyaris on a treacherous Bakhtiyari chief. Whatever the truth, both agree that Moʿtamed al-Dowleh was resolved to punish Sheikh Thamir for having protected Mohammad Taqi and for having resisted his troops. In 1841, Moʿtamed al-Dowleh demanded from Sheikh Thamir: (i) the handing over of "Mirza Kurna" of Behbahan, (ii) payment of 9,000 *tumans* to the shah, and (iii) presents and supplies (*sursat*) for himself and his troops. Sheikh Thamir refused; he had 8,000 followers and the support of the Muntafiq. The British therefore believed that he would resist an attack on Falahiyeh, for he might always retreat to Mohammareh. If paid, they also believed that Moʿtamed al-Dowleh was likely to leave. As soon as the summer was over, Moʿtamed al-Dowleh declared Sheikh Thamir to be an enemy of the shah and marched against him. Moʿtamed al-Dowleh constructed a bridge at Umm al-Zakhar, but it was attacked at night by the Kaʿb and he retreated. Then the *Vali* of Hoveyzeh and the Bawi Arabs suggested to float his troops down the Karun to Mohammareh and from there attack Falahiyeh. He did so in the fall of 1841. Not having enough faith in his support from the tribes, Sheikh Thamir felt he was unable to defend himself against the even larger Qajar force that had been amassed and fled with his family, guns, and property. Sheikh Thamir first went to Kut al-Sheikh and then to Ottoman territory in the Shatt al-Arab.[118]

Moʿtamed al-Dowleh marched unopposed to Falahiyeh, but did not destroy it. He made Sheikh ʿAli Reza chief of the Kaʿb. Sheikh Thamir had hoped that the Qajar army

---

116. Layard 1971, pp. 253-63; Sipihr 1377, vol. 2, pp. 771-72.

117. Kasravi 1333, pp. 131-32.

118. Kasravi 1333, p. 132; Schofield 1989, vol. 1, p. 126; Layard 1971, p. 343; Ibid. 1846, p. 41; Sepehr 1377, vol. 2, p. 775.

would not stay during the hot season, and then he could return, but since they did, the Sheikh went to Kuwait. Sheikh ʿAli Reza and his brother Moslem fled, and so did Sheikhs Fadʿam and Morid from Shushtar. Moʿtamed al-Dowleh then gave the governorship of Khuzestan to Mowla Farajollah, *Vali* of Hoveyzeh. Moʿtamed al-Dowleh ordered him to leave troops at Falahiyeh to ensure that Sheikh Thamir would not return; he also gave orders to make Mohammareh flourish. He further sent a message to the governors of Baghdad and Basra stating "you either rebuild Mohammareh or Basra will become a ruin like it." The government in Tehran did not allow Moʿtamed al-Dowleh to pursue this matter any further, because of Russian and English opposition, and so Moʿtamed al-Dowleh desisted in carrying out his attack on Basra. He left some troops with Mowla Farajollah to watch the Kaʿb at Falahiyeh.[119]

The immediate result of Moʿtamed al-Dowleh's threat were the Erzerum Boundary Commission negotiations under British-Russian auspices. During the negotiations the Ottomans kept a watchful eye on what passed at Mohammareh. When Rawlinson visited the place in 1843 on his fact-finding mission an Ottoman brig of war was lying off the Haffar canal to prevent vessels from Mohammareh entering the Shatt al-Arab with Indian goods, which these vessels easily circumvented. "Vessels bound for Mohammareh sail through the Bahmanshir instead of the Shatt al-Arab, or if they draw too much water to pass the bar they unload their goods on Abadan island, a few miles below the mouth of the Haffar Canal, then pass the Turkish guard ship empty, anchor at Mohammareh and the goods follow by land. The town thrives by being a free port. If Basra would apply a tariff equal to that of Bushehr and Bandar ʿAbbas Mohammareh would decline. Sheikh Jabir knows this and wants to protract the Erzeroum negotiations as long as possible."[120] The governor of Khuzestan, Moshir al-Dowleh noted that Dervish Pasha, one of the Erzerum negotiatiors, had promised the Kaʿb that if they said that they were subjects of the Ottoman Sultan he would not ask the 10-years arrears of taxes due to him. Meanwhile, Moshir al-Dowleh had added 2,000 *tuman*s to the Kaʿb taxes.[121]

As a result of these negotiations Mohammareh was recognized as Qajar territory and the Banu Kaʿb as Qajar subjects. Although the Ottoman government was a signatory to the 1849 Erzerum Treaty, the local authorities in Basra still found it difficult to accept the new reality. Mashuq Pasha, the governor of Basra in 1851, for example, had enlisted two refugees of the Kaʿb tribe, Soleyman al-Ghazban and "Musa al-Gendeel" who attacked shipping in the lower Shatt al-Arab. Soleyman had a camping ground assigned to him opposite to Mahalla against which Sheikh Jaber protested. The pasha also had assigned a house to Soleyman in Basra, which belonged to Sheikh Jaber.[122] These were but the first of further problems that would arise between the two countries about the Shatt al-Arab.[123]

Another result was the permanent ouster of Sheikh Thamir as part of Qajar policy to break Kaʿb resistance to its rule and establish firm control over Southern Khuzestan once and for all. Layard considered Sheikh Thamir a remarkable man, for an Arab.

---

119. Sepehr 1377, vol. 2, pp. 772, 776-77; Kasravi 1333, p. 132.

120. Rawlinson 1989, vol. 1, pp. 300-01.

121. Sepehr 1377, vol. 3, p. 995; Kasravi 1333, p. 134.

122. Schofield 1989, vol. 2, p. 226.

123. Much of that history may be read in the other volumes of Schofield 1989.

The country over which he ruled owed much of the prosperity which it then enjoyed to the encouragement which he gave to agriculture and commerce, and to the protection which he afforded to strangers and merchants in his territories. Canals and watercourses for irrigation, upon which the fertility of the soil mainly depended, were kept in good repair, and new works of the kind were frequently undertaken. He also had declared Muhammera a free port, and it had become an important depot for merchandise, not only for the supply of the province of Khuzistan, but of the adjoining Turkish territories.[124]

Lieutenant Selby also gave a positive account of Sheikh Thamir's administration, who "by a more temperate government than is usually exercised by the rulers of that province, and a real desire to benefit his country, had succeeded in rendering it comparatively prosperous, and was perhaps approaching a state to indepednet for the wishes of the Persian court."[125] He had his bad side, of course. According to Layard, the Sheikh was untrustworthy, who furthermore had killed many relatives on his way to the chieftainship. "He was very generous to seyyids and mullas, who, in consequence, flocked to Fellahiyah and condoned his evil deeds."[126]

The countenance of Sheikh Thamer was not prepossessing. He was tall and had a somewhat commanding appearance, but his features were coarse and vulgar- unlike those of the generality of high-bred Bedouins. His forehead was almost as prominent as that of a negro, and he probably had black blood in his veins. ... He wore an 'abba, cloak, richly embroidered with gold, over a gown of figured muslin. In a girdle round his waist he carried a long gold-mounted pistol, and the sheath of his sword was ornamented with the same precious metal. His head-dress consisted of a 'tarbush,' or red cap, round which was twisted a 'lung,' or long shawl, of Indian manufacture, one end of which was allowed to fall far down his back. ... The sheikh's hands and feet were dyed almost black with henna. Like a true Arab, he wore no drawers nor trousers, and went bare-footed.[127]

With the ouster of Sheikh Thamir, the last independent and vigorous supreme ruler, the Ka`b permanently lost their independence and became tax paying subjects of the Qajars. In an ironic turn of events the Al Bu Nasir ruling clan later lost the rulership over the Ka`b confederacy, which came into the hands of the Sheikh of Mohammareh.

---

124. Layard 1971, p. 245.

125. Selby 1844, p. 219.

126. Layard 1971, p. 245.

127. Layard 1971, pp. 244-45. According to Stocqueler 1832, vol. 1, p. 70, "the sheikh Samur was stone blind at his left eye since birth, but did not like it being told so."

The End of Ka'b Independence

Although in 1838 Sheikh Jaber had warned Sheikh Thamir that if threatened he would ask for help from the Qajars, this was not what he really wanted. It was only his most convenient and safest fall-back position, for when four years later Mo'tamed al-Dowleh and his troops came to Mohammareh en route to Falahiyeh, Sheikh Jaber fled to Kuwait rather than welcoming his 'master and savior'. He left it to his nephew Hajj Mohammad to do so. After the Ottoman attack of 1837 Mohammareh had been rebuilt and was starting to flourish again. Mo'tamed al-Dowleh ordered the new governor of Khuzestan Mowla Farajollah Khan to build a fort at Mohammareh and equip it with a garrison to protect pilgrims going to Mecca and solidify Qajar control over the port.[128]

After the departure of Mo'tamed al-Dowleh, Sheikh Jaber returned from Kuwait and sent his nephew Hajj Mohammad to Falahiyeh to agree with Sheikh Fares (who had been appointed to replace his uncle Sheikh Thamir in 1842) on a concerted policy of protection with regard to the Qajar regime. This shows that his flirtation with the Qajar authorities was one of political expediency and not what he really wanted. Shortly after his arrival, Hajj Mohammad was shot by the Ka'b chief as a rebel and traitor to his tribe and this led to intertribal warfare. Hashem brother of Fares and governor of Kut al-Sheikh crossed the Haffar to try and expel Sheikh Jaber, who then for his own protection asked for Qajar help. Troops from Dezful occupied the town in the spring of 1843 and remained there for a few months, when Sheikh Jaber contrived their withdrawal claiming problems with supplies. However unwelcome the Qajar troops were, they did not all leave, for an officer with a small detachment continued to stay to represent Qajar interests. Sheikh Jaber's fears were realized, for he was now less independent than before.[129]

Mohammareh was not the only place where changes had taken place. After Mo'tamed al-Dowleh's devastating operations, the government in Tehran imposed changes on the Ka'b and brought their manner of administration in line with other parts of the kingdom, (i.e. appointment of chiefs, hostages given, garrison of troops, regular payment of annual taxes). In 1849-50 Ardashir Mirza was appointed governor of Khuzestan, Lurestan, and Bakhtiyari. He was specifically charged with bringing order to the Ka'b territory and Ramhormuz (nazm-e arazi-ye Cha'b va Ramhormuz). He marched into southern Khuzestan, undertook a land assessment according to the value of the produce and collected the taxes, which in the case of Falahi he raised from 4,000 to about 20,000 *tuman*s annually.[130]

---

128. Rawlinson 1989, vol. 1, p. 299; Kasravi 1333, p. 134; Sepehr, vol. 3, p. 776.

129. Rawlinson 1989, vol. 1, pp. 299-300. Sheikh Thamir told the boundary commission in 1849 that Sheikh Jaber "is a rebel against Sheikh Faris and he has Persian soldiers to protect him." Schofield 1989, vol. 1, p. 108. Administration Report 1889-90, p. 13 has Sheikh Fares b. Gheyth rule from 1840 onwards.

130. Rawlinson 1989, vol. 1, pp. 289-90; Sepehr 1377, vol. 3, p. 1003. Despite the imposition of Qajar rule there still remained the annual problem to make them pay. According to Loftus 1857, p. 282, "tribute or *pishkesh* is now extracted from the Chab whenever the shah or provincial governor have enough strengths to get it." According to Najm al-Molk 1342, p. 119 the Ka'b even paid 70,000 *tuman*s when Heshmat al-Molk was governor in 1866-67.

After the ouster of Sheikh Thamir, the last strong Sheikh of the Ka`b, his successor did not oppose the Qajar government and did not withhold taxes. Also, thereafter the Khamis of Ramhormuz, the Bawi Arabs and the Al Moheysin accepted the authority of the Sheikh of Mohammareh and soon, according to Kasravi, the chief of Falahiyeh lost the title Sheikh al-Mashayekh.[131] This development resulted in the independence of the Sheikh of Moham-mareh. Rawlinson observed in 1842 that Sheikh Jaber was hostile and bent on revenge to the family of Sheikh Thamir.

> Mohammareh will not accept soon submission to the Chaab. Mohammareh and Hizan belong to Sheikh Jabir and are dependent on Persia now. Boojidi and Kut al-Nawasir pay their revenues to the Bawi Arabs, who consider themselves Persian subjects, either depending on Dezful, Hoveyzeh or Fellahiyeh. Tamar, al-Jadeed, Khomeisah, Shakhura, Nahr Yussef, Darband, El Khayin and El Haffar are under the Chief of Kut al-Sheikh as deputy of the chief of Fellahiyeh and are subject to pay 300 tons of dates to Basra. Apart from occasional presents from Sheikh Jabir the Persian government gets nothing else, no revenue, in kind or military, from these lands.[132]

131. Kasravi 1333, p. 135. According to Curzon 1892, vol. II, p. 324, the Sheikh of Falahiyeh continued to have the title of *Sheikh al-mashayekh*. This is also confirmed by Fasa'i, according to whom only the true descendants of Sheikh Salman were called *sheikh al-mashayekh*, which therefore remained the title of the chief of Falahi. Fasa'i 1378, vol. 2, pp. 1413, 1616; see also Mafi 1361, vol. 1, pp. 110-17.

132. Rawlinson 1989, vol. 1, p. 301.

Table of the ruling Sheikhs of the Banu Ka`b (1690-1889)

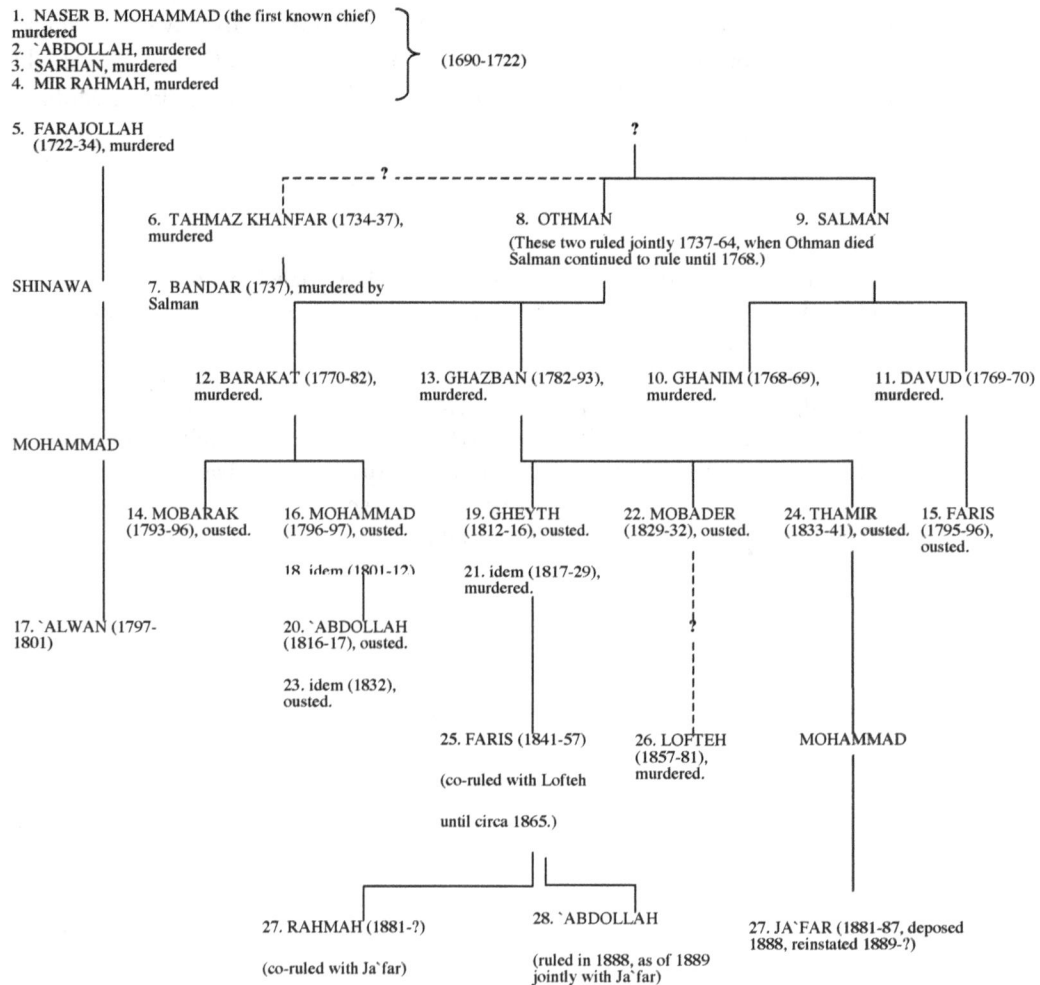

1. NASER B. MOHAMMAD (the first known chief)
murdered
2. `ABDOLLAH, murdered
3. SARHAN, murdered   (1690-1722)
4. MIR RAHMAH, murdered

5. FARAJOLLAH   ?
   (1722-34), murdered

- - - - - - ? - - - - - - - - - - - - - - - -

6. TAHMAZ KHANFAR (1734-37),   8. OTHMAN   9. SALMAN
   murdered   (These two ruled jointly 1737-64, when Othman died
                                  Salman continued to rule until 1768.)

SHINAWA   7. BANDAR (1737), murdered by
               Salman

            12. BARAKAT (1770-82),   13. GHAZBAN (1782-93),   10. GHANIM (1768-69),   11. DAVUD (1769-70)
                murdered.   murdered.   murdered.   murdered.

MOHAMMAD

            14. MOBARAK   16. MOHAMMAD   19. GHEYTH   22. MOBADER   24. THAMIR   15. FARIS
            (1793-96), ousted. (1796-97), ousted. (1812-16), ousted. (1829-32), ousted. (1833-41), ousted. (1795-96),
                                                                                                                 ousted.

                           18. idem (1801-12)   21. idem (1817-29),
                                                       murdered.

17. `ALWAN (1797-   20. `ABDOLLAH
1801)   (1816-17), ousted.

                    23. idem (1832),
                    ousted.

                                   25. FARIS (1841-57),   26. LOFTEH   MOHAMMAD
                                                          (1857-81),
                                   (co-ruled with Lofteh murdered.
                                   until circa 1865.)

                     27. RAHMAH (1881-?)   28. `ABDOLLAH          27. JA`FAR (1881-87, deposed
                                                                       1888, reinstated 1889-?)
                     (co-ruled with Ja`far)   (ruled in 1888, as of 1889
                                               jointly with Ja`far)

   In 1852, Loftus referred to Sheikh Fares as the "current Chab chief," and mentioned that Sheikh Jaber had become almost independent from his chief. He further considered Sheikh Jaber a shrewd man, who possessed several vessels and carried on extensive trade with Muscat and Bombay, and could field many musketeers and horsemen. He added that "He would be a formidable rival for Faris in case of conflict."[133] This conflict did not materialize, for Sheikh Jaber got a break and in some way his revenge. This was due to his support of the Qajar army during the attack of Mohammareh by the British expeditionary force in the Anglo-Persian war of 1857. In March of that year British forces shelled and took Mohammareh and pursued the Qajar army as far as Ahvaz. Contrary to Sheikh Jaber's support, that of Sheikh Fares seems to have been less forthcoming. Also, Ka`b tribesmen along the Karun supplied the British force with information on the movements of the Qajar army, its garrison

---

133.   Loftus 1857, pp. 282-85.

at Ahvaz and the supplies of that town to which they also helped themselves.[134] As a result, at the end of the Anglo-Persian war in 1857, Sheikh Jaber was recognized by the Qajar government as the independent Sheikh of Mohammareh. He was no longer dependent on the Ka`b, whose supreme chief was shortly thereafter taken to Tehran. This did not mean an end to their conflict, for in 1863 Pelly noted that both Sheikhs had been summoned to Dezful "for the settlement of their mutual grievances."[135]

Mohammareh just after the British conquest, *The Illustrated London News,* May 23, 1857

Shaikh Fares was probably deposed in 1857, or earlier, for not paying taxes and the governor of Khuzestan appointed Sheikh Lofteh b. Badr in his place. This was only for a time, because in early 1863, Pelly reported that Sheikh Lofteh's deputy at that time was his nephew Fares b. Gheyth (Farass-ibn-Graith).[136] These two Sheikhs co-ruled the Ka`b of Falahiyeh

134. Hunt 1858, pp. 235-86; Watson 1976, pp. 446-54. However, according to the British the following chiefs volunteered information about the Qajar troops: "Shaikh Faris al Ghadhan, Chief of Fellahiah, Mulla Abdulla, Chief of Hawizah, Shaikh Jabir-el-Mardao, Chief of the Mohaisen tribes, and Shaikh Suwaila, Ferhan and Darwish, Chiefs of the Nasara tribe of Khushab." Saldanha 1986, vol. 7/1, p. 53. Unidentified Arabs, probably Banu Ka`b, assisted the British. "Not less than 300 of their number [i.e. the Persian army] were killed, and in addition large numbers were killed by the Arabs, who butchered all Persians they came across. The loot of the Persian camp is still a popular theme amongst the greybeards of Muhammarah." Government of Great-Britian 1917, p. 14.

135. Lorimer 1915, p. 1253; Pelly 1865 a, p. 38; Ibid. 1865 b, p. 124.

136. Pelly 1865 b, pp. 124-25, who described Sheikh Fares as "the old gentleman seemed about 40 or 50, but rather dissipated in appearance," which was due to alcoholism. According to Administration Report 1889-90, p. 13 he ruled for a long time, and became blind. One son was Mohammad Sartip. Sheikh Fares Khan was still *sheikh al-mashayekh* in 1860. *Ruznameh-ye Ettefaqiyeh-ye Vaqaye`* 1373, vol. 4, p. 3039 (27 Ramazan 1276/14 April 1860). According to the British Resident, "Sheikh Lufti was an exhausted debauchee and at times suffered from delirium trements." Saldanha 1986, vol. 2, p. 4. Curzon calls Lofteh b. Badr by another name, i.e. Lotfollah Mohammad Khan. Curzon

and changed places for a number of years depending on the circumstances and the whim of the governor of Khuzestan until finally his cousins, Jafer (sic; probably Ja`far) and Salman, sons of Sheikh Mohammad al-Fares at Jerrahi, killed Lofteh and his son Gadhban in May 1878.

> The immediate causes for the murder were:-Sheikh Lufti was collecting money from the Kaab, for which he had rendered himself responsible to the Prince-Governor [of Khuzestan] on being made Sheikh, and was accompanied by the two lads, Jafir and Salman, sons of his cousin, Mahomed al-Faris. The elder of these, Jafir, was reported to have written three times to his father complaining of the way Lufti treated him, but in reply his father told him to have patience.

> This it seems he could not do, and as Sheikh Lufti was "writing a letter and using abusive language to the people around him as usual," Jafir drew a pistol and shot him, and Salman shot Ghathban, the eldest son of Sheikh Lufti. Jafir and Salman then rode off together.[137]

The Persian government in reaction to the murder of the Ka`b chief appointed another cousin, Sheikh Rahmah grandson of Gheyth, as his successor as governor of Falahiyeh. The tax (*divan*) and governor's present (*pishkesh*) of the district were fixed at 10,000 *tumans*. Furthermore, the sub-districts of Deh-Mullah, Jarahi, Hendiyan and Bandar Ma`shur were separated from the district of Falahiyeh and reconstituted as a new district. The governor of Khuzestan appointed Amir `Abdollah of Deh Mullah as the chief of this new district, on condition that he paid 12,000 *tumans divan* taxes and *pishkesh* as well as 9,000 *tumans* arrears of Deh Mullah. He was only able to pay 9,000 *tumans* and the British Resident commented that he "will probably either have to fight for the balance or seek safety in flight." However, he was able to hold on to his function as is clear from later developments. Because Sheikh Rahmah was a weak administrator and only was able to collect 4,000 *tumans* in taxes from the tribes, he asked the governor of Khuzestan for help. The latter sent his vizier Asadollah Khan with a battalion of troops, but the Sheikhs of the important Ka`b clans refused to visit him. Meanwhile, the governor of Khuzestan agreed with Sheikh Mohammad Khan, oldest son of Sheikh Jaber of Mohammareh, that the latter should jointly farm the district of Falahiyeh and Ramis (Ram-Hormuz) with Asadollah Khan the following year. Due to the impasse at Falahiyeh, Rahmah Khan was replaced by his cousin Fares after a few months. However, he was soon reinstated thereafter, and ruled "in a feeble and unpopular manner." He remained in office paying 15,000 *tumans* in taxes in 1880, while Amir or Sheikh `Abdollah remained governor of Deh Mullah paying 12,000 *tumans*.[138]

1892, vol. 2, p. 324, while Administration Report 1889-90, p. 13 has only Lotfollah and mention four other co-rulers Mohammad Khan b. Fares, Rahmah, `Abdollah and Ja`far Khan.

137. Saldanha 1986, vol. 2, p. 4. This violent behavior stood in contrast to that of Sheikh Jaber of Mohammareh, who "though according to report past 90 years of age, governs his district with all the vigour of youth, and his earnest endeavours to promote the welfare of his subjects afford a pleasing contrast to the stolid indifference to all advancement which is characteristic of so many oriental rulers." Administration Report 1874-75, p. 4.

138. Saldanha 1986, vol. 2, p. 5; Administration Report 1878-79, pp. 7-9 (Mohammareh paid 33,000 *tumans* ad Falahiyeh 22,000 *tumans* in taxes); Administration Report 1879-80, p. 6;

In 1881, Sheikh Ja`far Khan son of Mohammad Khan, son of Sheikh Thamir Khan Sheikh al-Shoyukh became co-ruler of Falahiyeh with his cousin Sheikh Rahmah grandson of Gheyth. Zell al-Soltan deposed Sheikh Ja`far Khan in 1885 and Sheikh Mez`al of Mohammareh was forced to accept the governorship of Falahiyeh on behalf of Sheikh Rahmah. However, then Zell al-Soltan reappointed Sheikh Ja`far Khan in Sheikh Rahmah's place. According to the British resident, this game of musical chairs was a subterfuge of the Persian authorities to have a pretext to interfere in the affairs of the Arab chiefs of Khuzestan. When Sheikh Rahmah died in 1885 or 1886 his place was taken by his brother Sheikh `Abdollah with Sheikh Ja`far as co-ruler. The latter was deposed in early 1888, but, when in September 1888 Nezam al-Saltaneh, governor of Khuzestan approached Falahiyeh with 500 troops and some Bakhriyari cavalry with a view to impose a Persian governor, so the Ka`b sheikhs reinstated Sheikh Ja`far b. Mohammad. The chiefs of Falahiyeh refused to negotiate and broke the Jerrahi dams and flooded the country around Falahiyeh. Nezam al-Saltaneh, therefore, had to abandon his plan to take the Ka`b stronghold.[139]

In 1891, Sheikh `Abdollah was reinstated as chief of Falahiyeh, but the major Ka`b clans deposed him in 1892 and appointed Sheikh Ja`far b. Mohammad. Sheikh Mez`al of Mohammareh supported Sheikh `Abdollah and Hosam al-Saltaneh, governor of Khuzestan unware of tribal sentiments, therefore, reappointed Sheikh `Abdollah. However, when he became aware of the tribe's hostility to his appointee he cancelled the appointment and in January 1893 named Sheikh Ja`far b. Mohammad as the governor of Falahiyeh. In 1894, the tables were turned, because the Ka`b clans opposed the nomination of Sheikh Ja`far b. Mohammad and, therefore, the governor of Khuzestan appointed Sheikh `Abdollah. However, the latter was unable to resolve outstanding fiscal issues (arrears), which led to a cabal to unseat him. As a result, before the end of 1894 Sheikh Ja`far b. Mohammad was reappointed as governor of Falahiyeh.[140] By that time the Al Bu Naser had lost most of its influence and three years later lost control of Falahiyeh.

According to Lorimer, the Falahiyeh district was placed under Sheikh Jaber, the Moheysin rival of Sheikh Fares in 1857, and, except for 1860-62, the former supreme Ka`b Sheikhs were subordinate to the Sheikh of Mohammareh, who henceforth called himself the Sheikh of the Ka`b. The Moheysin were as of then the paramount division, although they were outnumbered by the Ka`b.[141] However, according to Kasravi, the change in the balance of power took place in 1898 when Sheikh Khaz`al Khan of Mohammareh received

Administration Report 1880-81, p. 5; Administration Report 1883-84, p. 9 (Sheikh Rahmah was appointed governor of Falahiyeh and Sheikh `Abdollah of Deh Mullah). Curzon mentioned a third co-ruler for Sheikhs Ja`far and Rahmah, viz. Mir `Abdollah of Deh Mullah (see figure 2), who, as is clear from above, was governor of a new district that had bene part of Falahiyeh in the past. Curzon 1892, vol. 2, p. 324.

139. Kasravi 1333, p. 135; Saldanha 1986, vol. 2, p. 8; Administration Report 1888-89, p. 13 (the operation was part of the pacification campaign against the Bakhtiyaris and the decision to open the Karun for navigation). Sheikh Ja`far b. Mohammad fled to Kuwait in early 1888 and was replaced by Sheikh `Abdollah; for the events resulting in this flight see Mafi 1361, vol. 1, pp. 110-17; vol. 2, p. 59; Administration Report 1889-90, p. 13 calls Sheikh Ja`far b. Mohammad Khan "the present ruler and is known by the title Sheikh el Mushaikh."

140. Saldanha 1986, vol. 2, p. 10; Administration Report 1893-94, p. 9; Mafi 1361, vol. 2, p. 107 (in 1891 Sheikh Ja`far had been disposed again). Saldanha 1986, vol. 2, p. 10.

141. Lorimer 1915, p. 1253

and paid the taxes for Falahiyeh and then appointed one of his own people as chief of the Ka'b, which was the end of the long rule of the Al Bu Nasir family.[142] In the years thereafter the governors of Falahiyeh were not of the Al Bu Nasir family anymore, but agents from Sheikh Khaz'al. In 1905, for example, Mullah 'Abdollah Ka'b was in charge of Falahiyeh and in 1910 Sheikh 'Abdol Majid, the little son of Sheikh Kaseb Khan, Nosrat al-Molk, the governor of Ahvaz.[143] The hostility between the two ruling families persisted. In 1924, when the Iranian army marched into Khuzestan one of the descendants of the Al Bu Nasir family, 'Abdol-Hoseyn Khan went with a group of Arabs of Falahiyeh to Behbahan to join the forces led by Reza Shah.[144]

The Composition of the Ka'b Tribal Confederacy

The Ka'b confederation had increased in size since its departure from Iraq. By the 1840s it had grown to some 12,000 families, probably due to the fact that other tribes had joined, Chirikov surmised.[145] This was indeed the case as is clear from Table 4.1 and from the observations made by Lorimer, who observed that "the tribe consists partly of original and partly of adscititious families and groups, the divisional name Dris being closely associated with the former and that of Khanafireh with the latter of these two classes. The more minute classification of the Ka'b depends not on blood relationship but on political accidents, for the name of a headman's family or section is generally extended to include all who find (or place) themselves under his authority; it follows that there are many semi-obsolete names as well aliases both exact and partial."[146] He further remarked that "The Dawariqeh are said to be an aboriginal race distributed among the various branches of the Ka'b as herdsmen and almost as serfs. The Dris and Nassar are universally regarded as true Ka'ab; the Khanafireh and Muqaddam mostly as non-Ka'ab, but described as tava'ef or 'dependent tribes.'"[147] The Moheysin were also not part of the original Ka'b tribe. They "are said to be descended from a man named as such and his son in law Kasib (pronounced Chasib). They belonged to a tribe in the Mohammareh district according to tradition which were driven away by the Ka'ab to the Tigris, where they are known as Al Hoseyn Pasha. Muhaisin and Kasib having bought

---

142.   Kasravi 1333, p. 135. Kasravi is borne out by Mafi 1361, vol. 1, pp. 75, n., 110-17 and vol. 2, pp. 74-75, 80, who mentions the interference by the Sheikh of Mohammareh in the appointment and administration of the Sheikh of Falahiyeh in 1888 and 1890, thus indicating that the latter was not yet subordinate to the former. However, Sheikh 'Abdollah was in the pocket of Sheikh Mez'al of Mohammareh, who, therefore, made trouble for Sheikh Ja'far *Sheikh al-Mashayekh*. According to Gordon 1891, p. 14, Sheikh Mez'al "is the only powerful Arab chief now left in Arabistan: all have been broken but him."

143.   Administration Report 1905-1906, p. 31; Administration Report 1910, p. 38 (he was the eldest son of Sheikh Khaz'al). For the later period see Zarrabi 1342, pp. 285-86.

144.   Kasravi 1333, p. 135.

145.   Chirikov 1989, vol. 2, p. 471.

146.   Lorimer 1915, p. 948.

147.   Lorimer 1915, pp. 959-60. The proper rendering of Dris and Nassar is Idris and Ansar, according to Kazeruni 1367, p. 33.

land in Mohammareh from the Ka`ab returned to their native land and founded the Muhaisin tribe."[148] The Moheysin were not only residing in Iran, but also in Ottoman lands. "Threefifths of these live on the right bank of the Shatt-el-Arab between Bassorah and the fort of Zen and on the island of Umm-ul-Hsasif, in the Shatt-el-Arab, opposite the fort of Feiliyeh, belonging to Sheikh Hadji Jaber; while two-fifths live on the left bank of the Shatt-el-Arab, in the tract between Mohammareh and a point about 2 miles above it on the Karun as far as the Chetiban Canal."[149]

Table 4.1 shows the composition of the Ka`b confederacy around 1840 as reported by Layard. Around 1900 this composition had changed significantly as a result of the political changes in S. Khuzestan (see Table 4.2). The Dris still existed, but their arch-rivals the Nassar became a subdivision of the Dris. The Khanafireh instead of being a subdivision of the Moheysin became a major division of the Ka`b. In place of the Bawi and the Banu Tamim, who may have split off, the Moqaddam and the Hazbeh had become the other major divisions of the Ka`b. These changes show that the composition of tribal confederacies like the Ka`b were in constant flux as a result of both internal and external pressures.

The supreme chief of the Ka`b, who was based at Falahiyeh, bore the title of Sheikh al-Mashayekh. He was always from the Al Bu Nasir, of the descendents of Sheikh Salman. They formed the leadership lineage of the Idris one of the main groups of the Ka`b confederacy. The supreme Sheikh's vizier was always from the Nasara, the other main and original Ka`b group. Layard believed that these two functions were hereditary in these two tribal divisions. The later-comers to the Ka`b included a branch of the Banu Tamim, a large tribe in Central Arabia, under Mir Mazkur, a sayyed. The Bawis had joined the Ka`b from the late eighteenth century, while the Moheysin had been co-opted when the Ka`b had taken the left bank of the Shatt al-Arab.[150] There was constant rivalry between the two leading divisions of the Ka`b, the Idris and Nassar. However, this had little effect on Mohammareh. Sheikh Jaber allowed few of them into his town. He had his own troops that served him loyally.[151]

Table 4.1: Composition of the Ka`b Arabs

Great Tribes	Division	Subdivisions	Name of Sheikhs	Residence
Cha`b (Ka`b)	Ali Bu Nasir Idris		Thamer	Fellahiyah
	Idris	El Sakhereh	Salman	Left bank of the lower part of the Karun and the Bahmeh-shir
		Ali Bu Ali		
		Ali Bu Badi`		
		El Ghanam		

---

148. Lorimer 1915, p. 1253.

149. Chirikov 1989, vol. 2, pp. 464-71 (including the a mode detailed description of the extent of their territory); see also Ibid., pp. 111-21; 139, 226. For the situation around 1900 see Lorimer 1915, pp. 1249-52.

150. Layard 1846, p. 38.

151. Rawlinson 1989, vol. 2, pp. 374-75.

Great Tribes	Division	Subdivisions	Name of Sheikhs	Residence
		Ali Bu Dalleh		
		Ali Bu Suf		
		El Haffadelleh		
		Thawame		
		Shileishat		
		Rubahat		
		Soweilat		
		Rawajileh		
		Toweijat		
		El Fayyal		
		El Koweiseb		
		Ali Bu Mahmud		
		Ali Bu `Alafi		
	Nasara	..	Haji Mash`al and Kerreyyid	Right bank of the Bahmeh-shir and southern part of Mohammareh.
	Mohaisen	Mejd-ed-din	Haji Jaber	Right bank of the lower part of the Karun and the northern part of Mohammareh.
		Khanafirah		
		El Matesh asfer		
		Motuwwar		
		Buweisher		
		El Hallalat		
		Derarijeh		
		El Mahamid		
		Beit Mosahil, or Ebn `Ali Basha		
		Morazijeh		
		Mo`awijah		
	Bawi	Motarideh	`Ajil	Right and left banks of the Karun, above and below Isma`iliyah and that village.
		Newaser		
		El Wasseyin		
		El Wurumi		
		Al `Ajajat		
		El Jebbarat		
		El Mosabbeh		
		Ali Bu Haji		
		El `Awud		

Great Tribes	Division	Subdivisions	Name of Sheikhs	Residence
		El Zerkan		
		Bem Khaled		
		El `Omur		
		El Erkither		
		El Shamakhiyeh		
		El Berashideh		
		El Hardan		
	Branch of the Beni Temim	Sherifat (Beni Ershed, Soleyyeh, El Farud, &c.)	Mir Mazkur	Hindiyan, Deh-Mulla, right bank of the river of Hindiyan and Zeitun Hills.
	Haideri; Hiyader (i.e. Haideris)	..	Ahmed	Banks of the Jerrahi. Near Fellahiyah.

Source: Layard, "A Description," p. 37.

The authority of the supreme Sheikh was not absolute as is clear from the foregoing discussion and the family tree of the ruling Sheikhs. Many of the supreme Ka`b Sheikhs were killed by their own tribesmen. Stocqueler reported that Sheikh Mobader when in his *divan-khaneh* or public audience hall, had a considerable guard. He further described him as being "the most powerful chieftain in south-west Persia."[152] Despite the fact that, according to Stocqueler, he was held in great veneration, and that he had a body-guard, he nevertheless was deposed one year later. Sheikh Mobader was of "middle stature, of a pleasing countenance, and graceful demeanour. He is reputed to possess much kindness of heart, and, at the same time, the courage of a lion. He is liberal and tolerant and anxious for improvement, reason why he encourages artisans and Europeans in his territory."[153] The Ka`b at that time were not just buffalo-herders, for they also had their men of learning and literature such as Sheikh Fathollah, who studied in Shiraz, was qadi in Basra for some time, and wrote a history of the Ka`b, which was the main source for Kasravi's account. However, he seems to have been an exception, for otherwise the tribal leadership had no use for bookish learning and all that it entailed. Sheikh Thamir b. Ghazban b. `Othman "sheikh of sheikhs of the Chaab tribe and commander of the district of Gobban [Qobban]" as his title was noted in an official document of the Erzerum negotiations, declared in 1843 that he had no documents, "we do not understand such things."[154]

Table 4.2: Composition of the Ka`b around 1900

I. Dris	II. Muqaddam	III. Khanafireh	IV. Hazbeh
1. Dris	1. Ishaq	1. (Al Bu) Hamdi	1. Ghuwainim

152. Stocqueler 1832, vol. 2, pp. 74, 78.

153. Stocqueler 1832, vol. 2, p. 79. His brother Sheikh Thamir employed a Greek advisor named Nicholas in Kut al-Sheikh, Ibid., vol. 2, pp. 68-69.

154. Schofield 1989, vol. 1, p. 108. On other learned persons in Falahi around 1800 see Shushtari 1363, p. 182.

2. (Al Bu) Nasir	2. Maiyah	2. Kawamil	2. Hazbeh
3. Nassar	3. Muqaddam	3. Shawadiyeh	3. (Al Bu) La`ateh

Source: Lorimer 1915, vol. 2, pp. 949-60.

According to Layard, the Sheikh's "authority is respected if he can enforce it with sufficient force, but the Bawis and Sherifat are large and powerful tribes and consider themselves under the protection rather than under the authority of Sheikh Thamir. But they are as yet not strong enough to oppose him if he is supported by his own tribes."[155] This did not only hold for weak Sheikhs, but even for the strongest such as Sheikh Salman. When the Ka`b were under pressure by the joint Basra and EIC force in 1765 two Sheikhs of the Ka`b surrendered and reconciled with the *mutasallim* of Basra, while the majority of their fellow-tribesmen under Sheikh Salman continued to hold out.[156] A similar situation existed under another important and strong leader, Sheikh Thamir. For example, Mir Mahanna, chief of the Sharifat opposed Sheikh Thamir and tried to defend himself in his mud-castle at Deh Mullah. He was forced to surrender, retired to Falahiyeh and Sheikh Thamir gave the chiefship to Mir Mazkur.[157] Despite the change in leadership the Sharifat did not join Sheikh Thamir in his opposition to Mo`tamed al-Dowleh's invasion, but in fact displayed a rather neutral-hostile behavior. They did not unite with Sheikh Thamir, but pretended to remain neutral joining with the Qajar troops. Even after the departure of the Qajar troops the Sharifat still did not obey Sheikh Thamir.[158]

Often, the Bawi Arabs had openly opposed Sheikh Thamir. When the Ottomans destroyed Mohammareh they supported his rival `Abdol-Reza, who replaced him after the Ottomans left. Thamir then sought refuge with Mohammad Taqi, the Bakhtiyari chief. On his return, the Bawis sought forgiveness for their defection and the Sheikh received them back under his protection. Some time later a Bawi Sheikh was invited to Falahiyeh, while drinking coffee in the council meeting (*majles*) he was shot death together with

---

155. Layard 1846, p. 39.

156. Perry 1971, p. 146.

157. Layard 1846, p. 39.

158. Layard 1846, p. 39; Ibid. 1971, pp. 252, 265-66.

A Ka`b Sheikh, Stocqueler 1832, vol. 1, frontispiece

one of his principal supporters. Sheikh Thamir replaced him with ʿAqil, who was his client. However, during Moʿtamed al-Dowleh's second invasion of Kaʿb territory he deserted his patron and armed the tribe against him. The Zarkan and Banu Khalid refused to join the rest of the Bawi Arabs and joined Sheikh Thamir. After the departure of the Qajar army Sheikh Thamir expelled the rebellious Bawis from Esmaʿiliyeh. They fled to Ahvaz and the lower part of the Ramhormuz plain.[159]

A Kaʿb woman, Stocqueler 1832, vol. 2, frontispiece

159.   Layard 1846, p. 39; Ibid. 1971, p. 241 (they were scouring the plains for plunder). Rawlinson wrote in a marginal note to Kazeruni 1367, p. 30 that "the date groves of Bujidee, cultivated by the Chaabies, subject to Fellahieh, but paying revenues to the Bawee Arabs." Schofield 1989, vol. 1, p. 99 showing that the Bawi Arabs only had a patron-client relationship with the supreme chief of the Kaʿb, but did not consider themselves Kaʿb Arabs.

The position of the Sheikh of Mohammareh was a delicate one. First, Hajj Yusof was the son of one of the Sheikh Gheyth's slaves and secondly, he led a group of dependents within the Ka`b confederacy. Nevertheless, the advantageous location of Mohammareh and above all its rising revenues gave its governor wealth and ideas, one of which was to be more his own man. Already a second-generation governor, Hajj Yusof ignored the Sheikh of Fala-hiyeh when he could afford to do so. Given his antecedents and the fact that he was at the head of a small division of the Ka`b, he could not openly challenge the supreme chief's authority. He supplied his share of troops when the Qajar government asked for them, and supported Sheikh Thamir when hostile forces threatened Falahiyeh, but reluctantly, it would seem. Moreover, he settled directly with the Basra government regarding the land rent and gave presents to governors of Dezful and Hoveyzeh without the knowledge of the Sheikh of Falahiyeh. Clearly, he was jockeying for an independent position.[160]

Also, outsiders such as the Government of India dealt with the Sheikh of Moham-mareh without first bothering to contact the supreme chief of the Ka`b or the government in Tehran or Basra. Sheikh Thamir also carried on correspondence with the EIC political agent at Basra.[161] In 1837, Sheikh Jaber, governor of Mohammareh allegedly felt embarrassed to be addressed by the British about the establishment of a coal station at his port, because he had been appointed by Sheikh Thamir, or so he professed. But this coy attitude was but a negotiating ploy, for in that same year he refused the coal station unless 9,000 "Eyrie piasters" ground rent was paid to him.[162]

There was clearly a state of confusion about who was the actual suzerain of Moham-mareh and the Ka`b. When Stocqueler was set upon by the Ka`b Sheikh in Weys, despite his laissez-passer from the Sheikh of Kut al-Sheikh he rather than addressing himself to the Qajar authorities or even to the Sheikh of Kut al-Sheikh wanted to return to Basra to complain to the *mutasallim* about this behavior and obtain redress from the Ottoman authorities.[163] This seems to have been a logical step, for Basra's governor considered the Ka`b as its subjects. Even as late as 1831 the *mutasallim* of Basra had asked for military support from the Ka`b against the invading Muntafiq as discussed above. The Government of India believed, however, that Mohammareh was Qajar territory and that the Sheikh of Mohammareh has been independent or subject to the Sheikh of the Ka`b. Since the days of Karim Khan, the captains of Ka`b boats operating in the Shatt al-Arab delta had carried the Persian flag on their vessels, but probably more as an indication of being Shi`a than being a Zand or later as a Qajar subject. Since then Mohammareh had been considered Persian even though its Sheikhs

---

160. Rawlinson 1989, vol. 1, pp. 296-97. "Sheikh Jabir in Mohammareh had gradually amassed an enormous fortune." Loftus 1857, pp. 282-83.

161. Layard 1971, p. 243; Schofield 1989, vol. 1, p. 126.

162. Schofield 1989, vol. 1, p. 126. In the original, *qorush-e `eyn*, i.e. piaster equivalent; 10 of which equaled 15 rupees or 15,000 dinars current (*rayej*) at Shiraz. Kazeruni 1367, p. 29.

163. Stocqueler 1832, vol. 1, pp. 60-67. Because Weys and Ahvaz were held by the Moheysin and thus owed allegiance to the Sheikh of Mohammareh rather than his alleged superior the Sheikh of Kut al-Sheikh or southern Mohammareh. The Sheikh of Ahvaz told Stocqueler as much, when "he said he was shocked at the conduct of *his brother*, the sheikh of Weiss, and was quite sure that the sheikh of Mahummarah woud send for both his and his brother's head, when I told the story of my distasters." Ibid., vol. 1, p. 67.

occasionally sent presents to Baghdad.[164] Although the Sheikh of Mohammareh nominally acknowledged Qajar rule he opposed any force if threatened with demands with which he did not want to comply, when supported by the Ka'b Sheikh. He never supplied troops or paid taxes. *Pishkesh* has been given annually directly or via Ka'b Sheikh.[165] The covert and later open rebellion of the Moheysin was that most serious challenge to the authority of the supreme chief of the Ka'b. In fact, the rebels ended becoming the masters as already has been discussed.

The supreme chief of the Ka'b, therefore, did not have an easy task. He had to play his political cards well, marry girls from the right families, have enough funds and then judiciously use them to be able to sway the Sheikhs to come or keep on his side and if everything else failed use brute force. However, that only worked if you had enough force and could use it in a sustained manner. To the outside world, the Ka'b were a bloodthirsty lot. Najm al-Molk described them as "a strong-hearted, fearless, bloodletting people, who are always at war and in conflict with each other and who do not hesitate to shed the blood of a father or brother as evidenced by many of such occurrences."[166] Correct outward behavior was the first requirement to establish proper decorum and give respect where it was due. Stocqueler noted that Sheikh Mobader had an open mudif or audience hall where chiefs and others came to call. "These chieftains were received with a ceremony proportioned to their rank and consequence, and a cordiality bearing reference to their zeal, courage, or interest in Mobader Khan's bosom. Those of the highest rank merely bowed and took their places, others advanced and kissed the sheikh's hand, while the humblest officers knelt on one knee to perform the same ceremony." Age was always paid great respect to and transgressed rank.[167] In his reception hall, Sheikh Thamir behaved in a similar manner. He sat alone and the petty Sheikhs and armed retainers were kept, sitting or standing, at a distance.[168]

If the Sheikh commanded enough respect, authority and power to back it up, he could rely on these other chiefs to come to him with their own weapons and supplies. Kinneir stated that the revenues of the Ka'b Sheikh amounted to five lakhs of piasters (about £50,000) and that he was able field 5,000 horse and 20,000 foot. Kinnier was not impressed by this number, because "it is an undisciplined rabble armed with matchlocks, lances and swords, without order or officers.[169] The Ka'b horsemen trained their skills amongst other things by the throwing of the javelin (*jarid-bazi*) and other horse games.[170] In 1831, Sheikh Mobader was able command 6 to 7,000 cavalry and about 15,000 infantry.[171] "His revenues arising from the exportation of the date, the manufacture of the abbah, and the custom levied on

164. Schofield 1989, vol. 1, p. 124.

165. Schofield 1989, vol. 1, pp. 124-26.

166. Najm al-Molk 1342, pp. 110-11.

167. Stocqueler 1832, vol. 1, p. 76.

168. Layard 1971, pp. 244-45.

169. Kinneir 1973, p. 91. According to a Persian manuscript, the Ka'b allegedly were 100,000 families strong around 1800. Kunke 1991, p. 85.

170. Stocqueler 1832, vol. 1, p. 87.

171. Stocqueler 1832, vol. 1, p. 79.

Indian imports, may amount to about sixty thousand tomauns annually."[172] According to Layard, Kinneir's estimate was much too high. He maintained that Ka`b chief's revenues were barely one-third of that.[173] According to Chirikov, in 1850 the Ka`b could "field 20-25,000 men; they have paid 13,000 *tuman*s in tribute."[174] In 1863, according to information collected by Pelly, the main Ka`b tribes could field 68,000 men as shown in Table 4.3. However, Pelly remarked that he thought this number was overstated.[175]

The numbers reported by Chirikov and Pelly are much higher than an earlier estimate by Layard and a later one by Lorimer. According to Layard, at the time of Mo`tamed al-Dowleh's expedition, Sheikh Thamir was able to mobilize about 7,000 armed men of which 3,000 were well-armed with muskets and matchlocks; 1,000 were horsemen, and 3,000 were indifferently armed with spears, swords, etc. The Bawis had about 1,000 horsemen; their foot amounted to some 3,000, but without good weapons. The Sharifats had about 2,000 foot and 700 horse. Thus, the total force at the disposal of the supreme Sheikh was 12,700 men, if he was obeyed.[176] This number is more in line with that the Ka`b had fielded in the eighteenth century and the estimate given by Lorimer, according to whom the fighting strength consisted of 15,722 men (see Table 4.4). This would mean a total tribal number of some 55,000 not counting those outside S. Khuzestan and Hendiyan (1,500 in the latter of the Sha`bani group). At the end of the nineteenth century, many long-barreled muzzle-loaders were still seen, for "almost every fighting man among the Dris and Khanfireh have these or better arms."[177] By 1890, the number of the Ka`b was estimated at 62,000.[178] About 50% of these were women, who were involved in all kinds of economic activities (animal husbandry; weaving, etc.). As among other tribes in Iran, "The Chabean women enjoy a much greater degree of liberty than either the Persians or Turks. They do not veil even in the public streets, nor scruple to hold any communication with the other sex which modesty and fidelity permit."[179]

Table 4.3: The principal Ka`b tribes, chiefs, fighting force and location in 1863

Name	Name chief	Number of grown men	Observations
Albooghesh	Moraid	6,000	Bozeeah, their principal town
Asarkeerah	Zair Kraidee	4,000	Oushar, near Boozeeah
Mukasebeh	Saadoon	2,500	Anayetee more S. & E.
Albooalee	Saadon	2,500	On a creek, no name

172. Stocqueler 1832, vol. 1, p. 78.

173. Layard 1846, p. 44.

174. Chirikov 1989, vol. 2, p. 471.

175. Pelly 1865 a, p. 36.

176. Layard 1846, p. 39.

177. Lorimer 1915, p. 960; Najm al-Molk 1342, pp. 79, 105 (the Ka`b can field 12,000 horse and foot). In 1863, the men at Falahi all had "long flintlocks manufactured in Baghdad." Pelly 1865 b, p. 125.

178. Curzon 1892, vol. 2, p. 322. For particulars about the remaining tribal groups of the dispersed Ka`b see Zarrabi 1342, pp. 286-92.

179. Stocqueler 1832, vol. 1, pp. 84-85 (picture of a woman on the frontispiece of 2nd volume).

Sowayhut	Showash	2,500	Do. do.
Almukhudum	Shureeb	4,500	Khoot, near Dorack
Al Khanaferah	Hajee Hamdan	5,000	On road to Dorack, from Mahomerah
Bhawee	Akheel	8,000	On the Jerahee creek or mouth
Zoorgan	Jubbur	8,000	On pastoral grounds
Sherayfat	Meer Muhanna	10,000	Hindeean and on the plains
Amoor	Shooheetee	10,000	Wandering and pastoral
Beni Khaled	Shadee	5,000	Ditto ditto
Total	-	68,000	-

Source: Pelly, "Remarks," p. 37.

The number of 15, 722 fighting men (see Table 4.4) does not include the number of the Moheysin of Mohammareh, who, in 1850 numbered 2,000 families and could field 4,000 men.[180] However, their willingness to collaborate with the supreme Sheikh after 1838 was close to zero.[181] By the turn of the twentieth century, they had a force of 6,000 men; the Sheikh of Mohammareh claimed that it was double that figure. The total number of Moheysin in Qajar Iran was estimated at 12,000. About three-quarters of the men had rifles and about 15% had a horse.[182]

Table 4.4: Number of fighting men of the Banu Ka`b per sub-division (ca. 1890)

Dris	` Asakireh	4,750
	Ghubais (Al Bu)	3,042
	Nassar	1,200
Khanafireh		4,680
Muqaddam		2,050
Total		15,722

Source: Lorimer, *Gazetteer,* p. 960.

180. Chirikov 1989, vol. 2, p. 471; Amanat 1983, p. 190.

181. Curzon 1892, vol. 2, p. 322.

182. Lorimer 1915, p. 1253; see also Administration Report 1905-1906, pp. 32-33 that provides updated figures.

As is clear from the above, the supreme Sheikh of the Ka`b could not always count on the support of his tribesmen. Both the Qajar and Ottoman governors used bribes and other means to play the subordinate Sheikhs against each other and to fan dissension among them. Therefore, the supreme Sheikh had his own military force, in addition to other means, to enforce his authority. Sheikh Thamir, for example, "chiefly relies on 3 small guns (4, 8, 12 lbs) better mounted that those in the Persian army and worked by 40 Persians, who had been drilled by a fugitive Tehran artillerist. They are very effective, because Arabs hate to face artillery, but the gunners were not very good and could not be relied upon in a serious fight." Again, he had several other unmounted guns that were placed on the walls of Falahiyeh. They were old and hardly fit to be used. Sheikh Thamir also owned three bombs and mortars, but he was unable to use them. After Mo`tamed al-Dowleh had taken Falahiyeh he destroyed the guns on the walls.[183]

Extent of Ka`b Territory

The Ka`b occupied most of Khuzestan. The limits of Ka`b territory extended north as far as territories of Shushtar and Ramhormuz; more in particular from above Weys, a village on the river Karun, to Khalifabad, a village on the river Jarrahi. To the east it was limited by Behbahan (the Zeytun hills to the Zuhra or the river of Hendiyan), including Hendiyan, which was in their possession. To the south they were spread along the Persian Gulf as far as Basra. To the west they were limited by the Karun, where they inhabited the western or right bank of the river, but did not extend far into the interior. They also occupied its banks from Weys and Samaniyeh (two small villages) and Ahvaz to its junction with the Shatt al-Arab, and both banks of the Bahmanshir, to the Persian Gulf. Their land was mainly watered by the Tab, Jarrahi and its tributaries and the Karun on the west. The most important rivers in Iran thus traversed the country controlled by the Ka`b. It was a large country certainly taking into account its small population. Between the rivers and their adjacent swamps there were vast sandy plains without any supply of water except during the rainy season and the few months thereafter. The most fertile area was that around Falahiyeh. The main products of Ka`b territory were dates, rice, grains, while it was famous for its horse breeds. Otherwise the Ka`b tribesmen had herds of goat and sheep.[184] Despite the abundance of water, man-high grass was only available in spring during good years. In dry years it was too short for horses and other cattle and thus only fit for sheep and goats. Young grain was only available in small quantities near towns when reserves of old chopped straw had run out.[185] The principal towns were Falahiyeh, Ahvaz, Hendiyan, Ma`shur, Qobban and Jarrahi.[186] In 1850 the Ka`b terri-

---

183. Layard 1846, p. 39. Qajar governors behaved in the same way. Mafi 1861, vol. 1, p. 111.

184. Kinneir 1973, pp. 85-86; Layard 1846, pp. 36, 44; de Bode 1845, vol. 2, p. 112; Stocqueler 1832, vol. 1, pp. 88-90; Loftus 1857, p. 287; Pelly 1865 a, pp. 34-36, 39-40; Lorimer 1915, p. 962; Fasa'i 1378, vol. 1, p. 780, vol. 2, 1616.

185. Pelly 1865 a, pp. 35, 40; Ibid. 1865 b, pp. 129-30.

186. Kinneir 1973, p. 88

tory had 50 villages.[187] Many of these were scattered, "many of them like most of the Jerrahi, composed of huts built of reed. Villages come and go every day, due to disappearance of pasture, destruction of watercourses or other causes."[188]

Table 4.5: Names of districts in Ka`b territory and their number of villages (ca. 1850)

Name district	Number of villages
Falahi	9
Jarrahi	8
Hendiyan	3
Ahvaz	3
Mohammareh	27
Total	50

Source: Amanat, *Cities & Trade*, p. 189.

Falahi or Falahiyeh or Falahiyeh-ye Dowraq

In the past the town was called Dowraq, but once cultivation started the area the name was changed to Falahi or Falahiyeh. It was here where the Sheikhs lived in houses built from reed and mud, so wrote Fasa'i.[189] Falahi was situated on a low marshy ground, on the banks of two of the branches of the Jarrahi. The high and thick walls of the citadel (the ancient limits of the town), were about a mile and a half to two miles in circumference, built of mud, sixteen feet in thickness, and flanked, at regular distances, with round towers, which by 1840 were almost in ruins. In 1863, when Pelly visited the town, the walls also had become broken down. He further noted that "between the wall and the houses it is all swamp: beyond all marsh. The whole affair looks like a bad edition of Baghdad on a small scale." Although the wall was not very strong, the town had a strong barrier against Persian attacks in the many deep canals and water courses around it. The Jarrahi was two miles above it, and divided into two branches, one was called Nahi Busi and ran into the sea at Khur Musa near Bandar Mash`ur; the other ran through Falahiyeh and was lost eventually in irrigation, except for one artificial branch that ran into the Karun about 10 miles above Mohammareh. There were but few houses within the walls, as the majority of the about 8,000 inhabitants preferred living in the suburbs, under the shade of date- and pomegranate trees. In fact there were so many date trees, that "you cannot see it [Falahiyeh] at all at once," Pelly noted. According to Stocqueler, the style of the houses was different from those in the Persian Gulf and Euphrates

---

187. In the 1880s the Falahi district had 45 villages that are listed by Fasa'i 1378, vol. 2, pp. 1414-15; see also Kazeruni 1367, p. 30 who mentions 46 fortified villages (*qal`eh-ye ma`mur-e abad*).

188. Layard 1846, p. 44.

189. Fasa'i 1378, vol. 2, p. 1413 (he also gives a description of the extent of the district); see also Kazeruni 1367, p. 30. The weight of Falahiyeh was still known as *man-e Dowraq* throughout Khuzestan in 1888. Mafi 1361, vol. 1, p. 119 (with a description of the town). For a modern description of the town, which is now called Shadegan, see Zarrabi 1342, p. 281.

area, for they resembled English cottages, "having a sloping roof of compact thatching," but otherwise unsubstantial, that walls only being thick layers of long reeds, "whose summits are interwoven with the thatching." Within this citadel, on the left bank of the river "there is the Koote or palace of the sheikh," which by 1840 was in partial decay. According to Kinneir, it was "a miserable structure, build of sun-dried bricks." There was a spacious square or *meydan* in the center of the palace; "one side is occupied by the sheikh's artillery (8 pieces of brass long 9-pounders and 2 iron howitzers) all ornamented with the arms of Portugal." Shustari complained about the filthy and unhygienic conditions of the town as well as its bad water and climate; he did not stay long. The town was famous for the production of *'aba*s or cloaks, which were exported all over Iran and Arabia. Otherwise around 1810, there was little trade, while the bazaars were badly supplied. This situation improved somewhat with the growth of Mohammareh, for Falahi had become to some extent a depot for goods for Dezful and Shushtar and Khuzestan throughout. According to Pelly, "From one to two hundred vessels of from 50 to 60 tons burden are said to arrive here yearly and carry away rice, dates, barley, wheat and horses." Despite increased trade the commercial infrastructure remained rather basic. Pelly remarked that "the bazaar is a miserable place built of sun-dried bricks, imperfectly covered with matting. There are not above twenty shops in it; most of the shops are in reed huts."[190]

There was communication between Mohammareh and Falahiyeh via the canals leading to the Jarrahi and goods were transported in small boats locally called balam and shvuya; the latter was a smaller sailing boat than a baghaleh. Rawlinson did not believe that Kazeruni was right when he claimed that one also might ride along the banks of the canals on horseback, because he believed that these banks were so densely covered with reeds that no horseman could pass. However, Stocqueler walked on the shore, for "the river's banks presented merely a narrow range of tamarisk and other wild shrubbery."[191] The canals were not always passable for this depended on the time of the year and other circumstances.

> These canals are of little importance during the dry season, only the Junjari, Kulli and Umm al-Zakhr (Oom-l-sakhar) are not fordable during the rains and succeeding months. The Jerrahi is deep, its banks steep, and in its narrowest part (above its division into 3 large canals immediately above Fellahiyeh) 55 yards in width and often 100. A large dam at the separation of the three canals of Ghiyadhi, Fellahiyan and Boteinat, form a barrier in the progress of the river, this insuring a supply of water in the smaller canals for irrigation. The dam or kashwah when in repair the 3 canals beyond it are fordable; when it is destroyed, which is always done on the approach of an enemy, the canals become deep and broad and the land is flooded all around. The dam is made of mud and reed is easy made and broken. In the smaller canals there are smaller dams to regulate water. Vessels from Koweit and Arabia can sail on the Junjeri and Kolfi. The tide rises from 5-6 feet even above the village of Bust.[192]

190. Kinneir 1973, pp. 88-89; Stocqueler 1832, vol. 1, p. 73; Layard 1846, pp. 40, 43; Pelly 1865 b, p. 124; Shushtari 1363, p. 182. Rice was cultivated in the marshy districts of Falahiyeh. Administration Report 1878-79, p. 20.

191. Kazeruni 1367, p. 31; Schofield 1989, vol. 1, p. 376; Stocqueler 1832, vol. 1, p. 61.

192. Layard 1846, p. 40.

Ma'shur

Bandar Ma'shur was a port and situated at about 55 km ESE from Falahiyeh. It was situated at about 8 km from the sea, but via a manmade canal small vessels could reach the port 3 km away. There they unloaded their goods at a place called *sif* or port, where these were then loaded onto pack animals. Kinneir described Ma'shur in 1810 or thereabouts as a village with 700 people that had some small trade. It had good water from a well outside the gate.[193] Stocqueleur visited Ma'shur in 1831, which clearly had grown in size. "Mashoor is a walled town with about a mile in circumference," with about 1,000 people, who were mostly engaged in trade. They were well-off, their houses, though small, had many European luxuries. The only source of drinking water was brackish from wells outside the town.[194] By 1860, Ma'shur had fallen on bad times and was much smaller in population and importance. According to Pelly, Ma'shur was by then "a miserable place, half in ruins and built on a mound apparently artificial," where not more than 300 people lived in addition to some visiting merchants. Most of the population dressed like Persians, and only a few spoke Arabic. During winter time it looked as if the town's entire surroundings were swamps and flooded lands. "From 40 to 50 bugalows of about 60 tons each arrive hear yearly, bearing coarse cloth, corn, and dates from Bushehr, Koweit, and Bussorah, and carrying away wool."[195]

Deh Mullah

In 1831, "*Dere Mullah* is a considerable town on the left bank of the *Tab*, or Endian river" at 8 farsang from Ma'shur. "It is surrounded on three sides by a wall of mud and stone, the river occupying the fourth. Above the postern, or principal entrance, is a high circular tower, armed with loopholes for the defence of the town against assaults."[196]

---

193. Kazeruni 1367, p. 34; Kinnier 1973, p. 91.

194. Stocqueler 1832, vol. 1, p. 84 (Sheikh 'Ali Khan was its chief in 1831).

195. Pelly 1865 a, p. 35; Ibid. 1865 b, p. 130. The possible reason for the decline was the outbreak of the plague around 1840 that had decimated the population. Kazeruni 1367, p. 34 (Bandar Ma'shur paid Sheikh Thamir 1,200 *qorush-e 'eyn* and one excellent colt; Ibid., p. 35). For the situation in 1882 see Najm al-Molk 1342, p. 106.

196. Stocqueler 1832, vol. 1, pp. 85-86 (Sheikh Ahmad was its chief in 1831); Najm al-Molk 1342, pp. 105, 110.

Ahvaz

Ahvaz, according to Kinneir, was a miserable place of 60 inhabitants in 1810 or so.[197] Mignan estimated its population in 1827 at not more than 1,600 people. The town occupied only a small portion of the site of ancient Ahvaz, the remnants of whose buildings were built with stones from its ruins. According to Layard, it was but "a mere collection of Arab huts."[198] In 1857, the situation of Ahvaz had not changed much for it was described as "nothing beyond the usual collection of miserable hovels, constructed of mud and stone, grouped together without attempt at regularity of streets or thoroughfares ... utterly without drainage or provision for cleanliness or ventilation. It may contain from fifteen hundred to two thousand inhabitants."[199] In the 1870s, the population had dropped significantly to some 200 to 300 people.[200]

Hendiyan

Around 1810, Hendiyan occupied both banks of the Tab River and was "almost 2 miles in circumference; it has a wall, but broken down in many places, and are nowhere above three feet thick." The town was estimated to have between 4-5,000 inhabitants and lived from the trade with Basra and Behbahan.[201] In 1842, it had 1,200 families that were doing well, and 300 that were in dire straits. In the past, before the plague, the town did quite well. In 1842, the bazaar had 40-50 shops representing all crafts and trades, most of them originating from Bihbahan. There were four mosques, three of which were in use; the fourth being in ruins. The town paid 1,200 *tuman*s per year to Sheikh Thamir.[202] Although Hendiyan was an entrepot for Behbahan, around 1861 Pelly found no ferry to cross the river, which was only "navigable for light boats and canoes [*balam*] to within a short distance of Behbehan." He further found the town in ruins with not more than 4-500 inhabitants. Trade was small with only some buggarahs coming from Kuwait and Bushehr.[203]

---

197. Kinneir 1973, p. 89.

198. Mignan 1829, p. 301; Layard 1971, p. 239; Selby 1844, p. 225. Around 1850 the chief of Ahvaz was "Sheikh Ibbara." Loftus 1857, p. 290.

199. Hunt 1858, p. 283 (with a color drawing of Ahvaz).

200. In 1876, Ahvaz was described as a village with some 200 inhabitants. FO 60/383, f. 326. Najm al-Molk 1342, p. 34 called Ahvaz a village in 1882 where 60 Arab families lived.

201. Kinnier 1973, pp. 90-91.

202. Kazeruni 1367, p. 37.

203. Pelly 1865 a, p. 35; Ibid. 1865 b, pp. 132-33; Najm al-Molk 1342, pp. 105, 110.

Mohammareh

The district and town of Mohammareh was also called Dura; it acquired its new name "from the redness of the earth."[204] Kasravi relates that in the *Tarikh-e Ka'b* the new settlement was first mentioned during the rule of Sheikh Gheyth as Kut al-Mohammareh.[205] The town was built by Mirdow and his son Hajj Yusof in about 1812 on the orders of Sheikh Gheyth at the time when the Ka'b withdrew before the Muntafiq from the left bank of the Shatt al-Arab. Sheikh Thamir told the Boundary Commission: "My brother walled Mohammara to protect it against the wild Arabs." The original construction was a petty fort on either side of the Haffar canal, which at that point was 150 meters across. Its palm groves extend to the Shatt al-Arab.[206] Sheikh Thamir further declared that Mohammareh was walled, with permission of Da'ud Khan Pasha of Baghdad, after Mohammad 'Ali Mirza had attacked Falahiya, "when my brother Ghais was chief of the Chaab."[207] This statement, made when he was supporting the Ottoman claim to Mohammareh, is at odds with another statement of his, viz. that his brother believed the fort to be strong enough to oppose the governor of Baghdad.[208]

Given its defensive nature against attacks from the other side of the Shatt al-Arab and the fact that it was built on a canal with the new walled fortification built on both banks of the Haffar canal mirrored the original settlement of Qobban. Mirdow, the slave of Sheikh Gheyth, lived in the fort on the northern bank of the Haffar. When he died his son Hajj Yusof replaced him, and on his death in 1819-20 his younger brother Hajji Jaber took over.[209]

---

204. Schofield 1989, vol. 1, pp. 104-08.

205. Kasravi 1333, p. 128. The area where Mohammareh was built has been inhabited since ancient times and earlier urban settlements, such as Alexandria and Bayan, are said to have existed there. Eqtidari 1348, p. 845; Kasravi 1333, p. 124. Before it became known as Kut al-Sheikh or Kut al-Fares the southern village was known as "Maharzi." Schofield 1989, vol. 1, p. 175.

206. Rawlinson 1989, vol. 1, p. 296. According to Chirikov 1989, vol. 2, p. 464, Mohammareh was built in the 1820s. However, according to captain Kemball, Mohammareh already had acquired some importance as a town at the end of Karim Khan's reign and seems to have thrown off the dependency off Basra at that time and placed itself under the protection of the Ka'b whose Sheikh appointed its governors. Schofield 1989, vol. 1, p. 125. In view of the other evidence Kemball seems to be mistaken about the existence of Mohammareh in the 1770s. He may have mistaken it for Haffar. According to Administration Report 1878-79, p. 21, the orthography of Mirdaw is Mardaw and Mardao, according to Administration Report 1881-82, p. 5.

207. Schofield 1989, vol. 1, p. 175.

208. Schofield 1989, vol. 1, p. 108.

209. Rawlinson 1989, vol. 1, pp. 296-97; Kasravi 1333, pp.125-26.

Mohammareh's European quarter around 1900

The fort on the southern bank of Haffar was invariably held by the Sheikh-in-waiting, because HajjiYusof from the very beginning tended to disregard the authority of the chief of Falahiyeh. "The next heir to the chiefship of the tribe was usually stationed in the fort on the southern bank of the canal, to hold him in check, and to administer the Chaab affairs upon this, their western frontier."[210] During Sheikh Gheyth's rule, his brother Mobader acted as his deputy on the Haffar, and when Mobader succeeded him, the third brother Thamir took over the command of southern Mohammareh. Thamir on becoming chief, placed his nephew Fares at Mohammareh. When he became the chieftain of the Ka`b and moved to Falahiyeh his brothers Hashem and Mohammad were placed at Mohammareh. The southern fort although originally part of Mohammareh was called Kut al-Sheikh, while the northern part was just called Mohammareh. Kut al-Sheikh, later Kut al-Fares, depended directly from Falahiyeh, but the chief at Mohammareh sometimes acted without acknowledging the authority of the supreme chief.[211] Kut al-Sheikh was also smaller than Mohammareh. In 1850 it had a population of only 150 families or some 800 people, who lived in huts made of mud or date palm-leaf matting. The place only had one caravanserai.[212]

In 1850 there were 600 brick houses covered with reeds and huts made of palm-leaf matting in Mohammareh. The number of people was about 2,000 consisting of Arabs, Turks, Persians, Parsis, Indians, Sabeans and African slaves from Abyssinia, Nubia, Barbary and the coasts of the Persian Gulf. There was a mosque with a minaret, two prayer-houses, a most

---

210. Rawlinson 1989, vol. 1, p. 296; Saldanha 1986, vol. 7/1, p. 114.

211. Rawlinson 1989, vol. 1, p. 297; Stocqueler 1832, vol. 1, p. 67.

212. Amanat 1983, p. 90.

miserable bazaar, two caravanserais and the walled house or citadel of Hajj Jaber, which also contained some of the town's public buildings. The bazaar had about 100 shops, of which 17 were well-stocked with Manchester goods. There were in all some 70 traders from Bushehr, Behbahan, Shushtar, Dezful, Basra and Kuwait. The town was most filthy with dead animals lying around, other filth, stagnant pools, dust and an awful stench. The town as before had a wall on three sides, which was ruined in many places. The wall was made of soft, slimy earth and had towers. The two closest to the canal were defenses against the approach by water. There was a moat or rather a trench around the wall, which was only filled with water near the canal. The rest of the trench was just muddy. There were three small bridges across the trench that gave access to the town. They were simple constructions consisting of palm trees covered with earth and brushwood. There were, however, no town gates, which would have made no sense given the many breaches in the wall as well as holes through which anyone could enter, but only on foot, because they all were too low for a rider. The holes were part of the town's defenses. The fourth side was protected by the Haffar canal, which forms its anchorage (len-gargah) and separated it from Abadan Island. The wall was in particular ruined on the S.W. and N.E. sides. Only the walls of the citadel were in a good condition, but none of the mud walls could withstand artillery fire. The three walls and the shoreline formed almost a quadrangle. The S.W. wall was 720 paces long, the front parallel to it 670 paces; the third part on the opposite side from the river was 520 paces. Outside the town were brick kilns, and N.W. of the town was a small shrine. On the way to it there were the remains of the burst cannon, which had stood on the wall, and had triggered the assault of Mohammareh in 1837.[213]

In 1876, although its trade had diminished much, due to the decline of Shushtat and Dezful, Mohammareh was still "the market for dates, grains, and wool, produced in the neighbouring district, and supplies the Arabs with calicoe, coffee, sugar, &c. The houses are generally built of sun-dried brick, and ruinous, while the streets are filfthy beyond conception. The population is about 3,000. In 1870 the Shah had ordered the construction of fortifications round the town, and a mud wall, twelve feet in height and two in thickness, was built. Rain and wind have, however, made numerous and large breaches in it."[214]

In 1891, its population was about 2,300. The Arabs were cultivators, while the Persians were engaged in trade and handicrafts.[215] Around Mohammareh, "near the Shat-ul-'Arab, the

213. Chirikov 1989, vol. 2, pp. 465-66; Amanat 1983, pp. 89-90 (three caravanserais; 500 families); see also Saldanha 1986, vol. 7/1, pp. 114-16 (Rawlinson in 1844). The town had clearly grown between the time of Rawlinson's visit in 1842 and that of Chirikov in 1850. The former reported that the rebuilt fort of Mohammareh "is a quadrangular enclosure of about 350 yards by 300. It has the usual mud wall with no artillery. It has one caravanserai for merchants, the other buildings in the fort are mud and reed huts for the Arabs living in the fort." Rawlinson 1989, p. 300. According to Loftus 1857, p. 284, "In its present state, Mohammareh consists of a wretched assemblage of huts, containing about three hundred families, and is tolerably furnished with bazaars." For a description of the new defenses in 1857 see Hunt 1858, pp. 238f and Watson 1976, pp. 446-47. For a description of Mohammareh at the end of the nineteenth century see Lorimer 1915, pp. 1255-62 and Najm al-Molk 1342, p. 93.

214. FO 60/383,"Robertson's Report on his visit to the Karoon River 20th May 1876," f. 326. In 1874 it was reported that "exports from the eports of the Beni Kaab in wool, ghee, and grain are considerable. Mohammareh has doubtless a large and important trade, but it is not intended at present to attempt to estimate it." Administration Report 1873-74, p. 10.

215. Administration Report 1891-92, p. 50.

[palm] groves are kept in good order, but elsewhere the trees are dying of age and neglect. They are the property of the Persian Government, and the Arabs who inhabit tem have little interest in their welfare. The cultivator and his Shaikh are aware that any appearance of prosperity would be followed by unduly increased tazation, and they prefer to let decay take its course."[216] In 1892, the population had grown to 3,500, half of whom were from Bahrain. Many immigrants came from districts where security of property was poor, or trade was bad, and/or to avoid conscription, if they came from Ottoman territory. Due to continued immigration from Ottoman lands the population increased to 5,000 in 1895.[217] In 1896, the population grew to 5,600 due to an influx of people from Iraq and Fars where there was scarcity.[218]

Assimilation

Not only had the Ka`b increased in strength and landholdings, also they had changed. From buffalo herders in Wasit with a nomadic lifestyle, they became sedentary to a great extent. In 1840, according to Layard, "Most Cha`b have become deh-nishin or villagers. ... The Cha`b have lost much of their genuine Arab character" The Sheikh exercised despotic power over his subject, and Layard therefore opined that the relationship with the Ka`b Sheikh was not like that of an Arab Sheikh and his tribe. The Ka`b tribesmen also intermarried with Persians especially with natives from Shushtar, Dezful and Behbahan. The principal wife of Sheikh Thamir was the daughter of a chief of Zeytun.[219] Pelly in 1863 observed three distinct groups among the Ka`b. (i) "The Bedouin- wandering, pastoral, tent-loving, disdaining to trade, yet avaricious, and willing to sell his ghee, his mutton, or his horse." They depended on the availability of pasture and followed what nature allotted them. For trading purposes they suffered Jews or Sabeans among them; (ii) Semi-pastoralists, who were partly settled. They cultivated crops, wove `abbas or cloaks, traded, and replaced tents with huts of reeds, and finally (iii) Settled merchants in towns. The Ka`b had become partially Persianized in custom and habits, reason for other Arabs to consider them 'foreigners'. According to Perry, "The Aseel Arab on the other river bank would never intermarry with a Chaab. But a Chaab would not only marry thence if he could, but accept also a Persian in his bed."[220]

Lorimer by the beginning of the twentieth century confirmed the sedentarization process, which although sustained was a gradual one. While the Ka`b had become settled, they were not as yet completely sedentary. They cultivated dates, as well as wheat and barley on the Karun as far as Weys. In November they went to their wheat lands on the Karun leaving

---

216. Administration Report 1878-79, p. 20.

217. Administration Report 1892-93, p. 55; Administration Report 1894-95, p. 56

218. Administration Report 1895-96, p. 76. In 1898, the population was about 7,000. Administration Report 1897-98, p. 97.

219. Layard 1846, p. 44 (properly Zeydan, but locally pronounced as Zeytun).

220. Pelly 1865 a, pp. 37-38, 40, note (with other examples of mutual contempt between Sunni and Shi`i Arabs and between Arabs and Iranians); see also Ibid. 1865 b, p. 125 and Najm al-Molk 1342, pp. 70, 105.

Mohammareh, which was the chief town. In February after having sown they returned to Mohammareh to fertilize their date trees; in May they returned to the Karun to reap wheat and barley; in June-July they reappeared at Mohammareh to the date harvest which began mid-July. They also owned many sheep and goats, some cattle and a few buffaloes. When they returned from Ahvaz they left part of their herds with the Bawi (or plural: Bawiya) tribe.[221] In short, the Ka`b were slowly transforming from nomadic to settled life. There were still some true Bedouins, but the tendency was towards a settled life. "Among the former selling things for money is an alien activity. They cultivate wheat, barley and rice; if they herd they have buffaloes, cattle, sheep, goats and even donkeys. They move around in canoes, fish and fowl." In Falahiyeh they made very fine and light `abas for summer wear.[222]

The Ka`b Arabs "have adopted various Persian ways and customs, such as bowing instead of raising the hand to the forehead, which is the ordinary Arab salutation. Their manners on ceremonious occasions are altogether rather Persian than Arab, and their dress, with the exception of the head-dress is Persian. Persian women, being excellent cooks, are highly esteemed by them as wives.[223]

The assimilation process was not only one of lifestyle (social and economic) but also a cultural and linguistic one. In 1831, according to Stocqueler,

> The language of the Chabeans is, to the west, Arabic; but the traveller will find, as he advances eastward, that it is gradually amalgamates with Persian." Their dress was also a mixture. "They wear the Persian *kabah*, or green tunic, loose trowsers and slippers, the *cummr*, or girdle, and a lilac cloth turban of the same form as the Arabs. The sheikhs wear crimson and gold brocade dresses on extraordinary occasions, but for ordinary use content themselves with crimson chintz, variegated with yellow flowers in imitation of gold.[224]

Loftus who was among the Ka`b some 15 years later came to a similar conclusion. He wrote that the Ka`b were mixed with Persians, and in dress they were more Persian than Arab. "The national black and white striped abba is thrown over the blue cotton tunic and short drawers of the Persian, while an ample black turban, tied in the peculiar fashion of Shuster and Dezful, shields the visage from the sun. Each man carries an immense long musket slung over his shoulder, a sword, and round target of tough bull's hide, studded with large copper nails or bosses."[225]

---

221. Lorimer 1915, pp. 1252-53 (They were all Shi`as, except for the Beyt Ghanim).

222. Lorimer 1915, p. 961. For rice cultivation at Falahiyeh see Mafi 1361, vol. 1, p. 120.

223. Administration Report 1878-79, p. 22.

224. Stocqueler 1832, vol. 1, pp. 79-80.

225. Loftus 1857, p. 285.

Discussion

The history of the Banu Ka`b shows that even when a tribal group is located in an inaccessible area, it can be and will eventually be subdued by the states that encompass it. For borderers it may have been easier than other similar groups to maintain their independence, because they could cross borders when threatened or play one state against the other. However, the larger states also showed a pattern of behavior. For example, Karim Khan's first attack was partly due to the non-payment of revenue that had been paid to the *Vali* of Hoveyzeh and Sheikh Salman actually paid him a considerable sum when he withdrew. Unlike the first one of 1757, Karim Khan's second campaign was not a revenue collecting expedition, but one to subdue a rebellious territory and enforce the regular payment of tribute. The same pattern may be found among the Qajars. First there were a number of revenue collecting expeditions (1818, 1830) and then finally in 1841 there was the expedition mounted by Mo`tamed al-Dowleh to punish and subdue the rebellious Ka`b and incorporate their territory into the Qajar state. These activities did not make the Persians liked by the Arabs.

> Although the upper classes mix familiarly and the Arabs learn from the Persians, their mutual dislike and contempt are inwardly strong, the Persian looking on the Arab as a dull fellow only fit to be multed and cozened, and the Arabs regarding the Persian as a cowardly rogue who has got the better pf hom by stratagem and intrigue. The Arabs firmly believe that if they could but combine, the expulsion of the Persians would be an easy matter, but they know that for them combination is impossible, for no man can be sure of the members of his own family, far less of the Chiefs of other districts and tribes. Between the lower classes of Arabs and Persians the hostile feeling is undisguised.[226]

From the history of Banu Ka`b it is also clear that the only times that they enjoyed independence was either when the central authorities were too weak to intervene in Ka`b territory or when the Ka`b asserted their independence in a proactive manner. For example, when Sheikh Salman in the 1760s fought the Basra government and the EIC to a standstill it got everybody's attention. Rawlinson has rightly characterized the objective of that stage of Ka`b history as "The emancipation of the tribe from any further political dependency upon Bussorah may be regarded as the actual and legitimate issue of the contest."[227] Apart from the difference in economic and military resources between the Ka`b and the Qajar state, the undoing of the Banu Ka`b's independence was their own internal structure. The paramount chief of the Ka`b not only had to deal with two outside powerful centers (Ottoman Baghdad and Qajar Tehran), but also with his own periphery. The Ka`b Sheikhs were often killed by their own tribesmen due to the infighting among the family of the chief and most importantly their authority was constantly being challenged. In particular the behavior of the Sheikh of Mohammareh undermined Ka`b strength and unity. In his challenge of central Ka`b authority the Sheikh of Mohammareh not only weakened the allegiance of

---

226. In 1882, Najm al-Molk 1342, p. 66 opined that Khuzestan could not really be considered to be a part of Iran.

227. Rawlinson 1989, vol. 1, p. 284.

other tribal groups of the Ka`b confederacy, but, more importantly, he allied himself with the Qajar authorities. In doing so, he was able to maintain his independence vis à vis the Ka`b, but the Ka`b lost theirs and initially so did he. For all parties concerned henceforth became obedient subjects of the Qajar Shah. The Sheikh of Mohammareh got the better deal, for he became the major power in south Khuzestan, who even for some time, was able to carve out an autonomous role for himself using the British government in a similar fashion as he had used the Qajar government earlier. But finally he went the same way as the Sheikh of Falahi-yeh and was incorporated into the modernizing state of Iran, when there was no further place for independent peripheral forces.

CHAPTER FIVE

THE BANDAR ʿABBAS - ISFAHAN ROUTE IN THE LATE SAFAVID ERA (1617-1717)

Introduction

In a detailed article published in 1979,[1] Heinz Gaube made an important contribution to our knowledge of the various stages of the important trade route which connected Bandar ʿAbbas with Lar, and onwards with Shiraz and Isfahan. In addition, Gaube gave us detailed information on the three types of *khan*s or caravanserais which provided the traveler with shelter and often with food and fodder supplies on this route. By comparing the description of this trade route by Wilson in 1907 with those of some seventeenth century travelers Gaube concluded that very little had changed in 300 years. He was able to identify most of the buildings listed and/or described by these earlier travelers during a field trip that he made along this route in 1977. However, as will be clear from what follows, the halting places along this trade route were far more numerous than Gaube and the sources which he has used indicate. Also, when going beyond Lar on the same route, we note that there had been changes in the halting stations, especially on the Shiraz-Isfahan stretch in the 19th century. Unfortunately, I have not been able to follow Gaube's example and travel the same route, whilst identifying the various historical locations and buildings. Nevertheless, the number of additional known and regularly used halting places on the Bandar ʿAbbas -Lar stretch, including caravanserais, is twice that of the number listed by Gaube. It is therefore of historical geographical interest to discuss these other locations. Also, because some of them indicate that the manner of seeking shelter was not limited to caravanserais. The additional new data have been mainly taken from Dutch sources, in particular, from the routes taken by the Dutch embassies in 1652,

---

1. Gaube 1979, pp. 33-48.

1691, 1701 and 1717 as well as by regular Dutch East Indies Company (VOC) caravans such as in 1645 and 1685, which indicate that the route described was the standard normal road taken by trade caravans and other road users. In addition I have used a modern Persian description of the route in 1896, because that describes the road all the way to Isfahan (and beyond).[2] I will not discuss the other route from Bandar ʿAbbas to Shiraz (to the north of the route that is discussed here), which was more difficult to travel and has been described in detail by Preece in 1884. This route passed Tarom, Forgh, Rustak, Darab, Darakan, Fasa, Sarvestan and then Shiraz, and from there onwards to Isfahan. This was the normal trade route prior the reign of Shah ʿAbbas I (1587-1629). It has been suggested that the road from Suru (old Gamron) to Lar, close to the site where later Bandar ʿAbbas would be established, as well as that of Lar-Shiraz probably was principally used for local trade before 1600. However, this seems unlikely given the fact that the road was dotted with caravanserais and that commercial and other travelers regularly used it.[3]

Road Amenities

Two things struck all travelers: (i) the caravanserais and (ii) in the area between Lar and Bandar ʿAbbas, the multitude of water cisterns. Not only were there so many caravanserais, and their form often peculiar, but their use was also free of charge. Usually, they had been built for the public weal as well as their own greater glory by this show of piety by black court eunuchs, other high court officials, governors, rich widows, and merchants who had grown rich in trading along these routes plus others. For not only were they often palatial in design and size, covered with glazed tiles and artwork as well as adorned with gardens and trees, water works and other amenities, but the founders made sure that everybody knew whose money had built the caravanserai, by having his/her name on the wall in beautiful script. Though the use of the caravanserai and cisterns was free of charge (*moft*) it was appreciated if lodgers said a prayer (*doʿa*) for the benefactor. Though many travelers would spend the night in the open air, caravanserais were not superfluous, because the weather was often inclement and both man and animal required shelter. Therefore, if private philanthropy failed to provide a caravanserai on certain stretches of the road (at half a stage distance) the local governor often would take care of the oversight.[4]

Apart from the beauty, size and gratis use of the caravanserais, travelers, noted that as of Lar, all caravanserais till Bandar ʿAbbas were of a different design than elsewhere in the country. For in the Garmsirat (Persian Gulf littoral) all caravanserais were of the same basic

---

2. Sadid al-Saltaneh 1362, pp. 53-71, 579-85.

3. Preece 1885, pp. 403-37. Le Strange 1966, pp. 295-97. This seems to have been the road usually taken by the Portuguese embassies in the early 16th century. Smith 1970, pp. 39-42, though later they also took the route via Lar, Ibid., pp. 64-67; Gabriel 1952, pp. 76, 62. John Newbery took the same route in 1581 as described here. Newberie 1905, pp. 460-63.

4. Kaempfer 1968, pp. 141-42; Ibid. 1976, pp. 729-35; Silva y Figueroa 1667, pp. 52, 104; Richard 1995, vol. 2, p. 189. For a translation of the text commemorating the founder on the caravanserai at Biriz see Chardin 1811, vol. 8, pp. 477-78. See also Membré 1993, p. 48.

type, viz. the square cruciform design open to all four sides to stimulate a stream of air. They all had a *bad-gir*, or wind catcher, where the forced air was cooled by water which it had to pass. Those not accustomed to the climate were advised not to sleep close to this cooler stream of air. The animals all stayed outside, because these sarays did not have stables.[5]

However, there was also another side to caravanserais. Though built at no cost to the public by the donator, they were often not or inadequately funded to ensure their upkeep and maintenance. The custodian or *dokkandar* or *oda-bashi*, who infrequently resided near the caravanserai to sell provisions to travelers (in particular in the Garmsirat), was but a local man, making some extra money as a sutler working on his own account.[6] Therefore, over time these admirable buildings decayed and became dilapidated. In other cases their frequent and indiscriminate use and their being a public good meant that nobody felt responsible for them and some turned into pigsties in the worst of cases, others were just not clean. They were a far cry from the inns and hostels that travelers were accustomed to in Europe.[7]

> Coming to our Inns [karavansarays], we have no Host, or Young Damosels to bid us Welcome, nor other Furniture than Bare Walls; no Rooms swept, nor Cleanly Entertainment, Tables neatly Spred, or Maidens to Attend with Voice or Lute to Exhilarate the Weary Passenger; but instead of these, Apartments covered with Dung and Filth; Musick indeed there is of Humming Gnats pricking us to keep an unwilling Measure to their Comfort: So that there is neither Provision for Man or Beast, only an open House, with no enlivening Glass of Pontack, or Poniant Cheer to encourage the Badness of the March; but every Four or Five Pharsangs, i.e. Parasangae, a German League, on the King's High way, a Caravan Ser Raw, as dirty as Augeus his Stable, those before always leaving the next comer work enough to cleanse where they have been; that after coming in Tired, they are more intent to spread their Carpets for Repose, than remove the incrusted Cake of Sluttery, the constant Nursery of Flies and Beetles, they often bringing their Horses into the same Bed-Chamber.[8]

Although the presence of many caravanserais along the trade artery between Bandar ʿAbbas and Isfahan suggests that travelers stayed there as a matter of course, this was not necessarily the case. Depending on the circumstances such as the weather, the availability of space, the state of cleanliness, the availability of victuals, or some other reason, travelers decided whether they would stay at a caravanserai or not. Oftentimes they did not, even where, such as at Gichi (or Gachin), there were two beautiful caravanserais. A Dutch party in 1645, e.g. did not stay at one of the caravanserais, but rested in the open air near a water

---

5. Tavernier 1930, p. 322; Silva y Figueroa 1667, pp. 53, 94. For detailed studies on the types of caravanserais see Siroux 1949; Kleiss and Kiani 1367.

6. Le Gouz 1653, p. 115; Richard 1995, vol. 2, p. 189.

7. Chardin 1811, vol. 8, pp. 225, 221, 477; Fryer 1909, vol. 2, pp. 197-98.

8. Fryer 1909, vol. 2, pp. 178-9, vol. 3, pp. 26-28; see also Herbert 1929, p. 51, who, though more complimentary, also remarked that service could not be relied upon.

tank.[9] In fact, it was quite normal that the travelers stayed in tents outside the caravanserai.[10] If the heat was too oppressive or just because it took the travelers' fancy they might just stay out in the open, in a garden, or a date grove, or just in the 'wilderness'. It also happened that travelers would stay for the night with nomads.[11] However, more frequently, travelers lodged in houses in one of the villages they passed through, a practice that was usual whenever the caravanserais were full, or when these were considered to be inhabitable. Important travelers often stayed in the village chief's house (*kalantar, ra'is*).[12] Also, the travelers would lodge in some other building in the village such as a mosque.[13] At roads that were not frequented much, or were far off the highway, villagers usually had a dilapidated house set aside for travelers, though important persons usually stayed in the best house in the village. Peasants were very friendly to travelers unlike their European counterparts. Travelers were welcomed with a carpet, flowers, fruit and whatever the village had to offer. The village elders came to keep the guests company and divert them, while the rest of the village's population came for *tamasha*, i.e., to ogle the strangers. Eventually a loose woman would show up offering her service, if it was wanted.[14] Of course, in the majority of cases the travelers used the caravanserais, but it is quite clear from the available evidence that the various alternatives were used on a regular and frequent basis.

The second road amenity that drew the appreciation, if not the admiration of travelers, was the many water cisterns which made both living and traveling in the Garmsirat possible. For in many areas there was no water to be had and therefore artificial means had to be applied to provide the peasant and/or traveler with this basic need. The Persians distinguished the following sources of water. First those filled with rain water or cisterns were known by various terms such as *ab-e anbar, ab-e berkeh*; second there were those springs gushing forth from the rocks known as *ab-e bongerd, ab-e ghadir*. Then you had dug wells or *ab-e chah*, and sources of fresh natural running water, known as *ab-e cheshmeh* and *ab-e rud*, and finally the more pedestrian variety the *ab-e howz* or the domestic water pond, which did not lack in either urban homes or public buildings of any kind.[15] The rain water cisterns or *berkeh*, like the caravanserais, were built by rich persons to assist their fellow human beings. It also helped, of course, that they used the same road or town, and was it not useful to have water cisterns?

Water cisterns came in different types and the travelers noted that variety. The cistern of Mokhak was large and circular, four to five fathoms in diameter and very deep. "It is covered with a great Dome of rough stone, that hath six Entries, by so many Doors that are round it, by which they go it to draw water, which in the Spring-time is so high, that it comes almost

---

9. *NA,KA* 1057, f. 359-85, "Dagh Register gehouden bij den oppercoopman Leonard Winninx 'tsindert den 6 Julij anno 1645 dat uijt Gamron naer Spahan vertreckt, tot den 24e November, daeraen volgende, als wanneer in gemelte Gamron wederom gearriveert is." October 11, 1645 (Henceforce cited as Winninx, referring to the dates rather than folio numbers for easier reference). Winninx, July 7 (Gitsj).

10. For various instances see Valentijn 1726, vol. 5, pp. 260-66.

11. Winninx, November 14 (at Banaru).

12. Stodart 1935, pp. 74-75; Tavernier 1930, p. 323.

13. Stodart 1935, p. 75; Silva y Figueroa 1667, p. 140.

14. Kaempfer 1968, pp. 141-42; Ibid. 1976, p. 731.

15. Kaempfer 1976, p. 728.

up to the Doors, swelling so high by the Rain-water in the Winter-time, by means of a Trench that comes from a neighbouring Hill: at each Door there are steps to go down to the bottom, when the water is low, for there is no other water in that place. They make, besides, in those Quarters Cisterns after another manner; they are of an Oblong Square, covered with a long Convex Vault, shaped much like the Roof of a Coach, with a Door at each end: and one of these ways are all the Cisterns from that place to Bender [Abbas], built."[16]

The same problem that bedeviled other public goods also affected the water cisterns. When the first rains fell the cisterns were not filled, for these rains were used to clean out the dirt etc. from the storage tanks. Also, not all cisterns in Lar e.g. were open to the public at the same time. Usually three were open, and despite the fact that the quality of the water was not very good, it was a very precious good in this arid zone. Because the stored water was not used for years sometimes, the water was filled with Guinea worms, which, if the water was not boiled or passed through a cloth sieve, caused considerable discomfort to the consumer.[17]

Because there was neither real supervision in the manner of their use beyond their rotation and annual filling, nor of their maintenance, the cisterns became dilapidated overtime. Rather than rehabilitating them, benefactors preferred to build new ones. It was better to be known as the builder of something new than as the maintenance person of somebody else's construction.

> These Cisterns or Storehouses for Rain are digged out of the Ground deep into the Earth, beyond the Surface of the Sand, and are curiously covered above with Stone, and plastered within with excellent durable Plaster; some Spherical, others Transverse, cutting one another in manner of a Cross; others, and the largest, Oblong, Square, Orbicular, or Oval; which being once finished, like their Caravan Seraws have no Endowment to maintain them, either to keep them clean, or from falling to Decay; so regardless are they of Futurity, that no one is suffered to repair them; On which account it is, that about their great Cities so many of all sorts are found, newly built, superannuated, defiled, (which they esteem so, if either Man or Beast have dropped in and been drowned), unfrequented, and full of Nastiness; so pervicaciously Vainglorious, that they will have the Repute of an entire Founder, or none.[18]

Another item of interest was other constructions that formed an important part of the road network, to wit: bridges and causeways. In the description of the route we will find mention of a few of these road constructions which were built by government officials, merchants or other benefactors. However, money for their

16. Thevenot 1971, vol. 2, p. 128; Chardin 1811, vol. 8, p. 463. The cisterns were circular and about 50 paces in diameter, and all with a dome.

17. Tavernier 1930, p. 320; Herbert 1929, p. 52, who gives a description of the cisterns, was initially more positive about the quality of the water, which was drawn out using *hoseyni*s or leather bags or other vessels, but he was rather negative about the rain water (*ab-e baran*) cisterns in Lar (Ibid. p. 59).

18. Fryer 1909, vol. 2, p. 169.

upkeep was as usual lacking and we observe also gradual decay in the case of these essential components of the road network.

Travel Cost

Though the Bandar Abbas - Isfahan road was a much frequented trade route, we have hardly any information on the cost of traveling or what kinds of food supplies were available to the traveler. We learn from the occasional remarks by several travelers that they were able to buy supplies en route such as butter, milk, cheese as well as to get game such as partridges, deer, and not to forget goat or sheep meat. Finally, many fruits that were cultivated along the route are mentioned and travelers availed themselves of all these excellent products. However, we have no idea how much the cost was for these supplies and in what quantities they were available.

As an appendix to this study a translation of a document from the VOC records has been reproduced. This document details day-by-day, and at what location, how much was spent on food, fodder, repairs, messengers and the like by a group of VOC staff traveling from Bandar Abbas to Isfahan between 10 July to 4 August 4 1645. From this document it is clear that items such as rice[19] and oranges were available in Laristan in addition to normal products such as chickens, bread, yogurt, clarified butter (ghee), fresh butter, and meat. Also of interest is the purchase of dates by the Dutch party to make beer.[20] Necessary repairs of horse tack, horse-shoeing and the like as well as veterinary procedures such as bloodletting could be carried out in the road without any problem, an indication that there was the necessary infrastructure in the villages dotting the trade route.

Description of the Route

Though the starting point of this article is the Bandar Abbas-Lar road, given the fact that this road was but a part of the important trade route to Isfahan, and that a detailed description thereof would be as useful and of historical interest as that for the road to Lar, I have extended the scope of this article to include the road to the Safavid capital city. There will be no discussion of the economic context of the trade route described here for I limit myself to the description of the route itself and the cost of traveling, a subject about which we know very little. Travelers taking the road from Isfahan to Bandar ʿAbbas usually stayed at the same halting places or *manzel*s. However, there were many alternative halting places, especially

---

19. Rice grown in small quantities in southern Fars was known as *champa*. Despite this local production, rice never became a staple in Fars, being too expensive for most. Wulff 1966, p. 242.

20. One traveler mentioned a liquor "distilled chiefly of dates and liquorice leaves [probably the root]. It is called arequy." Teixeira 1902, pp. 197-98. Another traveler mentions that in Lar *eau de vie* was sold which was produced from dates. Le Gouz 1653, p. 114.

near large cities such as Isfahan and Shiraz. But even elsewhere on parts of the road, alternative *manzels*, or even routes, existed. Travelers would change halting places depending whether they were traveling up-country or down-country. In what follows I describe this road in detail, not only by listing the numerous halting places, but also detailing what information is available for each of them. This will give the reader an idea on the size and physical endowment of each location and their relative importance and of what they had to offer to the traveler. I will not detail the time that each traveler took to arrive at the various halting places. This varied per traveler, and depended on the weather, the season, and the haste with which the travelers wanted to get to his next stop. For example, it was not exceptional that travelers reached Mahyar in one day. Others, however, preferred to travel more leisurely and did the same distance in three days. Some did not even stop at Mahyar but continued their journey.

The total distance of the route described here is 180 German miles (each mile = 7407.41 m) or 1,333 km long. Travelers, who were in a hurry, such as the Dutch merchant Leonard Winninx, who had been charged with an important diplomatic mission in connection with a military conflict which had broken out between Iran and the Dutch East Indies Company (VOC), traversed this distance in about thirty days, which included resting days at Shiraz and Lar. He left Bandar Abbas on 6 July 1645 and arrived in Isfahan on 5 August 1645.[21] His return trip began on 25 October and he arrived in Bandar Abbas on 23 November 1645. However, embassies traveled much slower. For example, the Dutch ambassador Jacob Hoogcamer left Bandar `Abbas on 7 April and arrived on 4 June 1701 in Isfahan, while his return trip took from 18 February to 12 April 1702.[22] A normal VOC caravan traveled faster and took about one month to make the journey.[23]

The Isfahan - Shiraz Road

On leaving Isfahan all travelers went to Mahyar. But before reaching this village, travelers had quite a choice of places to stop at before arriving at their next destination. This was due to the fact that the hinterland of Isfahan was heavily populated and that various alternative roads or paths existed, which all went to Mahyar. Our first traveler, Don Garcia de Silva y Figueroa both arrived and left Isfahan via Iarustan.[24] According to Chardin, all travelers for Bandar `Abbas left Isfahan through the Karun city quarter (mahalleh-ye Karan). He himself left via the Bagh-e Qol-e Padeshah (Bag Koullou pad cha; the royal slave garden), then he went

---

21.   On the origins and the conflict itself, including Winninx's mission, see Floor 2004 b, pp. 116-50; Matthee 1999, chapter six.

22.   Valentyn 1726, vol. 5, pp. 272-76, 284-85. The Dutch ambassador Johan van Leene, whose itinerary is also listed here in appendix 1, left Isfahan on 18 October and arrived on 29 December 1691 in Bandar `Abbas. Ibid., vol. 5, pp. 259-67. The English embassy of 1628, led by Sir Dodmore Cotton, left Isfahan on 12 October and arrived on 19 December 1628 in Bandar `Abbas. Stodart 1935, pp. 73-85.

23.   Kaempfer 1968, pp. 85-124. The caravan left Isfahan on 21 November and arrived on 28 December 1685 in Bandar `Abbas. See also appendix 5.2.

24.   Silva y Figueroa 1667, pp. 173, 335.

through the Cheik-Sabanna suburb (mahalleh-ye Sheikh Sabana) and crossed the river at the Shahristan (Chereston) bridge, which was another suburb with many beautiful gardens; he then left Isfahanak (Spahanek) village on the left, and then via Kotal-e Orchini (Koutel hurt chiny) to Mahyar.[25] In 1685 a Dutch money caravan said its farewells, to the staff remaining behind, also in the Bagh-e Qul-e Padeshah (Koli padsja) and after 4 hours, via the village of Osgewan and the Orchini pass, the caravan then arrived at the caravanserai-ye Mirza ʿAli Reza.[26] This caravanserai was named after its founder, who had married one of the shah's sisters. It was badly constructed from clay, its water was brackish and there was no wood. After one hour of further traveling there was a *rahdar*[27] or road guard station, then followed the village of Deh-e zard (Dehserd), and after one *farsakh* the caravanserai Gonaresh? (Gonoresj), which also was a clay building. Then the traveler finally arrived at the village of Mahyar.[28] Another Dutch traveling party, led by the Dutch ambassador Joan van Leene, left Isfahan on 18 October 1691 from the beautiful pleasure garden Bagebatsjaron at 1.5 miles from Isfahan.[29] The caravan then went via the village of Agag Hadi, which had a large, but dilapidated caravanserai, which was built from clay like the houses in the village. Due to the weight of the snow the buildings collapsed. The Ketelaar embassy traveled via the Goes-Jaroen garden (Bagh-e Jush Aran) and Paaij-ammarek, which was half a German mile from this garden. Via the Kotal-e Orchini the van Leene embassy then also passed the small village and caravanserai of Mirza ʿAli Reza and finally arrived at Mahyar.[30] Some went via Lalibeek direct to Mahyar, whilst others rode to Isfahanak, which was as miserable a village as its caravanserai called Takht-e Pulad or Barabaruk, and then via the caravanserai Mirza ʿAli Reza, while Fryer went via Marg, which had an old lonely caravanserai, three miles from the Orchini pass.[31]

25. Chardin 1811, vol. 8, pp. 192-93.

26. Kaempfer 1968, p. 85; Winninx (August 5) stayed in Mohammad ʿAli Beg Isfahani's (Mamet Ali beecq) garden, the shah's steward or *nazer-e boyutat* from 1640-1651; Fryer 1909, vol. 2, p. 239. (Urchin Hills). The Kotal-e Orchini or Stairs Pass is not high, but it was very difficult to get up, because it was very slippery rock. The travelers went one after the other, also because mules fell and threw their baggage, and because most of the traveling was done at night. Thevenot 1971, vol. 2, pp. 119-20. Even during the day people dismounted and went on foot. Speelman 1908, p. 132; see also Chardin, vol. 8, pp. 193-95 and its road guards.

27. For a discussion of the role and functioning of the road guard system see Emerson & Floor 1987, pp. 318-27.

28. Kaempfer 1968, pp. 85-86; Hedges 1967, vol. 1, p. 209 (Moyar); Winninx (26 October - Maijaer); Silva y Figueroa 1667, pp. 173, 336 (Mahier).

29. For a description of this garden see Valentijn 1726, vol. 5, pp. 259, 275.

30. Valentijn 1726, vol. 5, p. 275 (Cotali Ortsini; Miseralisa; Majaart); NA, KA 1793, Dag-Register off Dageljkse aenteijckeningen, nopende het principaelste voorgevallene in d'opreijse, uijt Gamron naer de Coninglijke Residentie Stad Spahan van den E.E. Agtbaeren heer Joan Josua Ketelaer etc. beginnende den 27e maart, en Eijndigende 30e maij A. 1717, f. 1034; Strauszens 1678, p. 186 (Majar). But not every caravan stopped at Mahyar. For example, the Dutch ambassador Hoogcamer on leaving Isfahan on February 18, 1702 stopped at the village of Poskoen or Kietsje and from there went straight to Commesia. Valentijn 1726, vol. 5, p. 284.

31. Speelman 1908, pp. 132, 319 (Spahanek); Herbert 1929, pp. 120-21 (Spahawnet); Winninx (October 25 - Spahannecq); Tavernier 1930, p. 294 (Ispehanek) which was a *rahdar* station; LeBrun 1718, vol. 2, pp. 253-54, 300 (Spahanek; Miersa alresa). For a drawing of the caravanserai see plate 112; Fryer 1909, vol. 2, p. 239 (Mirge). van Dam 1993, vol. 3, p. 328. Another road led from Isfahan, via Vazudar (?) to Mayar. Anonymous 1939, vol. 1, p. 218, n. 4, which refers to the situation before 1622.

What do we know about Mahyar? According to Silva y Figueroa it was a prosperous small and extended village with a nice caravanserai.[32] Herbert wrote that "Moyeor, [was] a considerable town, for it consisted of about a thousand houses: and, albeit their houses were neat, yet there were in no wise comparable to their dove-houses for curious outsiders."[33] In 1651 Speelman described it as small settlement, which was entirely surrounded by villages and gardens. Its caravanserai was a total ruin, reason why travelers were lodged in a large dilapidated castle. This had been the practice already for 30 years according to Speelman judging by the Dutch, English and French names written on the walls. This castle represented the largest area of the village, and in some areas, that were still usable, was used as housing by local families. Based on the size and the cellars and corridors, Speelman believed that the clay and burnt brick building must have covered a considerable area. According to the village chief, the castle was already 600 years old.[34] In 1665, Mahyar was described as a ruined village, though formerly it had been of note, with many gardens and an important agricultural production. However the grand vizier had cut off the village's water supply for a pleasure garden that he had constructed nearby, so that the inhabitants had to satisfy their needs by bringing their victuals from elsewhere because nothing grew there anymore. Water was only to be had from a large pool in the village. Tavernier, who was at Mahyar at the same time as Thevenot, described it as a large village with a good caravanserai[35] Chardin, in 1674, wrote that Mahyar was a large village of 300 houses, which you had to pass through, because it was situated right between two mountains. However, travelers did not stay at the old decayed caravanserai, but rather in houses of the villagers, of whom there were many and who wanted to earn some extra money. The surroundings of the village were rather arid, treeless and without verdure. Nevertheless, it was a nice village where you could obtain all kinds of provisions.[36] This sad situation apparently did not last, for Kaempfer wrote in 1685, that it was a long stretched out, rather populous village, close to the Kuh-e Baba Hoseyn. Its caravanserai, made of bricks, was called Alabek, had been built around 1510.[37] In 1691, it was qualified as a large village with a large new unfinished caravanserai, which had been built by Shah Soleyman. It was unfinished, for laborers were still completing it. The caravanserai had much space for travelers as well as water tanks. It also had many shops where the traveler could buy everything he needed. The caravanserai had a large open space in which a nice *talal* [sic; *talar*] or veranda had been constructed, which was covered with blue tiles, where the traveler could smoke his water-pipe or have a cup of coffee. The stable, which could hold more than 1,000 horses, was still under construction. There were many sheep in the neighborhood, but the water was bad, so much so that ambassador Cuneaus warned his staff not to drink much of it.[38] In 1717, this same caravanserai was still very nice, situated in a garden, which was linked via a tree lined

32. Silva y Figueroa 1667, p 173.
33. Herbert 1929, p. 120.
34. Speelman 1908, pp. 132-33 (Mayaar).
35. Thevenot 1971, vol. 2, p. 121; Tavernier 1930, p. 294 (Mahiar).
36. Chardin 1811, vol. 8, pp. 195-96 (Mayar).
37. Kaempfer 1968, pp. 85-86.
38. Valentijn 1726, vol. 5, p. 259; Fryer, vol. 2, pp. 238-39 (Mayar).

road to Qomisheh. Just outside the caravanserai was a nice small building equipped with a copper tap from which one could get very good and plentiful water.[39]

Continuing from Mahyar the traveler, after 15 minutes, arrived at a Chahar Bagh with an excellent caravanserai which in 1685 was still under construction. The bricks were white and burnt on the spot as was the lime. Via a number of villages (where travelers usually did not stop) [named Isba, Schafid Alibad, Waas nun, Gewabad, Germascha, Dedengun] the town of Qomisheh was reached.[40] In 1617 it had about 400 families and an old caravanserai, and in this town very good arrows were made, while in a village at one day's travel, the best bows of Persia were produced. By 1628, Qomisheh boasted 1,000 houses especially some of great antiquity according to Herbert, though it was described in 1645 as a dilapidated town. Speelman noted that in former times Qomisheh had been a large and populated town, but in 1651 it was an open, rather neglected and run-down one. It was inhabited by inferior artisans and only had some repute because of its gardens and the pigeon towers, which were sometimes inhabited by their owners for two months during the summer time. Tavernier wrote that Qomisheh was a reasonably sized town with a number of caravanserais which though constructed with clay he considered beautiful. The town, in effect, consisted of a string of villages, about half a mile long. According to Chardin, Qomisheh was a small town, though it looked more like a village. The town was more than 3,000 feet all around and its ruins showed that it had been much larger in the past. Its pigeon towers were quite a sight, but the various caravanserais were too small.[41] In 1685, it was considered to be a rather large town which was very densely built. It had a long bazaar, 24 caravanserais, a rather small Friday and other mosques. The town was well supplied with water and rich in agricultural production and you could get wine there. In 1717, the caravanserai was a new and spacious building.[42]

From Qomisheh it was only 15 minutes to the tomb of Shah Reza.[43] In 1645, Winninx visited the village of Shah Reza, where he observed water tanks with fish "from which you may not fish on pain of death." Thevenot confirms the fishpond and says the garden therefore was called Howz-e Mahi and that there was a darvish who prevented anybody from catching the fish therein. He also describes Shah Reza as a pleasant place with many gardens. Tavernier stated that at about three-quarter's of mile, just beyond the town of Qomisheh there was a nice mosque with a fish pond, which the mollahs did not allow anybody to catch because they were dedicated to "their prophets." But travelers used to camp near the pond during summer because of the shade of the trees and the fresher air rather than go and stay in Qomisheh. Kaempfer wrote that this place was known for its fish ponds, water wells and

39. KA 1793, f. 1033 r-vs (Mhaa-Jaar).

40. Kaempfer 1968, p. 87 (Gommosja); Anonymous 1939, vol. 1, p. 218, n. 4.

41. Chardin 1811, vol. 8, pp. 197-98 (Comicha).

42. Silva y Figeroa 1667, pp. 171, 337; Herbert 1929, p. 119 (Commeshaw); Winninx 3 August and 27 October (Comissa; Commischa); Speelman 1908, p. 131 (Commesja); Kaempfer 1968, pp. 87-88; Valentijn 1726, vol. 5, p. 260; Thevenot 1971, vol. 2, p. 120; KA 1793, f. 1032 vs. (Commisja); Tavernier 1930, p. 294 (Comche); Hedges 1967, p. 209 (Comesha); LeBrun 1718, vol. 2, pp. 254, 302, 307 (Cominsja; Kominsja).

43. Kaempfer 1968, p. 87 (Scharesa); arrived at Sjaresa at 0.5 mile from Commissia. Valentijn 1726, vol. 5, p. 260; Winninx, August 3; LeBrun 1718, vol. 2, pp. 254, 307 (Zja-reza) It had a caravanserai. For a drawing see Ibid., p. 308.

its many gardens as well as the cemetery. Fryer went there because the mud caravanserai at Qomisheh was too hot.[44] The road from Qomisheh to Shah Reza was lined with trees and on both sides with gardens.[45]

From Shah Reza, the road went via the Mirza Kuchek garden (after 2.5 *farsakh*), and after 30 minutes to the caravanserai called Mirza Kuchek Qalʿeh (Myrsa Kuczik Kala). It was well built and elegant, but already becoming dilapidated here and there.[46] After half a *farsakh*, one passed the village of Hajji and thereafter the village of Maqsudbegi. This village had only 10 houses and many gardens. The first pigeon towers were evident here. In 1665 it had been described as a new caravanserai, the old one being demolished, which Speelman had qualified as a sober building. The water was drinkable, but the fish were small and had an earthy taste. Fryer had a good opinion of the caravanserai where he stayed in a room, formerly designed for a coffee-house, having a water-tank in the middle and broad seats around to lie or sit on. However, Hedges in 1685, wrote that it was a sorry old ruinous caravanserai, which had bad water. He added that there was a good new caravanserai within half a mile of it, which were not much frequented, for want of provisions. The Dutch, probably referring to the new caravanserai considered the karavasaray of Maqsudbegi still a reasonable building in 1691.[47]

Some 30 minutes distance from Maqsudbegi was another caravanserai built with clay and sun-dried bricks. After 3 *farsakh* the large royal village of Amanabad was reached, which, in 1628 had high, strong walls with battlements resembling a castle and it housed 30 families, mostly Georgians. It was under the administration of Daʾud Khan, brother of the governor of Shiraz. There was a neat caravanserai and banqueting-halls for his own delight, with some rooms painted with imagery and embossed with gold. However, in 1685, it boasted of about 100 houses, many gardens, and a square fortress, built to protect the travelers against bandits who had infested the area. At the entry of the village was a large place with a Qalʿeh-ye Hammam, a mosque and the very beautiful octagonal Allahverdi Khan caravanserai, which was an excellent building.[48]

---

44. Winninx, 3 August (tSara); Thevenot 1971, vol. 2, p. 120; Kaempfer 1968, pp. 87-88 for a detailed description of the tomb; Fryer 1909, vol. 2, p. 237 (Come Shaw; Shaw Rezin); Tavernier 1930, p. 294; Chardin 1811, vol. 8, pp. 198-202 (Cha Reza) with additional information on the fishpond and the tomb.

45. Valentijn 1726, vol. 5, p. 260.

46. This was one of the most pleasant places in Iran, because of its many beautiful gardens and the buildings that Mirza Kuchek (who was *sadr* during 1661-1664) had constructed there. Chardin 1811, vol. 8, p. 202 (Mirza-Kut-chec).

47. Kaempfer 1968, p. 89 (Hadji; Mag sud Begi); Valentijn 1728, vol. 5, p. 260 (Misakoetsiek; Matubeki); Thevenot 1971, vol. 2, p. 120; Speelman 1908, p. 129 (Macsoubegy); Herbert 1929, p. 119 (De-Moxalbeg); Winninx, 2 August (Machsoetbeecq); Fryer 1909, vol. 2, p. 236 (Moxutebeggy); KA 1793, f. 1032 (Magh-Zoet-begie); Tavernier 1930, p. 295 (Maksoubegui); Hedges 1967, p. 209 (Macksood Beigh); Chardin 1811, vol. 8, p. 202-03 (Maxud Begui); LeBrun 1718, vol. 2, pp. 254, 302, 307 (Magsoetbegi).

48. Herbert 1929, p. 119 (Amno-baut, also called Boyall by some; see e.g. Purchas 1905, vol. 8, p. 463 [Boial]); Kaempfer 1968, p. 89 (Amnabad); Allahverdi Khan was governor of Fars and Shah ʿAbbas I's most important general. He was amongst other things the builder of the famous bridge in Isfahan that also carries his name. Valentijn 1726, vol. 5, pp. 260, 275 (Amnabat; Aap Nabaat); Winninx August 1 (Amnabath); Speelman 1908, p. 129 (Amnadabath); KA 1793. f. 1032 (Amnabaath); Tavernier 1930, p. 295 (Amnebad) who states that the builder was Imamqoli Khan, the son of Allahverdi Khan. For a description see Kaempfer 1968, p. 89 (Kala Hammum; Ala Werdi

The next stop after 2-2.5 *farsakh* was Yazdekhvast a peculiar village perched on the mountain, with gardens and a caravanserai, which according to Herbert was the best since Bandar Abbas. Next to the caravanserai was a stone castle with round towers. Winninx recorded that despite the precarious construction of the village, its population did not want to leave, for in their mosque was a wooden pillar, which they believed the patriarch Abraham himself had ordered to be placed there. Their mosque, which had been repaired many times, was built on this pillar. Because of the danger of earth-quakes the population, nevertheless, had started to build houses outside the village with a view to establish a new village there, which would be less vulnerable, according to Thevenot. The village had a nice large caravanserai (a magnificent brick building according to Fryer) built by the merchant, Mirza `Abud (Mirsa Abud). In 1717, the caravanserai was a new strong building.[49]

Bifurcation: Winter and Summer Route

From Yazdekhvast a bifurcation of the route began, which determined whether one took the winter or the summer route. On the left hand, eastwards was the lower road, and the other on the right hand and westward was the higher road. In wintertime, the higher road was filled with snow and could not be used and thus, travelers were obliged to take the lower, so-called winter road which, wrote Thevenot, was one travel day, or according to Chardin two days, longer.[50]

Summer Route

The first location on the summer road was the Kotal-e Na`l-shekani, i.e. the Hill that pulls off the horses' shoes.[51] Afterwards one passed a little castle called Gonbad-Qal`eh, where there

---

Chan) a drawing is in his original manuscript. Chardin 1811, vol. 8, pp. 203-04 (Amnaabad) writes that it was Da'ud Khan, Imamqoli Khan's brother who had build the fortress. Silva y Figueroa 1667, pp. 170, 337 did not mention the village by name, though he mentioned a small village where the governor of Shiraz had built a new caravanserai; LeBrun 1718, vol. 2, pp. 254, 302, 307 (Ammanabaet; Anabaet); Anonymus 1939, vol. 1, p. 218 mention the caravanserai Khan.

49.   Thevenot 1971, vol. 2, pp. 120-1; Winninx, 28 October (Jassegas); Speelman 1908, pp. 126-28 (Jasdegas), Chardin 1811, vol. 8, pp. 204-07 (Yezdecast), and Kaempfer 1968, pp. 89-9 (Jesdegas; Jesdechas), all have detailed descriptions of the village and its water supply. They also mention that here the best wheat of Iran was cultivated and recount the often repeated maxim: *Sharab-e Shiraz, Nan-e Yazdekhvast va Zan-e Yazd*. Chardin added a description of the Cha Resourg [Shah-e Bozorg] mosque. Valentijn 1726, vol. 5, p. 260; Herbert 1929, p. 119 (Yezdecawz); Fryer 1909, vol. 2, pp. 233-34, had the finest wheat (Esduchos); KA 1793, f. 1031 vs (Jes de ghaes); Tavernier 1930, p. 295 (Yesdecas); Hedges 1967, p. 209 (Yes-de-gas); Silva y Figueroa 1667, pp. 169, 337(Hies-de-Gas); LeBrun 1718, vol. 2, pp. 254, 302, 307 (Jesdegaas) and plates 113 and 114; Anonymus 1939, vol. 1, p. 219, note.

50.   Thevenot 1971, vol. 2, p. 121; Chardin 1811, vol. 8, p. 242.

51.   Chardin 1811, vol. 8, p. 220 (Koutel nalt che Keny); Thevenot 1971, vol. 2, p. 121 (Chotali-

was a ruined village. Speelman called it a small village, in which a few families lived. It was an old fortress, with a tomb in which a holy man named Imamzadeh-ye Mohammad Hajji was buried, the reason for its name [Gonbad = dome]. The latter is confirmed by Chardin, who like Tavernier also referred to a ruined castle with four towers. Kaempfer mentioned the dilapidated fortress, which had good water, and was inhabited by some Lurs and a recently arrived *rahdar*.[52] The Dutch embassy in 1691 considered Gonbad-Qal`eh to be a miserable caravanserai, which formerly had been a fortress of rebels. Also, close by was a square old tomb with an Imamzadeh, which was still partly tiled. The water was of reasonably quality.[53] The rebellion referred to must have taken place after July 1645, for Winninx mentioned the stronghold as having been built a few years ago to provide security to travelers, because the area had been infested with bandits.[54]

The next stop was Dehgerdu a small village in a very barren place, but with good water, though Winninx called it a miserable village.[55] Thevenot, who tried his hand at the etymology of the name of the village, writes that Dehgerdu meant the village of nuts, of which there were very few there, for the ones the inhabitants ate came from Lar. Chardin wrote that it had the best water in the world and all kinds of provisions. Kaempfer found it a small compact village, with small flat houses, and an old square brick-built caravanserai and, in 1691 Dehgerdu was qualified as a nice place with a good caravanserai, but by 1717 it had become totally dilapidated, but the embassy stayed there anyway.[56] In addition to the caravanserai and quite opposite to it, there was square circumvallated building constructed by Tahmaspqoli Beg, governor of Bandar Abbas in 1651, who had built it on the orders of Imamqoli Khan to lodge important persons, because the old caravanserai offered little comfort. In 1702, LeBrun called it a sorry caravanserai.[57]

After Dehgerdu the road led to a small fortress, Kala Kewilar, in the village of Kivilaar which had a beautiful caravanserai with very good water, but had become totally dilapidated by

---

Naar-Schekeni).

52. Speelman 1908, pp. 125-26 (Gommesella; Mansada Mahometh Hasi; Gombes = dome); Thevenot 1971, vol. 2, p. 121 (Chotali-Naar-Schekeni; Gombez Cala); Kaempfer 1968, p. 91 (Gumber allalah); Winninx, July 31 (Combazala); via the mountain Naatsikan; Valentijn 1726, vol. 5, p. 260 (Combesilala); Tavernier 1930, p. 295 (Kotal innal tekeheni; Gombeslala); Herbert 1929, p. 118 (Gumbazelello) ascribed the best wheat-bread to this town; Chardin 1811, vol. 8, p. 220 (Gombes lala).

53. Valentijn 1726, vol. 5, p. 260; LeBrun 1718, p. 308 (Gombes-Lala) very small village.

54. Winninx, 31 July.

55. Stodart 1935, p. 74 (Dehegerdow); Winninx, 31 July; Herbert 1929, p. 118 (Degardow); Silva y Figueroa 1667, pp.169, 338 (Derguiguer) in which a small house belonging to the governor of Shiraz; LeBrun 1718, vol. 2, pp. 255, 302, 308 (Degerdoe).

56. Thevenot 1971, vol. 2, p. 121 (Dehi Ghirdoen); Kaempfer 1968, p. 91 (Degerdu); Valentijn 1726, vol. 5, pp. 260-1 (Degerdoe); Smith 1970, pp. 39, 40, 42-3 (Diager, Diaguer); Chardin 1811, vol 8, p. 221. It would seem that della Valle was the last traveler who found nuts there; Fryer 1909, vol. 2, p. 233 (Degurdu); KA 1793, f. 1029 vs (Dhee-Girdoe); Tavernier 1930, p. 295 (Dehigherdou); Hedges 1967, p. 209 (Deregherdoo); Winninx, 31 July (Degerdoe); Chardin 1811, vol. 8, p. 221 (Deguerdou).

57. Speelman 1908, p. 125 (Digerdou).

1717.[58] Speelman also mentions the old caravanserai Da'ud Khan (Davudchan), named after its founder, in which some farmers lived, and then the village of Siyah Kuh, named after the bridge over the river. Ketelaar stayed in a house in the village.[59] Continuing the journey after 3 *farsakh* and crossing the Domboneh River, via a stone- and then a five-arched bridge, the next halting place (*manzel*) was situated, the village of Khoshk-e zard. It was a poor village on a very large but barren plain. At its outskirts there was a little hillock with a castle, seen from 5 leagues' distance. Thevenot had a better opinion of Khoshk-e zard, which meant 'silver pavilion'. There were 2 caravanserais, one newly built of burnt bricks and free stone with many embellishments, the other was old. The land showed signs of rich agricultural production, while it also boasted of pastures for the royal studs. The inhabitants were Circassians, who made wine from grapes from Ma'in. Chardin called it a large village which had 200 houses and which derived its name 'Golden Pavilion', from the two gilded domes in which were entombed Cheik Gulendon, a famous dervish and Imamzadeh-ye Esma`il, son of the sixth Imam Musa Kazem; it was an important pilgrims site. The caravanserai was large and well kept, and the best that Kaempfer had seen so far, though it was old. It had been built by a merchant from Surat, Hajji Hoseyn, for 100 *tumans*. Van Leene also considered Khoshk-e zard to be a fair village, and admired its beautiful brick-stone caravanserai with tiles. The village had some trees and good water. According to Fryer, Khoshk-e zard had a small but delicate caravanserai. The upper part was too heavy, which were pressing down the walls, which were adorned with painted bricks and polished marble. In 1717 the caravanserai was old and dilapidated.[60]

From Khoshk-e zard, after half *farsakh* the traveler, leaving Madar-e Dokhtar (Mader dochter) to the left, which was the beginning of another shorter but much more difficult road to Shiraz, arrived at the caravanserai Domboneh. This had been built by the well-known eunuch, Aqa Kafur, and after another 7 *farsakh* at the village of Asupas. It was a fine village at the bottom of a high hill that in 1617 had a Circassian population and about 100 houses. There was a good store of water, and some good wine sold by Georgian Christians, of whom, Herbert was told, some 30,000 were living in the area. Asupas had an old castle, which had been razed before 1645. Speelman only described it as a hill with a wall around it, which until 30 years ago had been occupied and maintained. He estimated its population at more than 200 houses, of which the caravanserai was the best building. Thevenot described it as a sorry old ruinous castle, inhabited by Circassians. He also noted that they made wine, and so did

58. Kaempfer 1968, p. 91 (Kala Kewilar); Valentijn 1726, vol. 5, p. 261 (Kivilaar); KA 1793, f. 1029 vs. (Serae Kwilaer); LeBrun 1718, vol. 2, p. 302 (Kiavielar).

59. Speelman 1908, pp. 124-25 (Chiakon); Chardin 1811, vol. 8, p. 221 called this bridge the Polichiokou. It crosses the Polvar river, which joins the Kur at Persepolis. Nowadays the location is called Shahkuh. This must be close to (or the same as) what Herbert, p. 118 called Bazeba-chow. KA 1793, f. 1027 vs (Pool Chachon); LeBrun 1718, vol. 2, pp. 302, 308 (Poel-Sakoe; Pol-Siakoe) which had no caravanserai.

60. Stodart 1935, p. 75 (Cuskezar); Thevenot 1971, vol. 2, pp.121-22 (Keuschkzer); Kaempfer 1968, p. 91 (Kuskiserd); Valentijn 1726, vol. 5, p. 261 (Cuchesaar; Koskoser); Smith 1970, p. 43; Speelman 1908, p. 124 (Coscosaar); Herbert 1929, p. 118 (Cuzcuzar). The next stop Herbert 1929, p. 118 made, Whomgesh, I have not be able to identify; Fryer 1909, vol. 2, p. 232 (Cuscuzar); KA 1793, f. 1027 (Khos-kie-zhaar); Tavernier 1930, p. 295 (Kouchkizerd); Hedges 1967, p. 209 (Coskezar); Winninx, 30 July (Kuskesaer); Chardin 1811, vol. 8, pp. 221-22 (Keuch Kezar); Silva y Figueroa 1667, pp. 169, 340 (Cuzcuzar); LeBrun 1718, vol. 2, pp. 255, 301, 308 (Koskiesar).

Tavernier, who also mentioned the presence of fish in the brooks, the ruined fortress, and the old disorderly caravanserai. The caravanserai of Asupas was a nasty one in 1665. Chardin recorded that Asupas was a large village of 300 houses and surrounded by water and marshes just like Khoshk-e Zard. The population was Circassian in origin, but had become Moslem to have an easier life, but continued to make and drink excellent wine. Here, there were as elsewhere in the villages along this route, quite a few Indians living for part of the year. Chardin spent the night with a peasant, because the caravanserai was unusable and in ruins. However, the Dutch embassy in 1691 found it a reasonable caravanserai. There was another *saray*, standing alone in the high mountains. In 1717, however, the caravanserai was old and dilapidated.[61]

Leaving Asupas, the caravan passed after 1.5 *farsakh* an unnamed caravanserai[62] and continuing, passed inter alia over a bridge with seven arches and after another 3 *farsakh* arrived at Ujan a poor village. Thevenot did not stay at its caravanserai because it stank from the carrion and the filth that was in there, which was confirmed by Tavernier. A river went through the village, which had a bridge with seven arches. The population also made wine from grapes from Ma'in. There was a tomb of the Shahzadeh-ye Imam Jaʿfar, with many tall plane trees in front in which storks nested. Chardin wrote that Ujan had 50 houses, and he described and provided a translation of the text on the freeze of the tomb of Sultan Sayyed Ahmad, a brother of Shah Esmaʿil I. This village was still inhabited by Georgians in 1685. Ujan was a large village, which had a fairly sizeable caravanserai but very bad houses, and little to offer in supplies, though it had good water. All travelers mention the famous tomb, though they disagree who was entombed there. Kaempfer believed that it was Shah Esmaʿil's brother, while according to Stodart it was the king's uncle. According to the Dutch embassy the tomb was a small chapel with a cupola, in which a wooden bier was located, where an *imamzadeh* was entombed. In his memory, every morning trumpets were blown. The building, which was rather well constructed, was situated in a garden. The caravanserai was rather good, while there were also many rose trees. In 1717 the caravanserai was totally dilapidated and the embassy lodged in the shrine.[63]

61. Stodart 1935, p. 75 (Assepose); Winninx, 29 July (Asepas); Thevenot 1971, vol. 2, p. 121 (Asoupas); Kaempfer 1968, p. 92 (Aszpasz); Valentijn 1726, vol. 5, p. 261 (Asepas; Haspas); Speelman 1908, p. 125 who also suggests that Haspas means cook or *ashpaz*, which is unlikely; Herbert 1929, p. 117 (Asseposse); Winninx 29 July (Assepas); Fryer 1909, vol. 2, pp. 231-32, the Georgians were farmers and planters of vines. Many had become Moslem (Asspass); Hedges 1967, p. 209 (Assapos) good water; KA 1793, f. 1026 vs (Haasepaas); Tavernier 1930, p. 295 (Assoupas); Chardin 1811, vol. 8, pp. 225-26 (Haspas); Silva y Figueroa 1667, pp. 168, 340-1 (Acopas); LeBrun 1718, vol. 2, pp. 255, 301, 309 (Dombaeyne; Assapas, Aespaas)

62. This caravanserai mentioned by Kaempfer may be the same as the halting place Herbert 1929, p. 117 stayed in, which was called Tartang, a small town, with a mosque and a remarkable tomb, in which a great-uncle of the shah was entombed. However, given the description Herbert may have made a mistake, for it seems that he described Ujan, see e.g. Chardin 1811, vol. 8, pp. 226-27.

63. Stodart 1935, p. 75 (Yeioone); Thevenot 1971, vol. 2, p. 122 (Oudgioun; Schah-Zadeh-Imam-Dgiafar); Kaempfer 1968, pp. 91-92 (Udjan); Valentijn 1726, vol. 5, p. 261 (Oedjaan). For a detailed description of the tomb see Chardin 1811, vol. 8, pp. 226-8 (Ujon; Sultan Sahied Ahmed) and Kaempfer 1968, pp. 93-94; Speelman 1908, p. 122 (Oedjangh); Herbert 1929, p. 117 (O-jone), see also previous note; Fryer 1909, vol. 2, p. 229 with tomb and many fruits (Ojoan); KA 1793, f. 1024 vs (Oojhoen); Tavernier 1930, pp. 295-98 (Oudjan); Winninx, 28 July and 31 October (Oldjoen); Silva y Figueroa 1667, pp. 167 (Vgion); LeBrun 1718, vol. 2, pp. 255-26, 310 (Oesjoen, Oedjoen, Aedioen)

The next major halting station was Ma'in by a stony and craggy way, having a great hill to pass over, the Kotal-e Imamzadeh-ye Esma'il (Chotal-Imam-Zadeh-Esmael; Isma'il mountain pass]). This was between Ujan and Imam Esma'il (Imomismoile). In the latter place there was excellent water. Right on top of the Kotal-e Imamzadeh-ye Esma'il there was a well with good water. At the foot of the mountain, called Kuh (Goe) de Kinjari, was a village called Esma'il (Esmaal), which had an *imamzadeh* and a beautiful new caravanserai. Tavernier, who has the same information, also mentions that practically all trees there were bitter almond. The almonds (*badam*) were exported to Gujarat where they were used as currency. The caravanserai was still in good condition in 1717. This was the most forested place that the Dutch embassy had seen so far. The mosque, in which a certain Isma'il was interred, looked like a castle [of which a description was given]; and a village close by with many gardens. The village of Imamzada Isma'il was circumvallated and well equipped.[64]

From there one arrived at the Circassian village of Ma'in, a large populous (600 houses according to Silva y Figueroa, but 300 houses according to Chardin). It was a beautiful village, with good water, provisions and much agricultural production. Its brick caravanserai was large, nice and comfortable building, where you could buy everything. There were many gardens with all kinds of fruit trees, as well as grapes from which excellent wine was made. It was one of the largest villages Speelman had yet traveled through. According to Fryer the best walnuts grew there as well as the choicest tobacco. Silva y Figueroa praised its many nut trees, while Chardin lauded its grenade apples, which were excellent and sometimes as big as a child's head. There were two small tombs with *imamzadeh*s, which had been badly built and since then totally neglected so that it hardly was worthy to note them.[65]

From Ma'in the traveler had two choices. He could go straight for Shiraz, or take another road that led to Persepolis. Continuing to Shiraz, the traveler crossed the Ma'in River over three bridges, also called Band-Amir River close to where the dam was built. The first bridge was the Pol Jesnejoen, [?] which in 1617, was broken in the middle. This was the reason why Imamverdi Khan, governor of Fars, had built Pul-e Khani [Pol Chanje].[66] In addition there was a five-arched bridge called Pul-e Now [Pouli-now] or New Bridge, though it

---

with the 280 year old tomb of the prince Sultan Hossen Mameth.

64. Kaempfer 1968, p. 94 (Majin; Mahin); Stodart 1935, p. 75 (Moyeeme); Thevenot 1971, vol. 2, p. 122 (Maain); Valentijn 1726, vol. 5, p. 261 (Majien; Majur); Speelman 1908, p. 122 (Monsada). The *imamzadeh* is Esma'il, son of Musa al-Kazem, the seventh Shi'ite Imam. Herbert 1929, p. 117 placed it in Ma'in, and its description under Ujan; Hedges 1967, p. 208 (Woo-John); KA 1793, f. 1020 vs (Imoen Sada); Tavernier 1930, p. 298 (Iman-Sade); Hedges, p. 208 (Imaum Zade) a pretty village; Winninx 27 July (Monsada); Chardin 1811, vol. 8, pp. 229-30 who stated that Esma'il son of Imam Ja'far was entombed here. He gave a translation of the inscription on the tomb that said so. Silva y Figueroa 1667, pp. 165-66, 343-4 (Amanzada); Valentijn 1726, vol. 5, p. 262 (Cotali Imames Esmaal; Imam Sadas Mal); LeBrun 1718, vol. 2, pp. 257 (ruined caravanserai), 301, 310 (Imansada).

65. Thevenot 1971, vol. 2, p. 123; Valentijn 1726, vol. 5, p. 262; Speelman 1908, p. 121 (Mahien); Herbert 1929, pp. 116-17 (Moyown); Fryer 1909, vol. 2, p. 228 (Maijm); KA 1793, f. 1017 (Mhaaiem); Tavernier 1930, p. 298 (Mayin); Hedges 1967, p. 208 (Moyeen); Winninx, 27 July (Majein); Chardin 1811, vol. 8, pp. 231-32 (Mayn); Silva y Figueroa 1667, pp. 165, 344 (Mahin); LeBrun 117-18, vol. 2, pp. 257-58, 301, 310 (Majien) with vineyards.

66. Silva y Figueroa 1667, p. 344; LeBrun 1718, vol. 2, pp. 258-60, 294 and plates 172 and 173 (Pol noof); Kaempfer 1968; Ibid. 1976, p. 295 (Pyli Chaan, Pyly Noo).

was somewhat ruinous in 1665. The bridge had been built by an Indian merchant, and at this point the river was locally called Ab-e Pol-e Now (Abpulneu), the New Bridge River. He then arrived at a caravanserai which had been built by a *vaqf* or endowment left by a rich man from Shiraz called Ab-e Garm, because there was a hot spring, with fish. Chardin reported that this area was full of hot springs and there was more than one caravanserai. From here onwards there were several ways to Shiraz. According to Tavernier the caravanserai at Ab-e Garm was half completed.[67] Thevenot and LeBrun choose the road which passed via the villages of Fagrabaet and Assaf over the Pol-e Gorg (Poligorg), a causeway, which had many arches and was 2,000 paces long. In the middle there was a bridge of 100 paces long. Continuing the journey there was a caravanserai and a little further there was another much better one, which had been built by the governor (vizier) of Shiraz. It was very large and extraordinary well-built with room for 500 persons and their equipage, though its spacious rooms were infested with gnats. It was called Agassef. From here a road went straight to Chehelminar. Continuing, the traveler came to the caravanserai Bajgah, from there it was 2 *farsakh* to Shiraz.[68]

Following another road the traveler would arrive at Bajgah (Basigaar), which was a rather sorry caravanserai, with a dilapidated cistern at the entrance. Going further, the traveler passed a beautiful caravanserai near a village, where he traveled over a mile long bridge, thus crossing several brooks. Near this is the Kotal-e Bajgah (Cotali Basighaar) which had to be crossed.[69]

Winter Route

From Yazdekhvast there was the alternative longer winter route to Shiraz, which was followed by Fryer in the 1670s and by the Dutch ambassador Hoogcamer in 1703.[70] After having left

---

67. Abigerne was at 5 German miles distance from Persepolis. Valentijn 1726, vol. 5, p. 262; Speelman 1908, p. 120 (Germawa), p. 323 (Aab de Germ); Winninx, 1 November has Germoens [may be my transcription error for Germaweh], which had much water, livestock and grains; KA 1793, f. 1016 vs (Ghermabe); Tavernier 1930, p. 298 (Ab-Gherme); Chardin 1811, vol. 8, pp. 234-39 (Abguerm); LeBrun 1718, vol. 2, pp. 260, 311 (Abgerm).

68. Thevenot 1971, vol. 2, p. 123 (Poligorgh); Tavernier 1930, p. 298, the cause-way was 1500 paces long and 15 paces wide, and was interspaced by 4 bridges to let the water pass (Pouligor); Speelman 1908, pp. 323-24 (Badsjega); Winninx 26 July (Agaseff). The caravanserai Poulou Gor, though old, was still one of the most solid and commodious caravanserais in Iran. It had been built by the old governor of Shiraz, Aga Seff, whose son, Miersa Hady was the current governor of Shiraz; Chardin 1811, vol. 8, p. 240 (Piligourc; caravanserai Assef; Bagsga). Tavernier mentioned that after this beautiful but gnat infested caravanserai three hours later there was another caravanserai, which was very wretched (Agassef; Badgega); LeBrun 1718, vol. 2, pp. 258-60, 294, 311 (Baeits-goedie).

69. Valentijn 1726, vol. 5, p. 262 (Basighaar; Baasga; Basgona); Thevenot 1971, vol. 2, p. 123 (Badgega).

70. The description of the winter route is based on Valentijn 1726, vol. 5, p. 284; van Dam 1993, vol. 3, pp. 327-28; and Frye 1909, vol. 2, pp. 316-19. Their alternative renderings of the localities are given between brackets in the text. The route was also traveled by a Spanish Carmelite monk. Anonymous 1939, vol. 1, p. 219, note. The same route was traveled by Sadid al-Saltaneh 1362, pp. 58-67, who mentions the following halting stations: Yazdekhvast, Abadeh, Surmaq, Dehbid, Khaneh-

Yazdekhvast the route went for 6.5 miles via the village of Shulgestan (Spilkestoen; Sirgistan) to the village of Abadeh (Abad; Obedeah) for another 6,5 miles, continuing to the village of Surmak or Surmeh (Soerna; Surima) for 4 miles, arriving after 6,5 miles at the caravanserai of Khan-e Khureh (Goengora; Gonnegaroe; Conacaraw). From here it was 4 miles to the village of Ajubsja[71] Dehbid (Debit; Dehid), which had a caravanserai and was at 0.25 miles from the caravanserai of Khan-e Kargan (Goenkergie; Goentergoe; Conacurgu). The next stop was the village of Mashhad-e Morghab (Mesdjid Madresa Soleyman; Mijtchiet; Mushat). After 4 miles, having crossed two bridges, was the village of Sivand (Ziwent; Sivand; Zivan), and after 4 hours the village of Zepahoenia which was also called Ayun (Ajoen). Continuing, Hoogkamer arrived after 4 miles at the village of Mirgaskan (Miergascoen; Meergoscoon; Mikashi). Because of the rains (it was 7 March) he could not cross the river Kur (Cur) via the Pul-e Now or Pul-e Khan (Pole Mouw or Polechan), and thus moved three miles further to the village of Mesdabat. After 5 miles he arrived at the long Pol-e Gorg (Polegorse) bridge and after crossing various brooks arrived at the caravanserai of Bajkhaneh (Basgona or toll-house). After two miles was the Chahar Bagh [Tsaarbag], which was just outside Shiraz.[72]

Merging of the Summer and Winter Routes

Both the winter and summer route merged in the plain of Marvdasht in which Persepolis is situated. This did not mean that the traveler had no choice in roads, for the Marvdasht plain offered various roads which led, via Persepolis or elsewhere, to Shiraz. Stodart reached Marvdasht, which was within half a league of Chehel Minar, and "sometimes difficult because of crossways on this plain which led to several villages. At Marvdasht there is a good water store."[73] From Marvdasht, after 7.5 *farsakh*, there was the village of Myrgascun, which was half a *farsakh* from Chehel Minar. It was a village of a reasonable size with a number of houses and a small bazaar, which had a public kitchen, and where one could by paper and other trifles. Its caravanserai only had some Persian merchants, who bought produce from the surrounding area and used the rooms of the *saray* as storage space. In 1685, its manager was an old ugly prostitute, who offered her services to the passing travelers. The road from Mirgaskan to Zarghan passed via a bridge with 4 arches, and Shiraz was at a distance of 15-18 km.[74] Continuing from Chehel Minar, Stodart arrived at Zarghan, which was a poor town

ye Gargan, Mashhad-e Omm al-Nabi, Qavamabad, Sivand, Takhteh-Jamshid, Zarqan, and Shiraz.

71. Strausensz 1678, pp. 187-88 (the villages Surina, Gusty, Siba, and Mardasch). See also Sjuabasar- Kaempfer 1968, pp. 102, 107, 109; Gabriel 1952, p. 144.

72. Valentijn 1726, vol. 5, p. 284 (Basigaar); Winninx, 25 July (caravanserai Bathiga); Speelman 1908, p. 104 (caravanserai Batsjega) at 2 miles from Shiraz; p. 107 (Mergaseon); Fryer 1909, vol. 2, p. 221, the plain was full of farms and villages (Meergoscoon); he continued via Zarghan [Zergoon]. The Carmelite monk also passed through Zarghan. Anonymous 1939, vol. 1, p. 219, note.

73. Stodart 1925, p. 76 (Mardasz); Herbert 1929, pp. 109-110; Strauszens 1678, p. 188 (Schilminar, Tzilminar); Chardin 1811, vol. 8, pp. 242-44 (Tchel monar).

74. Kaempfer 1968, p. 96 (Merdest); Chardin 1811, vol. 8, p. 407; KA 1793, f. 1013 vs (Mheerghas-koen), which was half a mile from Persepolis; Hedges 1967, p. 208 (Emer-Cascoon) at of a mile from Persepolis; Winninx, 11 November (Mirgascoen) where he also reproduced a number of

situated on the side of a hill one English mile from Rostam's tomb (i.e. Naqsheh-ye Rostam, the tomb of Darius I), which had been turned into a mosque. Here was good water. Speelman recorded that the village was divided into two parts, and built close to the slope of the mountain. Fryer called it a poor village inhabited by muleteers, while Hedges considered it a large and exceeding pleasant village, in a plain full of vineyards.[75] Struys stayed in the village of (Alikon) before arriving in Shiraz.[76]

The Shiraz–Lar Road

Leaving Shiraz, the traveler rode via the villages of Deh Ameris and Hasanabad, at one German mile from the city, crossed the 10 arched Pol-e Fasa bridge over the Qara Bagh river. The bridge was in need of repair, and was linked on both sides by a causeway[77] at the left of which a lake was situated. An alternative route was via the village of Ujval. The traveler, having passed over a bridge half-way, arrived after 5 *farsakh* at the caravanserai Baba Hajji. Ketelaar wrote that in the village of Ujval he camped in a walled garden where a saint's tomb was located.[78] Every traveler, but Hedges, considered Baba Hajji a poor caravanserai. It was situated at the end of the Shiraz plain, which is about 12 leagues in length and at some places 2 leagues in width. Water was not good here. The caravanserai was rather large, but partly dilapidated. It was standing alone, badly constructed of free stone, in one word 'wretched'. It had been named after its founder who was buried close by. It had no good water, though a little beyond the caravanserai there was some. The caravanserai was close to a cluster of seven villages, of which the most populous had the caravanserai. In 1717, the caravanserai was old though still a reasonable place to stay for the night. According to Hedges, Baba Hajji was situated in a fine, well watered plain and well stored with provisions[79]

---

letters in Old Persian script; Silva y Figueroa 1667, p. 144 (Margascan; Chilminara); LeBrun 1718, vol. 2, p. 301 (Mierchaskoen).

75. Stodart 1935, p. 76 (Zargoone); Speelman 1908, pp. 105-06 (Serghoen); Fryer 1909, vol. 2, p. 218 (Zergoon); Hedges 1967, p. 208 (Zurgoon); KA 1793, f. 1013 vs (Sergoen); Winninx, 3 November (Sergoe); Silva y Figueroa 1667, p. 140 (Zargan); LeBrun 1718, vol. 2, p. 301 (Sergoen); Anonymous 1939, vol. 1, p. 219, note (Band-e Amir; Zarghan; caravanserai).

76. Strauszens 1778, p. 190. This may be the caravanserai mentioned by Ketelaar, though he did not provide its name. KA 1793, f. 1013 vs.

77. Valentijn 1726, vol. 5, p. 284 (Polifasa); Speelman 1908, p. 84; Thevenot 1971, vol. 2, p. 127 (Poulifeza). The eight or ten-arched bridge is the Pol-e Fasa. There was also a caravanserai built by a rich Shirazi widow. Silva y Figueroa 1667, pp. 104, 351.

78. Kaempfer 1968, p. 111(Pylli Pessa); Speelman 1908, pp. 83-84 (Ousjouael); Fryer 1909, vol. 2, p. 209 (the Beggards-Garden called Udgewally); Valentijn 1726, vol. 5, p. 284 (Oesiwat; Osiwar); KA 1793, f. 999 (Oudsjou alla); Silva y Figueroa 1667, p. 105 (Ochiar). The lake refers to the Darya-e Mahalu, a salt lake, where there was also a caravanserai, p. 351. Aubin 1971, pp. 42-43 (Uxuan). Herbert 1929, p. 67 called the bridge near Baba Hajji the Pully-pot-shaw (Pol-e padshah).

79. Stodart 1935, p. 79 (Bobohogi); Thevenot 1971, vol. 2, p. 127 (Baba-Adgi); Valentijn 1726, vol. 5, p. 262 (Babaghasi); Kaempfer 1968, p. 111 (Baba Haddji); Speelman 1908, p. 83 (Babe Hasy); Herbert 1929, p. 107 (Bobbaw-hodgee); Fryer 1909, vol. 2, p. 208 (Bobba Hodge); Strauszens 1678, p. 193 (Dobba); Hedges 1967, p. 207 (Bobba Hadgee); KA 1793, f. 998 vs (Bha Bha Hadje);

From Baba Hajji, the traveler went to Mozaffari via Janjan, situated in the not so well watered Shiraz plain, over the small Cnonebande [?] Mountain, and after 4 *farsakh* arrived at the caravanserai Mozaffari which stood alone.[80] Opinions differed about the caravanserai Speelman was pleased with the comfort of the caravanserai which was situated in a nice valley, at about 400 meters from some villages where the traveler could get victuals. Tavernier wrote that the caravanserai was in an isolated spot, but that he had found black truffles there as big as those in the Dauphiné in France. Chardin wrote that the caravanserai was spacious and comfortable and well-watered by subterraneous channels from the Shah Bahman Su (Cha Bendmen Sou), just like the plain in which it was situated. According to Kaempfer it was a bad, but large, caravanserai built with free stones. According to Thevenot there was good spring water near the caravanserai Mozaffari, though according to Stodart the water was not good. The Dutch embassy in 1691 considered the caravanserai Mozaffari good, though lonely, while Fryer wrote that it was a very splendid caravanserai with which Hedges concurred. By 1717 it was an old, though spacious caravanserai situated in a nice valley, and housed a number of *rahdars*.[81]

Not far from Mozaffari, at the foot of the mountains, was another caravanserai called Mirsa Seri, and on the other side of the brook, the village Barajan, entirely in green foliage. After Barajan (Baradjun), via the villages (Charbi, Sendjan, Sagada, Bier, Fesjun and Asmunga),[82] it was another 3 *farsakh* to Khafr (Chafr) or Jen (Jesa), or rather its caravanserai which in 1617 was rather nice, but 30 years later was described as being rather small, octagonal and not too old. Close by were the remnants of a razed town which was called Barbar by the locals. Khafr was a rather large village (a couple of hundred houses) which was rich in agriculture (tobacco), and had many gardens with all kinds of fruit, and above all the choicest oranges. It was the first place that dates were seen by travelers coming from Europe. The Carmelites report that here `araq was made of Portuguese grapes.[83]

After the caravanserai Mirsa Seri, instead of going straight to Khafr, some travelers either stopped at the caravanserai Asmankard,[84] or, after 3 *farsakh*, rested at the large

Tavernier 1930, p. 310 (Babaadgi); Winninx, 22 July (Babba Hasi); Chardin 1811, vol. 8, pp. 461-62 (Babahaagi); LeBrun 1718, vol. 2, p. 312 (Babba hadjie); Anonymous 1939, vol. 1, p. 219, note.

80. Kaempfer 1968, p. 111 (Jansjun; Myrsa Feri); (caravanserai Mose Faril); Valentijn 1726, vol. 5, pp. 263, 285 (Moesaferie); Stodart 1935, p. 79 (Moozaferie); Herbert 1929, p. 67 (Moyechaw); Tavernier 1930, p. 310 (Mouzafferi); Winninx, 22 July (Mosaffri); Speelman 1908, p. 82 (Mossafry).

81. Kaempfer 1968, p. 111; Thevenot 1971, vol.2, p.127; Stodart 1935, p. 79 (Moozaferie); Valentijn 1726, vol. 5, p. 262 (Moesaserie; Mose Faril); Speelman 1908, p. 82 (Mosaffry); Fryer 1909, vol. 2, p. 208 (Mussaferry); Hedges 1967, p. 207 (Mussaferee); KA 1793, f. 998 (Mossa Ferhie); Chardin 1811, vol. 8, p. 460 (Mouza fari); LeBrun 1718, vol. 2, p. 312 (Mossefarie); Anonymous 1939, vol. 1, p. 219, note (Musafiri).

82. This village mentioned by Kaempfer may be the one that Herbert 1929, p. 66 stayed in, which he called Unghea.

83. Kaempfer 1968, p. 112 (Chafr; Jesa); Winninx, 20 July passed the ruins of town Gaffer, and later the village of Gaffar. Valentijn 1726, vol. 5, pp. 262, 285 (Chaffert); Thevenot 1971, vol. 2, p. 127 (Chafer); Tavernier 1930, p. 311 (Khafr); Speelman 1908, pp. 73-74 (Gaffer); Herbert 1929, p. 66 (Coughton); Fryer 1909, vol. 2, p. 206 (Caifer); Chardin 1811, vol. 8, p. 471 (Kafer); Silva y Figueroa 1667, pp. 96, 351 (Cafhra); Anonymous 1939, vol. 1, p. 219, note.

84. Kaempfer 1968, p. 113 (Asmugir); Valentijn 1726, vol. 5, pp. 262, 285 (caravanserai Asmongeert; Asmonger); LeBrun 1718, vol. 2, p. 312 (Asmongeer).

caravanserai Pa'in-e Rah, which was a reasonable building that had been built by Aqa Taqi, and was situated next to the village of Barajan. It stood alone, and there were no houses.[85] From here the road went via Cossir[86] to the village of Asmugir (not too far away), then to the village of Pacherabad, and, after 2.5 *farsakh*, the traveler arrived at the village of Tadavan. This was a pleasant large village which had ample water, cattle, fruit and large fish. Speelman added that it had not more than 100 mud dwellings and that it was a *vaqf* or endowment village. Tavernier observed that the road via Tadavan was not the normal route taken by caravans, which took the fork to the right, while he went straight on arriving in a plain, called Tadavan, which was full of orange, lemon and grenade orchards. Its brooks were filled with various kinds of fish, while the Europeans living in Bandar `Abbas often spent the summer here. Female dancers knew immediately when Europeans were here and soon came to dance and to drink wine. Hedges lodged in this most pleasant and fruitful plain he had yet seen in Iran, in a garden belonging to the Dutch, because there was no caravanserai. Winninx recorded a superstition among the population that anybody who had been born in the village, whether staying there or moving elsewhere, may not drink wine. He also saw a local peasant catch with his bare hands within 15 minutes five large fish of half and three-quarter's of an ell.[87]

From Tadavan, continuing along the Qara Agach (Mand) river as of Khafr, it was another 2.5 *farsakh* to the caravanserai Mukhak traveling through a fruitful and pleasant valley. The caravanserai of Mukhak was small, standing alone and situated in a craggy place and had good water and no want of provisions. Hedges ate there the best musk melons he ever tasted. About some hundred paces behind the caravanserai was a great cistern, 4-5 fathoms in diameter, very deep and covered with a dome. There was only one house near the caravanserai, while the only drinkable water was in a cistern at one musket shot distance. However Tavernier reported that a Jew had fallen into the cisterns and therefore the Moslems did not use it anymore, because its water became unclean. Chardin reported that the small caravanserai had been destroyed, and he considered this one of the sorriest halting places he had stayed in and its water was terrible. In 1685, the caravanserai had been recently built by a merchant of free stone. It was situated in the middle of nowhere, though it now also housed a number of *rahdar*s and had two new covered cisterns. Next to it was a warm spring in which one could take a bath. The old dilapidated caravanserai was still standing.[88]

85. Kaempfer 1968, p.111; (caravanserai Paira) Thevenot 1971, vol. 2, p. 127; (Pajera); Tavernier 1930, p. 310 (Paira); LeBrun 1718, vol. 2, p. 312 (Paroe);Valentijn 1726, vol. 5, p. 262 (Para); KA 1793, f. 997 vs (Serae Parhoe was old and bad). Aqa Taqi, who had built this caravanserai, had been *shahbandar* of Bandar `Abbas in 1640-43. He had an acrimonious relationship with the Dutch. He even imprisoned the VOC director in 1642. Speelman 1908, pp. 81-82, 338 (Acha Tachy). The place was called caravanserai Agatachi by Winninx, July 20; Fryer 1909, vol. 2, p. 207 (Aga Tocke); Hedges 1967, p. 207 (Agatakee); Chardin 1811, vol. 8, p. 461 (Aga Taki, a rich merchant). The Carmelites mention a caravanserai Camerbeik (Qanbar Beg?) 3 farsakh after Khafr. Anonymous 1939, vol. 1, p. 219, note.

86. Hedges 1967, p. 207.

87. Kaempfer 1968, p 113 (Tadejun; Tadewun); Winninx, 19 July and 11 November (Taddervangh); Thevenot 1971, vol. 2, p. 127 (Tadivan); Speelman 1908, pp. 72-73 (Taduwan), who also mentioned the old historical buildings in the mountains and gave a very detailed description of his visit to this site. Ibid., pp. 75-81; Tavernier 1930, pp. 311-14 (Dadivan); Hedges 1967, pp. 206-07 (Dottiuan); Chardin 1811, vol. 8, pp. 463-64 (Taduan); LeBrun 1718, vol. 2, p. 313 (Tadawoen).

88. Stodart 1935, p. 80 (Mochak); Thevenot 1971, vol. 2, p. 128 (Mouckek); Kaempfer 1968, p.

Before 1660 or thereabouts, travelers did not go over the Jahrom hill, but went eastward around it, three-quarters of a mile from Mukhak. Camel-drivers still took the old way, called the desert road, because the camels could not cross the alternative mountainous road. On the desert road, after having passed a village inhabited by camel drivers, the traveler did not find anything but nomad tents and many partridges till Lar. All other road users preferred the shorter (by three days) though more difficult and arduous road. Ketelaar, who traveled with elephants as a present, took the desert road.[89]

From Mukhak, after 2 *farsakh* one met the caravanserai built by Hajji Reza,[90] and after another *farsakh* the village of Deh-Manar, or alternatively the village of Fakhrabad (Fagrabaet), and then finally the famous date town of Jahrom.[91] Winninx described Jahrom as a town which in the past had been a nice, thriving commercial town, but now was in total decay. According to Thevenot, Jahrom was a little town or rather a large village, with a big bazaar. All around this town were palm plantations and gardens. Near the caravanserai was a cistern as at Mukhak, but larger, some 7 fathoms wide. Next to the caravanserai was a small house with a kitchen and room to lodge, for when the caravanserai was full. Chardin reported that Jahrom was a small town, known for its production of felt hats and a kind of camel hair robes called '*aba*, but above all because of its dates. Kaempfer wrote that it was a rather large, though densely built town, with more than 1,000 houses (a number also mentioned by Herbert) and that it looked like a large date grove. It also had a miserable bazaar, a large caravanserai Shah Hoseyn, in which the prostitutes seemed to be in charge. There was another caravanserai outside the town on the road, though rather filthy. Tavernier and Chardin reported that the caravanserai was 500 paces outside town and agreeaable. According to the Dutch, Jahrom was a nice place full of date groves and a very large caravanserai, the biggest they had seen so far. There was also a cistern and water hole. Struys called Jahrom a small town, without walls, located in a date grove. The town's trade consisted of cotton textiles and there were many weavers. The bazaar was quite pleasant, where all kinds of Indian and Persian goods were for sale, while twice a week there was a market when farmers from the neighboring villages came to town.[92]

---

113 (Musak); Valentijn 1726, vol. 5, p. 262 (Mokhak; Mochai Sughta; Mogagzoekte); Speelman 1908, p. 72 (Meggek); Herbert 1929, p. 66 (Mohack); Fryer 1909, vol. 2, pp. 205, 351 (Mocock Sugta; also *rahdar* station); KA 1793, f. (Mhochek-Soghti); Tavernier 1930, p. 314 (Mouchek); Hedges 1967, p. 206 (Moocack Sookta); Winninx, 18 July (Moggeck); Chardin 1811, vol. 8, pp. 462-63 (Moukak); LeBrun 1718, vol. 2, p. 314 (Mich-geak-sogte).

89. Tavernier 1930, pp. 314-15;

90. This caravanserai mentioned by Kaempfer 1968, p. 115 (Hadji Reza) may be located in the village of Bagar-Abad (Valentijn 17265, vol. 5, p. 274), which probably was identical to what Herbert 1929, p. 66 called Cut-bobbaw.

91. Kaempfer 1968, p. 115 (Schebsha-Djahrum); Stodart 1935, p. 81 (Goyreeome); Winninx, 18 July (Sjaron); Thevenot wrote after having left Paira, and after 3 hours he arrived at a ruined caravanserai with a cistern close to it, 5 hours later he arrived at large caravanserai just outside Dgiaroun. Thevenot 1971, vol. 2, p. 128; Hedges 1967, p. 206 (Jarroon). The 1691 Dutch embassy passed a small caravanserai, and rode over a rather long bridge before arriving at Sjaron. Valentijn 1726, p. 264 (Jaroen; Jarom); LeBrun 1718, vol. 2, p. 314 (Jaron) and plate.

92. Winninx, 18 July (Sjaron); Thevenot 1971, vol. 2, pp. 128-29 (Dgiaroun); Kaempfer 1968, p. 115 (Djarum); Valentijn 1726, vol. 5, p. 263 (Sjaron); Herbert 1929, p. 65 (Goyoom); Strauszens 1678, p. 193 (Scharim); KA 1793, f. 994 (Jharoen); Tavernier 1930, p. 315 (Djahroum); Chardin 1811, vol. 8, pp. 465-66 (Harron) and plate LXXVII with a map of the caravanserai of Jahrum;

From Jahrom the most dangerous part of the route began, because of the height and steepness of the road over the mountain, which was called Ajoudouchs or Jahrom Mountain. Because accidents had happened, the inhabitants had constructed a low wall half a foot tall to help the travelers and their mules pass in greater safety, while in another part there was a one-arched bridge across a ravine, which had been built by Imamqoli Khan. After the Jahrom Mountain, which had three cisterns on top, though these were most of the time empty according to Chardin, the traveler had to pass two others, one of which was equipped with a cistern. From Jahrum to caravanserai Chah-Talkh, which was the first stop, was 6 *farsakh*. Speelman considered Chah-Talkh had been correctly named, for it was a bad, dilapidated place that indeed had a bitter well. Thevenot, however, submits that the caravanserai Chah-Talkh was small and good, standing all alone in a valley, near to which were two cisterns, one covered with a dome, the other with a steep roof. The well near the caravanserai was bitter, hence the name. Tavernier confirms this and adds that the place abounded with bitter almond and turpentine trees (*Pistacia terebinthus*). There were *rahdars* who offered deer for a meal, of which there were many. The area also abounded with partridges as big as chickens. Hedges recorded that it had a spacious caravanserai with plenty of good fresh water and provisions, but Chardin called it a miserable place as was its water. Rich people, he wrote, took sweet water with them in goatskins or large copper flasks, in which the water remained cool. Next to the caravanserai was another one, which was partly in ruins in 1685. Fryer reported that the caravanserai was a new and an ample one, with a new cistern with not so bitter water. It had two new and two old cisterns in 1691. LeBrun wrote that the caravanserai was a comfortable one[93]

Going down from the Jahrom hill, the traveler passed the caravanserai Manjir-e Bozorg (Manjir besorg), then via the Kotal-e Hasani or Mamasani, at the foot of which was a cistern,[94] and then onwards through a stony plain, arriving at a fair caravanserai, called Manjir, in front of which was a basin that was filled by a brook. Because there was no one to sell food or fodder Thevenot did not stay there.[95] Kaempfer called it Manjir-e Kuchek (Mensir Kieschik), which had a large garden and cistern.[96] It was otherwise a sober caravanserai, which was standing alone, but had many fruit trees (dates, lemons, oranges) and several other kinds of fruit. There were no victuals for sale here; in 1702 its caravanserai was, though small, new.[97]

Anonymous 1939, vol. 1, p. 219, note (Giaru).

93. Valentijn 1726, vol.5, pp. 263-64 (Saithal; Satalk); Fryer 1909, vol. 2, p. 201 (Chawtalk); Winninx, July 17 (Schathalgh); Kaempfer 1968, pp. 115-6 (Tsjai Talg); Thevenot 1971, vol. 2, p. 129 (Tschai-telkh); Speelman 1908, p. 63, who also mentions the road protection at Sjatallig. Ibid., p. 65; KA 1793, f. 991 (Sjattalgh); Tavernier 1930, pp. 315-6 (Chakal); Hedges 1967, p. 206 (Chatalkee); Chardin 1811, vol. 8, pp. 468-69 (Chatalk); LeBrun 1718, vol. 2, p. 315 (Ziatalk). Membré in 1540 wrote that as of Lar people carried water in skins on donkeys. Membré 1993, p. 47; Anonymous 1939, vol. 1, p. 219, note.

94. Kaempfer 1968, p. 116 (Chotali Hasani or Chotali Mahhmaseni); Thevenot 1971, vol. 2, p. 129. The Cotal Hasani where travelers often had to dismount. Tavernier 1930, p. 316 (Hoseyn mountain); Valentijn 1726, vol. 5, p. 264 (Cotal Hasani).

95. Thevenot 1971, vol. 2, p. 129 (Momzir); Tavernier 1930, p. 316 (Mouezere).

96. Kaempfer 1968, p. 116; Fryer 1909, vol. 2, p. 200, an octogonal caravanserai (Mousar); Hedges 1967, p. 206 (Mowueseer) with an old dilapidated caravanserai and sorry water.

97. Valentijn 1726, p. 264 (Moesoer, Mossir; Mosetis). In 1651 there were some *rahdar*s who

Leaving Manjir the route went through the date villages of Gujum and Dschjuhum (behind which was Bahharru). From here, at 2.5 *farsakh*, was the Qal`eh-ye Tezerg (Tesorg), though despite its name the fortress was a ruin.[98]

After a quarter *farsakh* one came to a small caravanserai close to the village of Deh-e dombeh (Dehidombe), which in 1651 only had 15 houses. Chardin recorded that it had a large caravanserai with running water. It was a poor, but a reasonable building which was called caravanserai Deh-e Dombeh, while a ruined castle was nearby in the mountains.[99] The people of the village drank water from the cistern at the caravanserai which was four fathoms wide and covered with a dome.[100] En route, there were many water tanks and brooks before the traveler arrived at his next stop, after a half *farsakh*, the village of Scherafi, which had cisterns.[101] Then, after another 2.5 *farsakh*, was the caravanserai at the large village of Banaru; here many ruins were situated at the foot of the mountain. The caravanserai here had many big cisterns.[102] Banaru, was a pleasant, but not so large village, with many palm groves, and an old caravanserai called Kheyrat Khan [Cheirat Chan] after a Persian, who was an envoy from Golconda. When it rained, one took the road to Banaru via Bakhtiyari (after 2 *farsakh*) which had a fortress with two high towers. Banaru had a fortress and large cisterns.[103] The road went via the caravanserai Dehra, which was an ugly and miserable place (0.5 *farsakh*), and after another half *farsakh* there was a *rahdar* station,[104] one traveled over a plain, where

usually had some supplies for sale to the travelers. Speelman 1908, pp. 62-63 (Masuer); Winninx, 13 November (Mouser); Chardin 1811, vol. 8, p. 470 (Mouhser); LeBrun 1718, vol. 2, p. 315 (Mouseer).

98. Kaempfer 1968, p. 116. The village of Dschjuhum is probably the same as the village of Ijehoen, through which the Ketelaar embassy passed. KA 1793, f. 990 vs; Anonymous 1939, vol. 1, p. 219, note (Jiyum – a good place, with a fort, a good road, with a water cistern).

99. Kaempfer 1968, p. 116 (Domba); Valentijn 1726, vol. 5, p. 264 (caravanserai Teduba; Dedombe); Speelman 1908, p. 61 (Dedomba); Tavernier 1930, p. 316 (Detadombe); Winninx, 16 July (Dedombaj); Chardin 1811, vol. 8, p. 470 (Dedomba); LeBrun 1718, vol. 2, p. 315 (Dombanja, a hamlet with a ruined caravanserai).

100. Thevenot 1971,vol. 2, p. 129.

101. Kaempfer 1968, p. 117; Ibid. 1976, p. 433; Floor 1998, pp. 72, 77 (Sarafiya, Sarafie).

102. Thevenot 1971, vol. 2, p. 129; Stodart 1935, pp. 81-82 (Carerow) which had a *darughah*. Winninx, 16 July (Bererovio).

103. Kaempfer 1968, p. 117 (Bachtiaru; Benaru); Hedges 1967, p. 206 (Bocktarea, a nice watered village, the home of his chief muleteer, at whose house he stayed); Valentijn 1726, vol 5, p. 264 (Benaroe). Winninx traveled from Ziaron, 9 miles to caravanserai Mouser, then to Benerouw after 6 miles. He then went the remaining 9 miles to Lar, not via Beri and Kourdgh, which was shorter but more difficult. Winninx, November 13-15, 1645. The fortress, high in the mountains, was in ruins in 1651; close to it houses had been built where the inhabitants lived in case of war or insecurity. Speelman 1908, p. 60 (Benaroe); Herbert 1929, p. 65 (Bannarow); Tavernier 1930, p. 316 (Benarou); Fryer 1909, vol. 2, p. 198; an octogonal caravanserai and fortress. He also mentioned the houses, a well as castles, water-tanks and grain store-houses in the mountains (Bonaru); Hedges 1967, p. 206 (Benarroo); KA 1793, f. 989 vs (Bhenaroe); Chardin 1811, vol. 8, p. 470 (Benarou or Benarhou); Silva y Figueroa 1667, p. 80 (Benaru); Floor 1998, vol. 1, p. 219, note.

104. Kaempfer 1968, p. 118 (Dehra); Valentijn 1726, vol. 5, p. 264 (Dera); Thevenot 1971, 2, vol. 2, p. 130 (Dehra); Speelman 1908, p. 60 (caravanserai Serara); Ketelaar mentioned, without naming them, a *saray*, and two large villages, after Tang-e Kuh and before arriving at Banaru. KA 1793, f. 989 vs. One of these villages may have been Aeszjerasie where LeBrun 1718, vol. 2, p. 316 stayed, but which had no caravanserai.

barley was being sown and over a craggy, hilly and twisty road arriving at Biriz. All travelers agreed that it was a large (200 houses) and pleasant village, with many palms and tamarisks, which were irrigated with groundwater. Thevenot, Kaempfer and Hedges considered the newly built caravanserai, the most beautiful that they had seen so far, and the latter added that it had very bad water, but plenty of provisions. It had been built in 1648 by `Evaz Khan, governor of Lar, or by his Georgian wife and the Dutch considered it in 1691 still a beautiful caravanserai. The caravanserai had five covered tanks and wells. Right in front of the caravanserai was a very large water tank with a diameter of 100 feet crosswise and 315 feet circular, which according to Thevenot was full of worms. Fryer said that it was the best caravanserai on the road, well adorned with white facing stone, large and stately and well-built. The village further boasted of a village school and an *imamzadeh*, known as Puseri Saada Ali. In 1717, the caravanserai was still spacious and pleasant.[105]

The distance from Biriz to Lar was 8 *farsakh* and led via the villages of Deh-e Kuh and Kurdeh which both had a caravanserai, many palms and tamarisks and several cisterns. At Deh-e Kuh was a road stone indicating the road to Darab, erected by a merchant who had taken the wrong turn. From here one arrived at the caravanserai Pa-ye Kotali (Pai Chotali), which had a cistern and a well. From there it was still 4-5 hours to Lar, over difficult terrain and having crossing various brooks. Fryer reported that there was a new caravanserai, well-built and spacious, for both men and animals, with three tanks and a deep well of over 100 fathoms (180 m!), with a pond for the cattle to wash in. At two musket shots from the caravanserai was the village of Deh-e Kuh, where Kaempfer stayed. It had a reasonable caravanserai and an old dilapidated one, but he stayed in a beautiful house with wall paintings belonging to the *kalantar*. It had a large cemetery with a tomb. Ketelaar also stayed in the house of the village chief, because at the caravanserai there was no water. According to Speelman, who considered the caravanserai of Gurdheh or Kurdeh the best he had seen so far, both the adjacent village and the next one (which was Deh-e Kuh) in which his party rested, were called Deh-e Kuh, because they were at the foot of the mountain.[106] Stodart wrote that Deh-e

105. Valentijn 1726, vol. 5, p. 265 (Biries); Thevenot 1971, vol. 2, p. 130 (Bihri) with a description of the caravanserai; Kaempfer 1968, p. 118 (Beriss); Silva y Figueroa 1667, pp. 80, 362 (Bir). For a detailed description of the caravanserai, which also had two rooms with doors, and the tomb see Speelman 1908, pp. 56-57 (Bery); Herbert 1929, p. 63 (Berry) with description of the tomb; Tavernier 1930, pp. 316-17 (Bihri) reported that the caravanserai was built by the mother of Aimas, khan of Lar. Fryer 1909, vol. 2, p. 198, he also mentioned the tomb and the school (Bury); Strauszens 1678, p. 195 (Barry); Hedges 1967, p. 206 (Beeres); KA 1793, f. 989r- vs (Beries); Winninx, 14 July (Beri); LeBrun 1718, vol. 2, p. 316 (Bieries); Chardin 1811, vol 8, pp. 474-75 (Behry). The caravanserai was constructed by the governor's mother. He provided a detailed description as well as of the saint's tomb, whom he identified as Amir Ahmad [Emir Achmed], a son of the Imam `Ali and his wife Fatima; Anonymous 1939, vol. 1, p. 219, note (Berre – a place with a fort in ruins, two water cisterns on the road).

106. Kaempfer 1968, p. 119 (Däaku; Kurdä); Thevenot 1971, vol. 2, p. 130 (De-hi Kourd; Pai Chotali; Dehi Kouh) confirmed the existence of the road sign, which was about one fathom high on a basis of free stone. He also reported that a man had been shut in it condemned for highway robbery as a warning to others. The Dutch embassy passed a good caravanserai Pa-ye Kotal (Pakoetel) where it was met by a delegation from Lar. Valentijn 1726, vol. 5, p. 265 (Dehacoe; Dehikoe); Speelman 1908, pp. 55-56 (Decoe; Corde); Herbert 1929, p. 62 (De-achow); Chardin 1811, vol. 8, p. 479 (De Kert and 4 leagues later Gourde); Tavernier 1930, p. 317 (Pai-Kotali); Fryer, vol. 2, p. 197 (Pokutal); Hedges, pp. 205-06 (Kuda-Poicotal) a large and convenient *saray*, well stored with provisions; KA 1793, f. 989 (Pakotal; unnamed *saray* at the foot of the mountain, Dhekoe); LeBrun

Kuh was a poor village lying on a craggy and barren plain. "The water is good; but tanck water as most of these parts be, wch the cuntrey peple call obe choodohe, wch by interpretation is as much to saye Godes water [Ab-e khoda]."[107] Those not taking the road via Kurdeh could stop at the caravanserai Rustehhennis, built by a merchant Aqa Jamal, which had a very deep well (built by a governor of Lar); this only yielded brackish water.[108]

Continuing the journey to Lar, one arrived at a small caravanserai standing alone, with a cistern called Hhormont named after the village.[109] Lar, the next stop, had a *rahdar* station and only two caravanserais. One, inside the town, was not so good; the other, outside the town (towards the Gulf side) was quite comfortable. However, it could not be used during the rainy season, because it overflowed with water. Europeans and Armenians usually stayed at the Dutch house on the town's outskirts, which the VOC kept there. The house was used both as a retreat for Bandar ʿAbbas staff during part of the summer as well as a halting place. For it was in Lar that camels had to be changed. The ones coming from Isfahan could not stand the heat of the Garmsirat and vice-versa. Both inside Lar and in its environs there were plenty of cisterns, because there were years when it did not rain at all.[110]

The Lar to Bandar ʿAbbas Road

The traveler left Lar through the suburb Bajgah, where road guards were situated right in front of the caravanserai with the same name.[111] Then the route passed first through the village of Kanaru,[112] then onwards to the village of Talkhab with its small covered caravanserai, which according to Stodart had good water. By 1672, a benefactor had built a new magnificent caravanserai.[113] Travelers then continued to Fariyab, while they saw many villages and cultivated land en route. The caravanserai was very good, but was isolated, while also there was an old sober caravanserai[114] Alternatively, travelers could chose to go two hours

---

1718, vol. 2, p. 316 (Dehakoe); Silva y Figueroa 1667, pp. 79, 362 (Diacuri, small village with ruined caravanserai; Dianin); Anonymous 1939, vol. 1, p. 219, note (Dirkuh with many water cisterns).

107. Stodart 1935, p. 82 (Dehcohibibia).

108. Kaempfer 1968, p. 120 (Aga Djumal).

109. Thevenot 1971, vol. 2, p. 130 (Hhormont); KA 1793, f. 988 vs. where Ketelaar lodged in a house (Chormoenoen).

110. Tavernier 1930, pp. 317-20; LeBrun 1718, vol. 2, p. 318.

111. Chardin 1811, vol. 8, p. 486 (Bagsea), and from there each league a caravanserai each with 3 cisterns; Valentijn 1726, vol. 5, p. 265 (Basga).

112. Kaempfer 1968, p. 121, 116 (Kanaru); Valentijn 1726, vol. 5, p. 265. (Kenneroen); KA 1793, f. 981(Kenanoen).

113. Thevenot 1971, vol. 2, p. 232 (Tschercha); Tavernier 1930, p. 322 (Tcherkab); Kaempfer 1968, p. 116 (Tjerg aab); Valentijn 1726, vol. 5, p. 265 (Sargab); Stodart 1935, p. 83 (Cherchoke); Fryer 1909, vol. 2, pp. 201, 340. Speelman 1908, p. 44 did not stop there, because it was full (Sera 'tSurgou); Winninx, 11 July (Sargab); Silva y Figueroa 1667, p. 64 (Charcaph).

114. Kaempfer 1968, p. 121 (Basti Parija); Valentijn 1726, vol. 5, p. 265 (Pariaap; caravanserai Basti Parija), 285 (caravanserai Paste Poeriouw); Strauszens 1678, p. 197 (Farate); LeBrun 1718,

after Talkhab to another small covered caravanserai named Tenghinoun.[115] Wherever one stopped, the next halting place was at the covered caravanserai Wasili, and then to another covered square caravanserai called Chasmeh-ye Zangi. These caravanserais were not built like the others and were wretched lodgings, according to Thevenot. In 1651, at Waseli victuals could be had from the *saraydar* who lived in the village one mile away. The Dutch embassy of 1691 reported that the entire area was covered with saltpeter and looked as if it was covered with snow. There were two other good caravanserais at Chashmeh-ye Zangi, but the water was brackish.[116] Chardin wrote that there were two small caravanserais here, which were different from the caravanserais that he had seen until then and which were not called caravanserai, but *chahar-taqi*, because they were small, squat, square and cruciform. He added that the same types of caravanserais were also seen in Kerman. However, few people went there, while the countryside was even more miserable. According to popular etymology, the *saray* was built by an Ethiopian, hence the allegedly correct orthography of Chashmeh-ye Zangi or the Ethiopian's well, which clearly may be wrong. However, due to lack of suggestions I have retained this rendering of the orthography. The Dutch had "a neat, but small dwelling" here where the staff in Bandar `Abbas came during the hot season to find relief. In 1717, the caravanserai Chashmeh-ye Zangi had been totally destroyed due to a recent earthquake.[117]

After 2 *farsakh* from the caravanserai Waseli, the traveler came to the large green village of Desgert, where in 1717 the caravanserai was totally uninhabitable. Continuing, for 1.5 *farsakh*, the caravanserai Tschenitsche Tschengi, which was a square caravanserai was built of free stone, and open on all sides, which was typical for this kind of building in the Garmsir to provide cooling by the wind. But there was nothing to be had at this caravanserai, neither water nor straw, thus the caravan pushed onwards to Badini or Bahadini, which had a cistern, but full of worms "as most tankes be." In 1717, the caravanserai was old and totally in ruins because of the earthquakes.[118]

After Bahadini one arrived at the caravanserai Chek-Chek, where also, there was a hut for the *rahdar*s.[119] Continuing the journey the traveler arrived at a pleasing large village,

vol. 2, p. 318 (Basta paryouw).

115. Thevenot 1971, vol. 2, p. 132.

116. Thevenot 1971, vol. 2, p. 132 (Ouasili; Schemzenghi); Kaempfer 1968, p. 121 (Wasili); Valentijn 1726, vol. 5, p. 265 (caravanserai Wasselee; Samsange); LeBrun 1718, vol. 2, p. 318 (Basieli; then followed an unnamed small caravanserai probably Shamsangi); Speelman 1908, p. 44 (Wassely; Siamse Sangy); Herbert 1929, p. 54 (Ourmangel) in view of the distance, 5 *farsakh*, this must be Wasali; Fryer 1909, vol. 2, p. 190 mentioned half-way between Sham Zangee and Lhor [Lar] a new caravanserai which either must be Waseli or Tang-e Nao. Ketelaar, without reporting their names, mentioned two sarays between Dastgerd and Kenanoen. KA 1793, f. 981.

117. Fryer 1909, vol. 2, p. 190 (Sham Zangee, an Abbasin); Tavernier 1930, p. 322 (Chamzenghi); Chardin 1811, vol. 8, p. 487-8 (Tchem sesengui); KA 1793, f. 980 vs (Sjeam Sang).

118. Kaempfer 1968, p.121 (Bahadeni; Desgert); Stodart 1935, pp. 83, 116 (Dascherd; Bohodonie); Valentijn 1726, vol. 5, pp. 266, 273 (Bahadini. Badeni, Disgirt); Winninx, 9 July (Badang); Speelman 1908, p. 44 (Bahadany); Herbert 1929, p. 53 (Duzgun is Dastgird). I have not been able to identify nearby Laztan-de. KA 1793, f. 980 (Bhadanie; Dest-gird); Winninx July 11 (Dasgard); Anonymous 1939, vol. 1, p. 219, note mentions a caravanserai with three water cisterns at one league from Dizkurd.

119. Thevenot 1971, vol. 2, p. 132 (Tschetschek); Valentijn 1726, vol. 5, p. 266 (the other water tank Sjek Sjek); Speelman 1908, p. 43 (Sekke-sek); Ketelaar, without mentioning the name,

numbering 70 houses in 1617, situated in a date grove, called Hormut. It had two small caravanserais, the one a little beyond the other, at a bow shot from the village. These boasted of some cisterns, which contained bad water, and according to Silva y Figueroa were thereafter of a different type, i.e. the open *chahar-taqi* design. Speelman considered it a friendly village, which had many animals, date groves and agricultural production watered by wells. He estimated that it was inhabited by 300 persons. Victuals were plenty and cheap. About one mile from Hormut was the caravanserai Agaya Nalie. According to Tavernier, the stretch between Lar and Hormut was the most difficult terrain in Iran, because often there was no water to be had. Coming down towards the littoral there was usually plenty of water in the cisterns at the start of summer. But on returning to Isfahan one often found the cisterns empty due to the many animals that had drunk there. This obliged the traveler either to make the Hormut-Lar stretch in one go, or to divert from the road by 3 leagues to find water.[120] After one mile from Hormut, there was the caravanserai Berkeh-ye Aqa Jamal,[121] followed by the caravanserai Bascomaakoe, and the caravanserai Sartang: all of them offered poor lodgings.[122]

After Sartang, the caravanserai Bedgia Paria was next; this had salt water. The route then continued to the Imamzadeh-ye Seh Tang-e Dalan, which had three caravanserais including one built by a certain Aqa `Arab, which was a reasonable one. Then, according to Kaempfer, it was another 3 *farsakh* to the caravanserai Tang-e Dalan,[123] where in 1652 two neatly built, but small cool caravanserais were located, where nothing could be obtained. The village itself had only 10 houses in 1685 and only 2 in 1691. The water was good, but there was nothing else to be obtained for man or horse. Tavernier reported that there was a new caravanserai, within its midst a small basin which was fed by a small mountain brook. However, the water was a little salty and therefore a cistern had been built. A canal had been constructed by a rich merchant to channel water from the mountain to a dry area of land, where since then two thriving villages had been established, which supplied the caravanserai with its necessaries. Chardin noted two caravanserais here with their cisterns.[124]

---

reported that there was a ruined caravanserai before arriving at Badahini. KA 1793, f. 979 vs.

120. Thevenot 1971, vol. 2, p. 132 (Hhormout); Silva y Figueroa 1667, pp. 62, 94, 356 (Horum); Stoddard 1935, p. 84 said there was good water at Churmoot; Winninx, 10 July and 19 November (Gormoedt); Kaempfer 1968, p. 122 (Hormuus); Valentijn 1726, vol. 5, p. 266 (Choeremoet; Goermoet); Speelman 1908, p. 43 (Germoet); Herbert, p. 53 (Whormoot); Fryer, vol. 2, p. 189 (Cormoot, town of dates); Chardin, vol. 8, pp. 488-89 (Gormouth); KA 1793, f. 979 (Ghormoet); Tavernier 1930, p. 322 (Kormout); Winninx, 10 July (Gormoedt); LeBrun 1718, vol. 2, p. 318 (Gormoet); Anonymous 1939, vol. 1, p. 219, note.

121. Valentijn 1726, vol. 5, p. 285 (Borka Aga Sjouwmaat; Ahasimaal [Aqa Jamal]).

122. Valentijn 1726, vol. 5, p. 266 (Serteng). The little covered caravanserai called Serten. Thevenot 1971, vol. 2, p.133; Strauszens 1678, p. 197 (Sarap).

123. Kaempfer 1968, p. 122 (Imam se Tengi dalun; Tengi Dalun); Silva y Figueroa 1667, p. 60 (Tangotalan); Valentijn 1726, vol. 5, p. 266 (Tanke Daloen; Tangedoeloe); Stodart 1935, p. 84 (Tanggetelon); Fryer 1909, vol. 2, p. 189 also mentioned the stream of living water at (Tangedelon), and so did Chardin 1811, vol. 8, p. 493 (Tenguedelan) and Ketelaar. KA 1793, f. 979 (Tangidaloen); LeBrun 1718, vol. 2, p. 319 (Tangboedaloe); Anonymous 1939, vol. 1, p. 219, note (Yanikidalin).

124. Thevenot 1971, vol. 2, p. 133 (Tenghidalan) with description of this fine specimen. Tengi Dalan at 6 *farsakh*. Kaempfer 1968, p. 122; Speelman 1908, pp. 41-42 (Tangedelangh); Herbert 1929, p. 52 (Tanghy-Dolon); Tavernier 1930, pp. 322-23 (Tenquidalen); Winninx, 9 July and 20 November (Delang; Dalongh).

From Tang-e Dalan, the road led, after 6 *farsakh*, to the caravanserai Gur-e Bazargan, via two caravanserais, to wit: the covered caravanserai called Berka-ye Duband, and later another covered caravanserai known as Jihan. The name Gur-e Bazargan, allegedly had been derived from the name of an Armenian who was buried there; his grave was still there when the Dutch embassy passed. This solitary caravanserai, though not too far from a village, had three cisterns, for otherwise there was no water. Fryer mentioned the water-melons which were a grateful cooler in the extreme heat, and he considered the name, merchant's grave, aptly chosen.[125] Following Gur-e Bazargan the next stop was a small covered caravanserai Berkeh-ye Soltan and later another like it, but a bad one, near the village of Kurestan or Kahurestan.[126] The caravanserai did not offer much accommodation. The village itself consisted of about 100 mud huts to house farmers, who worked the surrounding fields. Here was a bridge over the Rud-e Shur financed by a Moslem merchant in 1639 or so, which, despite enormous amounts of money spent, still had not been finished and work was still ongoing in 1651. Tavernier remarked that here the traveler could buy the best and largest water melons in Iran. The caravanserai of Kurestan was named after a tree growing there, according to Fryer. He also noted that the houses in the village "being the first we met with whose Houses were fixed." In 1717 the caravanserai was so dilapidated that the Dutch ambassador stayed in the *kalantar*'s (village chief) house.[127]

From Kurestan the traveler required a guide, because there was neither path nor road, but only sandy plains, with many dangerous spots close to the rivers and brooks. All other travelers had to pass a bridge which boasted of at least 50 arches. In fact there were two causeway/bridges. One of which had a length of a quarter league, while the causeway to the second bridge was even longer. The second bridge was as long as the Pont Neuf in Paris and passed over the salty river Kur. It was so wide that five to six horses could pass at the same time. The bridge had been built by a Persian who had grown rich in Golconda and through trading with Iran. To perpetuate his memory he decided to build the causeway and the two bridges. He had offered the local peasants two *qazbegi*s for two *mann* of rocks to construct the causeway. This was good business for the peasants, who during the six months off-season could earn no money from passing caravans and therefore transported these rocks with their camels and donkeys.[128]

---

125. Kaempfer 1968, p. 123 (Djahun; Guri Bessergun); Valentijn 1726, vol. 5, p. 266 (Berkei Dobend; Jehoen; Gioen; Goerbaseregoen.); Stodart 1935, p. 84 (Goorebazargoone); Thevenot 1971, vol. 2, p. 133 (Dgei Hhou; Kor Bazirghion); Tavernier 1930, p. 323 (Gourbasarghant); Chardin 1811, vol. 8, p. 494 (Courbazargan); Speelman 1908, p. 41 (Choure basere Chan) and (Sera Sehoen [Jahan]); Fryer 1908, vol. 2, pp. 188-89 (Goor-Bazergum; Jehun); KA 1793, f. 979 (Ghoerbasraghoen; Serae Jehoen); Winninx, 8-9 July and 21 November 21 (Courbesserzan = moordtkuil [killing hole]; Gijhean; Gehoen); LeBrun 1718, vol. 2, p. 319 (Goerbasergoen); Silva y Figueroa 1667, p. 60 (Gehun); Anonymous 1939, vol. 1, p. 219, note (Kinbazirkan).

126. Thevenot 1971, vol. 2, p. 134; (caravanserai Berkei Soltouni; Kahuiristan) Kaempfer 1968, p. 124; (Coristan; caravanserai Koeresson) Valentijn 1726, vol. 5, pp. 267, 285 (Coristan); Smith 1970, p. 64 (Cabrestam); Herbert 1929, p. 53 (Courestan); Winninx 8 July (Couristan); Chardin 1811, vol. 8, p. 495 (Courestan); LeBrun 1718, vol. 2, p. 319 (Korestan).

127. Speelman 1908, pp. 39-40; see also Kaempfer 1968, p. 124 (Kahuirestan); Tavernier 1930, p. 323 (Cauvrestan); Chardin 1811, vol. 8, p. 501; Fryer 1909, vol. 2, p. 187; Silva y Figueroa 1909, pp. 53-54, 366 (Cabrestan); Anonymous 1939, vol. 1, p. 219, note (Qabristran).

128. Tavernier 1930, pp. 324-25; Chardin 1811, vol. 8, pp. 498-99. The *qazbegi* was a copper

Leaving Kurestan the traveler passed a small covered caravanserai Dobrike or Barik, and then, via caravanserai Guni Godscji Mamed, Barik over the river Kur. The next stops were: the village of Pohel, then a dilapidated caravanserai, and after *6 farsakh* the village of Gichi or Gachin, a village of huts built from straw and pieces of fabric.[129] For another alternative halting place the traveler had to ride 4.5 miles to the gardens of Latidun, and then 2.5 miles to Gichi. Fryer also mentioned the stately bridge with arches, of some three miles, which he believed to be recently built, and a nicely built causeway through the fens. In 1702 the bridge was broken in the middle, and in 1717 it was in ruins.[130] In Gichi itself, the caravanserai was situated in the wilderness, where Stodart found to his surprise eggs, milk, dates and hay for horses. It was a pleasant place because of green bushes and in some places date groves. In 1645, there were two beautiful caravanserais at Gichi, which had a water tank. However, Speelman was rather dismissive of the place, where he mentioned but 8 straw huts and some poor folk herding goats. Tavernier was much more upbeat, one caravanserai was quite well situated, the other however, badly located, because the wind had blown it full of sand so that one could not stay there. Chardin considered the caravanserai, which was half blown under by the sand the worst place he had visited. In 1685, Kaempfer echoed Speelman, though he mentioned that Gichi still had 2 caravanserais; one of which was dilapidated, while the other was still usable. In 1717, the caravanserai was still rather dilapidated.[131] Two leagues from Gichi there was a bifurcation. If the traveler did not have a guide and chose the left road, which looked better, he would end up on the wrong and a very dangerous road. The road on the right hand was the indeed the right one and was nothing but a track over a sandy plain as far as Bandar Abbas.[132] If the traveler was not welcomed by a delegation from Bandar `Abbas in Gichi he had to ride on to Khun-e Sorkh which in 1665 had a small caravanserai, while in 1691 there were two dilapidated caravanserais. From here the traveler pressed onwards to the Sultan's Gardens or to the caravanserai Band-`Ali and then to Gamron.[133] The caravanserai of Band-`Ali, situated close to the beach, was of the *chahar taqi* type with an octagonal cupola and was very comfortable. In 1717, it was described as being reasonably large with small rooms.[134] An alternative starting point of the journey up-country was the

coin.

129. Kaempfer 1968, p. 124 (Barik, Guni Godscji Mamed; Gedjii); Valentijn 1726, vol. 5, pp. 266-67 (Getsie; Getje); Thevenot 1971, vol. 2, p. 134 (Dobrike; Ghetschi); Tavenier 1930, p. 324 (Guitchi); Winninx 7 July (Gitsji); Anonymous 1939, vol. 1, p. 219, note (to the river).

130. Valentijn 1726, vol. 5, p. 285 (Latidoen; Getje); LeBrun 1718, vol. 2, p. 319; Fryer, vol. 2, p. 186; KA 1793, f. 979.

131. Stodart 1935, p. 84 (Gochine); Speelman 1908, pp. 38-39; Kaempfer 1968, p. 124 (Gedjii); Herbert, p. 52 (Gacheen); Tavernier 1971, p. 325 (Guitchi) where there were some Arabs in tents who offered milk and butter and other supplies; also Silva y Figueroa 1667, pp. 52, 367 (Guichy). Fryer 1909, vol. 2, p. 184 (Getche). Travelers could purchase cheese and butter here; KA 1793, f. 987 vs. (Getschijen); Chardin 1811, vol. 8, p. 502-03 (Guetchy); LeBrun 1718, vol. 2, p. 319 (Gesje).

132. Tavernier 1930, p. 325.

133. Winninx, 6 July (Gonasorgh; Soltan's Gardens); Thevenot 1971, vol. 2, p. 135 (Houni Sourkh; Bendali); Valentijn 1726, vol. 5, p. 267 (Onesoor; Bandali); Kaempfer 1968, p. 125 (Bend Ali); Anonymous 1939, vol. 1, p. 219, note (Kishigan?, 6 *farsakh* to Bandar `Abbas).

134. Speelman 1908, p. 38; Silva y Figueroa 1667, p. 52 (it was the last place till Lar where you could get fresh water); Herbert 1929, p. 51 (Band-Ally); Tavernier 1930, pp. 325-26 (Bend-Ali); Fryer 1909, vol. 2, p. 178 (Band Ally); Kaempfer 1968, p. 126 (Bend Ali); Valentijn 1726, vol. 5, pp. 267,

small Moslem temple Khvajeh-ye Khezr, not far from Bandar `Abbas, where the traveler was welcomed by the road guards.[135]

Table 5.1: Halting places along the Isfahan-Bandar `Abbas route

1628 Stodart	1645 up Winninx	1645 down Winninx	1665 Thevenot	1685 Kaempfer	1691 van Leene	1701 up Hoogcamer	1703 down Hoogcamer	1900 Sadid al-Saltana
Isfahan	Isfahan	Isfahan	Isfahan	Isfahan	Isfahan	Isfahan	Isfahan	Isfahan
				Koli padsja				
					Bagebatsjaron	Baagoesja-roen		
				Osgewan				
					Agag Hadi			
				Mirsa Ali Resa	Miseralisa			
		Ortschin		Urzcini	Cotali Ortsini			
				Dehserd				
				K. Gonoresj				
							Poskoen/ Kietsje	
						K.Mirzah Serafa		
	K. Mamet Alibeecq							
Moyore (Mahyar)	Maijaar		Mayar	Mahjar	Majaart	Majaar		
		Spahan-necq						
		tSarasa	Schairza	Scharesa	Sjaresa			Shah Reza
Comushaw	Comischa;	Comissa	Komschah	Gommosja	Commissia	Commessia	Commesia	Qumishah
				K. Kar Myrsa Mortusa				
				K. Mirsa Kutschek Kala				
	Machsoet-beecq	Machsoet-beecq	Maksoud Beghi	Mag sud begi	Mika-koetsiek/ Matubeki	Maksoetbegi	Maksoetbegi	Maqsudbeg
saray	Ammnebath	Amnebath	Amnebad	Amnabad	Amnabat	Aapnawaat	Aap Nabaat	
Yeassechoze	Jassegas	Jassegas	Yez-de Kast	Jesdechas	Jesdegas	Jesdegas	Jesdegas	Yazdikhvast
			Chotal Naar-Schekeni				Spilkestoen	Followed the summer route
		Combazala	Gombez Cala	Gumber allala	Combesilala	Gombesehala		

272 (Bandali); Strauszens 1678, p. 197; KA 1793, f. 978 vs (Bandalie); Chardin 1811, vol. 8, p. 503; LeBrun 1718, vol. 2, p. 319 (Bandalie).

135. *NA*, KA 1559, Hoogcamer to GG 21/8/01, f. 286 (Chogay Cheder); Chardin 1811, vol. 8, p. 505.

1628 Stodart	1645 up Winninx	1645 down Winninx	1665 Thevenot	1685 Kaempfer	1691 van Leene	1701 up Hoogcamer	1703 down Hoogcamer	1900 Sadid al-Saltana
Dehegerdow	Degerdoe	Degerdoe	Dehi Ghirdon	Degerdu	Degerdoe	Degerdoe		
				K. Arun				
				Kewilar	Kivilaar			
			bridge of 5 arches	bridge of 5 arches		Poelesiakoe		
Cuskezar	Kuskesaer	Kuskesaar	Keuschkzer	Kuskiserd	Cuchesaar	Koskoser		
				Dombone		Dombeny		
Assepose	Asepas	Assepas	Asoupas	Aszpasz	Asepas	Haspas		
					Bagedoe/Goe de Kinjari			
Yeioone	Oedjoen	Oldjoen	Oudgioun	Udjan	Oedjaan			
						Sjafada		
			Chotal-Imam-Zadeh-Ismael		Co-tali Imames Esmaal	ImamZade		
			Esmael	Imam Sadas Mal	Esmaal			
Moyeeme	Maijien	Majein	Maain	Majin or Mahin	Majien	Majur		
			Abgherm		Abigerne	Abegerm		
			Poligorgh			Poligor	Polgorse	
		K. Agaseff	K. Agassef					
			K.Badgega		Basighaar	K. Baasga	Basgona	
	Germoens							
Mardasz				Merdest				
Chelminar	Misgascan			Myrgascun				
				Tschehil-Minar				Takhteh-Jamshid
		K. Bathiga						
	Vergoed							
Zargoone								Zarqan
							Tsaarbag	
Shiraz	Shiraz	Shiraz	Shiraz	Shiraz	Shiraz	Shiraz	Shiraz	Shiraz
			Oudgeval		Oesiwat	Osiwaar		
								Ja`farabad
								Pol-e Fasa
Bobohogi	Babbahasj		Baba-Adgi	Baba Haddji	Babaghasi	Baba Hhadji	Baba Hhadji	Baba Hajji
					Cnonebande			
Moozaferie	Mazaffri	Mozaffri	Mouzeferi	Myrsa Feri	Moesasari	Mosesarie	Mose Faril	
			Paira	K. Paira	Pajera	K. Para	Para	
		K. Agatachi						

1628 Stodart	1645 up Winninx	1645 down Winninx	1665 Thevenot	1685 Kaempfer	1691 van Leene	1701 up Hoogcamer	1703 down Hoogcamer	1900 Sadid al-Saltana
								Akbarabad
								`Abbasabad
Chaffer	Gaffar	Gaffer	Chafer	Chafr/Jesa	Chaffert/K.			
				Asmugir	Asmogeert	Asmonger		
	Tadde-wangh	Tadder-vangh	Tadivan	Tadewun				
								Tang-e Esma`ilabad
							Asmonger	Asmankard
Mochak		Moggeck	Mouchek	Musak	Mochai Sughta	Mogagzoekte	Mogag-zoekte	Mokhak
			ruined K	K. Hadschi Resa	small K		small K	
Charmoot								
						Bagar-Abad		
	Ziaron	Sharon	Dgiaroun	Djarum	Sjaron	Jaroen	Jarom	Jahrum
Dehuion		Schatalgh	Tschai-telkh	Tsjai Talg	Saithal	Satalk	Satalk	Chahtalkh
			Chotali Haseni	Kutelli Harseni	Cotal Hasani			
	K. Mourer		Momzir	Mansir Kieschik	Moesoer	Mosetis	Mossir	
				Kalha Tesorg				
wilderness		Dedombaj	Dehidobe	Domba	K. Teduba	Dedombe	Dedombe	
				Scharafi				
								Javim
Goyreeome								
Carerow	Benerouw	Bererovio	Benaru	Benaru	Benaroe	Benaroe	Benaroe	Banaru
			K. Dehra	K. Dehra	K. Dera			
	[Kourdagh]	Sarai						
Berrie	Beri	Beri	Bihri	Biriis/Beris	Biries	Beries	Beries	
								Sharfu
Dehcohibibia			De-hi Kourd	Daaku	Dehacoe	Dehikoe	Dehikoe	Dehkuh
				Rustehhennis				
			Pai Chotali Dehi Kouh	[Kurda]	K. Pakoetel			Kurdeh
			Hhormont K					

1628 Stodart	1645 up Winninx	1645 down Winninx	1665 Thevenot	1685 Kaempfer	1691 van Leene	1701 up Hoogcamer	1703 down Hoogcamer	1900 Sadid al-Saltana
Lar	Lar	Lar	Lar	Lar	Lar	Lar	Lar	Lar
				Kanaru		Kenneroen		
					K. Basiga			
Cherchoke		Sargon	Tscherchab	Tjerg aab	Sargab			
			Tenghinoun					
				Basti Parija	Pariaap	Pastepariouw	Paste Poeriouw	Qal`eh-ye Fariyab
			K. Ouasili	K. Wasili	K. Wasselee			
			K. Schemzengh	Tschenitsche Tschengi	Samsange			K. Hajj`Ali
Dascherd		Dasgard		Desgert		Disgirt		
								Char Berkeh
K. Bohodonie		K. Badeng	K. Bahadani	Bahadeni	Bahadini	Baderie	Badenie	Badini/Bahadini/ Badami
			K.Tschektschek		Sjek Sjek			Gardaneh-ye ChakChak
Churmoot	Gormoedt	Gormoedt	Hhormout	Hormuus	Choeremoet	Goermoet	Goermoet	Hurmut
							Borka Aga Sjouwmaat	
			Sarai	Imam se Tengi Dalun?	K. Ahasimaal			Aqa Jamal
					Bascomaakoe			
			K. Serten		Serteng			Sartang
			K. Bedgi-Pari					
Tanggetelon	K. Dalong	K. Delangh	K. Tengidalan	Tengi Dalun	Tanke Daloen	Tangadoeloen		Tang-e Dalan
	Gehoen	Gilhaen	K. Dgei Hhou	Djehun	K. Jehoen	Gioen		Jihun
						Bonko Bonpaan	Borka bon paan	
Goorebazar-goone		Cour-bassergan	K.Kor Bazirghon	Guri Bessergun	Goerebasir-gan	Goerbasir-goen	Goerbaser-egoen	
								Berkeh-ye now
								Berkeh-ye Taqi Khani
								Shiyuhravan
			K. Berki Soltouni					Berkeh-ye soltan
	Couristan	Coristan	K.Courestan	Kahuiristan	Coristan	Coristan	Coristan	
				K. Guni Godsji Mahmed	K. Koeresson			Kahurestan
								Jangu'i
			K. Dobrike					
							Latidoen	Latidun
Gochine	Getsi	Gitsj	Ghetschi	Gedjii	Getsie	Getje	Getje	Gachin-bala

1628 Stodart	1645 up Winninx	1645 down Winninx	1665 Thevenot	1685 Kaempfer	1691 van Leene	1701 up Hoogcamer	1703 down Hoogcamer	1900 Sadid al-Saltana
	Soltan's garden	Gonasorgh	Houni Sourkh		K. Onesoor			Khun-e sorkh
			Bendali	K. Bend Ali	Bandali	Bandali		
Gombroon	Gamron	Gamron	Gamron	Gamron	Gamron	Gamron	Gamron	Bandar ` Abbas

Table 5.2: Cost for food and fodder en route from Bandar 'Abbas to Isfahan in 1645

Dates	Locations	Food supplies	Expenditures	Fodder for 4 horses and 4 mules	Expenditures
6 July 1645	Bandar 'Abbas	unspecified	Ma. 56	consumed since ultimo June	Ma. 66.01
7 July (the date in the fodder list is given as 8 July)	Gitsie and Corristan	2 *man* of bread eggs butter dates for beer buttermilk water lemons and water	Ma . 1.8 .4 .10 .6 .5 .10	16 *man-e Tabriz* of barley at 8 *gas* each for 2 days 18 *man* of straw at 2 *gas* [*qazbeki*, copper coin], per *man* of water	Ma. 6.08 1.16 .10
10 July	Tangedalangh	onions half *man* of bread butter buttermilk dates 3 chickens	Ma. .2 .7 .10 .5 .5 2.5	9 *man* of barley at 7 *gas* each 9 *man* of straw at 2 *gas* each paid to an *amael/\hammal*, porter] who brought the barley and straw into the *sera* [*saray*]; paid to muleteer who carried the fodder for the horses from Bandar to Gitsie	Ma. 3.03 .18 .03 5.00
11 July	Cormoet	3 chickens each at 14 *gas* 0.25 *man* of butter 1 *man* of dates milk fresh butter 1 *man* of bread rice [fire]wood	Ma. 2.2 1.5 .10 .11 .18 .12 2.00 .5	8 *man* of barley at 7 *gas* each; 9 *man* of straw at 2 *gas* each; paid to the muleteer who carried the barley and straw from Coristan to Courbaderchan	Ma. 2.16 .18 2.10
12 July	in Samsesengie	2 chickens bread: 6 *gas* butter [fire]wood	Ma. 1.10 .6 .10 .2	8 *man* of barley at 6 *gas* each 9 *man* of straw at 2 *gas* each paid to the *docqwaendaer* [*dok-kandar*, shop keeper] who accepted to take the sick mule to Bandar ['Abbas] for fodder	Ma. 2.08 .18 10.00
13 July	in Laar	Bread Cheese and *maest* (*mast*, yoghurt) dates butter 3/8 *man* rice onions and *kismus* (*keshmesh*, grapes) [fire]wood	Ma. .10 .10 .6 2.00 1.16 .6 .16	8 *man* of barley at 5 *gas* per *man* 9 *man* of straw at 1,5 *gas* each Water	Ma. 2.00 .14 1.00

Dates	Locations	Food supplies	Expenditures	Fodder for 4 horses and 4 mules	Expenditures
14 July	in Laar	Bread 1.5 *man*	Ma. .15	8 *man* of barley at 5 *gas* per *man*	1.12
		fresh butter and		5 *man* of straw	.07
		buttermilk	.10	water	1.00
		butter to cook	2.00	for repair of the mule's saddle	5.00
		rice	1. 4	for shoeing of 5 horses and 3 mules with	
		oranges	. 4	new irons	5.00
		cream	1. 4	salt for the animals 2 *gas* and for bringing	
		[fire]wood	.10	the fodder to the house 6 *gas*	
		hair of three jars?	. 6	for repair of riding saddle	.08
					1.00
15 July	in Decoe	Bread	Ma. .12	8 *man* of barley at 5 *gas* each	Ma. 2.00
		dates	.12	8 *man* of straw	.12
		eggs	. 7		
		rice	.16		
		3 chickens each at			
		15 *gas*	2. 5		
		maest	. 8		
		onions	. 2		
		butter	.12		
		fresh butter	1.5		
		[fire]wood	. 6		
16 July	in Bennaroe	*man* of rice	Ma. .16	11 *man* of barley at 4 *gas* each	Ma. 2.04
		man of butter	1.5	8 *man* of straw	.12
		eggs	. 8		
		3 chickens	1.16		
		buttermilk	.5		
		fresh butter	.5		
		[fire]wood	.5		
17 July	in Manzeir	Dates	Ma. .18	8 *man* of barley at 8 *gas* each	Ma. 3.04
		bread	.14	8 *man* of straw at 4 *gas* each	1.12
		man of rice	.18		
		onions	.3		
		man of butter			
		3 chickens	1.10		
		maest and milk	1.19		
		[fire]wood	.13		
			.7		
18 July	in Shatalch	*maest*	Ma. . 5	8 *man* of barley at 8 *gas* per *man*	Ma. 3.04
		bread	. 8	8 *man* of straw at 4 *gas* each	1.12
19 July	in Jaarom	*man* of bread	Ma. .10	7 *man* of barley at 6 *gas* per *man*	Ma. 2.02
		1 sheep's hoof and		8 *man* of straw at 2.5 *gas* per *man*	1.00
		feet	1. 5	for water for the horses to drink	
		butter	1.00	for repairs to two reins and the tail piece	.10
		dates for beer	.18	of the *jachtandraeger* (carrier of the	
		3 chickens 16 *gas*	2.18	*yaghdan* or suitcase)	.18
		each			
		man of rice melons			
		[fire]wood	1.14		
			. 7		

Dates	Locations	Food supplies	Expenditures	Fodder for 4 horses and 4 mules	Expenditures
20 July	in Mecheek	Bread *maest* 2 chickens butter [fire]wood	Ma. . 8 . 3 1.16 .10 . 3	8 *man* of barley at 8 *gas* per *man* 8 *man* of straw at 5 *gas* each	Ma. 3.04 2.00
21 July	in Gaffer	2 chickens at 15 *gas* each *man* of meat 3/8 *man* of butter bread oranges milk onions grapes and cucumbers [fire]wood	Ma. 1.10 .10 .15 .11 . 6 . 8 . 3 . 6 . 4	8 *man* of barley at 6 *gas* per *man* 8 *man* of straw at 2 *gas* per *man*	Ma. 2.08 .16
22 July	Mossafrie	*man* of rice 3 chickens at 14 *gas* each butter bread dates for beer *kismus* and beans present to the *siatier* (*shater*, messenger) who helped fishing [fire]wood	Ma..16 2. 2 1. 9 . 5 .18 . 2 1.10 . 2	7 *man* of barley at 7 *gas* per *man* 8 *man* of straw at 2 *gas* per *man*	Ma. 2.09 .16
23 July	in Chiraes	Bread maest apples apricots food from the bazaar *pillauw* (*pilaw*, rice) and eggs	Ma. .10 . 8 .10 . 6 2.00 4.00	8 *man* of barley at 5 *gas* per *man* straw straw for the muleteers shoeing of 5 horses and 3 mules as well as for bloodletting one oil as medicine repair of 7 to *8 nochtas* [?] and new iron clasps for the same a new *nochta* [?] a rough cloth (*hayer doeck*; sic, *haardoek*) to wash the horses with and a broom green grass for the horse left behind	Ma. 2.00 .12 1.01 8.00 .08 6.10 2.10 1.00 .06
24 July	in Chiraes	Bread butter 1 *man* of meat vegetables food from the bazaar *maest* prunes eggs [fire]wood	Ma. .10 1.10 1.00 .10 4.00 . 5 . 5 .14 .16		

Dates	Locations	Food supplies	Expenditures		Fodder for 4 horses and 4 mules	Expenditures	
25 July	in Chiraes	6 *man* of wine at 16 *gas* per *man*	Ma.	4.16	8 *man* of barley at 4 *gas* each	Ma.	1.12
		4 *man* of aracq (`araq; acqua vitae) at 2.5 Ma. per *man*		10.00	Straw		.12
		bread		.10			
		food from the bazaar		7.00			
		1,5 *man* of dates		1.04			
		for beer		.10			
		drinking water		1.00			
		1 *man* of meat		.08			
		butter and apples					
26 July	in Chiraes	3 chickens at 12 *gas* each	Ma.	1.16	8 *man* of straw at 4 *gas* per *man*	Ma.	1.12
		butter		.09	straw		.12
					2 iron currycombs		1.15
					5 iron clasps for the *nochtas* [?] and 0.5 Ma. to renew a rein		1.10
27 July	in Poelegor	*Maest*	Ma.	.09	8 *man* of barley at 6 *gas* per *man*	Ma.	2.08
		butter		.04	straw		.10
		[fire]wood		.01	paid to the *mehter* (groom) Mameth Bahi as gastos to take the Soltan's horse to Chiraes		.10
28 July	in Mahie	*Maest*	Ma.	.14	7 *man* of barley at 6 *gas* each	Ma.	2.02
		eggs		06	straw 10 *gas* and butter for the horses		
		man of dates for beer and the table					.14
		bread		1.00			
		meat		7			
		butter		.14			
		[fire]wood		6			
				5			
29 July	Oedjangh	Fresh cheese	Ma.	.14	6 *man* of barley at 6 *gas* per *man*	Ma.	1.16
		bread		.14	Straw		.10
		fresh butter		1.10			
		2 chickens		1.04			
		eggs		.10			
		maest		.05			
		milk		.06			
		fresh fish		1.05			
		butter		1.18			
		[fire]wood		.11			
30 July	Gaspas	Fresh butter	Ma.	1.05	7 *man* of barley at 8 *gas* per *man*	Ma.	2.16
		cooking butter		.19	Straw		.18
		maest		.06			
		bread		.17			
		2 chickens		1.04			
		wood and onions		.05			
		apples, vegetables such as melon		1.08			
		present to the gardener who brought some apples and roses		1.00			

Dates	Locations	Food supplies	Expenditures		Fodder for 4 horses and 4 mules	Expenditures	
31 July	Coscusaer and Degerdoe	Eggs *maest* wood bread dates vinegar onions butter	Ma.	.19 1.00 .09 .13 .18 .03 .02 .12	*1 man* of barley at 8 *gas* per *man* Straw	Ma.	2.16 .18
1 August	Jasdegas	*Maest* bread *man* of rice cherries and apricots 5 chickens at 12 *gas* each butter wood	Ma.	1.04 .12 1.00 1.02 3.00 .05	*1 man* of barley at 8 *gas* each Straw	Ma.	2.16 .16
2 August	Machtsoetbeecq	1,5 *man* of meat bread *maest* wood melons butter, fresh and for cooking	Ma.	1.10 .10 .07 .03 1.12 3.00	*1 man* of barley at 8 *gas* per *man* Straw	Ma.	2.09 .16
3 August	Commecha	1,5 *mann* of meat wood bread butter buttermilk melons	Ma.	1.10 .12 .15 .12 .05 .07	*1 mann* of barley at 7 *gas* per *man* Straw	Ma.	2.09 .16
4 August	Mayaer	1 *man* of meat mann of rice butter wood melons bread dates for beer	Ma.	1.04 1.00 .15 1.00 1.00 .10 1.04	*1 man* of barley at 7 *gas* per *man* straw water	Ma.	2.09 .14 .05

Table 5.3: Paid for various presents given en route in 1645:

To the servant of Aga Araab Derroga (Aqa `Arab Darugheh) in Laer who brought some grapes as a present	Ma. 1.00
To the servant of Abdul Cassemaga (`Abdol-Qasem Aqa) in Laer who brought one sheep and 5 chickens	2.00
To the servants of the governor of Laer who brought three bottles of wine	2.00
To the *radaers* (*rahdar*s or road guards) at Laer	10.00
To the woman* who keeps the Company's house here in Laer	4.00
To the servant Hossen (Hosayn) in Laer	1.00
To the *mechter* (*mehtar* or groom) of the governor in Laer who retrieved two mules	4.00
To the *radaers* in Chiatalch	5.00
To the *radaers* in Mochek	4.00
To the servant of Godia Mameth Alie (Khvajeh Mohammad `Ali) who brought some water melons etc.	1.00
To the Armenian servant in the Company's house in Sieraes on our departure	2.00
To the Carwaense *radaer* in Mahie	1.01
In Casdiaer where we lodged the night in a house	2.00
To the *radaer* of the caravanserai in Diggerdoe who brought some melons and other fruits	4.00
To the *radaers* in Combessala	10.00
In Machtsoetbeecq where we were lodged the night	2.00
To the *radaers* in Combeschadie who had given some chickens	10.00
To the *radaers* at Spanneck	10.00
Total given as presents en route	75.00

- In 1674, there was an old man and his wives who was caretaker of the Dutch house. Strauszens 1678, p. 196.

Paid as freight to donkey drivers and muleteers to transport 274 *mantauris* [*man-e Tabriz*] consisting of provisions, luggage, four paintings (and given as a present to the muleteers Ma. 10.00) from Bandaer [Bandar `Abbas] to Spahan   Ma. 346.15

Paid to a muleteer in Laer hired to carry two chests and horse harness from Laer to Spahan   Ma. 90.00

Total for freight from Bandaer to Spahan Ma. 436.15

Various payments to messengers in Bandaer as well as en route as Bandaer, Gamron.

To the siatier Nossom for a month, 22 days. Paid both monthly pay and subsistence money at Ma. 45 per month To the same on settlement of his subsistence money for the month of August for 15 days a Ma 0.5 per day	Ma. 67.00 7.10
To the *siatier* Chedder for the month of July, both his monthly pay and subsistence money Ma. 45.00 To the same on settlement of his subsistence money for the month of August for 15 days	Ma. 45.00 7.10
Paid to Abdul L'Asseth (`Abd al-Asad) for messagering to and from Siras and to Spahan again	Ma. 35.00
Total sum for messenger pay	Ma. 162.00

Table 5.4: Payment of monthly wages and subsistence pay to mechters, chatiers and house servants in 1645

To the *siatier* Hossijn (*shater* Hoseyn) who came from the director from Bandaer for the month of July both his monthly and subsistence pay at Ma. 40 per month. To the same on payment of his subsistence pay for August for 15 days at 0.5 Ma. per day	Ma. 40.00 7.10 47.10
To the *siatier* Cheibie who came from the director from Bandaer for the month of July his monthly and subsistence pay a 25 Ma. per month To the same on payment of his subsistence pay for August for 15 days at 0.5 Ma. per day	Ma. 25.00 7.10 32.10
To the *mechter* Isoph for the past month of July both his monthly and subsistence pay at Ma. 40 per month. To the same 15 days subsistence pay for August at 0.5 Ma. per day	Ma. 45.00 7.10 52.10
To the *mechter* Mameth Bahi for the month of July as above To the same for 15 days of the month of August at 0.5 Ma.	Ma. 45.00 7.10 52.10
To the Douleth Geldie for 6 days wages and subsistence for July starting as of 25 ditto at Ma. 40 per month To the same as payment for August for 25 days	Ma. 40.00 7.10 47.10
To Johan, servant of the junior merchant Dulckens for the month of July both his wages and his subsistence at 20 Ma. per month	Ma. 20.00
Total paid to *siatiers*, *mechters* and house servants	Ma.292.10

Various domestic expenditures and others

To Mr. Sarcerius (VOC director) for what he has spent and paid in bills	Ma. 37.15
For the repair of a *logiehoeder* [?]	06
For two cases of wine bought in Sieras for the director each with 16 bottles at 1 Ma. and 14 *gas* per bottle	27.04
For straw to pack the said cases	7.00
For three greyhounds bought in Mayaer	15.00
Total of domestic expenditures	Ma. 87.50

Table 5.5: Summary of various expenditures in 1645

Total for food	Ma. 226.01
Total for fodder and other cost for horses	221.03
Various presents en route	75.00
Payment to the donkey drivers and muleteers	436.15
Various cost for messengers	162.00
Monthly wages for *mechters, chiatiers* and house servants	298.00
Various domestic expenditures and the like	87.05
Total expenditures	Ma. 1416.04

BIBLIOGRAPHY

Archives

Archief MinBuiza or properly Archief Ministerie van Buitenlandse Zaken (Archives of the Ministry of Foreign Affairs, The Hague, the Netherlands)

B 149, inv. 1. Keun to van der Does (2 August 1876) and appendices.

I consulted this archive in 1975, but since then it has been transferred to the National Archives (The Hague), where the B-dossiers are available under access code 2.05.38. The letters and documents referred to here may be found in the files numbered 1370-1386. Because I have not consulted these files in their new location I used the old file numbers.

NA or National Archief (National Archives), The Hague, The Netherlands. Eerste afdeling (first section).

Records of the Verenigde Oostindische Compagnie (VOC) (Dutch East Indies Company)

Overgekomen brieven en papieren (Letters and papers received).

These Records had a KA number until 1979, when they were given a VOC number. I use KA numbers when I don't have the VOC number. The NA has a ledger, which indicates which KA corresponds to which VOC number.

VOC 1747, 2323, 2448 and KA 1057, 1559, and 1793.

National Archives (Kew Gardens, London).

FO 60/383

Books and Articles

`Abbasi, Mohammad Reza and Badi`i, Parviz eds. 1372/1993. *Gozareshha-ye owza`-ye siyasi, ejtema`i-ye velayat-e `ahd-e naseri – 1307 HQ.* (Tehran: Sazman-e asnad-e melli).

Abbott, Keith 1857. "Notes taken on a journey eastwards from Shiraz to Fessa and Darab, thence westwards by Jehrum to Kazerun in 1850," *JRGS* XXVII, pp. 149-184.

Abdullah, Thabit A.J. 2001. *Merchants, Mamluks, and Murder* (Albany, SUNY).

Abru, Hafez (Shehab al-Din `Abdollah Khvafi a.k.a.) 1378/1999. *Joghrafiya-ye Hafez Abru* ed. Sadeq Sajjadi. 3 vols. (Tehran: Ayin-e Mirath).

Abu Hakimah, A.M. 1960-2009. "Banu Ka`b," *Encyclopedia of Islam*2.

Abu Hakima, Ahmad 1965. *History of Eastern Arabia. The Rise and Development of Bahrain and Kuwait.* (Beirut, Khayats)

Adamec, L. ed. 1981. *Historical Gazetteer of Iran.* 4 vols. (Graz: Akademie Verlag).

Administration Report = *Administration Report on the Persian Gulf Political Residency for the year (1873 to 1940)* in Government of India. *The Persian Gulf Administration Reports 1873-1947*, 10 vols. (Gerrards Cross, Archives Editions, 1986).

Afshar-Sistani, Iraj 1369/1990. *Negahi beh Bushehr.* 2 vols. (Tehran, Nasl-e Danesh).

Aigle, Denise 2005. *Le Fars sous la domination mongole. Politique et Fiscalité (XIIIe-XIVe S.)* (Paris: Association pour l'avancement des études iraniennes)

Ainsworth, W. F. 1846. "The Passes of the Persian Appenines," *The New Monthly Magazine* part 2, pp. 475-81.

———. 1888. *A Personal Narrative of the Euphrates Expedition* (London, K. Paul, Trench & Co.).

Akhgar, Sarhang Ahmad 1366/1987. *Zendigi-ye man dar tul-e haftad sal-e tarikh-e mo`aser-e Iran* (Tehran: Akhgar).

Alexander, James Edward 2000. *Travels from India to England* (London, 1827 [repr. New Delhi, 2000]).

Algar, Hamid 1960-2009. "Kazaruni, Shaykh Abu Ishaq Ibrahim b. Shahriyar," *Encyclopedia of Islam*2.

Amanat, Abbas ed. 1983. *Cities & Trade: Consul Abbott on the Economy and Society of Iran 1847-1866* (London, Ithaca).

Amin, A.A. 1967. *British Interests in the Persian Gulf* (Leiden: Brill).

Anderson, T.S. 1880. *My Wanderings in Persia* (London: James Blackwood & Co.).

Anonymous 1865. "A Brief Account of the Province of Fars," *Transactions of the Bombay Geographical Society* 17 (1865), pp. 175-185.

———. 1917. *Behind the veil in Persia. English documents* (Amsterdam: C.J. van Langenhuysen).

———.1937. *Hudud al-ʿAlam. 'The Regions of the World.' A Persian geography 372 A.H.-982 A.D.* translated by V. Minorsky (London: Luzac).

———. 1939. *A chronicle of the Carmelites in Persia and the Papal mission of the seventeenth and eighteenth centuries,* 2 vols. (London: Spottiswood).

———. 1368/1989. *Do Safarnameh az jonub-e Iran dar salha-ye 1256 h.q. – 1307 h. q.* ed. Sayyed ʿAli Al-e Daʾud (Tehran: Amir Kabir).

Ansari, Mohammad Rafiʿ al-Din 2007. *Dastur al-Moluk. A Safavid State Manual.* Translated by Willem Floor and Mohammad H. Faghfoory (Costa Mesa: Mazda).

Arnold, A. 1877. *Through Persia by Caravan* (New York).

Atabegzadeh, Sorush 1373/1994. *Jaygah-e Dashtestan dar Sarzamin-e Iran* (Shiraz: Navid).

Aubin, Jean 1959. "Shah ismaʿil et les notables de l'Iraq person," *JESHO* 1, pp. 37-81.

Aubin, Jean ed. & tr. 1971. *L'Ambassade de Gregorio Pereira Fidalgo à la cour de Chah Soltan Hosseyn 1696-1692* (Lisbon).

Al-ʿAzzawi, ʿAbbas 1956. *ʿAshaʾir al-ʿIraq* 4 vols. (Baghdad).

Balfour, J.M. 1922. *Recent Happenings in Persia.* (Edinburgh and London: William Blackwood and Sons).

Ballantine, Henry 1879. *Midnight Marches Through Persia* (Boston: Lee and Shepard).

Bamdad, Mehdi 1351/1972. *Sharh-e hal rejal-e Iran dar qarn-e 12, 13, 14 hejri.* 6 vols. (Tehran: Zavvar).

Barrow, Edmund; Hirtzel, Arthur; Napier, George and Yate, Charles 1921. "South Persia and the Great War: Discussion," *The Geographical Journal*, Vol. 58, No. 2 (August), pp. 116-119.

Bashiri, Ahmad ed. 1367/1988. *Ketab-e Naranji. Gozareshha-ye siyasi-ye vezarat-e kharejeh-ye rusiyeh-ye tzari dar bareh-ye enqelab-e mashruteh-ye Iran* 3 vols. (Tehran: Nur).

Bayat, Kaveh ed. 1381/1992. *Iran va jang-e jahani-ye avval. Asnad-e vezarat-e dakheleh* (Tehran: Sazman-e asnad-e melli-ye Iran).

Berchet, Guglielmo 1976. *La Republica di Venezia e la Persia* (Tehran [reprint of Torino, 1865]).

Binning, R.B. M. 1857. *A Journal of Two Years' Travel in Persia, Ceylon, etc.* 2 vols. (London).

Boehm, Edgar Collins 1904. *The Persian Gulf and South Sea Isles* (London: Horace Cox).

Bradley-Birt, F.B. 1910. *Persia, through Persia from the Gulf to the Caspian* (Boston).

Braunnagel, W. 1925. *Autofahrten in Persien* (Neustadt an der Haardt, Carl Liesenberg).

Brittlebank, William 1873. *Persia during the famine: a narrative of the east and of the journey out and home* (London: Basil Montague Pickering).

Brydges-Jones, Harford 1976. *An Account of the Transactions of His Majesty's Mission to the Court of Persia in the Years 1807-11.* (Tehran [reprint of 1834 edition]).

Buckingham, J.S. 1971. *Travels in Assyria, Media and Persia* (Westmead, reprint [London, 1829]).

Çağman, Filiz and Tanıdı, Zeren 2002. "Manuscript production at the Kazaruni Orders in Safavid Shiraz," *Safavid Art and Architecture*, ed. Sheila Canby. The British Museum Press: London, pp. 43-48.

Candler, Edmund 1919. *On the Edge of the World* (London: Cassell and Co).

Carré, Abbé 1947. *The Travels of Abbé Carré in India and the Near East (1672-74)*, 3 vols. (London: Hakluyt).

Caskel W. 1929. "Ein Mahdi des 15. Jahrhunderts. Saijid Muhammad ibn Falah und seine Nachkommen," *Islamica* IV, pp. 48-93.

———.1934. "Die Wali's von Huwezeh," *Islamica* VI, pp. 415-34.

Chardin, Jean 1811. *Voyages du Chevalier Chardin en Perse et autres lieux de l'Orient.* ed. L. Langlès 10 vols. (Paris).

Chesney, Francis Rawdon 1868. *Narrative of the Euphrates expedition* (London: Longmans, Green & Co.).

Chirikov, E. I. 1989. *Putvoj zhurnal russkogo komissara-posrednika po turetsko-persidskomu razgranicheniyu* (St. Petersburg, 1875) translated into Persian by Abkar Masihi as *Siyahatnameh-ye Musyu Chirikuf.* ed. `Ali Asghar `Omran (Tehran, 1358/1979) and partly translated into English as "Extracts from the Diary of Y. I. Tchirikof," in Schofield, Richard ed. 1989, 12 vols. *Iran-Iraq Border*, vol. 2, pp. 327-471.

Chick, H. G. 1911. "Upon Various Districts of Fars and of the Gulf Ports," in Government of India, *Administration Report of the Persian Gulf Residency* for the year 1911, Appendix II.

Clerk, Claude 1861. "Notes on Persia, Khorassan, and Afghanistan," *Journal of the Royal Geographical Society* 31, pp. 37-64.

Collins, E. Treacher 1896. *In the Kingdom of the Shah.* (London: T. Fisher Unwin).

Connolly, A. 1834. *Journey to the north of India overland from England.* 2 vols. (London).

Cronin, Stephanie 1996. "An Experiment in Military Modernization: Constitutionalism, Political Reform and the Iranian Gendarmerie, 1910-21." *Middle Eastern Studies*, Vol. 32, No. 3 (July), pp. 106-38.

Curzon, G. W. 1892. *Persia and the Persian Question.* 2 vols. (London).

DCR or *Diplomatic and Consular Reports*; DCR 4179, "Report on the Trade and Commerce of Bushehr for the Year 1907-08" (London, 1909), p. 17.

De Bode, C.A. 1845. *Travels in Luristan and Arabistan.* 2 vols. (London: J. Madden & Co).

De Bourges, Jacques 1666. *Rélation du voyage de Mgr l'évêque de Béryte* (Paris: Denys Bechet).

Demorgny, Gustave 1914. *Les institutions de la police en Perse* (Paris: Ernest Leroux).

De Panisse, Comte 1867. *La Russie, la Perse, l'Inde. Souvenirs de voyage 1865-1866* (Paris: Jouaust).

De Rivoyre, Denis B.L. 1883. *Obock, Mascate, Bouchire* (Paris).

De Vilmorin, Auguste Lacoin. *De Paris à Bombay par la Perse* (Paris: Firmin-Didot Co, 1895).

De Windt, Harry. *A Ride to India across Persia and Baluchistan* (London: Chapman & Hall, 1891).

Douglas, J.A. 1923. "The Bushehr-Shiraz Road," *Journal of the Royal Central Asia Society* 10/2, pp. 104-22.

Ebtehaj, G.H. n.d. *Guide Book on Persia* (Tehran).

Ehlers, Eckhart & Floor, Willem 1993. "Urban Change under Reza Shah," *Iranian Studies* 26/3-4, pp. 251-75.

Sistani, Malek Shah Hoseyn b. Malek Ghiyath al-Din 1344/1966. *Ehya al-Moluk* ed. Manuchehr Setudeh (Tehran: Bonyad-e Tarikh)

Emerson, John & Floor, Willem 1971. "Rahdars and their tolls in Safavid and Afsharid Iran," *JESHO* 30, pp. 318-27.

English, Barbara 1971. *The war for a Persian lady* (Boston).

Eqtedari, Ahmad1348/1969. *Athar-e shahrha-ye bastani. Savahel va Jaza'er-e Khalij-e Fars va Darya-ye 'Oman* (Tehran).

E'temad al-Saltaneh, Mohammad Hasan Khan 1368/1989. *Mer'at al-boldan* 4 vols in 3. ed. 'Abd al-Hoseyn Nava'i and Mir Hashem Mohaddeth (Tehran).

Farrashbandi, 'Ali Morad 1336/1957. *Tarikh va joghrafiya-ye Borazjan ya sangar-e mojehedin* 2 vols. (Shiraz).

———. 1359/1980. *Tarikhcheh-ye Hezb-e Demokrat-e Fars* (Tehran: Eslami).

Fars (Shiraz newspaper).

Fasa'i, Mirza Hasan Hoseyni 1378/1999. *Farsnameh-ye Naseri*. 2 vols. ed. Mansur Rastgar Fasa'i (Tehran: Amir Kabir).

Fattah, Hala 1997. *The Politics of Regional Trade in Iraq, Arabia, and the Gulf 1745-1900* (Albany).

Ferguson, Margaret 1941. *Bid Time Return* (London: Robert Hale Ltd).

Floor, Willem. 1971. "The Lutis-A Social Phenomenon in Qajar Persia," *Die Welt des Islams* 13, pp. 103-21.

———. 1979 a, "The bankers (*sarraf*) in Qajar Iran," *ZDMG*, vol. CXXIX (1979), pp. 263-81.

———. 1979 b, "A Description of the Persian Gulf and its inhabitants in 1756," *Persica*, 8 (1979), p. 172.

———. 1983, "The Revolt of Sheikh Ahmad Madani in Laristan and the Garmsirat (1730-1733)," *Studia Iranica*, vol. VIII (1983), pp. 63-93.

———. 1987, "The Iranian Navy in the Eighteenth Century," *Iranian Studies* 20 (1987), pp. 31-53.

———. 1988. "Le droit d'entreposage dans Qajar Iran," *Studia Iranica* (1988), pp. 59-77 and 179-182.

———. 1367/1988. *Hokumat-e Nader Shah.* translated by Abu'l-Qasem Serri (Tehran: Tus).

———. 1992 a. "Kalantar," *Encyclopedia Iranica*; available at http://www.iranica.com.

———. 1992 b. "Kadkhoda," *Encyclopedia Iranica*, available at http://www.iranica.com.

———. 1992 c. "Securité, Circulation et Hygiene dans les rues de Teheran a l'époque Qajar," in: Adle, Charyar et Hourcade, Bernard eds. *Teheran*, Institut Francais de Recherche en Iran (Bibliotheque iranienne, vol. 37).

———. 1994. "The Dutch and Khark Island, The adventures of the Baron von Kniphausen," in: Européens en Orient aux XVIIIe siècle. *Moyen Orient & Ocean Indien*, pp. 157-202.

———. 1998. *The Afghan Occupation of Iran* (Paris 1998).

———. 1999 a. *A Fiscal History of Iran in the Safavid and Qajar Period* (New York, Bibliotheca Persica).

———. 1999 b. *The Persian Textile Industry in historical perspective, 1500-1925.* Paris: L'Harmattan.

———. 2000. *The Economy of Safavid Persia* (Wiesbaden: Reichert, 2000).

———. "The Economic Role of the ʿOlama in Qajar Persia," in Linda Walbridge ed. *The Most Learned of the Shiʿa* (New York: Oxford UP), pp. 53-81.

———. 2003. *Agriculture in Qajar Iran.* Washington DC: MAGE.

———. 2004 a. *Public Health in Qajar Iran.* Washington DC: MAGE.

———. 2004 b. The First Dutch-Persian Commercial Conflict. The Attack on Qeshm Island, 1645 (Costa Mesa: Mazda).

———. 2006. *The Persian Gulf during the Safavid Period* (Washington DC: MAGE).

———. 2007. *The Rise of the Gulf Arabs* (Washington DC: MAGE).

———. 2009 a. *Labor and Industry in Iran 1850-1941* (Washington DC: MAGE).

———. 2009 b. *Textile Imports into Qajar Iran. Russia versus Great Britain. The Battle for Market Domination.* Costa Mesa: MAZDA.

———. 2009 c. *Guilds, Merchants and Ulama in Nineteenth Century Iran* (Washington DC: MAGE).

———. 2012. "The history of hospitals in Safavid and Qajar Iran, an enquiry into their number, growth and importance" in Fabrizio Speziale ed. *Hospitals in Iran and India 1500-1950s* (Leiden/Boston: Brill).

Francklin, William 1976. *Observations made on a tour from Bengal to Persia in the years 1786-7* (repr. Tehran [London, 1790]).

Fraser, David 1910. *Persia and Turkey in Revolt* (Edinburgh/London: William Blackwood and Sons).

Fraser, J.B 1984. *Narrative of a Journey into Khorasan in the Years 1821 & 1822* (Delhi [reprint of London, 1825]).

Fryer, John 1909-15. *A New Account of East India and Persia Being Nine Years' Travels, 1672-1681*, 3 vols. (London: Hakluyt).

Gabriel, Alfons 1952, *Die Erforschung Persiens* (Vienna).

Gaube, Heinz 1979. "Ein Abschnitt der safavidischen Bandar ʿAbbas - Shiraz-Strasse: die Strecke von Seyyed Gemal al-Din nach Lar", *Iran* XVII, pp. 33-48.

Ghaffari, Kashani, Abu'l-Hasan 1369/1990. *Golshan-e Morad (Tarikh-e Zandiyeh)*. ed. GholamReza Tabataba'i Majd (Tehran: Zarrin).

Gleadowe-Newcomen, A.H. 1906. *Report on the British-Indian commercial mission to southeastern Persia during 1904-1905* (Calcutta).

Golestaneh, Abu'l-Hasab b. Mohammad Amin 2536/1966. *Majmal al-Tavarikh* ed. Modarres Razavi (Tehran: Daneshgah).

Goldsmid, Frederic 1867. "Notes on recent Persian Travel," *JRGS* 27, pp. 183-203.

———. 1874. *Telegraph and Travel* (London: MacMillan & Co.).

Gollancz, Hermann 1927. *Chronicle of Events Between the Years 1623 and 1733 Relating to the Settlement of the Order of Carmelites in Mesopotamia* (London/Oxford: Oxford UP/ Humphrey Milford).

Gordon, T.E. 1891. "Journey from Tehran to Karun and Mohamrah etc." *Diplomatic and Consular Reports* 207 (1891), Miscellaneous Series.

Gouvernement Imperial de la Perse 1913, *Le Fars. La question des Tribus. Situation politique générale. Routes du Sud. La réforme administrative* (Tehran, June).

———. "Les réformes administratives," *Revue du Monde Musulmane* XXIII (1913), pp. 1-109.

Government of Bombay, 1856. *Selections from the records of the Bombay Government No. XXIV- New Series*. Bombay.

Government of Great Britain 1917. *A Sketch of the political history of Persia, Iraq and Arabia etc.* (Calcutta: Superintendent Government Printing, India).

———.1945. *Persia* (Naval Intelligence Division) (n.p., September).

Government of India, *Persian Gulf Administration Reports 1873-1957* 11 vols. (repr. Gerrards Cross, 1991).

Grummon, Stephen R. 1985. *The Rise and Fall of the Arab Shaykhdom of Bushehr: 1750-1850 (Iran, Persian Gulf)*. Unpublished dissertation (Johns Hopkins University).

Habibi, Mohsen 1992. "Reza Chah et le developpement de Teheran (1925-1941), in: Adle and Hourcade 1992, pp. 199-206.

Hamilton, Alexander 1930. *A New Account of the East Indies* 2 vols. in one (London).

Hamy, E.-T. 1911. "Voyage d'André Michaux en Syrie et en Perse (1782-1785) d'après son journal et sa correspondance." *Neuvième Congrès International de Géographie, Compte Rendu Des Travaux du Congrès*, vol. 3, pp. 1-38.

Hatami, Hasan 1375/1996. "Golabarun – do`a-ye barani-ye Kazerun," in Iraj Afshar and Karim Esfaniyan eds. *Namvareh-ye Doktor Mahmud Afshar*, vol. 9 (Tehran, Bonyad-e Mowqufat-e Doktor Mahmud Afshar), pp. 5185-90.

Hazin, Sheikh Mohammad `Ali 1830. *The Life of Sheikh Mohammed Ali Hazin*. Belfour, F.C ed.& tr. (London: Murray).

Hedayat, Rezaqoli Khan 1339/1960. *Tarikh-e Rowzat al-Safa* 10 vols. (Tehran).

Hedges, William 1967. *The Diary of William Hedges Esq*. ed. R. Barlow & H. Yule (New York).

Herbert, Thomas 1929. *Travels in Persia 1627-1629*. ed. W. Foster (New York).

Hollingberry, William 1976. *A Journal of Observations made during the British Embassy to the Court of Persia in the Years 1799, 1800 and 1801* (Tehran [reprint of Calcutta, 1814]).

Hotz A. ed. 1879. "Cornelis Cornelisz Roobacker's Scheepsjournaal Gamron-Basra (1645); De eerste reis der Nederlanders door de Perzische Golf" *Koninklijk Nederlandsch Aardrijkskundig Genootschap* 1907, pp. 289-405.

Houtum-Schindler, Albert 1911. "Persia," *Encyclopedia Britannica* (London).

Hunt, George Henry 1858. *Outram & Havelock's Persian Campaign* (London).

Ibn al-Balkhi 1912. *Description of the Province of Fars* translated by G. Le Strange (London: Roayl Asiatic Society).

Ineichen, Markus 2002. *Die schwedischen Offiziere in Persien (1911-1916)* (Bern/New York: Lang).

Issawi, Charles 1971. *The Economic History of Persia* (Chicago: CUP).

Jeyhani, Abu'l-Qasem 1368/1989. *Ashkal al-`Alam*, translated by `Ali b. `Abdol-Salam Kateb. Ed. Firuz Mansuri (Mashhad: Astan-e Qods Razavi).

Johnson, Lieut. Col. *A Journey from India to England through Persia, Georgia, Russia, Poland and Prussia in the Year 1817* (London: Longman, Hurst, Rees, Orme, and Brown, 1818).

Jonub, Ruznameh-ye 1371/1992. eds. Kheyr al-Nesa (Badr) Tangestani and Ahmad Tangestani. Tehran: `Ali Reza Tangestani.

Kaempfer, Engelbert 1968. *Die Reisetagebücher* ed. Meier-Lemgo. (Wiesbaden).

———. 1976, *Amoenitatum Exoticarum Politico-Physico-Medicarum Fasciculi V* (Tehran [reprint of Lemgoviae 1712]).

Kalantar, Mirza Mohammad 1325/1946. *Ruznameh-ye Mirza Mohammad Kalantar-e Fars* ed. Abbas Eqbal (Tehran: Yadgar).

Kasravi, Ahmad 1333/1954. *Tarikh-e Pansad Saleh-ye Khuzestan* (Tehran).

Kazeruni, Mohammad Ebrahim 1367/1988. *Tarikh-e Banader dar Khalij-e Fars* ed. Manuchehr Setudeh (Tehran).

Kazeruni, Sadr al-Sadat Salami 1381/2002. *Athar al-Reza* (dar tarikh va joghrafiya-e Kazerun va Shiraz), ed. Zahra Khoshbu'i and Musa Mottahari-zadeh (Tehran: Kazeruniyeh).

Kempthorne, G.B 1835. "Notes made on a Survey along the Eastern Shores of the Persian Gulf in 1828." *Journal of the Royal Geographical Society* 5, pp. 263-85.

Keyhan, Mas'ud. 1310/1931. *Joghrafiya-e Mofassal-e Iran* 3 vols. Tehran.

Khurmuji, Mirza Ja'far Khan Haqa'eq-Negar 1380/1960. *Nozhat al-Akhbar. Tarikh va Joghrafiya-ye Fars*. ed. Sayyed 'Ali Al Davud (Tehran: Ketabkhaneh, Muzeh va Markaz-e Asnad-e Majles).

Kinneir, J. Mc. 1973. *A Geographical Memoir of the Persian Empire* (New York [reprint of London, 1813]).

Kleiss, Wilhelm and Kiani, Mohammad Yusef 1367/1989. *Fehrest-e karavansarayha-ye Iran*. 2 vols. (Tehran).

Kunke, Maria 1991. *Nomadenstämme in Persien im 18. und 19. Jahrhundert* (Berlin: Klaus Schwarz).

Lambton, A.K.S. 1969. *Landlord and Peasant in Persia* (London: Oxford UP).

Layard, A.H. 1846. "A Description of the Province of Khuzistan," *JRGS* 16, pp. 1-105.

———. 1971. *Early Adventures in Persia, Susiana, and Babylonia* (Westmead [reprint of London, 1894]).

LeBrun, Corneille 1718. *Les Voyages*. 2 vols. (Amsterdam: Wetstein).

Le Bruyn, Cornelius 1737. *Travels into Moscovy, Persia and part of the East-Indies*, 2 vols. (London: Bettesworth, Hitch, etc.).

Le Gouz, François 1653. *Les Voyages et Observations du Sieur de la Boullaye-Le Gouz* (Paris).

Le Strange, Guy 1966. *The Lands of the Eastern Caliphate* (London [reprint of London 1905]).

Locher, A. 1889. *With Star and Crescent* (Philadelphia).

Loftus, W. 1857. *Travels and Researches in Chaldaea and Susiana* (London).

Longrigg, Stephen Hemsley 1925. *Four Centuries of Modern Iraq* (Oxford).

Lorimer, J. G. *Gazetteer of the Persian Gulf* 2 vols. (Calcutta, 1915).

Lumsden, Thomas 1822. *A Journey from Meerut in India to London in the Years 1819 and 1820* (Memphis, Tenn.: General Books, 2010 [reprint of London 1822]).

Lycklama à Nijeholt, T.M. 1873. *Voyage en Russie, au Caucase et en Perse*. 4 vols (Paris-Amsterdam: Arthus Bertrand-C.L. van Langenhuysen).

MacGregor, C. M. 1879. *Narrative of a Journey through the province of Khorassan* 2 vols. (London: Wm. Allen & Co).

Mafi, Hoseyn Qoli Khan Nezam al-Saltaneh. 1361. *Khaterat va Asnad-e Hoseyn Qoli Khan Nezam al-Saltaneh Mafi*. eds. Ma'sumeh Nezam-Mafi et al. 2 vols. (Tehran: Nashr-e Tarikh).

Mafi, Ma'sumeh Nezam, Mansureh Ettehadiyeh (Nezam Mafi), Sa'vandiyan, Sirus and Ram Pisheh, Hamid eds. 1361/1982. *Khaterat va Asnad-e Hoseyn Qoli Khan Nezam al-Saltaneh Mafi*. 3 parts in 2 vols. (Tehran: Tarikh-e Iran).

Mafi, Mansureh Ettehadiyeh and Sa'vandiyan, Sirus 1366/1987. *Gozideh'i az majmu 'eh-ye asnad-e 'Abdol-Hoseyn Mirza Farmanfarma 1325-1340 hejri qamari*. 3 vols. (Tehran: Nashr-e Tarikh-e Iran).

Majidi Kera'i, Nur Mohammad 1381/2002. *Mardom va sarzaminha-ye ostan-e Kuhgiluyeh va Buyir Ahmad* (Tehran: Baztab Andisheh).

Marvi, Mohammad Kazim 1369/1990. *Tarikh-e 'Alamara-ye Naderi*, 3 vols. ed. Mohammad Amin Riyahi. (Tehran).

Mahmoodian, Saeed 2007. *Encyclopedia Larestanica* (Richmond:Brandylane).

Mashayekhi, 'Abdol-Karim ed. 1377/1998. *Madraseh-ye Sa'adat-e Bushehr az chand zavayeh* (Qom: Markaz-e Bushehrshenasi).

Mazzaoui, M. M. 1981-84. "Musha'sha'yan. A XVth Century Shi'i Mouvement in Khuzistan and Southern 'Iraq," *Folia Orientalia* (Krakow) XXII, pp. 139-62.

Membré, Michele 1993. *Mission to the Lord Sophy of Persia (1539-1542)* tr. by A.H. Morton (London: SOAS).

Merritt-Hawkes, O. A. 1935. *Persia – Romance & Reality* (London: Nicholson & Watson).

Migeod, Heinz-Georg 1990. *Die persische Gesellschaft unter Nasiru'd-Din Šah (1848-1896)* (Berlin: Klaus Schwarz).

Mignan, Robert 1829. *Travels into Chaldea* (London).

Milburn, William 1813. *Oriental Commerce*. 2 vols (London).

Miles, F.B. 1966. *Country and Tribes of the Persian Gulf*. 2 vols. in one (London).

Moberley, F.J. 1987. *Operations in Persia 1914-1919* (London: HMSO).

Mokhber al-Saltaneh, Mehdi Qoli Hedayat 1344/1965. *Khaterat va Khatarat* (Tehran: Zavvar).

M[oney], R.C. 1828. *Journal of a Tour in Persia during the years 1824 & 1825* (London: Teape and Son).

Monteith, William. "Notes on the Route from Bushehr to Shiraz." *JRGS* 26 (1857), pp. 108-19.

Moore, Benjamin Burges. *From Moscow to the Persian Gulf*. (New York: G.P. Putnam's Sons, 1915).

Morier, James 1812. *A Journey through Persia, Armenia and Asia Minor in the Years 1808 and 1809* (London: Longman, Hurst, Rees, Orme, and Brown).

Mohammad Mofid Mostowfi. *Mokhtasar-e Mofid* 2 vols. ed. Najamabadi (Wiesbaden: Reichert).

Mostafavi, Sayyed Mohammad Taqi 1978. *The Land of Pars (The historical monuments and the archeological sites of the province of Fars).*)Chippenham: Picton Publishing).

Motahharizadeh, Musa 1383. *Naser-e Divan Kazeruni deh revayat-e asnad* (Tehran: Kazeruniyeh).

Mozayeni, A. 1974. "City Planning in Iran: evolution and problems", *Ekistics* 38/227, p. 264-67.

al-Muqaddasi, Muhammad b. Ahmad 1906. *Kitab ahsan al-taqasim fi ma'rifat al-taqalim* ed. M.J. de Goeje (Leiden, Brill).

Mustafa 1904. *Mit Sista Vandrigsår. Ströftåg i Persien och Indien* (Stockholm: Wahlström & Witstrands).

Mustawfi, Hamdallah 1919. *The Geographical Part of the Nozhat al-qolub*, ed. Le Strange (Leyden/London: Brill/Luzac).

Najm al-Molk, 'Abdol-Ghaffar 1342/1963. *Safarnameh-ye Khuzestan*. ed. Mohammad Dabir-Siyaqi (Tehran).

Nami Esfahani, Mirza Mohammad Sadeq Musavi 1363/1984. *Tarikh-e Giti Gusha. Tarikh-e Zandiyeh*, ed. S. Nafisi (Tehran).

Nasiri, Mirza Naqi 2008. *Titles and Emoluments in Safavid Iran*. Translated and annotated by Willem Floor (Washington DC: MAGE).

Nasiri, Mohammad Ebrahim b. Zeyn al-'Abedin 1373/1994. *Dastur-e Shahryaran*. Ed. Mohammad Nader Nasiri Moqaddam (Tehran: Bonyad-e Mowqufat-e Doktor Mahmud Afshar Yazdi).

Natanzi, Mahmud b.Hedayatollah Ashofteh-ye 1350/1971. *Noqavat al-Athar fi Dhekr al-Akhyar*.ed. Ehsan Eshraqi. (Tehran: Bonyad-e Tarjomeh).

Newberrie, John 1905. "The Voyages of Master John Newberie", in: Samual Purchas ed. *Purchas His Pilgrimes* 20 vols. (Glasgow 1905), vol. 8, pp. 460-63.

Nezam-Mafi, Reza Qoli ed. 1363/1984. *Ketab-e Sabz* (Tehran: Nashr-e Tarikh-e Iran).

Nezam al-Saltaneh 1361/1982. *Khaterat va asnad-e Hoseyn Qoli Khan Nezam al-Saltaneh Mafi*. 2 vols. ed. Mansureh Nezam Mafi, Sirus Sa'dvandiyan and Hamid Rambisha (Tehran).

Niebuhr, Carsten 1772. *Beschreibung von Arabien. Aus eigenen Beobachtungen und im Lande selbst gesammelten Nachrichten* (Copenhaguen).

―――. 1774. *Description de l'Arabie* (Amsterdam).

―――. 1997. *Reisebeschreibung nach Arabien und andern umliegenden Ländern* 3 vols. in one (Zürich).

Nilstrom, Gustav 1372/1994. *Shakheh-ye Nabat. Khaterat-e sargord-e Nilstrum afsar-e su'idi-ye zhandarmeri-ye Iran az vaqaye'-ye Fars va nahzat-e Tangestani (Avril –September 1915)*. Translated by Afshin Partow (Bushehr: Ershad-e Eslami-ye Ostan-e Bushehr).

Norden, Hermann n.d. *Under Persian Skies* (Philadelphia: McCrea Smith).

Nyström, P. 1925. *Fem År I Persien Som Gendarmofficer* (Stockholm: Albert Bonniers).

Oberling, Pierre 1974. *The Qashqa'i Nomads of Fars* (The Hague: Mouton & Co).

O'Connor, Frederick 1931. *On the frontier and beyond* (London: John Murray).

Okazaki, Shoko 1986. "The great Persian famine of 1870-71," *BSOAS* XLIX/1, pp. 183-92.

Olearius, Adam 1971. *Vermehrte newe Beschreibung der moscowitischen und persischen Reyse*, ed. D. Lohmeier (Tübingen: Max Niemayer).

Olivier, G.A. 1802-07. *Voyage dans l'Empire Othoman, l'Egypte et la Perse*. 6 vols. (Paris).

Ouseley, William. *Travels in various countries of the East; more particularly Persia*. 3 vols. (London: Rodwell and Martin, 1819-23).

Parsons, Abraham 1808. *Travels in Asia and Africa* (London).

Pelly, Lewis 1865 a. "Remarks on the Tribes, Trade, and Resources around the shore line of the Persian Gulf", *Transactions of the Bombay Geographical Society* 17, pp. 32-112.

———. 1865 b, "Recent Tour round the Northern portion of the Persian Gulf," *Transactions of the Bombay Geographical Society* 17, pp. 113-40.

Perry, John 1971. "The Banu Ka`b: an amphibious brigand state in Khuzistan," *Le Monde Iranien et l'Islam* 1, pp. 131-52.

———. 1979. *Karim Khan Zand, A History of Iran 1747-1779* (Chicago).

Persia 1910 = Government of Great Britain, Persia No. 1 (1910) *Further Correspondance respecting the Affairs of Persia*. London: HMSO.

———. 1911. Persia No.1 (1911) *Further Correspondance respecting the Affairs of Persia*. London: HMSO.

———. 1912. Persia No. 5 (1912). *Further Correspondance respecting the Affairs of Persia*. London: HMSO.

———. 1913. Persia No. 1 (1913). *Further Correspondance respecting the Affairs of Persia*. London: HMSO.

———. 1914. Persia no. 1 (1914). *Further Correspondance respecting the Affairs of Persia*. London: HMSO.

Philippi à SS. Trinitate 1649, *Itinerarium Orientale* (Lugduni: Antonii Ivllieron).

Pirzadeh 1343/1964. *Safarnameh-ye Hajji Mohammad 'Ali Pirzadeh 1303-06/1886-89*. ed. Hafez Farmanfarmayan 2 vols. (Tehran: Daneshgah).

Plaisted, Bartholomew 1757. *A Journal from Calcutta in Bengal, by Sea, to Busserah* (London: J. Newbery).

Preece, J.R. 1885. "Journey from Shiraz to Jashk via Darab, Forg, and Minab". *RGS, Supplementary Paper* 1, pp. 403-37.

Poverty Bay Herald, XLI, 13406. 13 June 1914.

Price, William 1832. *Journal of the British Embassy to Persia*. 2 vols. in one (London: Thomas Thorpe).

Purchas, Samuel 1905. *Hakluytus Posthumus or Purchas His Pilgrims*. 20 vols. (Glasgow: J. MacLehose & Sons).

Qa'em-Maqami, Jahangir 1354/1975. *Asnad-e Farsi, 'Arabi va Torki dar Arshiv-e Melli-ye Portoghal dar bareh-ye Hormuz va Khalij-e Fars* (Tehran).

———. ed. 1359/1980. *Nahzat-e Azadikhvahi-ye Mardom-e Fars dar Enqelab-e Mashrutiyat-e Iran* (Tehran: Markaz-e Irani va Tahqiqat-e Tarikhi).

Qomi, Qazi Ahmad 1359/1980. *Kholaseh al-Tavarikh* 2 vols. ed. Ehsan Eshraqi (Tehran: Daneshgah).

Ranjbar, Mohammad ʿAli 1389/2010. *Fars az mashrutiyat ta jang-e jahani-ye avval* (Tehran: Sazman-e Asnad).

Rawlinson 1989: "Memorandum by Major Rawlinson on the Subject of Mohammerah and the Chaab Tribe," in Schofield 1989, *Iran-Iraq Border*, vol. 1, pp. 281-344.

Al-Razi, Amin Ahmad 1972. *Haft Eqlim* (Calcutta: The Asiatic Society).

RMM - *Revue du Monde Musulmane*.

Rich, Claude James 1836. *Narrative of a Residence in Koordistan ... and of a Visit to Shirauz and Persepolis*. 2 vols. (London).

———. 1839. *Narrative of a Journey to the Site of Babylon ... with a Narrative of a Journey to Persepolis* (London: Duncan and Malcolm).

Richard, Francis ed. 1995. *Raphael du Mans missionnaire en Perse au XVIIe s*. 2 vols (Paris).

Risso, Patricia 1986. *Oman & Mascat, an early modern history* (New York).

Rivadeneyra, Adolfo 1880. *Viaje al interior de Persia*. 3 vols. (Madrid).

Roschanzamir, Mehdi 1970. *Die Zand-Dynastie* (Hamburg: Harmtmut Luedke).

Rubin, Michael A. 1999. *The formation of modern Iran, 1858-1909: Communications, telegraph, and society*, Yale University PhD, June 16, 1999 (UMI Microfilm of Ann Arbor MI; UMI Number 9954362).

Rumlu, Hasan Beg 1357/1978. *Ahsan al-Tavarikh*. ed. ʿAbdol-Hosein Navaʾi (Tehran).

Ruznameh-ye ettefaqiyeʿ-ye vaqayeʿ 4 vols. (Tehran, 1373-74/1994-95).

Sadid al-Saltaneh, Mohammad ʿAli Khan 1362/1883. *Safarnameh-ye Sadid al-Saltaneh* (Tehran: Bihnashr).

Sahab, Mohammad Reza et al. 2005. *Persian Gulf. Atlas of Old & historical Maps (3000 BC - 2000 AD)*. 2 vols. (Tehran: Center for Documents & Tehran University).

Sadri, Mehrdad 2002. *Standard Philatelic Catalogue. Iran-Qajar Dynasty* (N.p.: Persiphila).

Safiri, Felurida 1364/1985. *Pulis-e Jonub-e Iran. Es. Pi. Ar.* Translated by Mansureh Ettehadiyeh and Mansureh Jaʿfari Fesharaki (Tehran: Tarikh-e Iran).

Saldanha, J.A. 1986. *The Persian Gulf Precis* 8 vols. (Gerrards Cross: Archive Editions).

Sarvestani, Masʿud Shafiʿi 1383/2004. *Fars dar enqelab-e mashrutiyat* (Shiraz: Bonyad-e Fars-shenas).

Sayyah, Hajj 1346/1967. *Khaterat Hajj Sayyah ya Dowreh-ye Khowf va Vahshat* (Tehran: Ebn Sina).

Scarcia, G. C. 1971. "Annotazioni Mushaʿshaʿ," in *La Persia nel medioevo* (Rome), pp. 633-37.

Schofield, Richard N. ed. 1989, *The Iran-Iraq Border 1840-1958*. 11 vols. (Gerard's Cross: Archive Editions).

Schwarz, Paul 1993. *Iran im Mittelalter nach dem arabischen Geographen*. 10 vols. (Frankfurt: Institute Hitory of Arabic-Islamic Science).

Sistani, Malek Shah Hoseyn b. Malek Ghayath al-Din Mohammad b. Shah Mahmud 1344/1966. *Ehya al-Moluk*. ed. Manuchehr Setudeh (Tehran).

Sepehr, Mo'arrekh al-Dowleh 1336/1957. *Iran dar jang-e bozorg 1914-1918* (Tehran).

Sepehr, Mohammad Taqi Lesan al-Molk 1377/1988. *Nasekh al-Tavarikh*. ed. Jamshid Kiyanfar 3 vols. in 2 (Tehran).

Selby, W.B. Lieutenant 1844. "Account of the Ascent of the Karun and Dizful Rivers and the Ab-i-Gargar Canal, to Shuster," *Journal of the Royal Geographical Society* 14, pp. 219-46.

Shepherd, William Ashton 1857. *From Bombay to Bushehr and Bussora* (London).

Shirazi, `Ali Reza b. `Abd al-Karim 1888. *Tarikh-e Zandiyeh* ed. Ernst Beer (Leiden: Brill).

Al-Shushstari, Sayyid `Abdallah b. Sayyed Nur al-Din b. Sayyid Ni`matallah 1924. *Kitab-i Tadhkira-ye Shushtar*. ed. Khan Bahadur Maula Bakhsh (Calcutta).

Shushtari. Mir `Abd ul-Latif Khan 1363/1984. *Tohfat al-`Alam va Dheyl al-Tohfeh. Safarnameh va Khaterat* ed. Samad Movahhad (Tehran).

Silva y Figueroa, Garcia de 1667. *L'ambassade de Don Garcia de Silva Figveroa en Perse*. Trans. Abraham de Wicquefort (Paris).

Sirjani, Sa`idi ed. 1361/1982. *Vaqaye'-ye ettefaqiyeh. Gozareshha-ye khafiyeh-nevisan-e englisi* (Tehran).

Siroux, Maxime 1949. *Caravanserais d'Iran, et petites constructions routières* (Paris).

Slot, B.J. 1991. *Les origines du Koweit* (Leiden: Brill).

Smith, Ronald Bishop 1970. *The First Age. Of the Portuguese Embassies, Navigations and Peregrinations in Persia (1507-1524)*. (Bethesda).

Speelman, Cornelis 1908. *Journaal der Reis van den gezant der O.I. Compagnie Joan Cunaeus naar Perzië in 1651-1652*. Ed. A. Hotz (Amsterdam).

Spuler, Berthold 1952. *Iran in Früh-Islamischer Zeit* (Wiesbaden: Steiner).

———. 1985, *Die Mongolen in Iran* (Leiden: Brill).

St. John, O. 1868. "On the Elevation of the Country Between Bushehr and Teheran," *JRGS* 38, pp. 411-13.

Stack, Edward 1882. *Six Months in Persia*. 2 vols. (New York).

Stern, Henry A. 1854. *Dawnings in the East; with biblical, historical, and statistical notices of persons and places visited during a mission to the Jews in Persia, Coordistan, and Mesopotamia* (London: Charles H. Purday).

Stevens, Roger 1979. *The Land of the Sophy* (New York).

Stirling, Edward 1991. *The Journals of Edward Stirling in Persia and Afghanistan 1828-1829* ed. Jonathan L. Lee (Naples).

Stocqueler, J.H. 1832. *Fifteen months' pilgrimage.* 2 vol. (London).

Stodard, Robert 1935. *The Journal of Robert Stodart* ed. Sir E. Denison Ross (London).

Strauszens, Johan J. 1678. *Reisen durch Griechenland, Moscau, Tartarey, Ostindien und andere Theile der Welt* (Amsterdam).

Sykes, Christopher 1937. *Wassmuss.* New York/London:

Sykes, P. M. 1902. *Ten Thousand Miles in Persia* (London: Charles Scribner's Sons).

———. 1969. *The History of Persia.* 2 vols. (London: Routledge and Kegan Paul).

Tavernier, Jean-Baptiste 1681. *Les Six Voyages* 5 vols. (Paris: Gervais Clouzier).

———. 1930. *Voyages en Perse et description de ce royaume* (Paris).

Tayyebi, Mansur Naseri 1389/2010. *Asnad-e Fars dar dowreh-ye dovvom va sevvom majles-e shuray-e melli* (Tehran: Ketabkhaneh-ye Majles).

Teixeira, Pedro 1902. *The Travels of Pedro Texeira with his "Kings of Harmuz"* (London: Hakluyt).

Thevenot, J. de 1971. *The Travels of M. de Thevenot into the Levant* (Westmead [reprint of London, 1686]).

Trade Report = *The Persian Gulf Trade Reports 1905-1940.* 8 vols. (Bushehr 2 vols). (Gerrards Cross: Archive Editions, 1987).

Vahid-e Qazvini, Mirza Mohammad Taher 1383/2005. *Tarikh-e Jahanara-ye 'Abbasi.* Ed. Sayyed Sa'id Mir Mohammad Sadeq (Tehran: Pazhuheshgah-e 'Olum-e Ensani).

Valentijn, François 1726. *Oud en Nieuw Oost-Indien*, 5 vols. (Dordrecht).

Van den Berghe, L. 1959. *Archeologie de l'Iran ancient* (Leiden: Brill).

Van Dam, Pieter 1993. *Beschryvinge van de Oostindische Compagnie*, Tweede Boek, deel III. ed. F.W. Stapel ('s-Gravenhage).

Vahram, Majid 1351/1972. "Chand telegrafi az Sadeq al-Mamalek Hakem-e Dashtestan beh Farmanfarma-ye Fars," *Barrasiha-ye Tarikhi* VII/1, pp. 177-232.

Vahraman, Farraxmart I 1997, *The Book of Judgements (A Sasanian Lawbook)*, translated and annoted by Anahit Perikhanian/Nina Garsoïan (Costa Mesa: Mazda/Bibliotheca Persica).

Vatandoust, Gholamreza and Pourhasan, Jalil 1380/2001. *World War I and the Creation of the Gendarmerie in Fars* (Shiraz: Behdid).

Von Blücher, Wipert 1949. *Zeitenwende in Iran. Erlebnisse und Beobachtungen* (Biberach a/d Riss).

Vothuqi, Mohammad Baqer 1375/1996. *Larestan va Jonbesh-e Mashrutiyat.* Qom: Mo'assesseh-ye Farhangi-ye Hamsayeh.

———. 1375 b. *Beyramdar al-Ovliya-ye Larestan* (Qom).

Waring, Edward Scott 1973. *A Tour to Sheeraz* (New York [reprint of London, 1807]).

Waters, George 1876. "Report of a journey from Bushehr to Kazeroon and back," *Transactions of the Bombay Society NSR*, pp. 175-202.

Watson, Robert Grant 1976. *A History of Persia* (London).

Weeks, Edwin Lord 1896. *From the Black Sea Through Persia and India* (New York).

Williams, E. Crawshay 1907. *Across Persia* (London).

Wills, C. J. 1893. *In the Land of the Lion and the Sun* (London: Ward, Lock & Bowden).

Wilson, A.T. Captain 1916. *Report on Fars* (Simla: Indian Political Department).

Wulff, Hans E. 1966. *The Traditional Crafts of Persia* (Cambridge).

Yate, A. C. 1917 a. "Travel memories," *Scottish Geographical Journal*, 33/4, pp. 163-74; Ibid., b. 33/8, pp. 337-48.

Zarkub-e Shirazi, Mo`in al-Din 1350/1972. *Shiraznameh*. Ed. Esma`il Va`ez Javadi (Tehran: Entesharat-e Bonyad-e Farhangi-ye Iran).

Zarrabi, Manuchehr 1342/1963. "Ka`b-e Shadegan," *Iran Farhang Zamin* 11, pp. 281-92.

INDEX

South Persian Rifles 163, 167, 170
Sowlat al-Dowleh 135, 138, 163, 164, 165, 169, 171
Sowlet al-Dowleh 167
sparrows 97
Strike Force 169, 170
subvention of chiefs 150
Sultan Sayyed Ahmad 265
Sultan Selim 196
Sultan's Gardens 280
Sultan Soleyman 196
Sunnis, Kazerun 93
supplies en route 256
Surmak 268
sursaf 219
Sykes 163, 164
synagogue 43

T

Tab River 243
Tabriz 13
Tadavan 271
Talkhab 276
Tamar 203, 208, 210
tamasha 254
tamassok 120, 121
Tang-e Dalan 278
Tangestan 11
Tang-e Torkan 142, 148, 151, 165
Taqi Khan Bakhtiyari 215
Taqizadeh 139
tavazi fabrics 84, 89
taxes 44, 113, 135, 179
telegraph office 36
telegraph-station 75
Tenghinoun 277
teyul 118
timber 74
Timur Mirza 52, 68, 111, 112, 113, 118
tobacco 26, 37, 38, 39, 72, 99, 102, 104, 105, 141, 179, 266, 270
tofangchis 45, 54, 56, 110, 116, 145, 151, 160, 169, 170, 172
Trabzon 13
trade 38
trade, decline 138
trade Falahiyeh 241
trade, Kazerun 87
trade, Mohammareh 246
trade routes 131, 136
transport rates 141, 148, 150
Travel time 257
tribal economic activities 108
tribes, listed 106
tribute 205, 213

Tschenitsche Tschengi 277

U

Uggla 55, 150, 151, 154, 156, 181
Ujan 265
Ujval 269
Umm al-Zakhar 219

V

Vali Khan Mamasani 127
Vali of Hoveyzeh 198, 199, 202, 218, 219
Vazir-e Mahkhus 134
vegetables 37
villages, list 99

W

Wahhabis 210
wall 32
Waseli 277
Wasit 197
Wassmuss 55, 160, 162, 164, 171, 309
water 33, 101
water cisterns 95, 252, 254, 255, 275, 276, 277
water, Kazerun 94
wax 105
weather 31
weaving 38, 103
wells 16
Weys 235
women 84
wool 105
wrestlers 97
Wüstrov 162, 163

Y

Yazdekhvast 262

Z

zabet 43
Za'er Khezr 55, 56
Zafar al-Saltaneh 139
Zarghan 268
Zell al-Soltan 134, 227
Zepahoenia 268
Zireh 28, 48, 54
Zireh, district 61
Zirukh 53
Ziyarat 28
Zubayr 212